Singapore Politics Under t Action Party

This book is a comprehensive overview of politics in Singapore since its independence in 1965. The authors examine how this tiny island has developed into a global financial center, with one of the largest incomes per head, not only in Asia, but in the world. Its success has been due largely to the leaders of the party which has ruled it continuously, the People's Action Party. The party has coped successfully with the needs of a multiethnic population, claims for more extensive human rights, the nascent development of a civil society, and the problems of defending a small country in a turbulent region.

These key policies have been determined principally by Singapore's first two Prime Ministers, Lee Kuan Yew and Goh Chok Tong, and will be affected in the future by Lee's son, B.G. Lee Hsien Loong. All three personalities are here examined in depth. Mauzy and Milne also look at Singapore's response to its economic crisis, the elections of November 2001, and the challenges of the new century.

This major study of contemporary Singapore politics will be essential for both undergraduate and graduate students of Asian politics, as well as being of interest to business people and diplomats concerned with the region.

Diane K. Mauzy and **R.S. Milne** are professors at the University of British Columbia, Canada. They have published widely on Asian politics, including *Politics Under Mahathir* (Routledge, 1999) and *Singapore: The Legacy of Lee Kuan Yew* (Westview, 1990).

Politics in Asia series

Edited by the late Michael Leifer
London School of Economics

ASEAN and the Security of South-East Asia
Michael Leifer

China's Policy towards Territorial Disputes
The Case of the South China Sea Islands
Chi-kin Lo

India and Southeast Asia
Indian Perceptions and Policies
Mohammed Ayoob

Gorbachev and Southeast Asia
Leszek Buszynski

Indonesian Politics under Suharto
Order, Development and Pressure for Change
Michael R.J. Vatikiotis

The State and Ethnic Politics in Southeast Asia
David Brown

The Politics of Nation Building and Citizenship in Singapore
Michael Hill and Lian Kwen Fee

Politics in Indonesia
Democracy, Islam and the Ideology of Tolerance
Douglas E. Ramage

Communitarian Ideology and Democracy in Singapore
Beng-Huat Chua

The Challenge of Democracy in Nepal
Louise Brown

Japan's Asia Policy
Wolf Mendl

The International Politics of the Asia-Pacific, 1945–1995
Michael Yahuda

Political Change in Southeast Asia
Trimming the Banyan Tree
Michael R.J. Vatikiotis

Hong Kong
China's Challenge
Michael Yahuda

Korea versus Korea
A Case of Contested Legitimacy
B. K. Gills

Taiwan and Chinese Nationalism
National Identity and Status in International Society
Christopher Hughes

Managing Political Change in Singapore
The Elected Presidency
Kevin Y.L. Tan and Lam Peng Er

Islam in Malaysian Foreign Policy
Shand Nair

Political Change in Thailand
Democracy and Participation
Kevin Hewison

The Politics of NGOs in South-East Asia
Participation and Protest in the Philippines
Gerard Clarke

Malaysian Politics Under Mahathir
R.S. Milne and Diane K. Mauzy

Indonesia and China
The Politics of a Troubled Relationship
Rizal Sukma

Arming the Two Koreas
State, Capital and Military Power
Taik-young Hamm

Engaging China
The Management of an Emerging Power
Edited by Alastair lain Johnston and Robert S. Ross

Singapore's Foreign Policy
Coping with Vulnerability
Michael Leifer

Philippine Politics and Society in the Twentieth Century
Colonial Legacies, Post-Colonial Trajectories
Eva-Lotta E. Hedman and John T. Sidel

Constructing a Security Community in Southeast Asia
ASEAN and the Problem of Regional Order
Amitav Acharya

Monarchy in South-East Asia
The Faces of Tradition in Transition
Roger Kershaw

Korea After the Crash
The Politics of Economic Recovery
Brian Bridges

The Future of North Korea
Edited by Tsuneo Akaha

The International Relations of Japan and South East Asia
Forging a New Regionalism
Sueo Sudo

Power and Change in Central Asia
Edited by Sally N. Cummings

The Politics of Human Rights in Southeast Asia
Philip Eldridge

Political Business in East Asia
Edited by Edmund Terence Gomez

Singapore Politics Under the People's Action Party
Diane K. Mauzy and R.S. Milne

Singapore Politics Under the People's Action Party

Diane K. Mauzy and R.S. Milne

London and New York

First published 2002 by Routledge
11 New Fetter Lane, London EC4P 4EE

Simultaneously published in the USA and Canada
by Routledge
29 West 35th Street, New York, NY 10001

Routledge is an imprint of the Taylor & Francis Group

Typeset in Times by MHL Typesetting Ltd, Coventry
Printed and bound in Great Britain by
MPG Books Ltd, Bodmin

British Library Cataloguing in Publication Data
A catalogue record for this book is available
from the British Library

Library of Congress Cataloging in Publication Data
A catalog record for this book has been requested

ISBN 0-415-24652-0 (hbk)
ISBN 0-415-24653-9 (pbk)

To the memory of Michael Leifer

**Acclaimed scholar, percipient editor,
and good companion**

Contents

Acknowledgments ix
Key dates xi
List of acronyms xv

1 What is remarkable about Singapore? 1

2 How Singapore became independent: Lee Kuan Yew and the People's Action Party (PAP) 13

3 Locations of power: the state and the government 25

4 The People's Action Party: the structure and operation of a dominant party 38

5 Ideology of the leaders and for the populace 51

6 Economic policy for an independent Singapore 66

7 Supplying social services to the people 85

8 The dictates of ethnicity: language policy, education, and self-help 99

9 The successors: leadership trends in the PAP – the search for top talent 114

10 Authoritarian aspects of PAP rule 128

11 Elections, electoral innovations, and the Opposition 143

12 The growth of civil society 157

13 Deterrence and diplomacy 169

14 Singapore in the future 186

Further reading 198
Notes 202
Index 258

Acknowledgments

The extent of our indebtedness is evident from the notes. However, our special thanks are due to two "official" people who rashly offered to help with any queries that occurred to us after our interview. Lim Boon Heng, Minister Without Portfolio, and Ong Keng Yong, Press Secretary to the Prime Minister, provided this essential assistance. We are also appreciative of all the assistance we were given by the Ministry of Information and the Arts (MITA), particularly Madam Yeong Yoon Ying, the Director (Media Division) MITA and Press Secretary to the Senior Minister, and her capable secretary, Karolyn Poon. We are appreciative that politicians, both government and opposition, members of NGOs, journalists, and academics were willing to speak with us. Among academics, Professor Linda Low was particularly helpful, possibly because our research interests are so similar. We would also like to thank Professor James Cotton for his helpful advice on the organization of the book.

We cannot speak too highly of the assistance given us by the Institute of Policy Studies, particularly by its Deputy Director, Dr. Arun Mahizhnan, and Research Fellow Dr. Gillian Koh.

For library help we depended, as usual, on the marvelously well-stocked and knowledgably staffed library of the Institute of Southeast Asian Studies. We are particularly grateful to its librarian, Ch'ng Kim See, who provided, not only for our intellectual sustenance, but also some delicious, well-timed lunches. Her help continued after our departure from Singapore when recondite queries from afar were answered quickly and to the point by an expert library team headed by Gandhimathy Durairaj. We are much indebted.

As always in Singapore, knowledge of the political, social, and culinary ambiance was dispensed effortlessly by our friends, Pang Cheng Lian and Tan Joo San. In Vancouver, the services of the Singapore Consulate staff, especially of the Consul, Richard Grosse and Consular Assistant Josephine Zhang were indispensable. Finally, Diane K. Mauzy would like to thank the University of British Columbia for an HSS Research Grant that supported this research.

Key dates

1819	Stamford Raffles of the (British) East India Company founds a settlement, Singapore, at the southeast tip of the Malay peninsula.
1826	Singapore joins with Penang and Malacca to form the Straits Settlements.
1867	The Straits Settlements become a British Crown Colony.
1869	The Suez Canal is constructed, greatly increasing Singapore's accessibility.
1941	Japanese invasion conquers Malaya and Singapore.
1941–5	Japanese occupation. British rule resumes in 1945.
1948–60	Communist uprising in Malaya (the "Emergency").
1953	Constitutional changes provide for an elected legislature and the appointment of a Chief Minister.
1954	A new political party is inaugurated, the People's Action Party (PAP).
1955	Election with an enlarged but still limited franchise, which results in the victory of the Labour Front. Its leader, David Marshall, becomes Chief Minister.
1957	Marshall resigns and is succeeded by Lim Yew Hock, also of the Labour Front. Detention of 35 pro-Communists.
1958	New constitution with an extensive franchise promulgated.
1959	PAP wins legislative assembly election decisively. Its leader, Lee Kuan Yew, is the new Prime Minister.
1961	Tunku Abdul Rahman, Prime Minister of Malaya, in a speech made in Singapore, raises the possibility of forming a larger state, Malaysia, which would include Singapore. Two months later, left-wing dissidents in the PAP break away and form the Barisan Sosialis.
1961	Singapore creates its main organization for economic planning and implementation – the Economic Development Board.
1962	Singapore referendum on merger gives a majority in favor of Singapore becoming part of Malaysia, which occurs in 1963.
1963	PAP wins important general election against the Barisan Sosialis.
1963	GDP growth in Singapore is negative.
1963–6	"Confrontation" against Malaysia by Indonesia.
1964	PAP makes a "token" intervention in the Malayan general election; wins only one seat.
1965	Singapore exits from Malaysia; becomes an independent state.

1967	Singapore becomes a founding member of ASEAN.
1967	Registration for national service made compulsory in Singapore for males.
1968	Barisan Sosialis boycotts the Singapore Parliament and general election; PAP wins all the seats.
1968	Britain decides to withdraw from its Singapore military bases.
1971	Five Power Defence Arrangements concluded, which includes Singapore.
1971	ASEAN states endorse a Zone of Peace, Freedom and Neutrality (ZOPFAN).
1972	National Wages Council (tripartite) established.
1981	J.B. Jeyaretnam, leader of the Workers' Party, breaks the PAP parliamentary monopoly by winning the by-election in the Anson constituency.
1984	Legislation passed for Non-Constituency Members of Parliament to ensure some opposition in Parliament.
1984	PAP loses two seats in general election; seen as watershed confirming the return of the opposition.
1985	Association of Women for Action and Research founded.
1985–6	Economic recession.
1987	Institute of Policy Research set up.
1987–8	Controversial arrests under the Internal Security Act (ISA).
1988	Legislation passed creating Group Representation Constituencies.
1990	Relations established with the People's Republic of China.
1990	Goh Chok Tong becomes Prime Minister; Lee Kuan Yew is named Senior Minister; Lee Hsien Loong acknowledged as Goh's successor as Prime Minister "in due course."
1990	Nominated MP's proposal becomes law.
1991	Act passed to create an Elected President.
1991	PAP loses four of 81 seats in general election; Goh Chok Tong disappointed that his style of governance does not receive stronger endorsement.
1991	Deputy Prime Minister Lee Hsien Loong found to have cancer, but makes a good recovery.
1991–	Introduction and extension of the Internet in Singapore.
1993	Ong Teng Cheong elected President.
1993–	Goh Chok Tong introduces new ways of "topping up" Central Provident Fund holdings.
1994	The Roundtable is registered as a political policy discussion group.
1996	The ASEAN–Europe Meeting (ASEM), strongly supported by Singapore, holds its first meeting.
1997	PAP wins general election with increased percentage of the popular vote after three consecutive elections with a decline in its popular vote.
1997	Gradual introduction of Community Development Councils.
1998	Economic recession in Singapore, although less severe than in most neighboring countries.

1998–	Singapore government stresses the need to encourage the trend toward a Knowledge-Based Economy.
1999	S.R. Nathan elected President (unopposed).
2000	Launching of Speaker's Corner (Hong Lim Park).
2001	Economic recession in Singapore, as in most Southeast Asian countries.
2001	PAP wins resounding general election victory with a 10 percent increase in its percentage of the popular vote.

List of acronyms

AFTA	ASEAN Free Trade Area
AMP	Association of Muslim Professionals
APEC	Asia Pacific Economic Cooperation (forum)
ASEM	Asia–Europe Meeting
AWARE	Association of Women for Action and Research
BG	Brigadier General
CC	Community Centre
CCC	Citizens' Consultative Committee
CDAC	Chinese Development Assistance Council
CDC	Community Development Council
CDIS	Curriculum Development Institute of Singapore (Ministry of Education)
CEC	Central Executive Committee (PAP)
CEO	Chief Executive Officer
CIQ	Customs, Immigration and Quarantine
CLA	Criminal Law (Temporary Provisions) Act
CPA	Council of Presidential Advisors
CPF	Central Provident Fund
DBS	Development Bank of Singapore
DCAC	Directorship and Consultancy Appointments Council
DPM	Deputy Prime Minister
DSO	Defence Science Organization
DSTA	Defence Science and Technology Agency
EDB	Economic Development Board
EIC	(British) East India Company
EP	Elected President
EU	European Union
FDI	Foreign Direct Investment
FEALAC	Forum for East Asia–Latin America Cooperation
FPDA	Five Power Defence Arrangements
GDP	Gross Domestic Product
GE	General Election
GIC	Government of Singapore Investment Corporation
GLCs	Government-Linked Companies
GRC	Group Representation Constituency

HDB	Housing and Development Board
HQ Exco	Headquarters Executive Committee (PAP)
HUDC	Housing and Urban Development Company
IBM	International Business Machines
ICC	Inter-racial Confidence Circles
ICJ	International Commission of Jurists
IHT	International Herald Tribune
IISS	International Institute of Strategic Studies
IMF	International Monetary Fund
INGO	International Non-governmental Organization
IPS	Institute of Policy Studies
ISA	Internal Security Act
ISD	Internal Security Department
ISP	Internet Service Providers
IT	Information Technology
JBJ	J.B. Jeyaretnam
KBE	Knowledge-Based Economy
LF	Labour Front
MAS	Monetary Authority of Singapore
MCA	Malayan/Malaysian Chinese Association
MCP	Malayan Communist Party (later CPM)
MDA	Misuse of Drugs Act
Mendaki	Council of Education for Muslim Children
Mendaki II	Council for the Development of the Singapore Muslim Community
MITA	Ministry of Information and the Arts
MFA	Ministry of Foreign Affairs
MHA	Ministry of Home Affairs
MINDEF	Ministry of Defence
MNCs	Multinational Corporations
MP	Member of Parliament
MRT	mass rapid transit
MUIS	Majlis Ugama Islam Singapore (Islamic Religious Council of Singapore)
Nantah	Nanyang University
NASA	National Aeronautical and Space Administration
NCMP	Non-constituency Member of Parliament
NE	National Education
NES	New Education System
NGO	Non-governmental Organization
NII	Net Investment Income
NMP	Nominated Member of Parliament
NPPA	Newspaper and Printing Presses Act
NSP	National Solidarity Party
NSS	The Nature Society (Singapore)
NTUC	National Trades Union Congress
NUS	National University of Singapore
NWA	National Wages Council

OB	Out of Bounds (markers)
OCBC	Oversea Chinese Banking Corporation
OECD	Organization for Economic Cooperation and Development
OUB	Overseas Union Bank
PA	People's Association
PAP	People's Action Party
PCF	PAP Community Foundation
PEC	Presidential Elections Committee
PERC	Political and Economic Risk Consultancy (Hong Kong)
PERGAS	Association of Islamic Scholars and Religious Teachers
PIEU	Pioneer Industries Employees Union
PKMS	Pertubohan Kebangsaan Melayu Singapura
PLE	Promising Local Enterprises
PP	Progressive Party
PRC	People's Republic of China
PSA	Port of Singapore Authority
PSC	Public Service Commission
PSLE	Primary School Leaving Examination
RAdm	Rear Admiral
RC	Residents' Committee
R&D	Research and Developmentxvixvixvi xvi
RK	Religious Knowledge
RSAF	Republic of Singapore Air Force
SAF	Singapore Armed Forces
SAFRA	Singapore Armed Forces Reservists Association
SAP	Special Assistance Plan (schools)
SATU	Singapore Association of Trade Unions
SBA	Singapore Broadcasting Authority
SCW	Singapore Council of Women
SDF	Singapore Defence Organization
SDA	Singapore Democratic Alliance
SDP	Singapore Democratic Party
SILO	Singapore Industrial Labour Organization
SINDA	Singapore Indian Development Organization
SingTel	Singapore Telecommunications
SIP	Singapore Industrial Park (Suzhou)
SMEs	Small and Medium Enterprises
SPH	Singapore Press Holdings Ltd.
SPP	Singapore People's Party
SRS	Supplementary Retirement Scheme
S21	Singapore 21 (vision)
TC	Town Council
TCS	Television Corporation of Singapore
TDI	Total Defence Initiative
TFR	Total Fertility Rate
TUC	Trades Union Congress (Britain)
TWC	The Working Committee (network)

UMNO	United Malays National Organization
UOB	United Overseas Bank
UN	United Nations
US	United States
VWO	Volunteer Welfare Organization
WP	Workers' Party
WTO	World Trade Organization
YP	Young PAP
ZOPFAN	Zone of Peace, Freedom and Neutrality

1 What is remarkable about Singapore?

In 1965, the tiny, newly independent island-state of Singapore was not so different in its stage of development from much of the Third World then being decolonized, although its prospects were perhaps less promising given its almost total lack of natural resources. Why was it that Singapore was so successful at achieving socio-economic modernization and political stability in contrast to so many others? What is remarkable or exceptional about Singapore? What have been its achievements, and its mistakes?

Images of Singapore

Singapore can mean different things to different people. This is particularly true of the scenes that its pre-Independence mental images bring to mind. There is an early twentieth-century picture of rubber being transshipped from Malaya and bound for Europe. A 1920s Singapore might suggest dinner or dalliance at the Raffles Hotel, and a later impression would be of the 1941 Japanese invasion (see p. 14) and prison camps and civilian life under Japanese rule.

Later mental pictures might be less distinct, perhaps because the focus was more on its neighbor, Malaya, where the struggle to put down a Communist insurrection ("the Emergency", 1948–60) was more dramatic than anything that Singapore could provide. Yet there was indeed an anti-Communist struggle in Singapore, referred to in the next chapter of this book, which took the form not so much of open violence, as of intrigue, rumors and maneuvers, clandestine meetings, loyalties and defections. Singapore's Independence from the British, followed the emergence of the People's Action Party (PAP), led by political neophytes (see p. 38), who nevertheless used their political skills to achieve truly impressive results. After the PAP was elected to power in 1959, it governed into the next century and Singapore emerged as one of the top three or four states in income per head, not just in Asia, but in the world. Who were these people and how did they contrive to do what they did? This book tries to answer these questions.

After this introductory chapter, the sequence is: how the PAP came to power and built and maintained its political support base, the ideology and values of the elites and the socialization of the citizenry, and how it managed ethnicity and the vexing issues of language and education. The book tells how it constructed the economic "engine" which achieved prosperity – a significant achievement (see pp. 66–8) – and today emphasizes a Knowledge-Based Economy, founded on the application of ideas resulting in "value creation" rather than the production of material goods. It also relates how earlier, the PAP surmounted some of the challenges which come with affluence: housing the population; building hospitals and clinics, and providing schools that are now state-of-the-art. It further describes the services provided by the state, retirement schemes and social services, and recent plans to deliver services tailored to meet the needs and wishes of particular geographic areas.

Chapters in the latter part of the book are devoted mainly to various aspects of the relations between government and society: authoritarian aspects of government, such as control of the media and restrictions on civil and political rights, and the rule of law; democracy, elections, and the opposition; and the growth of civil society. Possible changes in the nature of the leadership are assessed, as well as foreign policy – vital because of Singapore's vulnerability in an area which is still unstable in spite of the existence of the Association of Southeast Asian Nations, of which Singapore is a member. Finally, there is a look into the future; how far is the government's policy towards more "openness" in tune with the changing demands of a more educated electorate, and what are the probable effects of globalization, eagerly embraced by Singapore, for better or for worse?

Singapore: old stereotypes and new

Present day Singapore is decidedly different from the old stereotypes. Modern perceptions would include the observations that "things work" – that it is an easy place to visit, a good place to shop, and, for most, a good place to live – and that there are no really ancient buildings, as there are in several other places in Southeast Asia. Singapore bears the stamp of PAP rule for over forty years. It is safe and orderly, and one of the first places to adopt new ideas that increase efficiency: the pedestrian waiting at a crossing for the traffic lights to change is informed by a digital clock telling precisely how many more seconds the wait will be.

Singapore, a former British colony, achieved self-government – but not control over its foreign policy – in 1959. In 1819, it was chosen as a settlement by the British East India Company because it was situated at a cross-roads for trade. It was essentially an "entrepot" economy (and remained so until the 1960s). It made money not by producing goods, but when goods were shipped through it in the course of trade. It was associated with the states of Malaya to the north, because both were under British rule and the administrations were linked. However, Malaya became independent in 1957.

Both Malaya and Singapore were hampered by the threat of Communism, and by the end of the 1950s, the Communists and pro-Communists in Singapore had established "bridge-heads" by winning control of some trade unions and Chinese middle schools.

When the right to vote at legislative elections was introduced in Singapore, not many people were given the franchise. Consequently, the political parties were working to win the votes of the few rather than the many. Even the Workers' Party, although striving for Independence, did not have a very radical program.

There was a political "gap" waiting to be filled after legislative changes enfranchised many more people before the 1959 election. The PAP did not quite emerge "out of the blue" to contest that election. It had put forward candidates in 4 of the 25 seats at the 1955 election, winning three of them. In 1959, however, it contested all 51 seats and won 43 of them.

In 1961, Tunku Abdul Rahman, the Prime Minister of Malaya, while visiting Singapore proposed that Malaya, Singapore, and the two sparsely-populated British territories of Sarawak and North Borneo (later called Sabah) should join to form a new state, Malaysia. There would be economic gains, through trade and investment, as well as security benefits to help fight Communist subversion. Malaysia was formed in 1963, but was followed by disillusion in Singapore. One of the main attractions for Singapore in joining the new state was the prospect of broadening Singapore's range of exports to Malaya. However, this was not encouraged by the Malaysian government, and, combined with other sources of disagreement, resulted in Singapore being forced to leave Malaysia in 1965, and become fully independent.

A completely independent Singapore

This was not the end of the world for Singapore. It was a well-disguised blessing. After Separation, Singapore no longer had any illusions about the prospects of promoting its ideals inside a Malaysia that had shown its determination not to change its policies. It now had full responsibility for making its own way in the world. Singapore had to chart its own economic course, which it did with the help of the U.N. Technical Assistance Board, which had already been advising it for several years.

After the PAP formed the government in 1959, its initial priority was dealing with unemployment, and providing housing, two objectives which, fortunately, were mutually supportive. Industrialization was an objective for a year or so, with Malaysia in mind as a destination for exports, then, when hopes of a common market were disappointed, the idea of "leapfrogging" exports to more distant destinations – borrowed from Israel – was adopted. But industrialization was slow in taking off. The Jurong complex, although an expensive infrastructure had been constructed (see pp. 8–9), was almost unoccupied. Tourism contributed to the economy, but it was not enough.[1] The first two attempts at manufacturing – paper products and ceramics – did not succeed.

Lee Kuan Yew writes in his memoirs that by the later 1960s he had resolved on two major thrusts of policy which led to Singapore's economic success. One was to make use of technology through cooperation with Multinational Corporations (MNCs), principally from the United States. He did not agree with the prevailing left-wing view that the MNCs acted as exploiters of the natural resources of developing countries – Singapore did not have many of these resources anyway. Lee Kuan Yew and, until 1965, Hon Sui Sen, a permanent secretary and then Minister of Finance, went through the applications from MNCs to decide which applicants should be strongly urged to come to Singapore. By the late 1980s, about three-quarters of Singapore's manufacturing output was produced by wholly- or partly-owned foreign firms. The second policy thrust was that Singapore should strive to attain the status of a First World "oasis" in a Third World region in respect of high standards in health, education, transportation, telecommunications, and services. This would help to re-educate and re-orient Singaporeans, as well as being attractive to foreigners who came to Singapore for business or pleasure. It is a corollary of the policy of encouraging the entry of MNCs: Singapore must have a competitive advantage and be attractive enough for them to locate there, or even choose it as the site of their regional headquarters.[2] These goals were assisted by the efforts of Singapore's Economic Development Board, and of UN officials, especially Dr. Albert Winsemius, who had acquired a deep knowledge of the Singapore economy over a long period.[3]

The two "new directions" of policy just referred to illustrate the connection between the values of the PAP leaders, examined in Chapter 5, and the economic policies pursued after the government achieved complete independence in 1965. Prime Minister Lee Kuan Yew seems to have taken a personal interest in "choosing the MNC path" as the preferred instrument in invigorating the economy. This was a significant decision – so many other Third World states chose, and stuck with, import substitution strategies.[4] What was important here was not only the presence of some values, but the absence of others. Lee himself has stated that (like Goh Keng Swee) his mind was untainted by the doctrinaire distrust of MNCs which influenced some politicians elsewhere. He was confident that, on his own territory, operating in an environment where corruption was minimal, he could stand up to any attempts by MNCs to assert control. Actually, some of the earlier MNCs, such as Shell,[5] were quite domesticated, and took part in local activities as well as being members of bodies such as the National Wages Council. This is an appropriate indication of the place of pragmatism in PAP decisions. If a proposed course of action conflicts with PAP values, it may be modified. If it does not, then pragmatism's dictates can be followed with vigor.

By about 1973, Singapore's leaders might have been excused if they felt that Singapore was well on the road to success,[6] not that it was in their nature to relax easily. Economic performance was always at the top of the PAP agenda, and remains so, but after the economic lines of advance were planned and set in motion, the government was able to give some attention to other important objectives. Four instances may be cited to illustrate the trend. Housing became less utilitarian and more gracious and stylish (see p. 90). Another topic was care of the environment, including "rescue" operations, such as the cleansing of rivers. Another was the promotion of planting and greening, which both benefited the atmosphere and was pleasing to the eye.[7] The fourth was the preservation of older buildings, perceiving them, somewhat belatedly, as assets and reminders of Singapore's history, rather than as relics which made no contribution to Singapore's "modern look".[8]

Changes in types of housing are discussed on pp. 90–1. The most spectacular, almost miraculous, examples of river reclamation were probably the restoration of the Singapore River and the Kallang Basin. Moving thousands of people who lived in boats or adjacent to the water was even more difficult than moving farmers from their land (see p. 91). Lee Kuan Yew led the way in encouraging a "clean and green" movement, not only planting trees and shrubs, but also ensuring that they were kept well maintained. This was complemented by constructing a bird park in

Jurong, until then a citadel of industrialization. Anti-pollution measures included bans on smoking and also restrictions on advertising tobacco products. Measures for controlling the use of firecrackers, however unwelcome to many Chinese, had the double merit of preventing injury and also checking noise pollution.

Singapore has no equivalent of the ancient buildings to be found in Cambodia, such as Angkor Wat, or Indonesia's Borobudur. But it has some agreeable buildings, now about 150 years old, or more – the Sri Mariamman Temple, Thian Hock Keng Temple, the Armenian Church and the Ali-Abrar Mosque.[9] Some official buildings, such as the new Parliament House and the old City Hall are also attractive. The area where most of these are clustered is becoming a cultural, historical and retail trade center. The policy of preserving noteworthy buildings and areas represents a change of heart by the government, symbolized by the establishment in 1971 of a Preservation of Monuments Board. The new policy applies not only to individual buildings, but also to historic areas, such as "Chinatown" and "Little India". The contribution of the new policy to tourism is indicated by the latest arrangements for two-hour tours which depart from the airport. One of the two includes Parliament House and the Colonial district, while the other includes Chinatown, Little India and other ethnic districts.[10] The achievements mentioned above were not as remarkable as the government's economic achievements. However, they showed that the PAP had a balanced agenda and that its program was concerned about more than the single-minded pursuit of economic growth.

Lee Kuan Yew and his "Lieutenants"

To consider the role of Lee Kuan Yew in this introductory chapter is neither an automatic nor a capricious choice; it is a considered one. The authors of a recent book on "Lee's Lieutenants"[11] have rightly made the case that the other leading figures in the PAP and in the government made important contributions to what was a team, not a one-man, effort. As usual, however, when making out a case for a "*primus inter pares*" role, the accent must properly be on the "*primus*".

History has amply demonstrated that leaders can make a difference. The most remarkable achievement of the PAP (and Singapore) was to have Lee Kuan Yew as its leader. This was not preordained. In a contest for the party leadership in 1959, Lee was elected by a single vote (Toh Chin Chye's) over Hokkien-speaking, and populist politician, Ong Eng Guan, who almost certainly would have led Singapore in different and probably disastrous directions.[12]

Lee's intellectual ability was demonstrated by his success at Raffles College, Singapore, and at Cambridge University. His entry into politics was somewhat fortuitous, arising from his meetings with other academics and professionals from Singapore and Malaya in Great Britain, when politics was discussed, pamphlets circulated, and feelings of anti-colonial nationalism were focused. The group was influenced by members of the British Labour Party, and by the Fabian Society. The meetings resumed after Lee's return to Singapore. Lee was confident – some say arrogant – and he had a good political sense. He gave evidence of this in the Assembly after the party had won three seats at the Legislative Assembly elections of 1955. When the PAP won a majority and formed the government in 1959, Lee had not yet demonstrated his complete range of political abilities. He was at the head of a divided party (non-Communist and pro-Communist). He achieved complete control after the latter faction broke off a few years later. This is one of the rare examples where, in a party divided along these lines, the non-Communist wing has triumphed. Lee has generalized about many new states: "In the first flush of the transfer of power to local nationalist leaders, a number of democratic socialists assumed authority over the apparatus of the state and the fortunes of the people. The history of the last two decades, however, is a sad commentary on their lack of understanding of the mechanics of power, and worse, their lack of expertise in the exercise of power." Lee continued by contrasting the emergence of Communist leaders in Asia: when they came into power, they stayed in.[13] The PAP under Lee was, of course, a conspicuous exception to the democratic socialist norm. It was part of the PAP's achievement not only to gain power, but to retain it. As Lee has observed, he was compelled to become a skilled exponent of street-fighting in order to match opponents who excelled at it.

He went on to lead the country for 31 years as Prime Minister. But one cannot judge the influence of Lee solely by his role as Prime Minister, or afterwards as Senior Minister. He left his indelible imprint on the party and on Singapore in two other ways. He conditioned future leaders to think and act in certain ways – although some of the ideas he advocated, such as the Graduate Mother Scheme, and some aspects of Confucianism, did not endure. Second, through his memoirs[14] Lee provides a more complete and more-widely-circulated account of politics in Singapore than any other politician has done or is likely to do.

There is no cult of personality in Singapore. Singapore's stamps and coins are not embellished with Lee's, or any other politician's, image. Lee's portrait or photograph is not apparent in classrooms and offices, and not found staring down from signboards, unlike many neighboring states. A gigantic bust of Lee has not been carved into the side of a mountain, as Marcos had done in the Philippines.[15] Perhaps unique in the region, tourists in Singapore are unlikely to know who the country's leaders are unless they read the local newspapers.

Lee Kuan Yew is a staunch believer in talent and the need to identify and encourage it (see p. 56). This support of meritocracy is expressed, as a parting message, in the last lines of the second volume of his memoirs,[16] where he reiterates the need to promote meritocracy, particularly at the highest level – political leaders. Lee is also a firm supporter in hierarchy, as are the PAP leaders in general, which is constitutionally correct in a parliamentary system like Singapore (although it does not operate in all parliamentary systems). Training courses given to civil servants in Singapore (see p. 27), made quite clear that the Minister, not the top civil servant, is in charge (see pp. 28–9).

Lee has voiced his skepticism about democracy, at least in the usual liberal "Western" version: The PAP founders (not too differently from Lee himself):

> ... believed that political stability was the top priority because it was a prerequisite for development and modernization. This belief accompanied a shared apprehension about the transferability of Westminster democracy to an Asian society and an underlying conviction that unfettered "democracy"... contained within it certain frailties always threatening to degenerate into mob

> rule. Although sacrifice of certain individual freedoms for the good of the whole (a concept traditionally part of certain Asian cultures) and for stability was necessary, at the same time they believed in constitutionalism and the rule of law as the only civilized alternative to arbitrary personal rule, the plague of the third world.[17]

Lee Kuan Yew's opinions on bribery and corruption are unambiguous. He is appalled by some Third World leaders' acquisition on a vast scale of wealth for their families and themselves. He has called this the "bane" of the Third World, and examples in the region abound, former Presidents Marcos and Suharto being among the most notorious.[18] The PAP has always stood for purity and anti-corruption, as symbolized by the white "uniform" worn by PAP members on official occasions. After the PAP became the government, it stiffened the rules in corruption cases in the prosecution's favor; for instance, it allowed the courts to treat proof that accused persons were living beyond their means, or were unable to explain the possession of property, as evidence that bribery had occurred. With these modifications, some quite high-profile cases became headline news. A Minister of State was sentenced to several years in jail for accepting bribes from a housing developer. Phey Yew Kok, the President of the NTUC and a PAP MP, was charged with, among other things, criminal breach of trust. He jumped bail and for some time spent an unglamorous life in Thailand. The saddest case was probably that of Teh Cheang Wan (see p. 91), who received payments in 1981–2 from housing developers for allowing improper construction. When an investigation began, he committed suicide. These examples show that even the high and well-connected were not exempt from anti-corruption laws.[19]

The primary reason for Singapore having the highest salaries for ministers and top civil servants is to attract and retain meritocratic candidates (see pp. 60–1). However, a subsidiary reason is to eliminate the smallest temptation to be corrupt.

Both Lee Kuan Yew and B.G. Lee were the subject of discussion in Parliament after investigations on their conduct had been set in motion by the Minister for Finance on the instructions of the Prime Minister, Goh Chok Tong (see p. 151). The investigations concerned alleged improprieties over discounts on the sale of some condominium units, and the matter was raised by J.B. Jeyaretnam of the Workers' Party. The finding was that no improprieties were involved. But the fact that questions could be asked and enquiries made about two very prominent ministers is significant. The question of the PAP leaders' probity in general was referred to by Thomas J. Bellows when he said that Singapore was an almost unique example of a country where "... national interests, albeit narrowly defined by a narrow elite, are consistently placed ahead of any particular benefits for the rulers."[20]

The problem of political succession has seriously destabilized many of the post-colonial states, particularly those with long-time rulers who will not name their successors and will not relinquish power, until eventually they either die or are violently thrown out of office. Lee Kuan Yew – always a worrier and a planner – recognized that this was a critical issue. By the late 1960s, when Lee was still just in his 40s, this problem came to the forefront of his mind – how to replace his almost irreplaceable self. He was so identified with Singapore's prosperity and well-being, that when he underwent a very minor operation, the stock market declined sharply. It is remarkable that Lee was willing to step aside voluntarily, and that he was able to identify, recruit, and train an able group of second generation leaders, who then chose from among themselves who should succeed Lee (see p. 114). It is also remarkable that he was willing to stay on in a new, somewhat less powerful role – that of Senior Minister. The succession to Lee Kuan Yew in late 1990 by Goh Chok Tong caused not a ripple of concern in Singapore (see p. 116). The gradual nature of the transition accustomed most of the public to the change. Also, initially, some believed that Lee was "really" still in charge. The smooth succession was a considerable achievement.

Singapore's achievements under the PAP

When countries are rated numerically to convey their performances in certain fields, Singapore usually comes out at, or near, the top. So many ratings are given, under so many headings, that it would be tiresome to attempt a comprehensive view. The following sample is just to give some impression of the respects in which Singapore has done well. In June 2001, Singapore was given the highest rating in Asia regarding health, and ninth in the world. On "leadership quality" and "economic policy effectiveness" it ranked top in both, but only fourth in its degree of government intervention. In 2001, it retained its Triple A rating by Standard and Poor, while in a World Competitiveness Report, it came second in the world for the sixth time, immediately after the United States. In 2000, it was rated second in the world in its degree of economic freedom, after Hong Kong. It won the competition for the world's best airline three times, but in 2001 was replaced by Air New Zealand, a victory for another small state.[21]

Unfortunately, it is impossible to measure another criterion for success, suggested by B.G. Lee – the number of disasters which governments have contrived to avoid! A good Singapore example is the way the PAP government steered the state through the serious 1997 Asian economic crisis, from which some states have still not recovered.[22] In Singapore, wages were frozen or cut back, as were employers' social security contributions, and the stock market and the Singapore dollar both fell somewhat, but, other than a few jobs lost, Singapore emerged almost unscathed by the devastating regional crisis (see Chapter 6, pp. 70–1).

Two other achievements of Singapore cannot be quantified, but nevertheless reflected great ability on the part of the government. After separation from Malaysia, Singapore had to construct both a department of defence (and armed forces) and a department of foreign affairs and a diplomatic corps (see Chapter 13, p. 169).

Construction of large-scale, useful projects (as opposed to "white elephants," which are solicitously nurtured around Southeast Asia) ranks among Singapore's competitive achievements Three projects stand out, two taken from the early days of Singapore's industrialization. Another is currently being completed.

An early EDB project was a planned, large industrial estate in Jurong, to be the site of an iron and steel plant. The plan included a waterfront heavy industry zone, which on completion would be followed by other industrial zones. In the early days of Jurong the undertaking seemed promising, although some impatient critics referred to it, affectionately, as "Goh Keng Swee's Folly".[23] Construction in Jurong was indeed a leap of faith. The leaders of the EDB were willing to expend much of their budget on building the infrastructure long before they had any clients to occupy it or pay for it. In the end, the accomplishment was universally acclaimed, meriting Goh Chok Tong's accolade of being a "Herculean achievement".[24]

A second construction achievement was in greatly expanding Singapore's port facilities, allowing it to become one of the busiest ports in the world, and in its early commitment to building the facilities to handle cargo containers (and 24-hour berthing). The PSA (Port of Singapore Authority) is the world's largest cargo container operator, if operations of its subsidiaries are taken into account.[25]

The third large-scale construction achievement is the new air terminal being built at Changi costing $1.54 bn, covering 350,000 square meters, and designed to handle 20 m. passengers a year, with four stories and three basement levels. Special lighting has been devised to allow the maximum amount of natural light.[26] The supporting infrastructure will be designed to handle the super-jumbo of the twenty-first century, the A3XX, twenty-five of which were on order from Airbus.[27]

Another achievement of Singapore's was unsought, and, unlike the Jurong project, container facilities, or the construction of the new air terminal, has been "unsung', in the sense that is too undramatic to be publicized or heralded. It concerns the perpetual fight against the dictates of geography – Singapore's location and small size.[28]

"Location! Location! Location!" is the slogan of estate agents, geographers and International Relations experts. The choice of Singapore for development in 1819 was appropriate because it lay at a "crossroads" of trade. But, as Michael Leifer has observed, from the point of view of security, it is subject to the tyranny of geography.[29] This point is elaborated on later (see p. 169). Singapore's location is of interest to Lee Kuan Yew, who believes that adverse climates are harmful to the prospects of good government. He has asked, rhetorically, how many well-governed states are situated on, or nearly on, the equator?

As regards size, steps can be taken to make slight additions to the amount of land available. Singapore has carried out a program of land reclamation, which has added 3,000 acres of land. One can visit a restaurant site where, thirty years ago, one ate chili crab near the water, but now, after reclamation, is no longer within easy walking distance of the sea. Other measures of adding to the stock of land and road space include tunneling, which provides underground space. Also, the Housing and Development Board intends to construct housing that rises even higher than before (see p. 93). Ironically, Singapore not only has a shortage of land; it also has a shortage of potable water, which makes it dependent on the good-will of its neighbors – an unenviable situation (see p. 174).

The need to extend foreign investment became evident by the 1990s (see p. 76). To compensate for Singapore's small size, it had to move business activity beyond its own restricted confines through foreign investment, by creating an "external wing" (see pp. 76–7).

Singapore's smallness has produced a number of social and economic consequences as well. One is that there is a shortage of talent, which has made it more difficult for politicians to pursue their aims of obtaining sufficient meritocratic recruits to strengthen government in Singapore. The talent which exists has to be spread too thinly, and this has led to "doubling up" of ministers and government workers so that one person often has two or more jobs, and as a result you "see the same people popping up everywhere".[30] It was mildly surprising, although pleasantly so, for the authors, after an interview with the Executive Director of the People's Association, to have him say that we would be meeting him again when we interviewed the Prime Minister in a few days time, since he would be present in his capacity as Press Secretary to the Prime Minister. Another reason for "doubling up" ministers is to broaden the experience of the younger ministers. A Minister may have a senior post in one department and also a junior position in another, mainly to provide training for the future. Additionally, occupying jobs in two ministries simultaneously may broaden vision, a quality much esteemed by Lee Kuan Yew.[31]

Another consequence of Singapore's small size is the "shortage of road space". Not only are there special charges for traveling on certain roads at times when they are heavily used, but to buy a car is costly; the required certificate of entitlement is in effect obtained by auction. It follows that new cars cost substantially more than they do in the neighboring countries of Malaysia and Indonesia.[32] Consumer budgets are skewed by the seemingly out-of-line high cost of owning and driving a car. Electronic road pricing was introduced in 1998. The corresponding achievement, or merit, is that traffic normally moves along smoothly in Singapore, unlike the ubiquitous traffic jams found elsewhere in the region. As B.G. Lee has noted, the high prices are painful, but the alternative is gridlock.[33]

Offsetting, to some degree, the disadvantages of smallness, are the administrative benefits which arise from it. "In no small measure the diminutive proportions of the island [have] contributed to the easy mobilization and the execution of public policies …".[34]

Government policy mistakes

After listing some of the government's achievements, it is fitting to mention several of its major mistakes, some of which are described in more detail elsewhere in the book.

One mistake was the "wage correction policy" (see p. 71), which represented a laudable effort to convert the economy from seeking principally to increase employment, to endeavoring to move from a low-technology economy to a higher niche by the use of more advanced technology. However, the attempt was premature, and the foreign demand was not enough to make it possible at a profit. One of the major problems of the Economic Committee (1986) (see p. 70) was therefore to make an appropriate correction to the wage correction policy itself.

Another ill-advised policy was persistence with the government's early "Two is Enough" population policy (see p. 52). It miscalculated the effects of affluence on the birth rate. It was not wrong for the government later to switch from discouraging population growth to encouraging it when the birth rate fell. The mistake consisted in taking too long to make the reversal.

The tangled question of Singapore's joining, and then parting, from Malaysia, constituted a minefield for politicians. One of the ensuing detonations followed the

PAP's decision to field a token number of candidates in the Malaysian parliamentary elections of 1964. Looking at this decision in hindsight, it seems not to have been a very good idea.

Political mistakes involving government policies

Some policies have merit and are not mistakes per se, but their unpopularity turns them into political mistakes. In retrospect, they could have been acceptable only by a disproportionate use of resources; even then, the effect might have been counter-effective. The Graduate Mother Scheme comes immediately to mind (see p. 60). It aroused too much emotional opposition to be worthwhile. The ends sought for needed to be attempted by other means – as, indeed, they have been (see pp. 60, 187–9).

An internal issue caused an outcry in 1984, and probably cost the PAP some votes in the ensuing election. The unpopular proposal was that the minimum age for withdrawal of savings from the Central Provident Fund should be raised from 55 to 60, or even 65. Dispassionately viewed, which it was not, the proposal made sense statistically; contributors' life expectancy was getting higher, and it would take them longer to save enough for their retirement. Once again, emotions were aroused, and defeated actuarial arguments. A cartoon, depicting a coffin and a long line of elderly people queuing to make their withdrawals, is captioned "Too late". The proposal was shelved.[35]

Hostility towards Singapore's PAP government

Finally, in considering what is remarkable about Singapore, one must consider the unusual degree of antagonism that Singapore and the PAP engender in some, mainly foreign, critics. Some of the criticism seems innately hostile, unwarranted, and based on preconceived ideas rather than the actual situation.

Criticism sometimes takes the form of tendentious "labeling", when, for example, housing blocks in Singapore are referred to as "barracks".[36] Another example of criticism, based on innuendo, is the misleading use of pictures. In one book, a photograph of marching police in Singapore is accompanied by the caption, "Police State Politics".[37] An endemic misunderstanding concerns the "banning" of chewing gum. The practice of chewing gum is not actually illegal (only importing it for sale is).

There have also been criticisms of government "campaigns" because they are said to be based on the premise that ordinary people (their target) are "immature".[38] To choose a few examples, there have been campaigns against long hair (on males), "killer litter" (thrown out of high-rise flats), spitting in public (originally to contain the spread of tuberculosis), and in favor of speaking Mandarin, behaving courteously, and flushing public toilets. Critics cite these campaigns to show that Singapore is a micro-managed "nanny state". However, such strictures often fail to take account of the fact that some behavior in Singapore has been lacking in civility, and some has been dangerous to health (see pp. 92, 196–7).

Image of the future

Singapore has come a long way from the image of rickshaws and death houses, to become an amazingly successful modern and globalized city-state. Perhaps later in this century the image invoked by the mention of Singapore will be one of a prosperous, cutting-edge Knowledge-Based Economy that is still extraordinary and remarkable.

2 How Singapore became independent

Lee Kuan Yew and the People's Action Party (PAP)

From Raffles to World War Two

To Western eyes, Singapore was discovered in 1819.[1] Of course, other eyes have since learned that it existed, and was populated – although not populous – before then. In spite of this, it seems appropriate here to follow the formerly conventional Western wisdom, and begin with Sir Stamford Raffles. His statue, erected in 1887, and undisturbed by the present government party, the People's Action Party, remains as a symbol of Singapore's commitment to trade. This book tells the story of how, after World War Two and the Japanese occupation, Singapore achieved independence and chose a quite remarkable group of people to rule it, Lee Kuan Yew and his colleagues in the People's Action Party, who raised Singapore from a Third World country to First World status.

Raffles, of the British East India Company (EIC), was instructed to find a port which could keep the Straits of Malacca open and protect that area from incursions from the nearby Dutch territories. Singapore, which he hit upon in 1819, was only sparsely inhabited. The first census (1824) showed that the population numbered only eleven thousand. "Malays", in a broad sense, were the largest group, but they were rapidly being overtaken numerically by Chinese. The rest of the population came from nearby areas, many from what is now Indonesia. The place had been given several different names, but the one used most was "Singapura", City of the Lion.[2]

By exploiting a succession dispute in nearby Johor in 1819, Raffles was able to conclude treaties with various local officials including the Johor Sultan, which allowed him to set up a trading post. By a further treaty, in 1824, the Sultan ceded Singapore island and all other islands within ten miles of its shores to the EIC. In 1826, the British government joined, administratively, Singapore with the territories of Malacca and Penang, as the Straits Settlements.[3] By 1860, Singapore's population has grown to over 80,000, of whom about 50,000 were Chinese, 13,000 were Indians, and 11,000 were Malays.[4] The Europeans had also grown in numbers, but remained a small minority, consisting mostly of merchants and administrators.

In 1867, the Straits Settlements was raised to the status of a Crown Colony. It was thought that the constitutional link with India was becoming less appropriate, and that Britain should become more involved in the neighboring Malay peninsula to protect its investments and trade, mainly in tin, from being disrupted.

Singapore's links with more distant countries were improved by the opening of the Suez Canal (1869) and by greater use of steamships.

Immigration from China was having social, and later political, repercussions in Singapore. Originally, the main security problem was "wars" between rival "triads" (secret societies). A "Chinese protectorate" was established in 1877 to regulate such organizations, as well as to control Chinese immigration. By the 1900s, these "wars" were not so troubling. However, in the 1920s and 1930s, the rivalry between the Guomintang and the Communists in China made it necessary to restrict the immigration of Chinese males, and led to the surveillance and suppression of some Chinese political organizations. While the interest in politics of most Chinese was centered on politics in China, some Chinese were now taking an interest in local politics, and, like their counterparts from other ethnic groups, were represented in the Singapore Legislative Council.

After World War One, Singapore became internationally significant, not only for trade, through its geographical setting near the Straits, but also for security reasons. By the Washington Naval Treaties of 1921, Japan's status as a naval power was confirmed and, maybe more important, Britain agreed not to construct a naval base which was east of 110 degrees longitude, which ruled out Hong Kong, but made Singapore eligible. Shortly afterward, construction of the Singapore base was started, and was completed in time for World War Two (irrelevantly, because it was claimed to ensure protection from a *naval* attack. As is well known, the invasion came from the north, by land). In December 1941, Japanese troops landed near the Thai/Malayan border, marched and bicycled the length of the Malayan peninsula, and the surrender of Singapore followed quickly. Even if resistance had been stiffer, Singapore's water supply had been fatally depleted once the Japanese had captured its main reservoir.

The Japanese occupation lasted until September 1945, when British troops landed and the Japanese surrendered. The Japanese occupation was a time of terrible hardship for many, including prisoners of war in Changi jail and elsewhere.[5] The economy had almost collapsed, and the British military administrators were hailed as liberators. As in most of Southeast Asia, the myth of "white supremacy" had been irrevocably shattered. During the occupation, the Chinese had been particularly harshly treated, because of Chinese resistance to the Japanese invasion of China and because Chinese resistance to the Japanese invasion of Malaya had been very effective. (This resistance, soon after the war ended, was largely converted into the Communist uprising (1948) that the British labeled "the Emergency".[6])

In Singapore, the British wished to promote constitutional advance, culminating in elections for a legislative assembly, from which a government for the Crown Colony of Singapore could eventually emerge.[7] A commission was appointed in 1953 (the Rendel Commission, under Sir George Rendel) to spell out the sequence referred to above. There were to be two main differences from the system which operated in Britain. Some powers would be "reserved" – would not be the concern of the legislature – because they would be retained by Britain. Also, in Singapore, although the chief minister could give advice to the governor, the latter would not be required to accept it.[8]

The first election held under the provisions of a new constitution in 1955 was contested by a wider range of parties than before. In addition to the relatively well-established, and well-off, Progressive Party, other contestants were the Labour Front, led by David Marshall, a lawyer of Iraqi-Jewish extraction, which was moderately left-wing, the Democratic Party which was conservative and communal (Chinese), and, finally, the PAP (People's Action Party) under Lee Kuan Yew (see p. 39). The Labour Front won the largest number of seats, and Marshall was appointed chief minister. The PAP contested only four seats, of which it won three. Lee and his colleagues thought it politically inadvisable to try to form a government at this stage. Lee made the observation that, "History has shown that those who take office before Independence never take office after it".[9]

> Some are critical of Marshall as a headstrong, hot-tempered, flamboyant, and egotistic individual, who never really seemed to anticipate or appreciate fully the consequences of his political words and deeds. Others view Marshall as a charming, principled idealist who, despite some honest blunders, believed himself to be a populist moving to the same rhythm as the people ... What is beyond doubt is that his tenure as chief minister was stormy and that later in his career he was badly used and misused by the pro-Communists.[10]

Marshall's period as chief minister was marked by riots, school sit-ins and strikes. The British were unhappy about Marshall's inability to govern effectively. In negotiations with the British concerning constitutional reform, Marshall said that he would resign unless Singapore were granted complete self-rule. The resulting All-Party Constitutional Mission to London (April–May 1956) won for Marshall almost everything that he sought, except that the British would not yield their control over emergency internal security powers. In June 1956 he resigned, expecting that his Cabinet would follow his example, but it did not.[11] However unrewarding Marshall's political career turned out to be, he was later transferred to Paris, as Singapore's ambassador. The PAP was inspired in making an appointment which matched the post with his talents.

The new chief minister, Lim Yew Hock, also of the Labour Front, was the antithesis of his predecessor – tough, action-oriented, hard-driving, a white-collar trade unionist. He used force to deal with strikes and sit-ins, without regard for the consequences of his decisive but ill-advised policies.

> Lim Yew Hock taught me how not to be tough and flat-footed ... Lim did not understand that the communist game was to make him lose the support of the masses, the Chinese-speaking people, to destroy his credibility as a leader who was acting in their interests. They were able to portray him as an opportunist and a puppet acting at the behest of the 'colonialist imperialists'.[12]

The worst violence occurred during the October 1956 riots that followed a student sit-in, and the arrest of most of the pro-Communist Middle Road (the location of MCP headquarters) trade unionists (incidentally relieving leftist pressure on PAP moderates). The riots left 13 dead, 123 injured, and more than 1,000 arrested, as well as extensive property damage.[13]

Politically, probably the most significant of Lim's actions was the arrest of thirty-five pro-Communists on August 20, 1957. Five of those detained were on the PAP Executive Committee (later known as the Central Executive Committee). The arrests were important in altering the balance of power in the top ranks of the PAP. At the party conference on August 9, 1957, pro-Communists had apparently gained control by having supporters turn up in unexpectedly large numbers, thus winning six of the twelve seats on the Committee. The arrests gave the moderates the chance (which they took) to regain control and alter the party constitution so as to prevent any such similar "coup" in the future (see p. 39).

Lim continued with the efforts to enlarge the powers which Singapore would enjoy under the new constitution. Two more Constitutional Conferences were held in London in 1957 and 1958. Singapore would be given almost complete self-rule, although Britain retained, not unexpectedly, control of defense and foreign affairs. The sensitive issue of internal security was ingeniously resolved by creating a national security council consisting of equal numbers of representatives from Britain and Singapore, and putting the deciding vote in the hands of a representative of the Federation of Malaya. This arrangement symbolized how closely, from the security perspective, the futures of Singapore and Malaya were intertwined.

The forthcoming general election (1959) would include compulsory voting, and more than half of the nearly 600,000 electors would be voting for the first time. The constellation of parties had altered somewhat. Marshall had left the Labour Front, and had formed the Workers' Party in late 1957. Lim Yew Hock reorganized his followers into the SPA (Singapore People's Alliance) in 1958.

Lim's new party did not fare well at the election. As foreseen, he had lost votes by his clumsy use of force, the economy was in poor shape, and some of his followers had been the target of allegations of corruption. The SPA gathered only four seats. Humiliatingly, with pro-Communist support withdrawn, the Labour Front did not win a single seat. The PAP enjoyed a decisive victory, winning 43 out of 51 seats contested. There were reservations about the PAP by some who were put off by the party's "leftness". However, others were attracted by its well-presented program and by its commitment to complete independence by seeking "merger" with Malaya (see p. 18). Additionally, by now the British had full confidence in Lee Kuan Yew.[14]

The PAP leaders, as an expression of their somewhat precarious solidarity with their pro-Communist wing, had promised not to take office until eight of the prominent detainees held by the British were released.[15] This was done, and celebrated appropriately. Nevertheless, none of the ex-detainees was appointed to high office, or was allowed access to top-secret files.

After the election, the PAP had some unfinished business to conclude. An early victory in the PAP's rise to power had been its gaining control of the Singapore city council in a 1957 election. The leading figure on the winning PAP team, Ong Eng Guan, helped by his use of the locally-prominent Hokkien dialect, was a successful vote-getter. However, once in office, he played to the crowd. His administrative abilities were limited and he did not work well with his staff. In 1960 he was appointed Minister of National Development, but was dismissed for incompetence. He was expelled from the PAP as well, and then started a small party of his own. For some time the PAP unfinished business remained unfinished. In the 1963 general election, Ong retained his seat against PAP opposition.[16] A small victory for the PAP was that, as promised in its 1959 election manifesto, it abolished the now superfluous city council, along with its troublesome mayor.

The decisive PAP win at the elections (in seats) was not an accurate indication of the PAP leaders' firm grasp of the top positions inside their own party. The small group, consisting mainly of professionals (see p. 38), which had conceived the idea of the PAP, still had to convert that group into a mass party ("mass" in the sense of size of membership, not the degree to which the policy of the party is controlled by the mass membership rather than by the leaders).

The PAP leaders went about their aim of forming a mass party in various ways. First, they attempted to use contacts which had been made and might be useful, for instance through various trade union leaders who had sought Lee Kuan Yew's legal advice on disputes which concerned their unions. Second, they studied, and followed in many respects, Communist methods and tactics for presenting their ideas to the greatest strategic advantage. Third, they sought to build up, take over, or defend from a hostile takeover, various associations (see p. 95). Fourth, as we have seen, they tried to defend, or recapture, the party organization from pro-Communist attack (see p. 39). Fifth, later, they sought to attract support by attractive programs, and by providing good government in implementing these programs. Sixth, they used their power in the capacity of acting as the government, to supplement their strength in intra-party or inter-party contests. A good example of this is the trade union legislation of the late 1960s (see p. 31). The second and third of these tactics are discussed in the next few pages.

The PAP moderate leaders were willing, indeed eager, to learn from their pro-Communist counterparts. They sought to understand their minds and know their methods of staging "campaigns" to impress people and harness their enthusiasm. "We wanted a series of well-publicized campaigns to clean the streets of the city, clear the beaches of debris ... It was a copycat exercise borrowed from the communists."[17] They saw no reason why all these exercises in symbolism should be the prerogative of the Communists alone. The PAP moderate leaders were no more reluctant to adopt such tactics of swaying the minds of the masses than they were in adopting a structure of party control, which would be exercised from the top down (see p. 39) which was also "copycat".

Another principal tactic was to capture and, if possible, hold "political space".[18] A prime example was the founding of the People's Association, which was of special importance because of its wide scope of operation, embracing voluntary associations as diverse as those concerned with sports, ballet, drawing and cooking. Another example was the Works Brigade, which recruited young unemployed people, housed them, and instructed them in farming and various kinds of construction work, "generally to put some discipline into them and, most important, to get them off the streets." Education and culture were given a negative, as well as a positive, interpretation. Not only was children's education and adult education to be extended, as in China there was a drive against "yellow culture" – the "decadent" culture that had afflicted China in the early twentieth century, exemplified by gambling, opium-smoking, pornography, corruption, nepotism and so on.[19]

In 1961, when tensions in the PAP had not yet reached the stage of an actual split, public interest in Singapore was captured by a speech made by Tunku Abdul

Rahman on May 21, 1961 on the possibility of merger between Malaya and Singapore.[20] Under the Marshall and Lim Yew Hock governments, Singapore had unsuccessfully approached the Malayan Prime Minister on this issue. It therefore came as a surprise to many when the Tunku mentioned such a possibility in 1961. Actually, Malaya had considered a number of schemes, in some of which a feature was the inclusion of the Borneo states. With the British about to relinquish sovereignty over Sarawak and North Borneo (soon to be renamed Sabah), failing some alternative arrangement, they would become independent. The Tunku's tentative suggestion included not only Singapore, Sarawak and Sabah, but possibly the protectorate of Brunei as well.

The Singapore government took the Tunku's proposals very seriously. Opinion in Malaya was also happier about the inclusion of Sabah and Sarawak. Merger with Singapore alone would have raised the specter of awkward ethnic numbers. Singapore's 75 percent Chinese would have raised the non-Malay numbers in Malaysia enough to negate Malaya's existing Malay numerical superiority. The inclusion of Sabah and Sarawak would not incur a similar "Chinese problem", the Chinese percentage was too small, and the others would help dilute Singapore's Chinese numbers.[21]

An important consideration was that having Singapore inside the new federation, where active pro-Communists could be restrained by the provisions of the tough Federation Internal Security Act (ISA) might be better than having it outside where it might have assumed the role of a "little Cuba". The broad shape of the agreement was as outlined but some quite important details remained to be settled.

The course of events was influenced by a number of national and international factors. The areas which would be included in Malaysia found the proposal attractive from the security point of view. Singapore and, to a lesser extent Sarawak, which also had an active Communist armed threat, would decidedly gain from greater internal security. Australia and New Zealand, which had already played a role in resisting Communist aggression in Malaya, 1948–60, were also supportive. Many of the documents cited by writers on the formation of Malaysia consist of correspondence with the leaders of these two countries. In Singapore, the PAP was split on the issue of merger until the breakaway of the Barisan Sosialis in 1961. There was also some disapproval by opposition parties in Sarawak, as shown in the Cobbold Commission Report (see below).

The greatest opposition in neighboring countries came from Indonesia and, to a lesser extent, the Philippines, which intermittently revived its claim to Sabah.[22] Indonesia was opposed because of President Sukarno's particular world view of history, and it supported a brief rebellion in Brunei in 1961.

One important consideration was that, for the Malaysia proposal to succeed, Britain had to agree.[23] Moreover, it had to be satisfied that the populations of Sarawak and Sabah were also agreeable. This was established by the visit of the Cobbold Commission and its report.[24] It did find enough support in the territories to justify proceeding with the proposal, although opposition was greatest in Sarawak. Additionally, it appeared that a union of the Borneo territories without Singapore would not meet with British approval. Nor did it seem that Singapore by itself would be strong enough to contain the Communists. The talks on the possibility of Brunei's joining in a new federation broke down in 1963. The disposition of Brunei's oil revenues was one obstacle. Another was the appropriate placing of the Sultan of Brunei in the existing order of precedence of the Rulers of Malaysia.[25]

There was general agreement that the federal government of Malaysia would have control over security, defense and foreign affairs with respect to Singapore, Sarawak and Sabah. However, other issues needed to be settled, some of which proved to be more contentious than others. The conclusion of this section will indicate what the main "sticking points" at issue were; key issues which could divide the two main countries concerned, Malaya and Singapore.

The common market between Malaya/Malaysia and Singapore was probably the outstanding attraction for Singapore to join in the creation of Malaysia (the other main incentive was increased security, including internal security through the ISA). But, just as Singapore had seen its advantages, some Malayan leaders, apparently believing that a "zero-sum" interpretation applied, regarded its implementation as disadvantageous. At any rate, the World Bank report and recommendations on financial arrangements were not quickly acted upon by the Tunku or his Finance Minister, Tun Tan Siew Sin, who was determined to ensure that Singapore paid "its share". The main obstacle seems to have been a number of related differences of opinion which coincided and reinforced each other. Financially, there were disputes about the method of collection of taxes in the new federation, and about how they would be distributed. Moreover, there were political aspects which exacerbated the dispute. Tan Siew Sin was not only Finance Minister, but also the leader of the Malaysian Chinese Association (MCA), the main target of the PAP's adventurous incursion into Malayan politics at the general election of 1964 (see p. 21), and the main Chinese party in the Alliance Party headed by the Tunku.

Two other issues were relatively non-contentious. Singapore wished to retain local autonomy particularly on education and labor. In exchange, on the related issue of representation in the federal Parliament, Singapore was willing to accept numbers fewer than its percentage of the population warranted. Citizenship qualifications presented some initial difficulty, the Malayan government wished to "insulate" the federation from the votes of 600,000 Singapore citizens who were born outside Singapore. Singapore citizens, it was now proposed, could run as candidates for a seat in a legislature only in Singapore. But they would automatically become "nationals" of the new federation. On the "special position" of the Malays, Malays in Singapore would enjoy that status, but the "special privileges" or preferences possessed by Malays in Malaya would have no counterpart in Singapore. Lee Kuan Yew was convinced that Malay special rights were not the solution to Malay poverty.

It did not bode well for the agreement on Malaysia that the final details, including some financial ones, were drafted only during the last two days before the deadline. It was confirmed that there would be a common market, but the details were not fully set out, nor, it seems, were the implications fully understood. Some of the outlines, including a proposed Singapore loan for the Borneo territories, were hurriedly sketched out and recorded on the back of an envelope from the Ritz Hotel in London.[26]

The Malaysia proposal and politics in Singapore

The prospects of merger provoked fierce opposition from the pro-Communists in Singapore. What worried them most was that, if Malaysia came into being, Kuala Lumpur would be in charge of internal security and the ISA would be rigidly enforced. Their hope was that, if the Malaysia project foundered, then the PAP government might be overthrown and existing security arrangements in Singapore might then be rescinded. What they desired was "full self-government". The focus was soon upon the Anson by-election of 1961, where the PAP candidate was a Malay. Some trade unionists expressed their support for full self-government, hinting that they might not vote for the PAP unless the party backed their stand. They added that all political detainees should be released immediately. No assurances were given by the PAP on either issue. Pressure was intensified two days before the by-election when eight PAP members of the Legislative Assembly declared their support for the recalcitrant unionists. The consequence was a narrow defeat for the PAP in Anson, and a victory, not of his own making, but from pro-Communist support, for David Marshall.[27] Three days later, a comic opera incident occurred when James Puthucheary and some other pro-Communists visited the British High Commissioner, Lord Selkirk, and talked to him, over tea. They asked him a question: if the PAP split and their group formed the government, what would the British reaction be? Selkirk replied, with deadpan constitutional correctness, that, if there were no riots or the like, the constitution would not be suspended.[28] The visitors were sufficiently elated (or insufficiently deterred) to force a vote in the Legislative Assembly. The government won, but the majority was slim, and precarious. The dissidents were expelled from the party and formed a new one, the Barisan Sosialis (Socialist Front).

For two months or so the PAP maintained a majority in the Assembly, subject to the vagaries of sickness, death, or changes of heart. It was dependent on the support of other, mainly right-wing, parties. (PAP support in the party branches fell so drastically that they had to be substantially rebuilt.) The results of the carefully-crafted and judiciously-interpreted, referendum of July 2, 1962 provided conclusive vindication of merger and the PAP. The government succeeded in fixing in people's minds the belief that merger was "... a tide so big that neither the Communists nor anyone else could stop it."[29] The message was conveyed through the media, through twelve explanatory talks by Lee Kuan Yew, and by illuminated signs, strategically placed, for instance, prominently in Orchard Road, proclaiming that merger would come as surely as the sun would rise tomorrow; beside it was a representation of the sun, in all its glory, behaving accordingly. The referendum showed a 71 per cent vote for "Alternative A", the PAP-preferred form of merger, while there were 23 per cent blank votes. During the campaign, every move made by the Barisan and other opponents of merger was, seemingly effortlessly, countered by the PAP.

Singapore's bumpy road after merger: Singapore's exit

During the two years or so that Singapore formed part of Malaysia, there were several occasions when disputes arose between Singapore and the federal government. Four examples may be cited to illustrate what kinds of issue were most likely to provoke such disputes. Probably, the one which led to the greatest acrimony was Singapore's decision to nominate a "token number" of PAP candidates to contest the 1964 parliamentary elections in Malaysia. Only nine PAP candidates actually contested. A second event was almost a mirror image of the first; United Malays National Organization's (UMNO) decision to fight three, Malay, seats at the Singapore elections of September 1993. A third, linked to the second, was incitement by UMNO "ultras" (extremists) to riot in Singapore in July 1964. The fourth was that when, in 1963, the date for Malaysia's coming into effect was advanced by a few days, the Singapore government declared that for the short period between the two dates that it was independent.

Singapore's participation in the Malaysian 1964 election was designed to expose the weakness of the MCA as a component of the Alliance in Malaysia. Lee Kuan Yew thought that, although the MCA was financially strong, its following was "soft" and could be attracted by the PAP's electoral platform. This judgment was reflected in the seats which the PAP chose to contest; none of them had an electorate that was predominantly Malay. Although PAP rallies were well attended, it won only one seat, Bangsar, where the Indian trade unionist, C.V. Devan Nair, was elected. Actually, the MCA was stronger than the PAP thought. It not only had large financial resources, but also benefited from the use of patronage. (The PAP, on the contrary, had not much of a foundation on which to build an organization in the area.) Also, if the PAP intervention was only a "token", why was it surprised that, apart from Bangsar, it had only a token effect? To contest more constituencies might have been more productive.

Noordin Sopiee makes the point that one of worst consequences of the intervention may have been the alienation of the Tunku, a man intensely loyal to his allies, including Tan Siew Sin. When Lee Kuan Yew remarked, just before the 1964 election that the intention was to save the Tunku from his "so-called 'friends'," the Tunku retorted, "The PAP wants to teach us what is good for us and what is bad".[30] Who, exactly, in the PAP made the decision to participate in the election? Lee Kuan Yew had left on a trip to Africa before it occurred. Previously, he had empowered the Central Executive Committee to take the decision after his return. Its decision was to take part in the election. According to Lee Kuan Yew, the Committee was persuaded by Toh Chin Chye, Rajaratnam, and Ong Pang Boon.[31]

In the Singapore election of 1963, the main contest was between the PAP and the Barisan. But also of great interest, particularly to Malays, was the effort of UMNO to win the three predominantly Malay seats. The Tunku was expectant; how could UMNO and its allies fail to reap the reward of being the champion of the numerous Malays in the area? Yet when Tunku came to Singapore during the election, it turned out that all three of the predominantly "Malay" seats had been lost, and he was devastated.[32] The third event, deeply disturbing to those who hoped for a peaceful and tolerant Malaysia, occurred in July 1964, when the UMNO secretary-general, Syed Ja'afar Albar, along with other Malay "ultras", started an inciting verbal offensive against the PAP in Singapore about Malay rights, which culminated in a race riot. As late as August 17, clashes continued to occur in the Singapore district of Geylang.

The fourth event was not a violent one, but nevertheless was unwelcome to the British. When the date when Malaysia was to come into being was changed from August 31 to September 16, 1963, Lee did not want there to be a time gap, which, for example, might be used to try to dissuade the Tunku from proceeding rapidly toward creating Malaysia. Consequently, Lee noted: "We therefore decided that on 31 August we in Singapore would hold our major rally as originally planned, and assume our immediate independence".[33]

Two other items might be added to the list. One was the formation of the PAP-led Malaysian Solidarity Convention, which, apart from the PAP, included: the People's Progressive Party and the United Democratic Party (both Malaya), the Sarawak United People's Party, and Machinda (both Sarawak). The aim of the Convention was to advance the cause of a "Malaysian Malaysia", in which all citizens would be equal, irrespective of race.[34] The remaining event was what Lee Kuan Yew has described as his most important speech in the federal Parliament. He spoke partly in Malay, spending some of his time quoting anti-Chinese remarks by Albar and speeches by Mahathir Mohamad.[35] However, these two events, although part of history, were probably delivered too late to have had an appreciable effect on the separation of Singapore from Malaysia.

Apart from events, there were certain stereotypes or misconceptions that lay behind some of the thinking and action which probably contributed to the separation of Singapore. One of these was the stereotype of the MCA held by the PAP. The MCA was indeed partly dominated by rich Chinese, but it did provide some benefits for poor Chinese, and acted as some kind of check on the ethnic predispositions of UMNO. As a junior partner in the Alliance, it still drew some rewards, although not proportionate rewards, from belonging to the Alliance, which was in power.

Tunku never got over the too-simple view that the Chinese wanted only to make money. This was rather a poor guide to the sophisticated mental operations of someone like Lee Kuan Yew. A variant of this stereotype was that the Chinese would be flattered, and content, to exercise financial, although not political, power by becoming the "New York" of Malaysia.[36] On the other hand, some Chinese quite often misunderstood Malays. They tended to underrate the potential of Malays who worked on the land. Nor were they fully sensitive to aristocratic-feudal characters such as the Tunku. They saw him, correctly, as naturally genial, and not opposed to people enjoying themselves. Some did not realize how tough he could be once he was "dug in" over an issue, and how his unfavorable views of people could become fixed.[37] On the other hand, as a prince, he exemplified the bounty of "noblesse oblige". He appreciated the virtue of loyalty and rewarded it, sometimes even beyond its deserts.[38]

There is evidence to suggest that, while Lee Kuan Yew was a brilliant political operator in the Singapore context, he showed an incomplete understanding of the Malayan theatre of politics. He seems sometimes to have misjudged the Malay feelings he aroused. Until near the time of separation he apparently believed that the PAP could win Malay support in Malaya and that the political pace the PAP set was "not too fierce, too rapid".[39]

Toh Chin Chye believes that Lee Kuan Yew, as a Chinese from Singapore, never understood Malay special rights.[40] On the other hand, although Toh was born and grew up in Perak and had opportunities to see Malay special rights in operation, he was not likely to appreciate a Malay point of view concerning them.

Comments after the event naturally find it relatively easy to explain and to understand what had gone wrong. Albert Lau writes that, according to Lord Head, the British High Commissioner, Malaysia was "something of a shotgun wedding".[41] A few lines later, Lau cites Noordin Sopiee as saying: "With the advantages of hindsight, it is clear that most of the major factors which were to lie at the base of PAP-Alliance dissension after the formation of Malaysia had raised their heads even before it".[42] The problem was that Malaysia was meant to achieve security and economic development aims for the two main participants. Yet, in the process of working together to reach these objectives, they encountered the bruising implications of concepts which had not been seriously considered by sufficient numbers of people, such as a "Malaysian Malaysia".[43]

In June 1965, certain *ad hoc* constitutional or "switching personnel" changes or "looser" arrangements were mooted, such as bringing a PAP minister, or ministers, into the federal Cabinet, but none of these "last-ditch" solutions was acceptable and separation occurred officially on August 9, 1965. Tunku's mind seemed to be made up that Singapore had to go. However, alternative explanations of Singapore's exit have been advanced, as opposed to simple expulsion. One was that the apparent expulsion was in fact a cleverly calculated "breakaway" by the PAP leaders. A variation was that there was indeed an expulsion, but that Singapore "acquiesced" in it.[44]

Until almost the last minute, uncertainty and ambiguity existed, notably in talks between the Tunku and Lim Kim San, Singapore's Minister for National Development, who visited him in hospital where he was recovering from shingles.[45] An important unresolved question was: Had Tunku irrevocably decided on separation or was some action still possible by the PAP leaders which could have swayed his judgment?

The main parts in Singapore's negotiations with the Malaysian leaders were played by Lee and Goh, although Toh and Rajaratnam followed their lead.[46] Goh seems to have been quite pro-separation, possibly because his original hopes for a common market had had so little success.[47]

The most powerful argument against the "breakaway" explanation (or against more than a minimal degree of acquiescence by Singapore) was the emotional appearance of Lee on Singapore television, when he expressed his hurt feelings about separation and his hopes for an independent Singapore (August 9, 1965).

Separation took place without violence, although not without acrimony, partly because the British Prime Minister, Harold Wilson, warned the Tunku that drastic action against the PAP leaders, except for treasonable activities, might lead to a British reappraisal of its attitude towards Malaysia, especially as regards its relations with Indonesia.[48]

A clue to the explanation of these events – although not a complete explanation – hinges on different politicians' use of "Malaysia" to mean different things. To put this in terms of the Singapore government's regret at having to leave "Malaysia", the Malaysia they mourned was not Malaysia as it was being interpreted by the federal government, still embodying special privileges for Malays but making no provision for an effective common market. It was a construct, based on PAP notions of rationality and equity, which were hardly compatible with the actual approach of the federal government.

The end of the Barisan Sosialis

Events in completely-independent Singapore fall within the scope of future chapters. Yet it seems fitting to deal with the disappearance of the Barisan here, because the party's days were numbered. The decline in its fortunes was indicated at a by-election in July 1965. It occurred in Hong Lim, and was occasioned by the resignation of Ong Eng Guan, until then seemingly the constituency's member-for-life. Lee Kuan Yew has interpreted the resignation as having been instigated by the MCA, which wanted to assess political support for the PAP. During the election rumors were current about the possibility of Lee's arrest. The PAP campaigned on a "Malaysian Malaysia" policy, which the Barisan leader, Dr. Lee Siew Choh, denounced as a communal and neo-colonial slogan. The PAP candidate won, with 59 per cent of the vote, reversing the result of the election two years previously, when the PAP had won only 26 per cent.[49]

When Singapore became independent, the Barisan, which had denounced independence as "phony", did not vote against the government, which would have made the party too unpopular, but boycotted Parliament. After a series of Barisan resignations from Parliament, and PAP victories at by-elections, the party's MPs had been reduced to two, who had fled to the (Indonesian) Riau Islands. The Barisan boycotted the 1968 general elections. In the absence of the leadership of pro-Communist Lim Chin Siong, Lee's most formidable rival, now no longer in politics, or an equivalent, those who were in "leadership" positions were "political innocents", weak in the theory and practice of struggle, who too readily abandoned a forum in Parliament and who "took to the streets" in order to accomplish very little.

3 Locations of power

The state and the government

The state

The first two chapters have dealt with Singapore's history and how the PAP became the government, which marked a shift in the way the party operated. Until then, it could act only as a party. After it became the government, or the state (see below), it acquired all the powers of a government and was restricted only by the constitution and the law. The state by definition (see below) has claims to superiority over other bodies in a polity. Additionally, James Cotton, in comparing its relationships with other "master discourses" – with class, with society and with ethnicity – demonstrates that in each the state is the "central phenomenon."[1]

This chapter begins by examining which ideas about the state in Singapore are most persuasive in explaining it, and showing how, under the PAP, a close relationship operated between party, government and state. Second, it attempts to survey efforts by writers to "capture" the nature of how power is distributed in the state in phrases such as "administrative state", "tripartism", etc. Finally, it tries to describe what social forces brought the PAP to power, and how its sources of support have changed since then.

One might start with some definitions of the state in general before considering Singapore in particular. A good definition, which takes account of both internal and external aspects of the state, must cover the following features: states claim legitimate control over territories and the people in them, if necessary by coercion. To expand this, but not to an unbearable length, one might arrive at the following: "The state must be considered as more than the 'government'. It is the continuous administrative, legal, bureaucratic, and coercive system that attempts to structure relationships between society and public authority in a polity, but also to structure many critical relationships within society".[2]

Actually, the terms "state" and "government" are used almost interchangeably, at least when referring to the internal aspects of the state. The main point in using the term is probably to indicate continuity and distinguish the state from any specific government which may happen to be in office at a particular time.

More should be said about PAP–government relations. The longer the PAP remains in power, the harder it becomes to distinguish between the two. Although the PAP has yet to declare, as King Louis XIV did, that it is the state, yet, significantly, a recent book on Singapore politics has only one entry in the index under "State" – "PAP". To be fair, Lee Kuan Yew once did declare, "I make no apologies that the PAP is the government and the government is the PAP", but he stopped short of calling the PAP the state.[3]

Sometimes it has been politic for the PAP not to stress party connections too much. In the PAP–Barisan Sosialis battle in the 1960s, each strove to take over associations which were ostensibly "community" and "non-political" (see p. 17). Later on, the PAP relied on several such bodies for political work. Also, when Community Development Councils were created (see pp. 96–8), it was sometimes claimed that they had no party orientation.

Cabinet, Parliament and President

In finding out what organizations play a major role in the state, one has to assume that most readers have an approximate notion of what they are and of their relative importance in the state's functioning. It is likely, for instance, that the powers of the Cabinet and of the Prime Minister are generally understood. It is the Cabinet that determines which legislation is submitted to Parliament, where the party system and a PAP majority guarantee its passage. The office-holders just mentioned are, have been, or will be pre-eminent party members, and also high in the pyramid of power, thus linking the government with the party. Where action is concerned, as distinct from legislation, an appropriate minister or ministers is/are responsible for taking action through civil servants. More than a century ago, an irreverent English witticism maintained that the country was not governed by logic but by Parliament. Appreciation of this quip was not entirely spoiled by its being dated. England had gone through a constitutional change, resulting largely from the rise of the party system, through which the Cabinet has replaced Parliament as the dominant force.[4] This appeared to be occurring already in Singapore when the PAP became the government in 1959, and the domination of the executive was quickly confirmed.

In Chapter 11 it is noted that Parliament still retains some useful functions; it supplies a forum for the Opposition, provided that its members are sufficiently numerous, vocal and constructive. It has been strengthened by the presence of NMPs (Nominated Members of Parliament), who are knowledgeable about particular subjects.

The role of President of Singapore has become less readily understandable. The President has a potentially weighty role as a unifier and as a symbol of goodwill, but the extension of his powers to include protection of the country's reserves initially resulted in misunderstandings and unhappiness (see pp. 153–5).

The President has an appointed presidential council with limited powers.[5] It can draw attention to any proposed legislation that it thinks may discriminate against any racial or religious community.[6] This is a useful check and a means of reassurance in a multi-ethnic state such as Singapore.

The judiciary

An account of the functioning of the judiciary is given on pp. 132–6. As in other countries, it is one of the three broad "branches" of the state, the others being the legislature and the executive. Its main characteristic in Singapore, which distinguishes it, for example, from the United States, is that the idea of "checks and balances" has limited influence. This is most evident, perhaps, in the relationship between the executive and the legislature, where the Cabinet system, bolstered by the influence of the continuously-governing PAP, ensures that these two institutions "keep in step". In a rather similar but less direct way, the judiciary follows the practice of "strict construction" in its interpretation of the law, as enacted.

One item may be referred to as an example. It concerns the government's decision that the *Asian Wall Street Journal* was engaging in domestic politics, and the legal action it took against the *Journal*. In the High Court, the Attorney-General argued that the Newspaper and Printing Presses Act, under which the law in question was made, could not be challenged. He claimed that the minister concerned had to decide whether the *Journal* had by its actions engaged in domestic politics, and claimed that the minister's decision was executive in nature and should be free from judicial interference. The *Journal*'s challenge was dismissed.[7]

On the other hand, there are constituent parts of the state about which less is known than those just mentioned, which might lead to their importance being underrated.

The civil service; the military

In 1959 most of the higher ranks of the civil service were products of colonial times. After independence, they retained the virtues of being competent and almost totally free of corruption. When the PAP took office, it wished to reinforce and extend the scope of anti-corruption measures by making examples of high civil servants who were corrupt (see p. 7). It replaced seniority by merit as a criterion for advancement, as it did for many other appointments. It also made it clear that the government expected civil servants to be loyal to it. (This was easier to obtain, as it became obvious that, unlike preceding governments, the PAP was destined to remain in power.) Civil servants, including those at the top, attended courses at a new Political Study Centre, which explained the party's ideals and programs, as well as exposing some clandestine Communist activities. These actions were entirely consonant with PAP values. The policies were backed up by legislation, which was strictly implemented. A new agency was created, the Corrupt Practices Investigation Bureau, placed directly under the Prime Minister's Office, thus indicating the high priority attached to it.

When the expatriate civil servants had been almost entirely replaced by local Singaporeans, other changes were made in accordance with PAP views on meritocracy. In the 1980s, highly-paid jobs in the private sector were adopted as a guide for determining the pay of top civil servants. (This policy was destined to become a contentious subject of debate in Parliament in June 2000.)

In and after 2000, the questioning spirit of the Knowledge-Based Economy (KBE) was pervasive. In spite of the high standards of administrators at the higher levels, criticisms grew that they tended to be too inflexible and were too often inclined to "play safe". "We cannot only aim for incremental improvements to the way we do things. We must also be willing from time to time to discard old ways of doing things and explore radical innovations as the operating environment changes."[8] In 2000, radical changes were mooted which would provide for quicker promotion, shorter tenure, and more emphasis on creativity and innovation.

The military, under civilian control, not only has a deterrent role (see pp. 169–74), it also, through "military technocrats", provides some of the country's top leaders (see pp. 125, 175).

Where does power reside in the Singapore state?

Other elements in the state are less well-known: for instance, statutory boards, except the familiar CPF and the HDB; the precise functions of GLCs are mysterious to many except that they are often believed to engage in high-level financial deals. While many people have a reasonably accurate notion of where power lies in Singapore, the finer points may be beyond them. What was the "presidential dispute" in 1999 (see pp. 153–5) all about? Sometimes people are slow to adjust their ideas about how things work. Many were unable to appreciate the timing and the stages of the shift of power from Lee Kuan Yew to Goh Chok Tong over several years, culminating in Goh's becoming Prime Minister in 1990 (see p. 116). Many people overestimate the role of Parliament. At present, correctly, some regard the functions of local councils, etc. as peripheral (unless some local concern is of burning interest to themselves at the time). However, when Community Development Councils (see p. 96) become fully operational, their impact will be more widely recognized. The role of the party vis-à-vis the state, or government is found confusing, leading to statements by members of the public that the PAP is very rich, when the speaker means that the government has just declared that it has a budget surplus.

The question of where power lies in the Singapore state has been discussed at length by many academics, especially by Chan Heng Chee. Among her contributions to analysis are two features especially germane to the topic. One is the PAP's policy of "depoliticization",[9] a climate favoring the PAP's rule unencumbered by the vexation of serious challenges by opposition parties. The other is the belief that in Singapore the politicians in power are not fully in control of the bureaucrats who are intended, constitutionally, to serve them. To take the first point, the PAP linked "depoliticization" with the existence of a state in which political decisions are "given", thus leaving administration as a matter of devising and applying detailed programs. This tends to limit the effectiveness of rival parties and of the electors.[10] However, there is another source of potential challenge to politicians' power: the bureaucrats. (Chan was *not* thinking of one way in which some bureaucrats were actually acquiring more power – being appointed as ministers. There was a constant shortage of people qualified to fill ministerial positions, and the top ranks of the civil service are sometimes used as a source.)

Chan's approach was tentative, but familiar in Western parliamentary democracies, for instance in Great Britain pre-World War II, as expressed in the knowing phrase, "it's the civil servants who really run the country." To cite one of Chan's passages:

> The presence of the top political leadership has not been overshadowed by the bureaucrats. In Singapore there is no doubt that the major policy initiative still lies most certainly with the Cabinet, but the bureaucracy is a close handmaiden of the party. But one trend must be borne in mind in any long-term analysis of politics in Singapore ... Because the economic strategy of the republic places importance on the participation of the Government in business, leading to a growth of governmental activities in statutory institutions and private [sic] companies, this has increased the power and scope of the bureaucrats in the system when they are placed in charge of the statutory boards and appointed as members of the Boards of Directors of the companies. In fact the consolidation of one party in power has seen the concomitant emergence of an 'administrative state' where political power is fast shifting to the administrative arena.[11]

Some of Chan's misgivings may have arisen from a consideration that was present in many minds until, say, the early 1990s, succinctly expressed in the question: "What after Lee Kuan Yew?" Unless there is a possible succession crisis through death or illness, as threatening as the one in 1992 when the two Deputy Prime Ministers, B.G. Lee and Ong Teng Cheong were stricken by cancer, that question is being answered and will be answered satisfactorily for some time to come by present and future leaders.

After reflection, a measured judgment would be that there was no prospect that the civil service could successfully take over from ministers – determined leaders had clearly established who were in charge.[12]

> As the ruling elite co-opted the civil service, so the civil service in turn became politicized to serve the ruling elite. As noted earlier, the two were naturally inclined to share the same values, and a close identification of interests developed between them ... The alliance, based on a convergence of interests between an increasingly technocratic civil service and the political leadership, has played a vital role in conferring legitimacy on the government.[13]

A few years later, Chan's briefly-stated remarks on government-linked companies (GLCs, as they came to be known) were expanded in a "Working Paper" by Werner Vennewald.[14] This piece is well-researched and clearly presented, with a number of lists and diagrams showing circles illustrating power relations in the GLC system. The paper is particularly useful because it places the GLCs in context. The members of the GLCs, like other high officials including top civil servants, are appointed by the DCAC (the Directorship and Consultancy Appointments Council), responsible to a Coordinating Board, which in turn reports to the Prime Minister. The Council consists of some leading ministers and civil servants.[15] It should be included in any exhaustive list of the components of the state, at the same time remembering that nearly everyone on it already qualifies for inclusion through membership of some other eminent body.[16] Below the Council are the GLCs, grouped under four holding companies, the biggest of which is Temasek (see pp. 30, 75).[17]

The GLC system works on a person-to-person basis without the tendencies toward corruption which are evident in some other Southeast Asian states.

Obviously criticism may be directed to the system's lack of transparency. Questions in Parliament are a source of information, but may also lead to some frustration:

> *Dr. Lee Tsao Yuan:* In light of public accountability, would the Government make the accounts of the holding companies public and transparent, for example, Temasek Holdings?
> *Dr. Richard Hu Tsu Tao*: Temasek does publish its accounts. But whether you have full access, it is a different matter. I think we will consider if it is necessary. At the moment, we would like to preserve our present arrangements.
> *Mr. Low Thia Khiang:* Why does the minister say that we want to preserve the status quo by divulging more information on Temasek Holdings' shareholding position?
> *Dr. Richard Hu Tsu Tao*: I think the list of companies in which Temasek Holdings has shares is, in fact, published in a book on Government-owned companies and their subsidiaries ... And each of these companies has its own balance sheet and therefore published. So you can quite easily aggregate the totals. I can make this book available to whichever Member is interested. The published book of Government holding companies, in which all the companies belonging to Temasek Holdings are, in fact, set out, with the Board of Directors, and so forth, and each of these companies in turn, particularly if they are public companies, would have annual reports.[18]

Vennewald's monograph is informative, and is worthy of respect for unearthing and analyzing hard-to-get information. Unfortunately, he goes further than this, contending that the "technocratic" thinking which occurs in such a system is "anti-democratic" because it takes insufficient account of the popular will, and could even result in dictatorship.[19] Two comments may be made, because the conclusions seem to go further than is warranted by the evidence. Complete transparency may sometimes be inadvisable, because some information disclosed might be useful to the enterprises' competitors, and therefore harmful to themselves.[20] Also, the allegation about the possibility of dictatorship raises the question: if it is correct, whose policies is Vennewald warning us against? If they are PAP policies, this seems unlikely: the PAP has very much the political and administrative system it wants to have, give or take a few non-vital arrangements. If they are not PAP policies, is there reason to doubt the resolution and toughness of the present, and succeeding, leaders for some time to come, to deal with them?

Balancing labor and capital

The notion of the government acting as a balance or mediator is quite common, for instance in Europe, as a means of moderating industrial strife.[21] It is hoped that, by agreeing on rules, both labor and capital will benefit, and that any damage to the economy will be contained. The activities of trade unions in Singapore preceded the formation of the PAP. When the latter was formed, the unions were a "given" in the industrial, and political, landscape. Their presence both aided and hindered the growth of the party. When Lee Kuan Yew began to practice law in Singapore, he acted for several unions, whose leaders provided him with union contacts. Yet the Communist Party, already active on the scene, was then in control of some powerful unions.

Politically, the sequence of events given in Chapter 2 (see p. 20) included the breakaway of left-wing members from the PAP to form the Barisan Sosialis, which was later crushed, principally by use of the Internal Security Act. After Singapore left Malaysia and became independent, the government started to remodel the labor movement so as to conform to its conceptions of a proper industrial order, one designed to achieve the objectives of the PAP's first economic guru, Goh Keng Swee, who saw industrialization as a priority, particularly for dealing with the then-current high unemployment rate. The PAP used the NTUC (National Trades Union Congress) to discipline and socialize workers to the values of hard work and loyalty. The legal embodiments of PAP industrial policy were the Employment Act of 1968 and the Industrial Relations (Amendment) Act of 1969. They applied to key issues including the basis of a trade dispute, collective bargaining, procedures for recruitment and promotion, etc.

A decade later, the place of unions in Singapore had been significantly altered. The government believed that the two largest, and leftist, unions, the Singapore Industrial Labour Organization (SIGO) and the Pioneer Industries Employees Union (PIEU) contained a disproportionate percentage of total union membership. Changes were made accordingly, resulting in a greater number of smaller unions. The process was made easier by inter-union rivalries which intensified contests for office within unions and for NTUC posts. Additionally, the strength of existing unions was reduced by the formation of some competing house unions.[22] The (Barisan-associated) Singapore Association of Trade Unions (SATU) ceased to exist in 1963 when its application for registration was refused, the NTUC being the main beneficiary. In the mid-1970s, Goh Keng Swee commented with some satisfaction on the new trade union orientation; "the labour movement took an enlightened long-term view of their group interests. They were willing to give the growth policy a chance to succeed. They reigned [sic] in the labour militants, who, either from past experience or individual disposition, believed that the right thing for the unions to do was to get at the employers' throats."[23]

These changes made it easier for the government to confirm its ascendancy over the unions. However, this process was modified by certain considerations. Among them was the frequently-invoked reminiscence that Lee Kuan Yew, in starting the PAP, had had the help of union leaders whose acquaintance he had made when representing them legally, thus establishing a special historical link. Less-often mentioned were the political connections of left-wing unions or the high percentage of unionists who left the PAP, mostly to join the Barisan, in 1963.[24] It certainly appeared to be government policy to associate, possibly even integrate, unions with the government as much as possible. Unionists were encouraged to join the party and some were persuaded to become PAP candidates for election to Parliament. Some – eighteen by 1980 – were appointed to statutory boards, and the like. Others were made members of committees set up to enquire into the state of the economy (see pp. 70–1). Naturally, they had a key role to play in the National Wages Council (see pp. 33–4).

Clearly the unions and the PAP were becoming closer, and an identifiable pattern at top levels emerged, beginning with Lim Chee Onn, NTUC secretary-general in the late 1970s, who had no previous solid party or trade union experience, in 1979 (see below). The arrangement seems to have been a version of the practice of appointing "technocrats" in the government, such as Goh Chok Tong, who became a Senior Minister of State in 1977. The practice (which still continues) was that the person in question would become, not necessarily at precisely the same time, both the secretary-general of the NTUC, and a minister in the government. Previous trade union connections are not necessary. Lim Boon Heng, the current secretary-general, had none, nor had his family, when he assumed his appointment. It is his, and his successors', function to explain government policy to the unions and vice-versa; he is the link between the two. For instance, if the government decides on a reduction in employers' contributions to the CPF (see pp. 70–1), it is his duty to explain such a policy to the unions. On the other hand, if the gap between the incomes of the better-off and the worse-off widens, he is obliged to convey to the government that some unionists need to be re-trained, and their subsistence costs may need to be partly met during retraining (see p. 80).

The new pattern of having one person combine the offices of NTUC secretary-general and government minister, demanded of the individual in question a very delicate balance. Lim Chee Onn sent many correct messages. When addressing the Central Executive Committee of the PAP, he underlined the duty of trade union leaders to be responsible. "When union leaders seek only to court popularity and defend their irresponsibility in acceding to wrong decisions on the ground that they are the servants of their members, they betray the responsibilities of their office".[25] This needed to be said. Yet "importing" leaders to office from outside demanded a nuanced approach to soothe union sensitivities. The NTUC had been too recently created to be as ossified as the British TUC. Yet there was some similarity, and it may be significant that in British cartoons the TUC was often portrayed as an elderly, stubborn, but at heart good-natured, horse, "Dobbin".

Lim Chee Onn was thought to be "on the way up". Appointed secretary-general of the NTUC in 1979, he also became a minister, and a member of several select committees. However, although the direction in which he steered the NTUC was in accord with PAP policy, he was seen as being "in too much of a rush". His reliance on "outside" (including civil service) advice irritated "old guard" unionists, particularly the influential Devan Nair, who felt the old guard were being marginalized. Their displeasure was conveyed to Lee Kuan Yew. Lim was dismissed from his trade union post, and soon afterward he retired from politics[26] to pursue a successful career in industry. While the top technocrats who were government ministers had the patience to outlast the grumbles of old guard detractors, in the NTUC Lim lacked the political clout to withstand *its* old guard.

Lim Chee Onn's most recent technocrat successor, Lim Boon Heng, had formerly been an executive with Neptune Orient Lines. He had been approached by Goh Chok Tong, who also had formerly worked for that GLC, and asked if he wished to offer himself for selection as a parliamentary candidate. In the course of the selection process, he was asked if he was willing to change jobs, and subsequently whether he might be interested in a NTUC post. He agreed. Lim

Boon Heng is an enthusiast who gets on well with people. He wants his staff to understand basic economics, which is now part of the core curriculum for NTUC leadership training programs.[27] Although by his antecedents he is a technocrat, in his capacity as the NTUC leader he is both acceptable and effective.

By the 1970s, the NTUC had extended its functions. Concern for wages and working conditions was supplemented by its providing services and acquiring profits for its members. Among other things it offered insurance and taxi services. Members were also provided with amenities and facilities for their enjoyment, such as the use of clubs and holiday chalets.[28]

The movements and changes of personnel between unions and the government has sometimes been described as evidence of a "symbiotic" relationship. This may be misleading, however. One helps the other, and vice-versa, but this does not imply equality of status. It was the PAP which nurtured the NTUC and used it to crush and supplant its arch-rival SATU.

Tripartism

In addition to the government–union relation, which is close and symbiotic, there is also the government–union–business relationship, in which the government plays the role of balancing the other two. This relationship, although evident in the tripartite National Wages Council (see pp. 33–4) is less firmly institutionalized than the government–union relationship. There are no really strong institutionalized government–business links, for example through a single person holding a post in each, such as the NTUC secretary- general/cabinet minister.

Other government–business linkages are also weak. Personal ties are not often strengthened by business ties. To be sure, in the early 1990s there was an increasing number of "business" MPs in the PAP ranks in Parliament,[29] but the PAP's inability to obtain as many candidates from business as it wants, especially people with ministerial potential, is an obstacle. Currently, however, the main PAP leader from business, the high-powered banking executive Dr. Tony Tan, a Deputy Prime Minister, is a political contemporary of Prime Minister Goh. Also, some Nominated MPs speak for business (see pp. 144–5). Government links with business are also hampered by the narrow recruitment range of business organizations, some of which are ethnically-based, or are limited to businesses below a certain size.

The contrast with labor is quite striking. Trade unions, practically all of which are affiliated with the NTUC, are connected with it hierarchically. Labor leaders' influence, as we have seen, is intimately linked with the government, and the exchange of "messages", as the Lim Chee Onn example indicates, is not unidirectional.

The National Wages Council

In Singapore, the "pride and joy" of tripartism is the National Wages Council, which in a tripartite form, has functioned since 1972. There are some peculiarities: it issues guidelines for wages which are non-mandatory, but are never rejected or amended; it had the same chairperson for over thirty years;[30] it is an institution which some say could work only in Singapore, yet many of the members representing business were not born in Singapore but attend because they are employed there by foreign MNCs.[31]

A large proportion of the work of the Council is done in preparation for its actual meetings. According to Lim Boon Heng, the NTUC prides itself on the strength of its research unit, founded with the help of government finance and seconded civil servants, which is sometimes better informed on a topic than the employers' organizations. Unlike the NTUC's acting as the sole voice for labor, the employers' representatives are chosen from the whole range of employers' organizations in Singapore. Civil servants put the point of view of the government. The materials discussed at the meetings take the form of "position papers." Some months after, the government announces its decisions on pay, based on the NWC guidelines. What happens if the NWC fails to agree? A well-known instance occurred in 1982. Apparently, at the eleventh hour the union leaders called the chairman into their room and said that, actually, they did not agree with the employers' position. They had been going over and over the matter, and found that after "an 8-hour marathon session" there was an impasse. They added, however, that, out of respect for the chairman, they would give way so that he could have a consensus.[32] The process outlined affects only the public sector, but some employers and unions in the private sector may take note of the outcome in their own wage settlements. Consequently, NWC guidelines have considerable effect, although some latitude is possible in the interpretation of them.

This basic account does not include ingenious modifications which have been evolved over time, such as arbitration procedures or "flexi-wage".[33] The system seems to work well in Singapore. Its success depends on the ability to reach consensus, and the PAP is known to support its efforts. Even the representatives from the MNCs include some who have been so exposed to Singaporean habits that they can emulate their local colleagues' behavior without too much effort.

Lim Boon Heng has found, from experience, that in talking to foreigners he now can convince them that tripartism can work in Singapore, but it is harder to persuade them that it could work in their own country.

Corporatism

Corporatism has similarities with tripartism. Like it, three elements are involved: the state, labor and capital. But, in analyzing the nature of the relations concerned, corporatism is more ambitious. Use of the term can be quite wildly off the track. One Western scholar [unidentified] has characterized Singapore as "corporatist" because "all political loyalty must be to the state".[34]

The earliest well-known use of the word, corporatism, was by Manoilesco in the 1930s,[35] then interest waned until a revival later in the 1930s and 1940s. The focus was Western Europe, as well as, linked with Spain and Portugal, Latin America. One of the leaders of the school, Philippe Schmitter, provided an inclusive, carefully-crafted definition, as follows:

> "a system of interest mediation in which the constituent units are organised into a limited number of non-competitive, hierarchically ordered, and

> functionally differentiated categories, recognised or licensed (if not created) by the state, granted a deliberate representational monopoly within their categories in exchange for observing certain respective controls on their selection of leaders and articulation of demands and supports."[36]

Schmitter identifies two varieties of corporatism. In the "state" variety, the state is the organizer and controller, and the groups are more constrained. In the "societal" version, the state exercises relatively less power, and the groups relatively more. The former is found mainly in Latin America, Spain and Portugal, while the latter is more typical of Northern Europe.

It is evident that there is an "imbalance" in the Singapore government–union relationship when compared with the government–business relationship. The difference between the government's stronger ties with the former, as compared with the latter, may be attributed to history. The main challenge to the PAP came from the Barisan Sosialis, whose main bastion was the left-wing unions. In order to overcome them, the PAP had to use its governmental power, and build up its own unions so as to crush the opposition forces, leaving it, not regretfully, allied with its creation, the NTUC.

Outstanding characteristics of the state under the PAP

Unless "corporatism" is acceptable as conveying the chief characteristics of the state in Singapore, can an alternative term be offered? One possibility is to see "control" as the outstanding feature. Yet, as has been suggested (see p. 92), there are some ambiguities about this term. Is the emphasis on successful control or on the will to control? Is the means of control to be force/enforcement or by persuasion/indoctrination? Another possibility might stress the state's persistence in attempting to penetrate many aspects of social life. This view has something in common with expressions such as the "nanny state" or the "Papa Knows Best" approach.[37] Without attaching pejorative labels, the state's "busyness" is well conveyed in the following quotations:

> We wouldn't be here, would not have made the economic progress, if we had not intervened on very personal matters – who your neighbor is, how you live, the noise you make, how you spit or where you spit, or what language you use ... It was fundamental social and cultural changes that brought us here.[38]

> It [the government] has over the years developed a complex battery of controls and incentives to influence the public's social and economic behaviour in many circumstances, including family planning, marriage, savings, home ownership, education and occupational choice, and land transport.[39]

Garry Rodan captures the essence of the matter, when he refers succinctly to the "general pervasiveness of the state in the social sphere" under the PAP.[40]

State autonomy under the PAP

The PAP has enjoyed considerable autonomy over forces, groups and classes during its long rule. Poulantzas deserves credit for making a good case that at least relative autonomy may quite often be achieved by the state vis-à-vis various classes and factions.[41] In Singapore, the core of the state might be perceived as (the higher ranks of) the party–Cabinet–government complex. In orbit circling it, so to speak, are two types of subordinate organizations. One consists of top civil servants and the corresponding levels in the GLCs. Each of these might have assumed powers beyond its constitutionally-indicated role, if the PAP leaders had been deficient in political will – which they were not. The second type represent the forces of labor and capital. These are obliged to occupy an ancillary position – the former because, although it was linked with the PAP, its status was clearly lower (see p. 31), the latter because, in Singapore, big business is overwhelmingly owned by foreigners (see p. 68), or by firms in associated with the government in the form of GLCs (see pp. 29–30).

The mere enumeration of state organs, or of private organizations influenced by state agents, is quite insufficient to explain the paramount position of the state in Singapore. Its strength is unimaginable without taking account of the calculated and concentrated energy which its leaders devoted to its operations (see p. 35). The state runs on dynamism, rather than on constitutions and organization charts.

Rodan develops the interpretation of the Singapore example of the state through looking at the roles of the PAP on various occasions. For instance, he makes the point that the state, when it acts through the NTUC, is not searching for a pre-requisite for acquiring autonomy, but, rather, is consolidating – or even displaying – its already established autonomy.[42] Elsewhere, referring to the government's restructuring of trade unions, he mentions that it took steps to guard against even the remote possibility of new power bases developing among organized labor which might challenge the PAP's hegemony in its economic policies.[43]

A memorable feat of the PAP is that it proved itself capable of switching part of its support base from one "constituency" to another. As Michael Leifer observed, it owed its initial success largely to the votes of the Chinese working class at the 1959 election – after the franchise had been widened. Yet, afterwards, following the PAP split, it won considerable middle-class backing, at the expense of the right-wing parties.[44] This partly made up for the votes it lost to the newly-constituted Barisan at the 1963 election.[45]

In applying the concept of class to the Singapore scene, there are some unusual features to be noted. To recapitulate the background, local capital was little developed and was politically weak. The PAP was persuaded to give it some encouragement (see p. 69) but, for the most part, it overwhelmingly chose MNCs as its prime instrument for promoting industrialization.

There was no substantial land-owning class, and initially during PAP rule, the government's need for land, to carry out its housing and other policies, led it to obtain substantial powers for acquiring land, which prevented any such class from developing (see p. 91). Labor's influence was limited, partly because it was divided. The PAP defeated left-wing labor's political arm though elections and the employment of the Internal Security Act combined with other coercive measures, while, eventually, left-wing labor itself was rendered practically powerless by the legislation of the late 1960s (see p. 31). The survivors on this field of battle, apart from the PAP/NTUC, were the MNCs and the GLCs (government-linked companies) which are sometimes thought to be too much "government-controlled" (see p. 73). Looking ahead, probably the government envisages a future in which more and more GLCs are transformed into local MNCs.[46]

Rodan takes his argument further by developing class themes. He diagnoses the PAP state as "very much a middle-class state", because decision-making is dominated by technocrats and professionals. However, he also thinks that the middle-class links may not be all that strong.[47] He suggests that the PAP has contrived to distance itself from ties with particular classes, thus projecting a rational image and avoiding the appearance of dependence on any class or classes. For example, the PAP attained office in 1959 without being substantially backed by capitalists, while its battles with the Barisan identified it as opposed to left-wing labor.[48] However, Rodan qualifies the former case by remarking that, as a government, the PAP was devoted to maximizing capital accumulation.[49]

It seems that, sifting through varying interpretations of the "middle class", one strand depends on which people make the main decisions, while another is based on who, or what class, benefits from the decisions made. These criteria may provide different answers.

Summary

PAP rule obviously effected change in the composition and behavior of the state actors. For example, the creation of GLCs led to the appointment of additional technocrats some of whom were drawn from the civil service. The larger statutory boards required a similar kind of recruit for their higher ranks, as did management positions in community organizations.

Apart from structural changes, a new spirit of energy was injected into state activities by the "busyness" (see p. 35) of the PAP leaders, as well as by their firmly-held values (see pp. 51–8).

Some constituents of the state, such as the civil service and the trade unions, modified their orientations, behavior, and recruitment criteria, as they became more attuned to PAP influence and example. The long-range effects of recent changes in presidential powers and their use are hard to predict, although the immediate effect seems to have been to incline PAP leaders toward making the choice of a President who is "safe"[50] as well as competent. The contours of the state have also been reshaped in less obvious ways. PAP leaders observed the proprieties in dealing with Parliament, and some useful changes have been made, for example the creation of Nominated MPs (see pp. 144–5). However, they have not increased the powers of Parliament. It has not benefited from a separation *of* powers, but, rather, is still undergoing almost a separation *from* power.

This chapter began with general statements about the relation between the state and the PAP government. The next chapter provides some more detail about the functioning of the PAP as a party, which should amplify its role in the relationship.

4 The People's Action Party

The structure and operation of a dominant party

Singapore has a dominant party system, as opposed to a one-party system. Other parties exist, around 20 are registered, and usually four to six parties compete in each election. In dominant party systems, only one party has the capacity to govern (in the short term at least), but the dominant party "must, in some measure, be responsible to other groups of political actors", and to the public, to ensure its legitimacy and continuing dominance.[1] The People's Action Party (PAP) is one of the world's longest surviving dominant parties, having been elected to power in 1959 and returned to power in every general election since then.

The PAP has retained its dominance by being a "catchall" party that fully controls the large political center.[2] It has done this without any mass membership or a complex party organization. The PAP is basically non-ideological (although its leaders subscribe to elitism), it is responsive, and it is obsessive about co-opting talent. As the government, its leaders control the media, make life difficult for and at times repress the opposition, and deliver the economic goods.

The best illustration of elitism by PAP leaders is found in the provisions for the operation of the party itself, especially centralization of power; efforts at party renewal, constantly replacing older MPs with the "best and brightest" young talent that can be recruited; and working to ensure smooth political succession at the top in order to avoid damaging splits and factions – often the undoing of dominant parties.

History

The genesis of the PAP was in the friendships which developed between a handful of young nationalist Singaporeans educated in Britain in the late 1940s. Lee Kuan Yew, Goh Keng Swee, and Toh Chin Chye knew each other earlier at the elite Raffles College in Singapore, where Lee and Toh were students while Goh was an economics lecturer. At Cambridge, Lee was a colleague of Eddie Barker, while in London, Goh and Toh, along with some others, formed the anti-colonial Malayan Forum. Back in Singapore, Lee was introduced by Goh to a left-wing journalist, S. Rajaratnam, who had spent twelve years in London until 1947.

In 1953, this group began meeting on Saturday afternoons to consider whether it was feasible to establish a left-wing nationalist party that would attract the trade unions, and hence the Chinese-educated majority, as its mass support base. Already Lee was the legal adviser to a number of unions and clan associations.

Having decided that the party must have trade union support, in 1954 Lee met with two Chinese trade unionists, Lim Chin Siong and Fong Swee Suan, about joining forces in a "united front". They agreed, after first checking with their Malayan Communist Party superiors, since the pro-Communists were vulnerable to arrest under the Internal Security Act (ISA) and in need of a cover for their activities (see p. 20). With this in mind, Lee was satisfied that "the new party would have a reasonably broad working-class base. We had the English-educated, the Malay blue- and white-collar workers, and we now had the Chinese clan associations, trade guilds, and blue-collar workers as well."[3]

The inaugural meeting of the PAP at the Victoria Memorial Hall was held in November 1954. According to Lee Kuan Yew, there was no electricity in the air, and the event stirred no great oratory.[4] An editorial in Singapore's pro-British *Sunday Times* ridiculed the meeting: "It was sad to see a socialistic movement kicking off in such middle class conditions ... Charming and clever people, but hardly sinewy toilers ... the people at the meeting ... will need more than shouts of 'Merdeka' to sustain them."[5] In fact, half of the pro-tem committee and 90 percent of those attending the inaugural meeting were trade unionists.[6]

The PAP started out seeking to be a mass mobilizing party. Lee and his group of English-educated moderates knew they needed the pro-Communists to mobilize the Chinese-educated workers, since the party managed to establish only a few branches in its first year. Lee called the united front "an inarticulate, inchoate, indefinable compact" that was held together only by the glue of anti-colonialism.[7]

The problem for the moderates was to avoid having the party captured "from below". This looked increasingly problematic. Singapore was seething with left-wing and nationalist activism. There were riots in 1954 against registering for the army draft; 1955 saw the Hock Lee Bus Riots; and there was violence during student sit-ins in 1956. Inside the party, the pro-Communists captured four out of 12 seats on the party's executive committee, and demanded that in future the branches, already under their control, nominate candidates to the executive committee. At the 4th party conference in August 1957, the pro-Communists made an all-out bid to take over the party by stacking the conference with non-members holding phony membership cards. They won six of the 12 executive committee seats, and had expected to win more. The moderates refused to take office to deny legitimacy to the "coup". It is unclear what more the moderates could have done beyond this. But fate intervened.

Nine days after the PAP party elections, the Lim Yew Hock government arrested 35 pro-Communists for subversion, including five members of the PAP executive committee and 11 branch officials. Although Lee states that Lim Yew Hock's actions were intended to save his own support base rather than assist the PAP moderates,[8] actually he greatly helped them. The moderates quickly set up an emergency council and held a special party conference in October 1957 to elect a new executive, now called the Central Executive Committee (CEC), and to take steps to regain and maintain control of the party by creating a new category of cadre membership, by instituting a bloc voting system for CEC candidates, and by re-registering members (discussed below).

Despite the internal incompatibilities, the party did not split in 1957. Both sides still believed they needed the other, and this seemed borne out by the PAP's convincing electoral victory in 1959. However, the efforts of the moderates to attain merger with Malaya – something the pro-Communists (and the MCP) strenuously opposed – and the increasing prospects of merger transpiring, led to the inevitable party split in July 1961.

It was a very messy break. Thirteen Assemblymen defected and formed the Barisan Sosialis, and nearly defeated the government in a no-confidence motion. The PAP branches were decimated, as were some of the auxiliary organizations. Lee Kuan Yew estimates that 20 to 25 branch organizing secretaries and their branch committees defected, many branch offices were trashed and equipment broken, and the Works Brigade was rendered useless and closed down.[9] In total, about two-thirds of the PAP membership and most of the party bureaucracy defected to the Barisan Sosialis.[10]

Because rebuilding the party organization was unavoidably slow, the assembly wing became predominant. PAP Assemblymen built support by regular constituency visits and by recruiting community grassroots leaders with influence in auxiliary or para-political organizations (see pp. 95–6), all in preparation for the 1963 electoral showdown against the Barisan Sosialis. A report by British Deputy Commissioner Philip Moore in December 1962 summed up the situation: The strength of the PAP resided in a highly effective government, while its weakness lay in lack of party organization, in particular as it pertained to the Chinese-speaking electorate.[11] The PAP survived its most crucial election in 1963, and soon emerged as a dominant party, winning most or all of the seats in subsequent general elections (see pp. 149–53).

Party structure and organization

Much of the organization and operation of the PAP has its roots in the struggle against the pro-Communists in the decade from the mid-1950s to mid-1960s. Power in the party is concentrated in the Central Executive Committee (CEC), which is led by the Secretary-General, the most powerful position in the party. Other officers include a Chairman and Vice-Chairman, a First and Second Assistant Secretary-General, and a Treasurer and Assistant Treasurer. There is a strong but not complete overlap between CEC membership and Cabinet members. Under the rules established after the attempted takeover in 1957, the outgoing CEC recommends a slate of candidates which the cadre members vote for or against *en bloc*. This has been amended to decentralize the process slightly. Now, the CEC nominates eight candidates for the party caucus to consider. The party caucus selects an additional ten candidates.[12] Care is taken to ensure that there is some ethnic diversity and that women are reasonably well represented. Twelve members are elected by the cadre and up to six can be appointed (those placing 13th and 14th in the election are automatically appointed) for two-year terms.

The CEC meets just before Cabinet meetings, a few times a year and more when an election is pending. The CEC appoints cadre members, and it is directly responsible for the Young PAP and Women's wings. Parliamentary candidates are selected by the CEC after a lengthy review process (discussed below).

Two to three years before an election, a PAP General Elections Committee is formed. It is led by the Secretary-General and includes about eight others, almost certainly from the CEC. It discusses new prospective candidates, MPs who should step down to make way for renewal, possible election themes and issues, and the strategic thrust of the campaign. The Committee appoints numerous sub-committees to deal with specific electoral tasks. For example, one sub-committee is delegated the task of preparing new candidates once they are selected. New candidates undergo "basic training", including mock press conferences and television appearances, primers on policies, and lessons on how to make campaign speeches and work the crowd.[13]

Cadre system

In 1958, the PAP instituted the cadre system to prevent any future hostile takeover attempts by the pro-Communists. Lee writes that he and other moderates noted the special strength of the system being used by the Vatican wherein the Pope appointed the Cardinals and later the Cardinals elected the new Pope. With this model in mind, the PAP established its cadre system – the CEC appoints the cadre and the cadre elect the CEC.[14]

Originally, there were about 500 "temporary cadre" appointed; since then the selection of cadre members has been meticulous, rigorous, and secretive.[15] A potential cadre member normally must be recommended by an MP, and he/she then undergoes a review or screening and an interview by a CEC panel of four or five ministers and MPs. About 100 are recommended each year. The PAP will not divulge how many are selected, and cadres are sworn to secrecy. It was always thought that there were only a few hundred cadre, but the party's Second Assistant Secretary-General, Home Affairs Minister Wong Kan Seng, has said that the number of cadre has been growing steadily, citing a figure of a thousand or so.[16] The only distinction between a cadre and an ordinary member is the formers' right to vote every two years for the party's top leaders. Even ordinary membership is not automatic. Lee Kuan Yew did not want a mass party and populist demands, and he wanted to avoid the Asian problem of "guanxi", or individuals seeking financial gain out of political affiliation. Prospective ordinary members therefore must demonstrate some involvement in grassroots work before their memberships are approved. Total party membership at the end of 2000, according to Wong Kan Seng, stood at 15,000.[17]

Party members are unpaid volunteers. There are no perks, except (since 1986) Family Day and PAP Community Day outings for members. There are some more significant rewards for grassroots leaders – priority in housing, school admissions, and parking at HDB estates – and often party workers are also community leaders in an overlapping network. Party members help the MPs during their constituency visits, serve on branch sub-committees, and help mobilize support during an election.

Young PAP and the PAP Women's Wing

In 1985, Goh Chok Tong, then the party's First Assistant Secretary-General, toured constituency branches to discuss what was needed in order to revitalize and strengthen the party. Among the initiatives was one to set up a Young PAP wing to attract the support of a new generation of Singaporeans and to get more youth to identify openly with the PAP and its policies. The Young PAP (YP) was formed in 1986, for members between the ages of 17 and 35. It was decided to channel all members in that age group into the YP. It was given resources to develop a parallel structure, including branches in every constituency. The leaders appointed to head the YP gave an indication of its importance. Its first chair was B.G. Lee Hsien Loong, now Deputy Prime Minister, and its second chair is B.G. George Yeo, the Minister for Trade and Industry – two political heavyweights. The focus of its activities is on political issues.[18] To this effect, the YP has Policy Study Teams that work like Parliamentary Committees to keep track of specific ministries, and it has an Internet group that participates in chat room discussions, sometimes to the chagrin of other participants. The YP members play as big or small a role in constituency matters and campaign efforts as individual MPs allow, according to B.G. George Yeo.[19] By 1999, some 20 percent of the PAP's 81 MPs had come from the YP.

Although women are entitled to join the YP, it was decided in 1989 to launch a Women's Wing to attract women members and to help integrate women into the national decision-making process. Initially some PAP women had reservations that it would turn into a "tea ladies" group. Despite assurances, it has in fact come to focus primarily on gender and family issues, because that is where it is most effective. By 1999, it had grown to over 3,000 members. Interestingly, the PAP had an earlier women's group, which had a much more aggressive style of political advocacy. In November 1955, a group of PAP women activists on their own initiative set up the Women's League. It focused on political education, getting women to vote, and, importantly, helping to get the Women's Charter formally adopted. However, the Women's League was torn apart by the PAP split in 1961, with most activists going over to the Barisan Sosialis. The League languished and then faded away.

PAP HQ Executive Committee and the party bureaucracy

In contrast to most ruling parties in dominant and one-party systems, and Western political parties, the PAP does not have a large party bureaucracy. In fact, it has a distinctly small bureaucracy. This is partly because Singapore's small size makes it unnecessary (there are no state party organizations, in contrast to India and Malaysia, for example), and partly because the PAP, as a result of its traumatic fight against the pro-Communists, promotes participation and support more through government para-political grassroots organizations than through the party branches.

On the party's flowchart, just below the CEC is the HQ Executive Committee, formed in the mid-1980s, which oversees the organization and administration of the party. The HQ Exco, comprising a small staff of nine party functionaries, maintains party accounts, membership records, and archival materials. It also oversees nine sub-committees (including constituency relations, publicity and publications, political education, and Malay Affairs), and coordinates feedback on issues through a network of the party branches.[20] The PAP HQ is now located inconspicuously and out of the way in Changi. PAP HQ is quiet most of the time, but comes alive as Ops Centre during elections.

The party branches

Branches are the basic unit of the party. The PAP has branches in all 84 constituencies; they are financially self-sufficient and have some autonomy. In constituencies held by the PAP (82), the MP is the branch chair. The chair is assisted by a Branch Secretary and Branch Exco. Clusters of branches are represented by District Committees, and since 1998, each Group Representation Constituency (multi-member constituency; see pp. 145–6) is linked to a Standing Committee headed by a Minister.

Despite this seemingly elaborate networking, the functions of the branch and district organizations are minimal. As mentioned earlier, the experience of losing so many branches to the Barisan Sosialis when the PAP split in 1961 has left the leadership wary of branch organization and party activists.[21] As a result, the PAP bypasses most of the functions normally associated with party branches in favor of governmental para-political organizations. The branches have no say in the choice of candidates (the selection is done by the CEC), virtually no policy input, nor can a party worker expect to be rewarded with a candidacy. Indeed, the party's 45th anniversary booklet notes that there is a feeling that the party has little to do except keep itself going until the next election.[22]

The main branch work is to help manage grassroots activities during election campaigns and to assist MPs in their meet-the-people sessions or walkabouts in the constituency. The meet-the-people sessions are weekly constituency clinics with the MP. The PAP considers these sessions important. In 1998, some fifty thousand Singaporeans met their MPs at these sessions.[23] Constituency walkabouts are half-day street walks to meet the people, and at least twice before an election each MP will visit every house or apartment in his/her constituency. Interestingly, the PAP stopped the walkabouts just after independence. They were restarted in 1982 when party renewal meant there were increasing numbers of new Ministers who were not very well known.

The party supports itself primarily by the contributions of Ministers ($1000 per month) and MPs ($600 per month), revenue from property on Napier Road, fund-raising events, and also donations from supporters.

The use of para-political organizations

As mentioned above, many traditional party activities are performed by governmental para-political institutions, in which the PAP MPs play an important role.[24] These include the People's Association, Management Committees of Community Centres, Citizen's Consultative Committees and Residents' Committees (see pp. 95–6 for details). All these are linked to the Prime Minister's Office (PMO) as the nerve-center. Because these are government organizations, their existence has served to blur the line between government and party, which has not been discouraged by the PAP. These auxiliary organizations have provided an opportunity for the PAP to "get to the ground" and to mobilize grassroots leaders who have been reluctant to identify openly with a political party.[25] They have functioned to mediate between the PAP MP, the government, and the people, instead of the party branch.[26] Not surprisingly, the PAP has kept opposition MPs out of most of these organizations.

The PAP has always sought to fill all available social and political space,[27] and it certainly did not want to leave pre-school education to chance, especially when the Barisan Sosialis began conducting kindergarten classes in the 1960s. So the PAP set up kindergartens and soon became the leading provider of pre-school education through PAP (now PCF) kindergartens. Until 1986, the kindergartens were run by the party branches. Since then, they have been run by the PAP Community Foundation, a charitable organization associated with the party. There are now 309 kindergartens, and 6 of 10 pre-school children attend PCF kindergartens.[28] Like many of these other organizations, the PAP saw affordable pre-school education not only in terms of its intrinsic value, but also as a good community outreach program to gain the support and loyalty of the parents.

Efforts at institutionalization

From the mid-1980s, Goh Chok Tong has taken an interest in strengthening the institutions of the party to reduce its reliance on personalities, and also to enlarge its membership. The Secretary-General now has four organizing secretaries instead of one, and there are some new committees, for instance, the GRC Coordinating Committee. *Petir*, the party journal, has been instructed to focus more on party news and political issues. The various activities of the party, including workshops, forums, walkabouts, and "Walkajogs", have been put on a more regular basis. This will serve to upgrade the branches to some extent. As mentioned above, the Young PAP and the Women's Wing were instituted. In 1996, "Friends of the PAP" was formed, comprising about 200 members, many of whom hold top positions in the private sector, who help with fund-raising dinners and contribute ideas to the party.[29] The PAP also established the PAP Community Foundation, a charity, to increase the party's involvement in various grassroots projects. The party endowed the PCF with $500,000.

Goh Chok Tong has also wanted to enlarge the party's membership, especially by attracting young people at the branch level. In 1998, he challenged the branches to recruit 50 new members each a year. The party has recruited about 1,000 a year since 1998, but this is well below its target of 4,000 per annum.[30]

Party renewal: replacing the old guard

The longevity of any political party depends upon its renewal capabilities. Lee Kuan Yew notes that there is an extensive history of nationalist leaders who successfully led anti-colonial fights for freedom, but who failed to groom honest and capable successors, and as a result their countries are steeped in veniality, corruption and nepotism.[31] Top caliber new talent must be recruited and nurtured, and the old guard must be asked – or if necessary, compelled – to step aside. Singapore is somewhat unusual in terms of renovation in two ways. First, normally when one considers the "circulation of elites", it is with regard to pressure from below exerted by the young blood – both to be admitted into the party and to rise quickly within it. This pressure has been absent in Singapore, that is, there are no "young Turks". Indeed recruitment of new talent of ministerial quality has been a problem that has absorbed considerable party energies, as will be discussed shortly. As Lee Kuan Yew has mentioned, he thought that the "orderly political processes would throw up men to carry on ...", but this did not happen.[32] Second, in the absence of pressure, the easiest course would be to put off renewal, as has happened in many states. However, Singapore had a strong-willed leader in Lee Kuan Yew, who has proven to be relentless in pursuit of a goal.

Lee Kuan Yew writes that he started the search for possible successors in the 1960s, when he was only in his forties.[33] By the early 1970s, he was committed to renewal in earnest, and he made it clear that he was not looking for successors from among the party stalwarts or activists. In 1979 in *Petir*, the PAP journal, he queried, "What is the most compelling task at present? It is self-renewal."[34] The first of the "second generation" leaders were recruited in 1976. In 1980, eleven MPs were asked to retire, and subsequently three old guard were dropped from the Cabinet. In 1984 there were 24 new candidates, and by the next year the new generation dominated Parliament, the Cabinet, and the party CEC. By 1988, only Lee Kuan Yew remained in the Cabinet among the old guard.[35] Not only were the talented newly recruited members given seats to contest, many were promoted rapidly and tested rigorously.

Renewal, however, was painful; it left considerable bitterness in its wake, and it certainly helps account for the drop in electoral support for the PAP in the 1980s and early 1990s. Some of the old guard, mainly the technocrats like Hon Sui Sen and Goh Keng Swee, asked to step down (Hon in 1978 and Goh in 1988). Ironically, these were men Lee was unhappy to lose at the time. Some others retired quietly, and yet others were eased into retirement. For example, S. Rajaratnam was relieved of his ministry but was made Second Deputy Prime Minister, and Lim Kim San formally retired in 1981 but was kept on in an important party recruitment position and became the chair of the Council of Presidential Advisors in 1992.

However, a number of old guard, mainly the "mobilizers" who had risen from the grassroots and who had strong links to the Chinese ground, were distinctly unhappy. These included Ong Pang Boon, Jek Yuen Thong, and Fong Sip Chee. They disagreed with the pace and timing of renewal – they were not ready to retire – and they were concerned about the "types" being selected, their lack of grassroots connections, and the generation gap. K.C. Lee (Lee Khoon Choy), who gave up his seat in 1984, reflected that "80% of our population speak dialects and Mandarin. But as for the kind of elites selected: they are all English-educated, who cannot even speak Chinese ... Can such candidates communicate with the crowd".[36] Some felt that to work under a younger leader who had not been through the struggle was an affront to their dignity. Lee Kuan Yew observes that, "they saw no reason why these bright, young, energetic men who had not contributed to the struggle should come in and displace them before they were ready to go. Yes, the Old Guard agreed that we needed to prepare successors, but quite a few did not agree that they were getting old and getting on that fast. One of them told me, 'Stop talking about our getting old, we are good for many more years ...' ".[37] Ironically, as pointed out in an article by Cherian George, the old guard mobilizers were victims of their own successes – as the opposition was neutralized, the mobilizers became less important.[38]

Also bitter was one of the founder leaders, a party organizer rather than a mobilizer, a Minister for 22 years, and the Deputy Prime Minister from 1959–68, Toh Chin Chye. Lee Kuan Yew writes that he left Toh out of the Cabinet "as a clear signal" to the old guard that renewal was irreversible.[39] Toh stayed on in Parliament as a backbencher, mainly because he might have run as a formidable independent in 1980 or 1984 if the party had tried to remove him. By 1988, redrawn electoral boundaries had eliminated his long-held constituency, and he retired. Of all the old guard, Toh became the most vocal critic of Lee, the second generation, and certain PAP policies.[40]

The transition from the old guard to the second generation stirred up internal divisiveness and contentiousness that had a devastating effect on the party machinery. Chan Heng Chee believes that it may explain the poor PAP performance at the 1981 Anson by-election and the 1984 general election.[41] In these elections and in 1991, Ong Pang Boon and some of the other old guard disagreed with the PAP election strategy and criticized the new generation for not being close to the "Chinese ground", among other things (see Chapter 11).

However, the transition was over by the 1990s, the old guard was honored at dinners, reassured they were appreciated and not forgotten, and ex-gratia payments were given to 47 former MPs who qualified for the gratuity under the Parliamentary Pensions Act. Interestingly, Chinese language and education has made a comeback (see pp. 106–9), and the 1991 election results went some way to confirm the fears of K.C. Lee and Ong Pang Boon about the Chinese ground being neglected (see p. 151). The lesson was absorbed and acted upon. Since then those Chinese who are recruited who have ministerial potential almost invariably speak Mandarin (or learn it quickly) and preferably a dialect, along with English. Mobilizers, as such, are still not being sought, but having political savvy and credibility have gained more prominence.

Systematic renewal in the party continues relentlessly. In the January 1997 election, there were 24 new candidates. There is less rancor about compelling MPs to step down now. The worst for any party is always getting beyond the founding stalwarts, who, in the case of the PAP felt entitled by their long service – conditioned by the Japanese occupation of Singapore, and fired by anti-colonial nationalism and the struggle against the Communist insurgency – to decide their own departure dates. The problem now, beyond recruiting new ministerial talent for the future, ironically, is keeping the top Ministers from resigning voluntarily. In the period after the 1991 election, three important Ministers resigned in favor of more appealing jobs outside of politics: S. Dhanabalan (who returned briefly), Yeo Ning Hong, and Dr. Tony Tan, although the last was successfully prevailed upon to return to the Cabinet.

Party recruitment: co-opting intellectuals and technocrats; selecting candidates and future ministers; political succession at the top

The PAP has always believed and acted upon the principle that the party which manages to recruit the "brightest and the best" will prevail. As early as 1959, in reference to the struggle against the Malayan Communist Party, Lee Kuan Yew said, "It is a battle of ideals and ideas. And the side that recruits more ability and talent will be the side that wins".[42] Lee has always had a strong preference for those who perform well scholastically, particularly in the sciences. Some of the other early party stalwarts had concerns about focusing so narrowly, but his view, modified a bit in the mid-1970s, has prevailed. Therefore, the "combing of every nook and cranny of Singapore" for political talent has typically gone outside the party, although the leaders must soothe the feelings of the party faithful by saying that all "PAP MPs are asked to nominate party activists who meet the criteria for consideration ...".[43] Lee Kuan Yew believes that having a few MPs from the party rank-and-file is permissible, but he is less sanguine about their prospects for rising, saying that maybe one day there will be cadre "good enough to be Cabinet Ministers," but, he adds, he "has his doubts." It is better, he believes, to headhunt those in their mid-30s who have an outstanding education and performance record.[44] The problem, as he explains it, is not one of getting "foot soldiers" but of finding "generals".[45]

Many of Singapore's first generation leaders were not born in Singapore and, especially after separation from Malaysia, the "catchment area" for political talent in the island-state has been very restricted. Lee Kuan Yew has regularly stated that, at any given time in Singapore, there are only about 400 to 500 people within the 30–45 age group who have the talent and qualifications that give them the potential that the PAP is looking for in recruits. Out of those, many are not interested in political careers, and of those selected and willing, there is a high attrition rate, or casualty list. In terms of recruiting potential "generals", Lee has said he would settle for ten for each generation.[46]

In the mid-1970s, according to Chan Heng Chee, PAP candidates were chosen to play one or more of four roles: technocrat, mobilizer, Malay vote-getter, and/or Chinese-educated intellectual.[47] In the 13-member 1976 Cabinet there were three journalists and a party professional – presumably mobilizers. Nowadays, there are no journalists or party professionals. There is always at least one Malay vote-getter,[48] and at least one Indian Minister in the Cabinet. Instead of the Chinese-educated intellectual, there are now bilingual-educated scholars, most of whom have attended the premier Chinese SAP schools (see pp. 106–9). There are many technocrats, both civilian (including trade union) and military. The type of person the PAP has been co-opting now is more narrowly focused: intellectuals and technocrats (a university degree is a basic requirement), with proven job competence. The fact that the person lacks political experience is not a handicap.

In the first major recruitment of new talent in 1968, the PAP fielded several PhDs, academics, professionals, including doctors and lawyers and some top administrators as electoral candidates. More were recruited in 1970 and 1972. However, most of these did not work out in their "baptisms of fire" as Ministers and MPs, and by 1980 most were gone.[49] In 1980, a new team of seven was introduced, but by 1984 only two remained. Lee Kuan Yew reflects that he soon discovered that a disciplined mind alone was not enough. Increasingly the PAP found success with its technocrats. Goh Chok Tong and S. Dhanabalan were recruited in 1976, from being CEOs of a government-linked shipping line and a bank, respectively. In 1979, Dr. Tony Tan, an academic but also a banker (and later chairman and CEO of a bank), was recruited.

By the mid-1980s, party recruitment also included a growing number of "scholar soldiers" from the Singapore Armed Forces (SAF) (while other military scholars moved in, at a high level, to the civil service and government-linked companies). The transition from purely civilian government to one including Brigadier-Generals and a Rear Admiral (the others do not use their ranks) was sudden, and it raised some qualms and presented Singapore with at least a minor image problem.

What happened was not planned, according to B.G. George Yeo.[50] To increase the prestige of the SAF (see p. 170), a major SAF scholarship scheme was introduced in 1971, and the "best minds" were channeled that route. Later, when the academic and professional recruits did not work out for the most part, and attracting candidates from the private sector or the Administrative Service proved difficult, the military scholars, especially from the first two scholarship batches (1971 and 1972), increasingly provided the PAP with its new talent.[51] Most of these scholar-soldiers were immediately appointed Ministers of State. As of October 2001, there were five SAF (reserve) Cabinet Ministers (one of whom is an acting minister) out of 17 members. Prime Minister Goh Chok Tong is aware that having too many military men in government is bad for Singapore's image, and he also believes it would not be good to have too many in Cabinet with the same military (engineering and mathematics) mindset. However, he does not see the present situation as constituting a problem.[52] What is a problem is the difficulty the party has in recruiting from the private sector.

Selecting candidates and future ministers

Since 1968, the PAP has averaged between 16–20 new candidates in each election. Before the late 1970s, the selection of candidates was less systematic and based mainly on recommendations coming through the old boy network, and some interviews. In 1976, Goh Chok Tong was put in charge of recruiting. By this time Lee Kuan Yew wanted a more formal and standard selection process, and such a system was worked out by Goh (see p. 117).[53] Basically, the selection process includes a number of stages, and it is rigorous and pains-taking in its deliberations.[54] On the recommendation of Ministers, MPs, senior civil servants, corporate leaders, and party activists, prospective candidates are invited to "tea parties" in groups of six to eight to chat informally with one of three Ministers, who take turns in meeting over 100 potential candidates a year. Some of these are invited to a second tea session, and those found suitable meet personally, first with Deputy Prime Minister Lee Hsien Loong and then with the party whip. Those who clear the process to this point then appear before the selection committee of PAP Ministers, who probe extensively into a prospective candidate's character and motivation, and ability to be a "team player". After this, those still being considered are interviewed by Goh Chok Tong and Lee Kuan Yew. If they agree to the selection, the candidate is then given a final interview by the party's CEC to ratify the selection. But this is not the end of it.

Candidates are then deployed in different constituencies to expose them to political work at the grassroots, and they undergo basic training, as mentioned earlier. Candidates are matched for linguistic affinity, meaning that in a Teochew-speaking constituency, the candidate must be able to speak that dialect during the campaign (PAP Chinese MPs try not to use dialects except for the election campaigns). Not all the selected candidates will necessarily be fielded in the next election.

Those among the selected candidates who are viewed as having ministerial potential go through an additional stage. They are given one-and-a-half days of psychological testing involving over one thousand questions. The PAP has adapted the system developed by Shell for its prospective new executives. The tests focus on three qualities – power of analysis, imagination, and sense of reality. As Lee Kuan Yew explained in his memoirs,[55] he was concerned that there were too many failures among those selected, and that the PAP needed a better way to assess a person's character. He was impressed with the coolness of the Apollo 13 astronauts in averting disaster, and concluded that NASA's psychological testing of astronauts had paid off.

The rigorous selection process and standards adopted by the PAP must be unique for a political party. They are meant to screen out those who may not perform to expectations while letting the most able, the "best and the brightest", rise to the top. And the PAP *is* very good at co-opting talent. However, there are some criticisms of the process. First, critics say the process is elitist (the PAP would say meritocratic) and leads the PAP to choose people with similar backgrounds and outlooks. Second, critics believe that the process is off-putting and many who could serve the government well are unwilling to put themselves through it, especially those who have already succeeded or who sense opportunities in the private sector and are busy chasing their careers.

As Chua Lee Hoong has observed, the PAP wants the same combination of ability, commitment, diligence and drive "sought after by employers everywhere".[56] Whereas the Information Technology age offers adventure for the daring, politics in a dominant party system can seem less than awe-inspiring. The result, as B.G. Lee has noted, is that it is harder now to persuade people to enter politics, and more are declining invitations from the PAP.[57] Thus, recruiting top-caliber new talent remains a very difficult and urgent task for the party.

How important is the party apparatus?

There is a widespread belief among Singaporeans and observers that the party exercises little influence on government. The PAP is everywhere, but it is the PAP government, not the party apparatus. As long ago as 1969, CEC member S. Rajaratnam noted that the party no longer played a key role in the political life of Singapore.[58] Chan Heng Chee observes that there is a widespread feeling "that the CEC is only a rubber stamp for government decisions, and that the party has lost its role in giving direction to society".[59] The reasons are clear – the party has been in office so long that the line distinguishing the party from the government has become faint, and this is compounded by the fact that the CEC membership overlaps extensively with the Cabinet. There is also an historical legacy: With the pro-Communists in the party and Parliament until the party split in 1961, the PAP government developed the habit of making the Cabinet the center for discussing ideas and developing policies, and of not using the party or Parliament as forums for policy discussions.[60]

Indeed, the PAP leaders view the party as a key "national institution" holding the country together, and not just an ordinary political party. There are other important institutions, they admit, but these are not designed to govern the state. Only the PAP can do this; there is no alternative. In fact, when they talk about the PAP, generally, they mean the government.

5 Ideology of the leaders and for the populace

The term "ideology" implies a coherent and interlinked set of ideas, beliefs and values leading to a plan of action. It is the systematic use of ideas and values to mobilize people, or to gain their support, for some goal or end. Ideologies reflect the beliefs, values and interests of those elites – usually state leaders – who produce or adopt them. The ability of elites to gain the consent of the people by defining and molding an ideology that is accepted by the masses is a powerful political tool that can serve to legitimize the political system and the leaders.

It is sometimes difficult to determine what constitutes an ideology. One way to identify an ideology is if it is a "theory" that has an "ism" – capitalism, socialism, etc. But nowadays "isms" are attached rather dubiously, for example "Mahathirism"[1] for the thoughts and actions of Malaysian Prime Minister Mahathir. Former Foreign Minister S. Rajaratnam once described Singapore's mass ideology as "moneytheism". Thankfully, no one has yet written, to the authors' knowledge, about "Lee Kuan Yewism" (this would indeed be a formidable task!). An ideology can be embodied in a constitution, but it need not be. Normally it has instrumental and cultural/symbolic aspects to it. Clearly an ideology is something more than just a social policy or a political theme or an organizing principle. It requires an intertwined network of thinking, and it needs logic and coherence. An ideology can be modified, reformulated, modernized or even be completely discarded.

The question is, has the PAP government an ideology? The leaders, while themselves logical thinkers, espouse no official ideology, having early on discarded socialism,[2] and they regularly reiterate that they are not enthralled by any "theories". After independence, it seemed that the nearest approach to an ideology was the theme of "survival". Singapore was, and remains, vulnerable (see pp. 169–70). This vulnerability was developed into a political discourse used to rationalize policies, such as the need for a tightly organized "rugged society", and to mobilize the people under a new banner.[3] Later, the "survival" motif was superseded by a reoccurring series of (not necessarily contrived) crises. One view is that the PAP leaders, and Lee Kuan Yew especially, believed in "the conflict theory of management: you either dominate or you are dominated", and this led to a "lifelong sense of insecurity that it could all be taken away with one uncontrollable spasm of social upheaval or regional chaos".[4] "Survival" may fall short of really being an ideology, but it had some coherence, it was symbolically important as a rallying cry, and instrumentally it helped justify a set of governing principles, as do the various crises. In the end, Chan Heng Chee concludes that the "politics of survival" was essentially a pragmatic ideology.[5]

Most analysts of Singapore conclude that the PAP government "ideology" comprises pragmatism, meritocracy, multiracialism, and, more recently and tentatively, Asian values or communitarianism. To these, we would add elitism as a foundation element of the complex ideology of the PAP.

Pragmatism

It is often said that the defining ideological characterization of the PAP is political pragmatism. Pragmatism tends to be loosely defined, meaning practical or useful and concerned with actual application rather than theory or speculation. It has become equated with rationality. However, pragmatism can also mean expediency – doing what is advantageous while motivated primarily by self-interest.

Pragmatism is sometimes viewed as non- (or anti-)ideology (leading to administrative or technocratic politics), and Chua Beng-Huat writes that the "prevalent understanding" of many Singaporeans is that it is non-ideological.[6] One critic disdainfully defines pragmatism as "action without theoretical guidance and rooted in pragmatic experience, spontaneity in the form of hunches, expediency of any means to the class end ...".[7]

It may not matter much to the PAP, but pragmatism has been considered an ideology or school of thought and there are some theoretical similarities to PAP practice. The school was founded in the US around 1872 by Charles Peirce and later popularized by William James and John Dewey.[8] They saw it as a method of testing the validity of all concepts by their practical results, and they disputed the notion of absolute truth and repudiated all forms of determinism. It is also found in early Confucian thought – something has value if it works or succeeds. Hsiao Kung-chuan writes that "Chinese political thought and learning were based on the idea of practical application" and thus never paid much attention to abstract theories, methods of thought, logical consistency, or to similarities and differences among conceptualizations.[9]

Lee Kuan Yew has described the PAP approach as "rational", meaning choosing the best available course of action and not allowing any option for achieving that goal to be excluded on account of dogma.[10] There are two aspects to PAP pragmatism. One is a commitment to rationality and practical results, the litmus test being "Does it work?", and the other is tactical. The PAP prides itself on not having any "sacred cows" to prejudice freedom of action, and on not getting locked into ideological or hard positions. Hill and Lian note that it is pragmatism based upon "purposive rational policies", meaning that policies are articulated on the principle that persons affected by it will respond in a calculated and predictable manner (for example, when the PAP ties electoral choice to housing improvements).[11] Such pragmatism requires planning and considerable quantitative analysis to complement a very strong strain of empiricism. If the leaders find that a policy is not working or that it is producing unintended results, the PAP will jettison it without any sentimentality. The "wage correction" policy, the "Two is Enough" population policy, and the moral education policy are three examples of such discarded policies.

If a major policy which the PAP wants incurs high political costs when initially implemented, the PAP usually does not just abandon the policy, although it might be withdrawn in the short term and reformulated. An example of this is the Graduate Mother Scheme (discussed below). Some others times, in the mid-1980s especially, the PAP persisted with some unpopular policies quite un-pragmatically and paid a political price for them electorally (see p. 150).

Pragmatism in a tactical sense involves prudent political management of the means, directions, timing, wording, and public presentation of policies, especially sensitive policies involving language, religion, and culture. It can mean slowly preparing the ground to bring the public around on a particular policy (for example, concerning the closure of Nanyang University in 1980). Rajaratnam explained, "When you are dealing with emotions ... you never meet them head on. You work your way around them. People don't keep pushing a door that is open".[12] Pragmatism sometimes gets accused of leading to the use of expediency. Political tactics and strategies are always expedient (everywhere) to the extent that they are usually designed to win support and votes. A number of policies over the last forty-eight years have served to help consolidate PAP support. However, the bottom line is that expediency has not been carried to the point where long-term interests and beliefs have been jeopardized for short-term popularity.

Elitism

Elitism is the belief that there is always a small group of people at the top who actually make the important decisions influencing society, whatever the political system, and whatever is claimed to the contrary. There is little doubt that the PAP leaders are elitists. They admire the power of the intellect, and they believe that only a few of the best and brightest are capable of leading well.[13] Likewise, they believe in logical calculation, rationality, and in the general superiority of science and technology in overcoming societal problems.

Elitism in the West was given theoretical rigor by the European scholars Gaetano Mosca, Vilfredo Pareto and Robert Michels. They posited similar propositions: government would always be by the few – a ruling class – who were distinguished in some ways as the best and the brightest. Further, in attacking Rousseau, they said that government might be *for* the people, but never *by* the people.[14] This is not far removed from the earlier thoughts of Thomas Jefferson who, in a letter to John Adams in 1813, wrote, "I agree with you that there is a natural aristocracy among men. The grounds of this are virtue and talents ...".[15] The later classical elite theorists (or positivists) were tainted, however, perhaps unfairly, by their identification with fascism,[16] and today many Westerners equate elitism with authoritarianism and political inequality.[17]

In Confucian political philosophy, elitism has a central position. Confucianism accepts that individuals are born with different capabilities, and that some are born to rule and the rest to be ruled. The ideal is that benevolent rule should be by the most able and virtuous. There is no concept of equality among men; instead there was an ordered social hierarchy, led at the top by the "ruler-preceptor" who possesses virtue and leads by example.[18]

Elitism in the PAP is found in the speeches of the leaders, in the high moral tone and paternalism of the government, in the party cadre structure, and in an assortment of policies. Lee Kuan Yew has regularly said, with reference to individuals, that "you either have the talent or you do not", and those who have extraordinary talent are always only a few. In 1967 he noted that in every society there is about five percent "who are more than ordinarily endowed physically and mentally and in whom we must expend our limited and slender resources in order that they will provide that yeast, that ferment, that catalyst in our society which alone will ensure that Singapore shall maintain its pre-eminent place in South and Southeast Asia".[19] Into the new millennium, the message is similar. At a law conference session, Lee said that out of a year's births of 45,000, there might only be about 150 to 200 who would meet top, world-class standards. "That's a hard fact of life", he concluded.[20]

Elitism can be seen in a number of policies. One is the commitment to a meritocratic system, based on ascriptive achievement criteria applied to students and government employees (discussed below). Elitism can also be seen in the determination of the government to pay extraordinarily high wages to government Ministers and civil servants, even though this policy has exacted some political costs. In Lee Kuan Yew's view, "From each his best, to each his worth".[21] The PAP leaders pragmatically believe that the only way they can attract scarce talent into government and the top echelons of the civil service is to pay wages competitive with the private sector. They also believe, perhaps because of a rather caustic view of human nature, that high salaries deter corruption. At the other end of the scale, elitism can also be detected in immigration policies governing unskilled foreign workers. They must have permission to marry while residing in Singapore, and females must take pregnancy tests every six months (and can be sent home if they become pregnant, so that the new child does not automatically acquire Singapore citizenship by right of birth in the state).

Elitism can also been seen in the style of the PAP leaders and how they conduct themselves. They accept that being the "best" carries with it the responsibility for being the most able and virtuous, and for leading by example. One can detect a certain sense of "noblesse oblige" in the PAP. They do not tolerate corruption or ostentatious lifestyles among themselves, and they are conscious that they must be seen to be living up to their own high standards. Goh Chok Tong, using a Chinese saying about corruption, notes that "If the beams on top are not straight, the ones below are bound to be crooked".[22]

Singaporeans on the whole seem unperturbed by the notion of elitism and seem to accept its utility for Singapore. Asad Latif writes that the "governing scholar-class" responds by making up "in ideas and organization what Singapore lacks so manifestly in size and population". Likewise, a *Straits Times* editorial remarks that "Singapore excels in producing elites. That is good, because a core of talented and motivated people is essential if a city-state is to prevail in the global jungle".[23] Where many Singaporeans seem to draw the line is with eugenics, which found its most obvious policy expression in the Graduate Mother Scheme (discussed below).

Eugenics is the belief that intelligence is largely inherited, and that selective breeding can improve the gene pool. The principles of genetics have long been used in animal breeding to improve desired traits and are well accepted. However, for humans it is controversial; Hitler gave it a bad name from which it has not recovered. Also, the validity of the scientific claims of the eugenicists is subject to debate.[24]

Lee Kuan Yew believes in eugenics. Among others, he has been influenced by Professor H.J. Eysenck, an expert on measuring intelligence, who visited Singapore in 1987.[25] Lee states that his views are a result of observation, empirical enquiry and study. "I started off believing all men were equal. Now I know that's the most unlikely thing ever to have been ...".[26] Commenting on the controversial Murray and Bernstein book, he opined, "the Bell Curve is a fact of life".[27] He states that the relevance of the Bell Curve became obvious to him by the late 1960s when he could see that equality of opportunity did not bring about equal results.[28] In a 1983 National Day rally address he said that 80 percent of talent and intelligence was inherited, and he lamented that the poorer and less well educated around the world have more children.[29] In Singapore now, the educated are reproducing only at a rate of 1.4 percent, despite incentives. Lee thinks that down the road this could be *the* most serious problem facing Singapore.[30] When asked if the other PAP Ministers shared his views on eugenics, he replied, "They know it isn't poppycock".[31]

Meritocracy

In explanations of Singapore's ideological foundations, elitism sometimes gets subsumed (and relatively neglected) under the rubric of meritocracy. However, it is the belief in elitist principles that has in turn led to the establishment of a meritocracy based on educational achievement and job performance. Meritocracy and elitism are sometimes described as the more and less acceptable sides of the same coin. Meritocracy is the idea that each individual's social and occupational position is determined by individual achievement, not political or economic influence; not race, class or parentage.[32] The principle is premised on the belief that merit can be determined objectively, or even scientifically.

While it might seem that the meritocratic principle of advancement based on achievement must be more fair than other criteria, it does have its critics. First, some believe that testing or job performance ratings are not as objective as often claimed, especially since, in Singapore, interview performance has been added to the criteria.[33] Second, meritocracy rewards certain kinds of talent (e.g. scholastic achievement) but may ignore other kinds of talent (e.g. originality). Third, educational meritocracy can "generate a status hysteria around admissions ...".[34] Finally, the meritocratic principle, as part of an elitist ideology, it is argued, can serve to legitimize socio-economic and ethnic inequality.

In Singapore, the meritocratic principle is applied to education, the civil service and armed forces, and government-linked companies. Ezra Vogel has characterized the political system as a "macho-meritocracy".[35] In education, great stress is placed on streaming and examinations (see p. 104). Students are streamed at various levels according to demonstrated scholastic ability (on the basis of tests primarily, but also teachers' reports), with the best students going to the best schools, which have the most resources and the best teachers, such as the elite Chinese Special Assistance Plan (SAP) schools.[36] Later, tertiary education scholarships are awarded on the basis of examination results and, more recently, interview performance. The merit principle is also applied to making appointments and promotions in government service, and civil service salaries, which are linked to private sector incomes, are another plank of the meritocratic system.

Singapore's leaders believe that the meritocratic system, which ideally is blind to race and class, has helped the brightest students rise to the top, and has made a major contribution to the establishment of a corrupt-free and efficient civil service. The PAP leaders realize that the focus on scholastic achievement often ignores those with artistic or athletic talent, and there have been efforts by Prime Minister Goh and the younger leaders to promote and reward these kinds of talent. As well, the PAP government is aware that a meritocratic system can elevate inequalities, and it has initiated a number of programs that help redistribute wealth (e.g. the HDB upgrading scheme). Deputy Prime Minister B.G. Lee explained the need for some redistribution as follows: "Meritocracy underpins the entire Singapore system. But equal opportunities generate unequal outcomes ... in the absence of periodic shake-ups, these inequalities will become more marked".[37]

Multiracialism

The concept of multiracialism will be dealt with only briefly here, as a part of the ideological review, since ethnicity and education are the themes of Chapter 8. Multiracialism represents a "founding myth". Singapore is a multiethnic state comprising Chinese, Malays, Indians, Eurasians, and others. From its inception, the PAP has made multiracialism a key principle, backed by strong sanctions against the use of inflammatory racial or religious utterances. Multiracialism is similar to "multiculturalism", meaning respect for and tolerance of all the ethnic groups and cultures represented in the society, and equality under the law. The meritocratic concept fits into this by basing rewards on achievement rather than on race or culture.

At independence, ethnic tolerance was strongly promoted, the four official languages were maintained, and Mandarin, Malay, Tamil and English schools continued. A Presidential Council was established to protect the rights of the minorities. However, side by side with multiracialism, and without disavowing it, there were strong PAP integrationist or "melting pot" strategies which gradually took precedence. The housing estates were integrated and English was promoted.[38] A Singapore identity was touted, and ethnicity was played down. Then, starting in the 1970s, there was a shift back to more vigorous multiracialism – described as an "idiosyncratic version of multiracialism"[39] – with reinforced ethnic identities and a high consciousness of race, but fortunately with no noticeable increase in ethnic tensions. Singaporeans "became hyphenated": Chinese-Singaporeans, Malay-Singaporeans, and so forth.[40] The new emphasis on ethnic identities was prompted by PAP worries about the impact of Westernization on Singapore, and was aimed specifically at revitalizing Chinese culture and language (see pp. 106–9).

Asian values, Victorian ethos, Confucianism and communitarianism

The Asian values[41] debate is often viewed in terms of a contest between the West, advocating the values of liberal democracy, and the East, representing the values of conservatism and tradition. The reassertion of Asian values has been in response to the West's, particularly America's, rigorous promotion of its own values.[42] It has generated considerable rancor. There has been indignation expressed in the West, that people who believe in human rights and liberal democracy have suddenly been depicted as "cultural and political imperialists".[43] Singapore has been one of the leading proponents of Asian values, and this has led to some tensions (see p. 180).[44]

While the Asian values discourse has at times been characterized an being "anti-Western", ironically these values have simultaneously been depicted as not being particularly Asian at all. Rather, it is said, most of these values can be recognized in past and present Western values – as part of the moral standards of the Victorian age (prudish and centered around family traditions). They can also be found in the hard work, thrift, and self-discipline of the Protestant ethic, and/or seen in the attraction to strong government, rejection of welfarism in favor of volunteerism, and the emphasis on community found in Western conservativism (or neo-conservativism).[45] One interesting thesis is that the values labeled as "Asian" are the values of 19th century Victorian England that were absorbed by Singapore's Baba Chinese, who admired what the British stood for when they ruled over Singapore and Malaya.[46]

Certainly former PAP Deputy Prime Minister Goh Keng Swee recognized a link between Asian and past Western values. In 1976, he said that Singaporeans should not discard their traditional values, such as belief in hard work, thrift, honesty, self-discipline, regard for education, respect for enterprise, and concern for family stability. He said that these virtues were not only Eastern: "These are the values that made America rich and strong", although these old values had now decayed.[47] Likewise, in one of his books, he wrote, "I think we can detect in contemporary Singapore a strange but striking similarity of intellectual climate and social values with Victorian England . . .".[48] Lee Kuan Yew has not been drawn into the debate. He says that "Asian values" is a label, and that while there is no single value system that encompasses all Asian societies, there are common principles. Further, he says, while these values may even be universal, they have developed differently in Asia and the West.[49] It seems clear that many aspects of Asian values are recognizable in traditional Western values, or vice-versa, but this does not mean that they have been imported to Asia from the West, or that they are not legitimately traditional Eastern values as well.[50]

Singapore's leaders have always been concerned about the "cultural roots" of Singapore's multi-ethnic society, especially the immigrant communities and particularly the Chinese. From the late 1970s, the PAP leaders became increasingly worried about the widespread use of English contributing to Westernization and eroding Chinese culture and values. With the technological revolution in the 1990s, the leaders decided it was imperative to promote traditional core values. This was critically important in their view because they saw a link between cultural values and economic growth. A study in mid-1991 confirmed that the core values of hard work, thrift, and group cohesion had to be stimulated in order to maintain Singapore's economic successes.[51] Prime Minister Goh explained, "We need Eastern values, not only to give us a sense of history and perspective, to know where we have come from but also because the values are still germane".[52]

Tamney claims that both Lee Kuan Yew and Goh Chok Tong publicly linked Singapore's economic successes to the prevalence of Chinese cultural values.[53] However, the belated attraction to reviving Confucianism for Singapore in the 1980s appears much more the inspiration of Lee Kuan Yew, who seemed to be undergoing his own voyage of discovery of traditional Chinese culture around that time. Rajaratnam explained that Lee was comfortable with Confucianism because it was a secular ethical system that fit his own conceptions of politics, filial piety, hard work, even submission to authority.[54]

The promotion of Confucian ethics began, at the suggestion of Lee Kuan Yew, with its inclusion in the new moral education program introduced in 1982.[55] Already, in 1979, a "Speak Mandarin" Campaign had been launched, which complemented the study of Confucian ethics. In 1983, an Institute of East Asian Philosophies was established. After this, a number of conferences were held in Singapore so as to downplay some of the undesirable aspects of Confucianism (such as the low status of women and the low value attached to entrepreneurship).

Professor Wang Gung Wu explains that Confucianism "is not some flag-waving ideology" and it "is certainly not a religion", but rather it is a rational approach to cultivating a moral awareness.[56] Although not a unified body of doctrine, Confucianism advocates a number of social and political ideas that are central to Confucian thought. First, as mentioned above, Confucianists believe that individuals are born with different capabilities. Therefore, rule should be by a morally "superior man" who is the most able and virtuous. Second, the goal of society is order and stability; thus Confucianism stresses obedience to benevolent and paternalistic hierarchical authority, and emphasizes societal duties and obligations. Third, Confucianism exalts the spirit of community, or communitarianism, which by the late 1980s was seen as a core value. Socially, Confucianism advocates strong patriarchal families and filial piety, self-reliance, the merit principle, respect for learning, and good moral behavior.

With some revision, Confucianism seemed to answer the question of how a society could be thoroughly modern and yet different from the West. Some, of course, view the Confucian revival in more conspiratorial terms. Wilkinson writes that "it is possible that the government, having drastically reduced any potential threat from the Chinese-educated, has tentatively concluded that the controlled use of its own version of traditional Chinese values many now be useful. This would explain the relatively recent emergence of an interest in Confucian ethics …".[57]

Ideology for the populace: socialization

The PAP leaders' own ideological beliefs can be seen in a number of policies designed to inculcate particular values and/or to channel social change and patterns of behavior amongst the populace. Values and traditions are durable, but not immutable. The cultural values for any society can change over time, albeit slowly and often with some enduring features. Unless isolated, cultures constantly absorb, borrow, and adapt, and individual values adjust accordingly.[58] Lee Kuan Yew has noted that more than half of Singapore's affluent and highly mobile population travels abroad each year, and the "speed in which they pick up social norms from abroad is startling".[59]

The evolution of cultural and political values in a society are naturally influenced by a state's ideology, constitution, and laws. However, beyond this, a government can try to save eroding values or inculcate new ones through policies, campaigns, and exhortations. This is known as political socialization (or, more pejoratively, "social engineering"). Socialization is a legitimate task of government, and all governments engage in it. It is also practiced by non-governmental organizations, such as religious bodies, social clubs, and interest groups; by families and, importantly, by schools and through educational curricula. Those who preach values contrary to the ones being promoted by the state are considered to be anti-establishment or counter-cultural (e.g. the anti-war hippies in the US in the 1960s or the "liberation theology" of radical Catholic priests in the Philippines in the 1980s).

Clearly, socialization is carried out by elites or counter-elites and absorbed in some degree by the masses. Traditions and values can be, and sometimes are, invented or manipulated, *but* they cannot be constructed successfully out of nothing – there must be some building blocks in the mass political culture. Likewise, traditions and political and cultural values can be imposed successfully from the top only if they are reasonably congruent with the mass political culture. A government will undermine its own legitimacy if it attempts to impose a set of beliefs and values that do not relate or conform to the experiences, traditions, and expectations of the people. As Goh Chok Tong has noted, Singapore's "leaders and the people must share the same broad ideas, the same core values, the same vision of what they want their society to be".[60]

Singapore's PAP government has actively engaged in political socialization since it came to power in 1959, but especially after independence in 1965, and particularly since the 1980s. Socialization up to 1965 was directed partly at achieving compatibility between the political cultures of Singapore and Malaya. Since independence, the PAP government has always stressed Singapore's vulnerability as a small state (see pp. 169–70) and the need for Singapore's society to be rugged and to have strong moral fiber in the face of constraints and challenges. Patriotism has been promoted in the form of a civic nationalism based on multiracialism, shared citizenship, and a common destiny. However, operating as it is in a multiracial but predominantly Chinese milieu, much of its political socialization has been directed at "people reared in the Chinese cultural tradition".[61] The PAP has tried to enhance those aspects of Singapore political culture that promote economic growth and accept authoritarian and paternalistic government in return for providing "good governance" (see pp. 192–3).

Policy problems when a gap exists between elite and mass beliefs

Although the PAP government in Singapore is acknowledged to have been quite successful in its socialization function, there are some examples of policies that reveal a gap between the ideology of the elites and the beliefs of the populace.

Perhaps the best example of a gap revealed in a policy can be seen in the 1984 Graduate Mother Scheme (although its replacement in 1987 with a less controversial but similarly motivated scheme served to close the gap). The 1980 census set off alarm bells. Women with the lowest educational levels and from families with the lowest incomes were having the most children. Conversely, many of the university graduate women were not getting married, and those who did were not having enough children to replace themselves.[62] By 1983, Lee Kuan Yew began talking about the problem of the lopsided pattern of procreation in Singapore (and around the world). He said that while some countries could tolerate this because of their size, Singapore could not, because its talent pool was numerically limited. A parallel but unstated problem was that the "lopsided pattern" had demographic implications: as the result of higher levels of education and affluence, the Chinese in particular were having fewer children.

Months of a "nature vs. nurture" debate followed, spawning catchy phrases such as "designer genes".[63] Despite negative public reaction in an election year, the government proceeded in June 1984 to introduce the Graduate Mother Scheme. The scheme provided direct financial benefits and special school enrollment privileges for graduate mothers having more than two children. It also offered financial and other benefits for the voluntary sterilization of women with little education who had at least one child and whose total household income fell below a certain specified level. Policies like the Graduate Mother Scheme and its successors attempt to influence values by according worth and status to the attainment of education, wealth, and motherhood.

The scheme was, however, very unpopular. The PAP government was accused of engaging in eugenics, attempting social engineering, and meddling in the bedrooms of the nation. It was also accused of trying to turn graduate women into prize breeding stock, and of ignoring the contribution of males. The scheme was an issue taken up by the opposition in the 1984 general election, and it no doubt cost the PAP some electoral support (see p. 150).

In mid-1985, the successor generation of PAP leaders had their way, and the Graduate Mother Scheme was withdrawn. Lee Kuan Yew later explained that it was unpopular primarily because it gave graduate mothers preferences in school enrollments for their children, but he noted that the idea of getting "more educated women to have more children has not changed".[64] In March 1987 a new bevy of measures was introduced. There was no mention of targeted educational groups, but the incentives were income-related in the form of large tax rebates and other benefits, and thus more beneficial to those with higher incomes. Since there is a strong correlation between levels of education and earned income, the refashioned policy was similar in its intentions.

Another PAP policy, that of paying high ministerial and civil service salaries, has also clashed with popular perceptions both of propriety and equity. It is an elitist policy that is justified by the meritocratic principle: those with the most talent should be "adequately" remunerated for it. Since the mid-1950s, when Lee Kuan Yew was in the opposition, he has favored paying top salaries to political office-holders and civil servants.[65] The reasoning is three-fold. The government will not be able to recruit or keep the best talent if these people can make much more money in the private sector. It is reminiscent of a common Singapore saying, "if you pay peanuts, you will end up with monkeys". Lee explained the problem thus, "That period of revolutionary change that threw up people with deep convictions and overpowering motivation is over. We are in an era of high growth, with fortunes being made by the enterprising".[66] Since the PAP has recruited technocratic types rather than political activists for high positions, the craving for power and position and the idea of power having its own rewards are perhaps dulled somewhat. Second, a salary commensurate with responsibilities encourages high standards of probity and protection against corruption. As Lee has noted, underpaying ministers and civil servants has contributed to the ruination of many Asian governments.[67] A third reason concerns prestige and honor, even credibility, in the eyes of the public since in Singapore, one's worth and status is often primarily determined by one's income and assets.

In 1994, a *White Paper on Competitive Salaries for Competent and Honest Government*, approved by Parliament, established a formula for ministerial and civil servant salaries, reviewable after five years, that made Singaporean officials the highest paid in the world (but they note, wryly, that highest paid does not mean the richest – just look at the corrupt leaders all around the world!).[68] Goh Chok Tong anticipated that the salary revisions would cost the PAP some votes, and undoubtedly they did in 1997 (see p. 151).[69] Nevertheless, after this, for a while, Singaporeans seemed more or less to accept the idea of payment based on the meritocratic ideal of ability and performance as this applied to politicians and government workers.

The salary revisions announced in June 2000, however, raised considerable resentment and dismay. "Public anger is rare in usually staid Singapore, but the pay issue has produced one of the loudest furors in years ... In coffee shops, Internet chat rooms and letters to papers, Singaporeans have been venting their anger".[70] In 1998 and 1999, in the midst of the Asian economic crisis, ministerial and civil service salaries were frozen, and the CPF public pension contributions of employers were scaled way back. As one letter writer to the *Straits Times* Forum page commented, "We will endure if our leaders endure with us".[71] In June 2000, sizable salary increases for Ministers (20 percent) and civil servants (averaging 13 percent) were announced. The Prime Minister's annual salary was now $1.94 million (the Senior Minister's salary is the highest and is likely to remain so), and that of the most junior Minister was $968,000.[72] Meanwhile, employers' CPF contributions had been only partly restored to 16 percent by May 2001 since some sectors had not fully recovered.

Damage control was clearly needed. This included previously unscheduled speeches in Parliament by the Prime Minister and Senior Minister. Goh Chok Tong focused on the idea of merit, implying that you get what you pay for, and saying that Singaporeans should judge the PAP government by the results it produces. If the economy had shrunk by 5 percent during the economic crisis, it would have knocked $9.5 billion off of the GDP. However, unlike virtually all the rest of the region, Singapore did not slip into negative growth. Thus, the price of good government was cheap and represented very good value, just $34 million more in wages – just $11 per Singaporean.[73]

The public has not been told exactly what the costs to them have been of lowering employers' CPF contributions for several years, but they know they have lost money. Said one, "We took a pay cut when things were bad, as we were told". Many acknowledge that the government did a superb job of steering the country through the Asian economic crisis. But beyond that, some or many remain offended that the government would raise its own substantial salaries before tending to restoring the people's pension contributions.[74] This was potentially a political mistake, and it might have become an election issue again if the economic downturn had not captivated all attention.

Another gap between elite and mass beliefs found expression in the policy enacting compulsory Religious Knowledge courses in schools. The teaching of Confucian ethics as an option for the Religious Knowledge course requirement in Singapore was intended to promote upright moral behavior, to educate students about the cultural and moral heritage, and the historical development and modern relevance of Confucianism.[75]

While there was an acknowledged lack of a Confucian intellectual tradition in Singapore, it was thought that the "little tradition" of transmitting Confucian moral teachings through the family over the generations would mean that elements of Confucianism were embedded in the mass Chinese popular culture and would not seem alien. Thus, for the Chinese, one could speak of a revival, or rediscovery of one's roots.[76]

However, Confucianism soon became caught up in issues of ethnicity and a Singaporean identity. The English-educated Chinese were not supportive on the whole, and some criticized it, along with some foreign observers, as a conspiracy to legitimize authoritarian government. Singapore's non-Chinese viewed Confucianism as yet another project to increase Chinese dominance.[77] Further, not very many students opted for the Confucian Ethics course anyway (Buddhism was considered an easier option). Finally, a six-report study showed that the Religious Knowledge courses were exacerbating religious consciousness and differences. In 1989 the Religious Knowledge courses were jettisoned.

In October 1988, Goh Chok Tong suggested that a "National Ideology" for all Singaporeans be developed. Clearly this was the biggest effort to inculcate specific values for the populace, and it too revealed an elite–mass gap. From the 1970s the PAP government had been concerned that Asian values were being eroded or superceded by Western values. By the mid-1980s, they believed they should try to counter this drift by institutionalizing values which they believed were necessary for Singapore's continued economic success; values which were also supportive of their world view. In Lee Kuan Yew's 1988 National Day speech he lamented that the promotion of English and its widespread use in Singapore had led to the country becoming a pseudo-Western society. In October 1988, Goh Chok Tong observed that over the last decade there had been "a clear shift in our values . . .".[78] He thought that Singapore's core values should be formalized into a national ideology that would define and encourage Asian concepts of morality and duty, obligations to society and community, in contrast to more individualistic Western codes of behavior.

In the President's opening address to Parliament in early 1989, he mentioned four core values and said that these fundamental ideas needed to be enshrined in a National Ideology. "Such a formal statement will bond us together as Singaporeans, with our own distinct identity and destiny. We need to inculcate this National Ideology in all Singaporeans, especially the young. We will do so through moral education and by promoting the use of the mother tongue, by strengthening the teaching of values in schools, and through the mass media ...".[79] Lee Hsien Loong was appointed to head a committee to formulate proposals and the Institute of Policy Studies was asked to prepare a background paper setting out various options. The challenge was to find a set of key values common to all the major communities and heritages and to avoid the appearance of the values being too Chinese or Confucian.

In January 1991, the *White Paper on Shared Values* was presented to Parliament, now with five core values. The term "National Ideology" had been dropped in favor of "Shared Values" because, as B.G. Lee Hsien Loong explained, it "more modestly and accurately described what the values attempted to do".[80] One commentator points out that Malay and Indian suspicions had been aroused that a National Ideology could be used to impose Confucian values on them, and that "probably in response to these criticisms", the proposal was modified to key values to be inculcated through the schools rather than promulgating an official state ideology.[81] The White Paper explains that the Shared Values should help in developing a Singaporean identity. It notes that "we need to take practical steps to weave them into our way of life ... The schools will play a major role".[82]

While the government stated that it was not "a subterfuge for imposing Chinese Confucian values" on the state, certain Confucian ideals were retained, such as praise for the idea of government by honorable men. Further, as Chua Beng-Huat recognized, the essence of Confucianism "was to be recovered and differently embedded in the concept of communitarianism." Further, he notes, communitarianism was now identified by Goh Chok Tong and others as a key variable enabling the East Asian economic miracle.[83]

The Shared Values are:

(1) Nation before community and society before self;
(2) Family as the basic unit of society;
(3) Community support and respect for the individual;
(4) Consensus, not conflict; and
(5) Racial and religious harmony.

The Feedback Unit had suggested rephrasing the third and fourth values. The fourth value was changed from "Consensus instead of contention", to "Consensus, not conflict" since "contention" implies discussion and legitimate debate. The third value was changed from "Regard and community support for the individual" to "Community support and respect for the individual" to make it clearer that respect for the individual was a major component of the idea. However, an earlier recommendation by the Institute of Policy Studies to modify "community ... before self" to "harmony or balance between individual and community interests" was not taken up.[84]

Public reaction to the Shared Values was muted and rather unenthusiastic, ranging from "unobjectionable, but so what?" to those seeing it as more evidence of an increasingly "Chinese Singapore". Some foreign commentators found more to criticize, noting that it was meant to shore up communitarianism and fend off "excessive individualism", liberal democracy, and human rights promoted by the West. John Clammer finds much to dislike. He writes that the values are primarily Chinese principles, that nowhere in the White Paper is the question of the effects of capitalism on Singapore society addressed; and that the document is silent on the subject of human rights. He sums up as follows: a closer reading of the White Paper "reveals it to be one recommending an ideology which is statist, patriarchal, Confucian, hides anti-democratic sentiments under the guise of 'consensus' and 'nation before community' [and] is at best ambiguous on the Singaporean understanding of human rights and social justice ...".[85]

In fact, although it started out conceptually as something more grandiose and far-reaching, PAP caution and pragmatism prevailed. These values are being taught in the schools (see pp. 103–6), which could possibly have a long-term impact, but beyond that, the Shared Values remain just a White Paper, "left quietly on the table", as Hill and Lian note.[86] Parliament approved the White Paper, but did not endow the Shared Values with any constitutional standing or legal power.

Conclusion

This leads to the question of whether there is a congruence between the ideology of the elites and their efforts at political socialization, and the political culture, beliefs and values of the masses. No doubt some gap exists in all systems anywhere, so the question is really whether there is *enough* compatibility so that the system functions smoothly and without political turmoil or tensions severe enough to require the use of force to suppress. Clearly in Singapore there is *enough* compatibility. How close the congruence is quantitatively would require more studies and surveys than are currently available. However, there are some indicators. Election results (see pp. 149–53) show that although Singaporeans complain about "elitism", they will rarely vote for a person who is not well educated and well qualified professionally. The meritocratic principle is widely accepted, even by most minority elites. One of the main criticisms of the Graduate Mother Scheme was that it offered school places as a reward, and this contradicted the merit principle. The *idea* of multiracialism, a founding myth, is fully ingrained and accepted (implementation is sometimes an issue, however: see pp. 106–7). No opposition party has ever challenged the concept. The PAP elite prides itself on its pragmatism, judging policies on whether they work, and, if unpopular, on whether the political costs are acceptable. It has withdrawn or modified some policies that had incurred negative popular reaction. Likewise, pragmatism permeates mass Chinese political culture.

However, more of a gap can be detected between the elite and mass values concerning communitarian values. It is widely accepted in Singapore that Singaporeans are materialistic, selfish at times, and somewhat individualistic. This is probably accurate. A consumer culture has been promoted – shopping is both a form of recreation and of social climbing – and meritocracy encourages fierce competition and rewards individual achievement. However, government exhortations about community needs and volunteerism have at least made everyone aware of the problem.

Surveys showing a strong streak of patriotism in Singaporeans and high levels of satisfaction with the PAP government (see pp. 196–7), indicate that the mass political culture is compatible with that espoused by the elites, and that the PAP's efforts at political socialization have contributed to a greater congruence between elite and mass culture.

6 Economic policy for an independent Singapore

Initial difficulties: foundations of success

By the time of Separation, Singapore had taken steps to build a sound, yet adventurous, economic future – economic planning, industrialization, manufacture for export, including the encouragement of multinational corporations (MNCs) to invest in the country. Some of Singapore's success economically must be attributed to luck. For example, in the early 1970s it benefited from the effects of the oil exploration boom in the region. Additionally, well-chosen policies helped to put Singapore on the right economic track. Under the guidance of its first Finance Minister, Goh Keng Swee, it was committed to economic stability through low inflation, along with liberal trade and foreign exchange policies.

In the short term, however, Singapore suffered economically in the mid-1960s. Two things in particular were responsible: confrontation with Indonesia, 1963–1966 (see p. 18), which interrupted trade, and the rapid rise in population growth to 4.5 per cent annually. In 1964, there was actually *negative* economic growth, –4.3 per cent. A third setback for the economy was Britain's decision to withdraw from its military bases in Singapore in 1968, which reduced Singapore's GDP by nearly 20 per cent through the loss of jobs.[1]

Economic policy from 1965 to 1985

When going into Malaysia in 1961, Singapore's leaders pursued economic policies which depended on the successful adoption of a Common Market. They were determined to reduce Singapore's dependence on entrepôt trade, and chose a policy of industrialization, combined with discarding import substitution and concentrating on expanding exports. They consulted United Nations experts, and were guided, in particular, by the counsel of an eminent economist from the Netherlands, Dr. Albert Winsemius, who quickly adjusted his mind to Singapore's perspectives and problems. He was struck by the, often informally acquired, skills of laborers in Singapore whom he watched undertaking effective repair jobs with simple tools. He was also impressed by the need for cooperation between employers and unions, which reinforced the PAP's preferences for a remodeled industrial relations system.[2]

Recommendations arising from UN surveys formed the basis of Singapore's first four-year development plan, which provided for an increase in the number attending schools, even larger than could be accounted for by the rise in the numbers in the relevant age groups, and in building both schools and housing.

The Economic Development Board

Goh Keng Swee had already formulated the main lines of Singapore's economic strategy before the 1959 election. He was not counting on foreign investment alone; he also wanted to mobilize capital internally. He proposed to set up an Economic Development Board – the EDB. Its function was to help financially sound projects from investors, both local and foreign, who were putting up factories in Singapore.[3]

To relieve itself of responsibility for industrial estates, in 1968 the EDB "hived off" its Jurong projects (see pp. 8–9) to a new Town Corporation. The investment functions were merged into the DBS (the Singapore Development Bank).

Enumerating lists of EDB projects would be tiresome. It might be of greater interest to look at how the EDB translated the "vision" of the PAP leaders into more specific terms in order to arrive at concrete decisions. On policy changes, a good example would be the government's rejection of the import substitution policy[4] and its replacement by manufacturing for export. Once Singapore left Malaysia, the idea of a Common Market disappeared, which entailed a great effort by the EDB to search for entrepreneurs in the United States, Europe and the rest of Asia who would be willing to locate their manufacturing facilities in, and export components or total products from, Singapore. The success of this policy resulted in a labor shortage, in a more liberal attitude toward the use of immigrant foreign labor, and, later, to a recognition of its need for more training of its own labor force.

On decision-making, the speeches and writings of the PAP leaders indicate that they speak or write with principles in mind (see pp. 51–2), which constitute a vision.

> It is possible and essential to have a vision and a master strategy for the development of Singapore and at the same time one must use all of one's practical intelligence to pragmatically and innovatively make it happen without at any time compromising the vision ... The common comment that "things work in Singapore" ... not only reflects the mundane observations about basic utilities functioning efficiently, but that the infrastructure is intelligently planned with a long-range vision in mind.[5]

Choosing the MNC path

Singapore was one of the first countries in Southeast Asia to make substantial use of multinational corporations (MNCs). Investors saw it as an efficient and relatively trouble-free place to choose as an initial investment.[6] Some investors moved on to later choices, although others remained committed to Singapore. One reason why Singapore was attractive to investors in the early 1970s was that its labor legislation in the late 1960s (see p. 31) gave it a competitive edge.

Some disciples of the "dependency school" believe that Singapore was beholden to the largesse of multinationals, thus becoming "dependent", ignoring the bargaining element on both sides.[7] Several Singapore economists, in conversation, have even suggested that sometimes the roles were reversed and that the investors were the more dependent party.

The decision to concentrate on MNCs as the main agents of industrialization made good sense. Small and medium business did have a part to play in Singapore's economic growth, but it was a subordinate role. It had to struggle to be listened to, but it had too much political support, from the Chinese, to be ignored (see below).

Some memories of the past may have contributed to Chinese dislike of government policies which have not conspicuously benefited the Chinese. Before the PAP came to power, it had been sympathetic to socialism, and the party had to reassure the Singapore Chinese Chambers of Commerce that it was not hostile to local Chinese business.

There is disagreement about the extent to which MNCs have made a contribution to the spread of technology in Singapore. One authority said that in at least two areas, petroleum products and electronics, there had not been much technology transfer by the mid-1980s.[8] Another source takes an opposite view. In summing up she states:

> In addition, the introduction of new technologies through the establishment of international firms in Singapore, rather than through licensing foreign technologies to local firms, produced three benefits. First, it implied that the multinationals would assume much of the start-up risk involved in implementing a new technology. Second, it allowed more rapid technological catch-up and upgrading of the capital stock than if local firms had had to go up the learning curve from the bottom. Third, to the extent that productivity gains that stem from learning-by-doing may accrue to local firms as well as to the multinational firm that is actually engaged in production, the presence of foreign nationals in Singapore may have facilitated the adoption of new technologies by domestic companies as well.[9]

The EDB's strategy in wooing MNCs had acquired a new dimension by 2001, when they numbered about 6,000. Its new policy extended its search from firms that had already "arrived" to those which were "emerging". In accordance with the Knowledge-Based Economy (KBE) (see p. 78), some new projects might not require heavy physical investments: "fabless" wafer fabs were an example – plants that designed computer chips, but did not manufacture, test, or assemble them.[10]

Small and medium enterprises: distinctions and roles

The place of small and medium enterprises (SMEs) in the economy – and the polity – may be indicated by the answers to three questions: How important is their role in the economy?; what services do they provide for MNCs?; what changes have occurred in the last twenty years or so in their status and their political clout?

Answers to the first question are indicated in the report of the Committee on Singapore's Competitiveness (1998). It found substantial differences in the roles

SMEs had vis-à-vis MNCs, which correspond closely with the distinction between manufacturing and non-manufacturing SMEs. The former tend to be dominated by a few large companies, while the latter are more diverse, containing commerce, community, social and commercial services, many of which are sheltered from international competition. Most of them employ fewer workers than the "manufacturing" category, yet account for more than half the total employment by SMEs. They have fewer links with MNCs than the "manufacturing" category.[11]

However, SMEs which interact with MNCs have an important role to play, and it is in Singapore's interest to encourage them to meet the needs of MNCs. These firms need not be Singaporean firms. Goh Chok Tong has given an account of Matsushita Electric's operations outside Japan. In Singapore it has an annual turnover of $5bn, and employs 12,900 people. Goh explained: "We are, in fact, stepping up our effort to develop local industries, not just to support the MNCs but to become world-class companies in their own right ... There will be a long-term partnership between equals".[12] As B.G. Lee has observed: "Not every SME will grow into a large firm. Some will remain small but successful companies, while others will leave the business. Such turnover of companies is normal, especially with small firms".[13]

SMEs are now held in higher regard by the government than in the early 1980s. An economist, Ian Chalmers, recommended that they forge more links with MNCs by seeking to act as their suppliers. He also observed that the policy-makers in government, at the 1991 election (see p. 151), had to be more sensitive to Chinese sentiments in the "heartland", where some small business was located.[14] Later in the 1990s there were further indications of support for small business. One was the Committee on Singapore's Competitiveness, whose recommendations led, among other things, to the encouragement of technology through constructing a Buena Vista science hub, near the Science Park in the National University of Singapore area.[15]

A recent development regarding SMEs has been a change in the kind of people who originate them. They tend to be better educated, more willing to face technological change, and less inclined to give jobs to family members.[16]

Economic success interrupted by recession (1985)

Singapore, after surviving the shock of Separation, geared up for industrialization and an export drive. For several years it had a stretch of rapid growth interrupted only by a mild world recession in 1974–5. Then growth resumed, although some flaws in economic policy were revealed. For instance, because of rising unemployment (which had been the great bugbear since Separation in 1965), the government held firm to a low-wage and labor-intensive policy for manufacturing for too long. It did not begin to relax on unemployment until the early 1970s, when labor had actually become scarce. Consequently, there was then a shift to jobs needing more technological skills, the employment of more foreign workers, and the opening of new training centers established by the EDB. Throughout this period there were attempts to stimulate the economy by offering financial incentives: examples in the 1980s included the use of the Skills Development Fund and Research and Development (R&D) assistance funds.

As 1985 approached, the shadows of the coming world recession were evident. However, Singapore was not just hit by the recession, it also contributed to it. From 1981 to 1984 Singapore's wage increases exceeded the National Wages Council guidelines and also outran gains in productivity.[17] Among external adverse factors were low petroleum prices, and a decline in the demand for shipping, which was damaging to exports from Singapore. Also, the United States growth rate declined in 1984–5, which reduced its demand for electronics imports from Singapore. Several other sectors of the economy suffered a decline in external demand, notably for oil rigs, oil refining and petro-chemicals. In 1985 the effects of the recession were plainly reflected in the statistics. Negative growth, a decline in exports, and a rise in unemployment to six percent, leading to Singapore's worst economic performance in twenty years.

An economic committee, headed by B.G. Lee, was appointed in 1985 to review the progress of the economy and identify directions for future growth.[18] It operated on a large scale, both as regards its membership (it functioned through subcommittees representing a wide range of views) and in the extent of the ground it covered. As a short-term measure, the committee recommended action on "rigidities", such as wages and CPF contributions. It also recommended a tax on expenditure,[19] acknowledging that it would be unpopular, but believing it would be preferable to high tax rates, which would drive foreign companies out of Singapore. The measures taken were instrumental in slowing down the recession; growth resumed, and reached double figures in the late 1980s.

Between 1960 and 1984 the shape of the economy altered. The percentage share of the GDP provided by manufacturing rose by about 80 percent, while financial business services almost doubled. Relatively, but not absolutely, the share of commerce fell. By 1984 four sectors accounted for about eighty per cent of the GDP – commerce; manufacturing; transport and communications; and financial and business services.

The 1997 economic crisis: Singapore's limited exposure

Why was it that, comparatively, Singapore was less affected than other places? Linda Low, referring to the 1997 crisis outside Singapore, wrote:

> Balance of payments deficits, poor positions in official reserves, fiscal deficits, high external debts, high extent of non-performing loans, gross financial indiscipline, and economic mismanagement stemming from corruption, nepotism, political patronage and cronyism and others were common symptoms in afflicted East Asian economies.[20]

She added that globalization and liberalization might have worsened the situation as funds poured into short-term speculative investments. Singapore might have become a victim of other countries' circumstances, but its strong reserves and strict policies kept it safe after the initial contagion.

The Singapore recession was comparatively brief and shallow. Singapore's relative immunity from damage during the 1997 crisis was probably due to its financial strength and to the measures it adopted to meet the challenge. Whatever problems the Singapore economy faced (see below), both Lee Kuan Yew and

Finance Minister Richard Hu defended Singapore's handling of the currency. In a Boston speech in 1997 the former referred to Singapore's annual budget, its strong official reserves, its current surpluses and its banks' highest credit ratings in Asia.[21] Overall, explained Hu, the Singapore dollar had emerged relatively unscathed. In its trade-weighted basket of currencies, it had lost against some, notably the United States dollar, the yen, and the Chinese and Hong Kong currencies, but had gained against most others.[22]

The downturn in real growth did not come until mid-1998. Individual components of the economy had certainly shown weakness. Among them was a downturn in exports. Manufacturing growth fell and so did productivity, which was the lowest for a decade. Estimates for 1998 growth had been between 5 and 8 per cent (below Singapore's average), bolstered by a surprisingly high growth rate for the third quarter of 1997. In fact, GDP growth in 1998 was only 1.5 per cent. Alarmingly, the annual unemployment rate also nearly doubled. The government believed that the economy had not performed well as regards cost competitiveness. Consequently it quickly set up a "Committee on Singapore's Competitiveness". Both the chair and the deputy chair were ministers in the Ministry of Trade and Industry. The other members came mainly from the private sector.

The Committee's Report recapitulated what had been accomplished, and what remained to be done, since the 1985 recession. It saw the outstanding problem as a loss of competitiveness resulting from cost increases outstripping productivity gains.[23] This was blamed on the "wage correction policy" (see p. 10). The Committee not only recommended more cost cutting. It also envisaged a "competitive knowledge economy",[24] and that Singapore would soon build up an infrastructure and a workforce to promote growth in information technology (IT) (see p. 80). Another facet of capability was a recommendation to develop local businesses and groom entrepreneurs. The major features of the Report were the importance of increasing capabilities, and the need to cut costs through reductions in wages and in CPF contributions. However, other government actions helped to reduce costs to business, e.g. reductions in the cost of land and factory rentals, charges for utilities, and tax reductions both to persons and to companies.[25]

It took some time to assess the damage to, and the consequent needs of, the economy. A $2bn package of cost reductions was implemented in June 1998. However, the economy slowed from 6.2 percent growth in the first quarter of 1998 to negative growth in both the second and third quarters (negative quarter-on-quarter growth technically constitutes a recession), which made further action necessary. B.G. Lee announced tax rebates in Parliament in November 1998.[26]

The Committee's diagnosis and recommendations were reminiscent of its 1986 predecessor's. The recipe was to cut costs as far as humanly and politically possible without causing undue resentment (see p. 123). Additionally, the apparently never-ending quest for capability in yet-higher spheres of technology and knowledge had to continue, which the government tried to do.

Privatization

This section is concerned with how some of the government bodies surveyed in Chapter 3, statutory boards and government-linked companies (GLCs), were privatized. The latter are grouped into four holding companies, the largest of which is Temasek. The emphasis here is on economic issues.

In many countries, privatization became fashionable, mainly in the 1980s, for a variety of reasons. Some states in Southeast Asia were interested in profiting from the sale of enterprises. These sales were a "one-shot" deal, but were attractive to governments which were short of money. In some countries sales were not always to persons of demonstrated competence, which left the way open for possible corruption. Singapore, however, was interested in issuing shares to a relatively large number of people, ensuring a widespread distribution of capital (and also gathering some political support), as well as strengthening Singapore's budding stock market (see p. 87).

A Public Sector Divestment Committee issued a report in 1987[27] (some privatization had already occurred, for instance of Singapore Airlines in 1985). It recommended that as many GLCs as practicable should be privatized. An economist has commented on a persistent problem: presently in Singapore there is a limited number of companies with the financial resources and management expertise required to take over the larger GLCs, if they are privatized.[28]

Still, realities dictated that the Committee recommend fewer than half the companies be privatized. It found the future of the (less numerous) statutory boards harder to determine, because the large ones were providing essential services or were monopolies. It reported that four of the seven boards it had considered were candidates for further study.

The process of handing over the functions of these bodies to the private sector was slow. Linda Low correctly judged that "... the privatisation programme is slow and cautious, suggesting the government's reluctance to surrender complete control of macroeconomic policies and targets".[29] In 1983, B.G. Lee announced that the Public Utility Board's electricity and gas operations would be privatized in the next few years (they were partially privatized in 1993). In 1999, the government's share of the Development Bank of Singapore was reduced slightly from 54 percent.[30] An example of privatization occurred in 2001. Keppel Corporation, Singapore's largest diversified conglomerate, restructured in order to facilitate more "hands-on" management.[31] Unlike in some neighboring countries, there were few good arguments for privatization on financial grounds. Most GLCs made profits, and most were efficient. Even in the economically-depressed mid-1980s, government enterprises made an average profit of about 5 percent.[32]

Government-linked companies: international transactions and near-transactions

The role of GLCs in the Singapore economy became more visible, by the dramatic appearance of one of them, Singapore Telecommunications (SingTel), privatized in 1993, on the international stage, early in 2000. As protectionism yielded to liberalization in Singapore and some other countries in the area, this spread of globalization was manifest in a bewildering series of takeovers and near-takeovers,[33] described below.

It was announced in January 2000 that the telecommunications market in Singapore would be open to all comers. This triggered off a series of merger proposals which transcended national boundaries in which the activities of SingTel were prominent. SingTel declared its interest in a merger with Cable and Wireless HKT Ltd, but Richard Li, son of Hong Kong billionaire Li Ka-shing, out-maneuvered SingTel by buying the company first.[34] Singapore then switched to Malaysia and attempted to buy a minority stake in Time Engineering, a heavily-indebted but well-connected part of the Renong group, and a subsidiary. SingTel's bid was not accepted, although Malaysian Prime Minister Mahathir denied that "bad blood" between Singapore and Malaysia was a factor.[35] The main conclusion drawn by some non-Singaporeans from SingTel's efforts was that it was "politically-influenced". Prime Minister Goh Chok Tong feared that Singapore would have to dispel the notion current among foreigners that GLCs had to follow the agenda of the Singapore government. If that were indeed so, then its GLCs could never easily expand beyond Singapore. In an attempt to disarm criticism that GLCs were controlled by the Singapore government and not merely linked to it, the government announced its intention to diminish its influence over SingTel through reducing its percentage share in the company.[36]

Distrust of Singapore's GLCs, because they were alleged to be "too close" to the government, was slow to disappear. A prominent example concerned Singapore Airlines' bid to increase its 25 percent stake in Air New Zealand, which owns Ansett Holdings of Australia.[37] A SingTel bid for Australian Cable and Wireless Optus Communications was approved by the Australian Defence Minister, but met with criticism in Australia.[38]

In spite of initial obstacles, SingTel later succeeded in extending its holdings. Apparently it was convinced (as some critics were not) that acquisitions, even at quite high costs, were justified by growth, particularly outside its narrow home market.[39] SingTel acquired further holdings, in Indonesia, in November 2001.[40]

A related issue is: Will Singapore become a telecommunications "hub" for the region, and, if so, which company, or companies, will be dominant? Two prominent firms have been rivals. One is SingTel, the CEO of which is B.G. Lee's younger brother, B.G. Lee Hsien Yang. The other, recently formed by local and foreign firms, is Star Hub, which has Ho Ching, B.G. Lee's wife, as president.[41] Such close connections between GLCs, government and the PAP make for good collaboration, but may also support the view that too great a concentration of power may exist.[42]

The future of Singapore's GLCs

A recent statement by B.G. Lee starts with the premise that the government wishes to groom a core of high technology companies to lead Singapore in this field. They could have their origin in GLC's, but would be less government-controlled than before. They would be the right candidates to form the nucleus of non-family owned sophisticated, technologically-powerful companies. On another occasion, B.G. Lee agreed that Singapore Airlines was an example, and that others had potential, but at present did not quite have an adequate scale of operations. He mentioned Sembawang Corporation, Keppel Corporation, Singapore Technologies and Singapore Telecommunications as examples. He favored the prospects of the Development Bank of Singapore (DBS), although it suffered a setback in 2001. He added that an adequate scale of operations had to be accompanied by a high quality of management.[43]

There is growing government awareness of the need to cultivate "ISCs" (International Singapore Companies). The theme has been elaborated by both Senior Minister Lee and Prime Minister Goh.[44] One benefit is to provide employment for local people.

The interest of the public and of MPs is mainly in the occasional GLC which makes losses. Two may be cited. One is Singapore Technologies (its President and CEO is Ho Ching) which deals partly with sensitive topics, such as defense; prices of items in which it deals may fluctuate greatly according to whether they are state-of-the-art or not. One example of losses made by Singapore Technologies related to its acquisition of Micropolis, a hard disk drive business in 1996. For a time things went well, but later heavy competition by rivals resulted in losses, and the expectation was that only about 10 percent of the debts incurred would be recoverable. Of course, as Richard Hu told Parliament, risk-taking was part and parcel of all investment decisions.[45] The other example, the Government of Singapore Investment Corporation (GIC), invests for the government. It was created in 1981, with Lee Kuan Yew as chair. Lim Chong Yah wrote that the size and composition of its investments had never been made public, and that when he discussed the topic he was dealing with "fragmentary evidence".[46] In 1996, a GIC manager was charged with eight cases of corruption, involving at least $2.4m. Richard Hu said that this was "the first important case we have come across".[47] The GIC was restructured in 1999 to make its operations more transparent and accountable.[48]

Excluding instances which have been marked by corruption, etc., profit or loss is not a very sophisticated criterion of acceptable performance. The test ought to be: has there been a return to the stakeholders larger than if the resources employed had been expended on alternative activities? Also, for GLCs such as the two cases cited, it is sometimes plausibly argued that transparency can be taken too far, that giving too much information to other parties, particularly competitors, can cost the government money.

A further question about GLCs is: which GLCs should do what? Should the GLCs' activities be interrelated in a tidy and logical way, or doesn't it really matter very much? B.G. Lee apparently does not intend to tell GLC CEOs what businesses they should or should not be in.

There has been an ongoing debate between the United States Embassy in Singapore and the Singapore government and Temasek. The main issue has been the GLC capitalization share of the Singapore stock exchange. The Embassy cited a higher percentage than Temasek. A similar dispute[49] concerns the GLCs share of the GDP. The Embassy again claims a higher percentage than Singapore. Two issues ought to be conceptually distinguished. One is the implications of GLC behavior for small and medium business in Singapore. The other is international perceptions of the degree of Singapore government control over GLCs and over firms with which they merge. Currently (in 2001) withdrawal of government stakes in GLCs is appreciable but slow.[50]

The extent to which small and medium business has been "crowded out" by GLCs was put in perspective by Trade and Industry Minister, B.G. George Yeo.

Business startups had increased in the last few years, which was not suggestive of severe "crowding out".[51]

Some light has been shed on the functions of Temasek by S. Dhanabalan, a former Minister, and later chairperson of Temasek, in an extended press interview in June 1999.[52] The interview was itself an example of transparency. Dhanabalan stated that Temasek companies account for about 10 percent of Singapore's economic output. He explained that a balance was required between "pro-activeness", his own view of its role, and a passive hands-off approach. On diversification of functions, Temasek would have no objection so long as the company concerned convinced Temasek that it needed to go in that direction. The emphasis would be less on promoting certain policies, but rather on choosing the right people to devise policies, and on creating appropriate checks and balances between them. Some changes in view were: the closer monitoring of diversification plans along with specifying performance not by actual profit but by comparison with how the money might have been spent otherwise. Checks and balances would include: limiting the tenure of chairpersons and directors to ensure fresh thinking at the top, and keeping separate the appointments of chairpersons and CEOs to prevent the views of one dominating the views of the other.

There have been some criticisms of recent Singapore economic policy, among which GLCs are a principal target. The critics support the thrust of the KBE (see p. 78), but claim that the instruments for achieving it are too often relics of the *old* economy. They contend that GLCs are still too often staffed by ex-scholars (see p. 170) and former civil servants,[53] who are efficient, but may not be sufficiently in tune with the KBE. Similar deficiencies exist in the stock market, they allege, which yields inadequate returns, and in procedures for investing abroad. Saving, through the public sector surplus and forced saving through the CPF, should be curtailed[54] and public consumption should be expanded.[55]

The liberalization of banking

In the late 1990s, B.G. Lee, the chair of the MAS (the Monetary Authority of Singapore), approximately the equivalent of a central bank, instituted a policy of economic liberalization, along roughly the same lines as he has been adopting towards telecommunications. He has exercised restraint as regards mergers among Singapore's larger banks. Three of these are private local banks, the Overseas Union Bank (OUB), the United Overseas Bank (UOB), and the Oversea Chinese Banking Corporation (OCBC). The leading state bank is the Development Bank of Singapore (but see p. 217, n. 56). Although Lee believes that it will not be possible for more than two local banks to survive very long, he seems inclined to let the market determine which will survive.[56] In exercising a "light touch", he has still kept up the pressure to merge. Local banks are now facing more competition for local customers and for commercial loans. A new, limited, number of licenses will allow some foreign banks to open a few branches and off-street cash machines. This is in addition to previously-existing regulations which permitted some foreign banks to operate. These changes are to persuade local banks to compete, not to displace them from their pivotal role.[57] MAS's powers over banks have been increased to allow it to make any necessary readjustments. Over the years, local banks acquired a number of "non-banking assets" – property and shares as well as soft drinks companies, etc. The government used moral persuasion to make banks act as "just banks". Now they are being forced to divest themselves of such assets within three years.[58] This requirement for local banks resembles that contemplated for GLCs (see p. 74). But action to put it into effect has been swifter for the former than for the latter.

Singapore investment abroad: the China–Singapore Industrial Park, Suzhou

Education Minister RAdm. Teo Chee Hean has drawn an informative contrast between Singapore's arduous, but successful, task in attracting investments after attaining Independence, and its current task of extending its investment abroad. In some ways, he believes, the second is harder than the first.[59]

Singapore's drive to invest abroad in the 1990s arose from observations made by Prime Minister Goh and the Senior Minister during their travels, where they found that vast areas in China, India and so on, were just waiting to be developed. These impressions led to a study of the possibilities there, which were embodied in a report. While the government would help, it encouraged the private sector to take the lead. To persuade Singaporeans to participate, it offered information on living conditions abroad, and on arranging for the education of any children involved on their return to Singapore.[60]

China was to be a focus for Singapore's investment. Lee Kuan Yew had close relations with its leaders, and Goh Keng Swee had several times been an economic adviser. After discussions, one of the main projects was to be a China-Singapore Industrial Park (SIP), estimated to cost US$30bn, and occupying 70 square kilometers. The official signing of the agreement was attended by Goh Chok Tong in May 1997.[61] Months later, ceremony had been replaced by a Singapore demand for assurances. What was required was a delineation of the respective roles of the SIP and a rival industrial park, set up nearby by the Suzhou government in 1994, which had already attracted US$2bn in investments. Suzhou was said to have accorded it priority. At a meeting with German business leaders the Suzhou vice-mayor had disagreed with German investors that SIP (the Singapore project) had the support of President Jiang Zemin, and asked German companies to go directly into China without Singapore. In Parliament, Deputy Prime Minister B.G. Lee said that if there was competition between the two Suzhou projects, investors would simply stay away.[62]

Lee Kuan Yew was still unhappy after protracted negotiations, and in June 1999 thought it best that only some of the original area should be completed as an industrial estate by Singapore. A comment was that Singapore had agreed to a "partial exit strategy". It lowered its share of the project to 35 percent (January 1, 2001) from 65 percent. It sold facilities, such as power or water treatment plants to the partners. Over eighteen months it led the development of only 8 square kilometers instead of 70. The cost that Singapore incurred financially was reportedly not all that great. The cost was more to Singapore's pride.[63]

In Parliament, B.G. Lee gave the following explanation:

> I should quote to the member what one very senior Chinese official told us. He said that if he had been aware of [the rival firm] he would not have advised us to go to Suzhou. Therefore this was a problem which we did not fully appreciate and their top leaders were not aware of either.[64]

In Lee Kuan Yew's memoirs, he brings out the ambiguity about whose interests were meant to be served by the negotiations about Suzhou. Singapore's view was that the talks were on a government-to-government level, while the Suzhou authorities considered that local interests were overriding.[65]

Suzhou may not have been the most typical, but it was the most discussed, Singapore venture in China. Apparently the Singapore leaders at first did not appreciate that China's size dictated that the way government operated in Singapore could not possibly work in China. The country was too large and too diverse, and, at least in the 1990s, communications were slow and central control was limited. Understanding of what went wrong in Suzhou had already been shown by Goh Keng Swee. He had concluded that in fact post-Mao China had become a federal state, but without a federal Constitution which would have defined the limits of authority of provincial governments (and lesser authorities). As a result, both center and provinces engaged in continuing negotiations over issues, including control over enterprises sited in provinces.[66]

Singapore leaders have been excited over the huge economic possibilities existent in China. But Singapore not only has to meet foreign competition in China, it also has to face competition *from* China, in trade, especially now that China is a member of the World Trade Organization (WTO) (see p. 82).

The Growth Triangle

An aspect of Singapore's economy that lies conceptually between the internal economy and its overseas "wing" consists of the "Growth Triangle" between Singapore and two other "poles", Johor (Malaysia) and the Riau Islands (Indonesia). The triangle took shape in the early 1990s from an idea, and a name, suggested by Goh Chok Tong.[67] The idea is based on complementarities. The objective is to coordinate projects that combine Singapore's industrial expertise, technology and financial strength, with less-developed Malaysian and Indonesian surpluses of land and labor. Singapore, on the other hand, is short of these factors of production (see pp. 9, 187). In the triangle, foreign investment would be encouraged by concessions on taxation, etc. Transactions between Johor and the Riaus were minimal.

The numbers immediately affected were small, only 3 million people in Singapore, just over 2 million in Johor, and about 150,000 in the Riaus. However, there was a "spread effect" north of Johor, and labor would be drawn to the Riaus from other areas of Indonesia. Apart from the appeals to self-interest just outlined, there would be wider benefits, such as increasing investment and trade, extending to other parts of ASEAN.

The two "poles" had different needs. Johor was already developing quite rapidly, but welcomed more investment from Singapore, while Riau was less developed. The Singapore EDB had to start from the bottom up in Riau, through constructing the near-equivalent of its own Jurong Industrial Park. The EDB was a central player in the planning and the implementation of the triangle, especially in attracting high quality investors such as Sumitomo Electric, Toshiba, Thomson Electronics and Philips. However, the Growth Triangle has been increasingly threatened by competition from China and Vietnam.

The Knowledge-Based Economy (KBE)

The Knowledge-Based Economy (KBE) is also known as the New Economy.[68] The emphasis is on human capital and its application in an increasingly competitive globalizing world.

To illustrate the KBE's pervasiveness, reference may be made to the forthcoming "super chamber of commerce", the Singapore Business Federation.[69] All firms in Singapore must join and pay a levy, including foreign companies. It will give Singapore business a stronger voice abroad. The key to the chamber's creation is not to improve government–business relations, or business–trade union relations. The motive is rather to work from the top in attuning business to the KBE better than can be done under present arrangements.

The KBE is predicated on risk-taking and on the creation of wealth rather than its preservation. There is a relentless insistence on profitability. Executives are highly paid, but shortcomings in performance are punished; it is said that two successive quarters of poor results[70] may be followed by the dismissal of the CEO concerned. With the KBE, a country's society and economy have to accept that business practices which had been successful and which people had become used to, may have to be discarded for new ones which are unsettling, uncomfortable and also disruptive to large sections of society.

B.G. Lee has contributed some insights (see pp. 79–80). The New Economy is partly fact and partly a slogan, an injunction to recognize, and follow its practices. It refers essentially to a new "knowledge-based mindset".[71] It refers to some knowledge-based industries, but these are not exclusively information-related; for example, they include pharmaceuticals. Lee has also stated, "The New Economy" implies that nowadays Singapore is a different world, of many opportunities but with fierce competition. His greatest fear is that, in becoming part of a globalized economy, Singapore might lose control of its carefully-nurtured identity. Yet Singapore has chosen globalization. Its policy has been to accept, rather than try to delay, its integration with the global economy; to become more competitive rather than try to shelter itself from competition.

It is B.G. Yeo's opinion that Singapore should take action quickly, while the New Knowledge idea is still new. Because of its small size and efficient government, Singapore is able to move quickly and successfully into a new kind of venture, e.g. in the life sciences. Later on, it might lose this kind of advantage, because the rate of change in the development of knowledge may accelerate.[72]

Talent and the New Economy

If the New Economy is defined in terms of knowledge, then it follows that it is closely related to the concept of talent (see p. 54). Government encouragement and employment of talent is clearly linked to its advocacy of meritocracy, as expressed in its educational and scholarship programs (see pp. 55–6). The need to develop and attract talent has been recognized by the government's setting aside US$1bn for a venture capital fund to be deployed during the next few years.[73] This will complement Prime Minister Goh's vision that Singapore will become an oasis of talent, with global links via telecommunications and transportation connections together with foreign investments and a number of training centers.[74]

The life sciences

Recruiting and retaining talent for developing the life sciences has been given a top priority. They are intended to complement the manufacturing sector, along with electronics, chemicals and engineering. In the opinion of B.G. Yeo, concentration on the life sciences will provide a viable fourth pillar. In the 1970s, he added, Lee Kuan Yew and Goh Keng Swee had been interested in concentrating on this field, but nothing came of it then.[75]

Emphasis on the life sciences seems to offer great advantages but also substantial drawbacks. It will not require much manpower or large supplies of material, but there will be a heavy emphasis on knowledge. The cost of testing its potential for production and export is reputed to be high, especially for items for human use.

So far, Singapore exhibits certain distinctive features in its approach to the life sciences, and some striking differences from Taiwan, with which it is sometimes compared. Government support for these sciences is usually more essential than for other sciences, because the "gestation period" is longer. In Singapore private funding has not been on a large scale, which has obliged the government to do more. There have been relatively few private "start-ups"[76] by comparison with Taiwan, even though the government provides incentives. It has been particularly active through the EDB, which administers three substantial biotech funds, including a $1bn (Singapore) Life Science Investment Fund. Singapore has attracted some important pharmaceutical firms, but, unlike Taiwan, has lagged somewhat in conducting basic research.[77] In 2000 a stem cell research center was set up by the EDB and Australian private investors.[78] The first biotechnology plant in Singapore is scheduled to be built in 2002.

Creativity, innovation, enterprise and risk

The heading of this section contains the most usual terms employed when referring to the New Economy. There has been some uncertainty about the meanings of creativity and innovation. How does one reconcile the finding of the World Economic Forum's "Economic Creativity Index" that Singapore achieved third rank in creativity, by being the leader in importing technology from abroad, with the finding that it was not included in even the top ten in the "innovation" category?[79] This discrepancy may indicate that innovation may be the hallmark of something which is *really* new, while creativity is used to describe a process that is essentially an adaptation. Government has a role, but it has its limits.[80]

B.G. Lee has linked innovation and entrepreneurship but provided a "twist", derived from Professor Michael Porter of Harvard; one requirement for innovation is "a local context ... encourages investment in innovation-related activity and vigorous competition among locally based rivals".[81]

There is a belief in Singapore that Singaporeans are averse to risk, although it is an essential ingredient in entrepreneurship (see pp. 78, 197). B.G. Yeo contributed two useful ideas on the topic – one was that advances in enterprise and innovation must be founded on the spread of IT.[82] The second, more novel, thought was that the bankruptcy laws should be made less punitive.[83] Conduct leading to bankruptcy has an element of enterprise which should not be completely stifled – the appropriate slogan should be: "Be bold, but not *too* bold!"

The Information Revolution

The New Economy depends on, indeed largely consists of, the range, ease and low cost of transmitting and processing information. The process has been summed up in the phrase, the "Information Revolution", which Singapore has embraced with fervor. The effects on education are indicated on p. 105, while the implications for government control and for confidentiality of information are discussed on pp. 140–1.

The government has catapulted Singapore into the Information Technology Age with a vision of an electronically-linked global city. Singapore's long-term program to develop IT began in 1991, and it aspires to reach the status of regional hub, or higher. The first leg of its IT strategy is to install the most advanced physical infrastructure. It is now required, by law, that every new home be equipped with broadband in the same way as it must have water and electricity.[84] In 2000, a nationwide broadband Internet system, Singapore ONE, was completed, "delivering bedazzling at-home services such as immediate access to traffic speeds on any street, thanks to global positioning systems set in all the nation's taxis, online schools, movies on demand and live news".[85] By 1996, Singapore already ranked third in the world (behind the USA and Finland) in Internet users per capita, and by 2001 half of Singapore households were linked to the Internet (ahead of the US). By 2006, 25 percent of Singaporeans will be living in "connected Internet homes" with computers and appliances hooked up to one another and the outside world.[86] Through a "Citizens Center" numerous transactions, income tax filing, applying for scholarships, receiving the balance in one's pension fund, etc., can be done over the Internet, twenty-four hours a day by all Singaporeans.

There are three potential "digital fault lines" dividing Singaporeans on IT: those between high- and low-income households; those between the English-educated and others; and those between early adopters of IT and later adopters.[87]

A recent technological discovery is that the bandwidth (the range of frequencies and wavelengths available to carry signals) is not strictly limited – as was previously believed – but is essentially infinite, thus extending the use of broadband.[88] Nevertheless, the broadband users were fewer than had been expected. Singaporeans appear to be slow in coming to prefer broadband, given the current (2001) cost. Even many businesses have been slow to choose broadband. Purely commercial calculations have not taken account of social habits. Many Singaporeans are so attached to their principal leisure activity, shopping, that they regard ordering by Internet not in terms of saving time but as depriving them of the joys of actual shopping.

Broadband's time will come. The introduction of a second broadband service, through the cable TV network, could lead to a cut in price. Also, the liberalizing of the telecommunications market may bring more choices for users such as Internet telephony, which may enlarge the market.

The "income gap": globalization, unemployment and retraining

In Singapore, many of those with higher incomes are employed in "international" occupations and earn "international" wages, which exceed those in other occupations; they are "cosmopolitans" rather than "heartlanders".[89] A rapid take-off in the higher incomes had been predicted as early as 1996 by Goh Chok Tong. "I expect the incomes of successful Singaporeans, those with professional skills, managerial ability, business acumen and drive to rise much more".[90] These predictions have been borne out.

Apparently, there is no simple answer to the problem. Just raising wages without upgrading skills is no solution. The only feasible remedy is training for those thrown out of work, while aiding those affected by helping them to subsist during retraining. The hardest hit have included the elderly, those with many children and those who have difficulties in understanding languages needed for training.

Goh Chok Tong is determined that living costs for such schemes should be firmly tied to retraining and not linked with welfare. He believes that training should not be associated just with taking courses. It should take the form of adapting to new types of employment, possibly in different surroundings and in different housing. There have to be expectations of change, rather than of continuity. Jobs are no longer to last for a life time.[91] Lim Boon Heng, the NTUC Secretary-General, made it clear the new target is to aim for lifelong *employability,* that is "portable" from job to job. He warned that if these issues are not handled successfully, social tensions will rise, possibly even breaking down social cohesion.[92]

The NTUC has launched a Skills Development Programme for workers who have been retrenched, which enrolled 53,000 workers between 1999 and mid-2001, by which time about 60 percent had completed their training. The government provided $100m for this. A NTUC Education and Training Fund was also set up, to support workers who took up part-time training courses on their own. It was expected to cover 20,000 trainees in 2001. Recognizing the importance of continuing retraining, a Lifelong Learning Fund was established, with a $1bn endowment.[93]

Recently the NTUC has been suggesting to the government and the employers that workers could build up more long-term savings if bonuses were paid in the form of unit trusts or some similar type of investment.[94]

The economic crisis of 2001

Although there were reports in Singapore toward the end of 2000 indicating an economic slowdown, they did not sound a note of urgency. The *Straits Times* announced a "dazzling 10.4 percent" growth for the third quarter of 2000, and expressed disquietude rather than alarm when it foresaw "a little fizzle next year".[95]

It turned out to be more than a "little fizzle". In contrast to the 1997 recession, which took the form of "contagious" regional currency speculation, this time the impetus came from a collapse of information technologies industries/electronics, prominent in Singapore's manufacturing exports to the United States. Unlike 1997 (see pp. 70–1), Singapore did not do better than its neighbors; it was one of the earliest Southeast Asian countries affected.

By August 2001, Singapore had reduced its growth estimate for the year, saying only that it could range from "a small positive to a small negative".[96] B.G. Yeo's explanation for this was that increased globalization had accelerated the speed with which events in one part of the world influenced events in another, thus disrupting existing models on the spread of crises.[97] Figures for the third quarter were 5.6 per cent less than for a year earlier, the greatest decline for an independent Singapore.[98] Employment was affected as well as growth. According to the Minister of Manpower, unemployment was likely to reach 25,000 by the end of the year.[99]

Prime Minister Goh Chok Tong's National Day Rally Speech (August 2001) explained what the government had done to overcome the crisis. Some of the measures taken to meet the 1997 crisis were still in effect, such as the cut in employers' CPF contributions which made Singapore more competitive (see p. 71). The budget for 2001 had cut corporate and personal taxes and had given relief from some charges, rentals and utility bills. B.G. Yeo also announced a "package" to help those affected by the current economic slowdown.[100]

Goh noted, in the "Rally" speech, certain increasingly important features of the external economic landscape, in China, and to a lesser extent, India. China was no longer competing with Singapore only at the lower end of the scale in manufacturing; it was becoming "an IT powerhouse".[101] Changes in investment followed a similar pattern. "In the early 1990s, China took 20 per cent of the total foreign direct investment into East Asia (excluding Japan), while ASEAN absorbed 50 percent. Today (2001) the numbers are reversed: China takes 50 percent and ASEAN 20 percent."[102]

Goh also developed the theme of "reaching out to new markets." He advocated the extension of Singapore's "external wing" (see pp. 76–7), and also asked his audience to look beyond the scope of its customary neighbors – mostly near-neighbors or high-income habitual importers. He extended the term to include the 2.8 billion people within a seven-hour flight radius from Singapore.[103] He also stressed the importance of promoting free trade; bilateral treaties had been concluded with New Zealand and Japan, and negotiations were being conducted with the United States, Australia, and some other countries.[104]

In coping with the recession, the government's primary purpose was to preserve jobs, even if there was an accompanying reduction in wages. Beneficial economic "packages" would be balanced by prospective wage reductions by the National Wages Council.[105] The package, announced in October, followed the concept of "topping up" (see pp. 87–8). Of the total package of $10.1bn, $2.7bn was to be spent on the allocation of "New Singapore" shares to all adult citizens. Finance Minister Richard Hu later explained that an annual dividend would be paid for a fixed period, plus bonus payments when the economy was doing well. The amounts would be based on income (more for those with lower incomes), and extra shares would be given to those who were over 62 and to those who had done national service. Shares would be redeemable in cash, but the total sum would not be paid out all at once.[106] Prime Minister Goh announced that the scheme was a principal component of a "social compact"[107] between well-off and lower-income Singaporeans.

There was a striking contrast with the 2000 decision to give greater rewards to ministers and top civil servants, while trade unions still felt grievances about cuts in employers' contributions not yet having been restored (see p. 61). In 2001, on the other hand, the new shares distribution was in effect a *redistribution*; at the same time, reductions were made in the salaries of ministers and top civil servants.[108] The appearance of equity was more prominent in 2001.

The critical question was whether the Asian economies' ills were mainly cyclical, or rather, structural.[109] Clearly, there had been an over-emphasis on electronics. In more general terms, there may have been too much concentration on manufacturing, in preference to more profitable enlargement of the services sector. If the sequence was partly cyclical, the revival of the US economy, accompanied by the kind of measures used by Singapore to combat the crisis, would likely enable the economy to recover, perhaps by 2003.[110] To the extent that structural deficiencies were to blame, part of the remedy may consist in emphasizing two related aspects of the KBE, innovation and risk (see pp. 78–80), which it seems particularly hard to promote in Singapore's culture. The Prime Minister's recent creation of a National Innovation Council might be helpful.[111]

A field offering diversification, which appears to have great potential rewards, as well as great risks, is the life sciences (see p. 79), particularly the bio-medical sciences (see p. 79).[112] Above all, education, particularly post-secondary, is vital, not solely for intellectual enrichment, but also for economic understanding and advancement.[113]

Prospects

The PAP leaders like their policies to work. They are unlikely to spend time lamenting the sad state of the economy; they are doing what they can to prevent it from getting worse by keeping up the number of jobs and maintaining existing living standards. Such an approach was successful in winning the 2001 election convincingly (see pp. 151–3). Their hope is that the economy will improve, partly sustained[114] by exports to the United States and elsewhere. In the longer run, the leaders are confident that some of the wide range of products arising from their adoption of the KBE will reap rewards on the export market. They also believe that they are more adept than their neighbors in extricating themselves from crises.

No economic crisis in Singapore is complete without its own committee, and a Review Committee was appointed in December 2001 to report in under twelve months.[115] Its scope is wide: there are to be no holds barred. Its task is to be complemented by the work of another committee, intended to study how Singapore could be remade, politically, socially and culturally,[116] acting almost like an extension of Singapore 21 (see p. 161).

Recent reports on the economy are indeed positive, although not conducive to early great expectations. They suggest that growth will be positive for 2002 and that the trends for both manufacturing and electronics may be "bottoming out". (The Deutsche Bank is more optimistic than most commentators about Singapore.)[117] It is also good news that actions based on recent ideas of the government about risk may soon have an influence on policy. Temasek's chair, S. Dhanabalan, has announced that it will now emphasize investment in high-risk growth sectors.[118]

7 Supplying social services to the people

Two of the three sections of this chapter are about the services provided by two statutory boards which, for Singapore, operate on a large scale – the CPF (Central Provident Fund) and the HDB (Housing and Development Board). Both of these have served increasing numbers of people. The CPF has also provided a greater variety of services – and has been criticized for having undertaken *too* wide a variety.

The third section concerns a totally different kind of organization, namely the CDCs (Community Development Councils). These are the latest in a series of community, or neighborhood, organizations, intended to instill community consciousness and to provide links between government and the people. A primary objective of CDCs is that some services now supplied by a central government department will be transferred to the councils, allowing easier feedback, thus improving responsibility and efficiency. Within a few years the officials heading these councils may possibly be elected locally.

Statutory boards

The CPF and the HDB are examples of statutory boards, providing services which are largely self-financing,[1] with different legal powers from departments, making them more flexible, and with employees who are not civil servants.[2]

Although the boards are different from the civil service in ways like these, they are still responsible to a minister. The two boards discussed here were created for different reasons. The HDB had existed previously under a different name. But, when the PAP had become the government, a new name was chosen, indicative of a new spirit of urgency. It was politically imperative that the PAP's promises on housing should be, as pledged, adequate and affordable. The party was determined that the housing constructed should provide a visible and massive testimony to the zeal and efficiency of a government which had dedicated itself to supplying the people's most urgent needs.

The HDB's functions were not closely linked to some other boards' activities. For example, at the opposite pole was the EDB (Economic Development Board) (see p. 67), the government's chief agency for planning and developing the country economically.[3] Although the EDB's work often results in vast projects, literally earth-shaking in their magnitude, the early stages require much paperwork. Lim Kim San, a prominent PAP leader, briefly with the EDB and later chairman of the HDB,[4] reminisced about an early encounter when in the

HDB, for which his EDB experience had provided little guidance. Some of the board's operations required evicting people from land which the board needed for its projects, but which owners or occupiers were loath to give up. On one occasion Lim and others were confronted by people who refused to give way to them on land in Bukit Merah. They were obstructed by a large crowd of determined women pig-farmers,[5] more aggressive by far than the EDB's customary clientèle.

The Central Provident Fund (CPF)

By 2001, the CPF had about 3 million members. A minister, S. Dhanabalan, has tried to explain the CPF's main function by clarifying the relation between the money paid in by a member during the person's working life, and the money paid back upon retirement. He made a reference to the CPF's original and basic function:

> "Because income and consumption streams are not perfectly coordinated throughout a person's lifetime, he or she has to save more in the prime working age so as to have enough savings in retirement to retain a certain lifestyle. Left to themselves, many individuals will make good plans for themselves and their children, but there will be a significant number who will not. The government has to step in and put in place a system which ensures that all will have a certain level of financial planning."[6]

Historically, the CPF was only one of a number of similar schemes, inaugurated or proposed by the British when about to leave their colonies.[7] It was unusual, even exceptional, in developing a "basic minimum" plan into an extensive and well-administered organization. Some of its most impressive features may be mentioned here. It was meant to provide for individual and family needs where applicable, until death, retirement age, or disablement. It was compulsory for employees, with some exceptions, and for employers. The exceptions included some unemployed and some day-laborers. The individual's contribution was put in a bank account. The amount was not what he/she was "entitled to", but what had been actually deposited, plus any interest due.[8]

Certain features of the scheme reflected PAP leaders' values. Anything which might weaken a person's will to work was discouraged. Few qualified for payments because of unemployment, and there was originally government resistance to insurance schemes.[9] Certain other aspects of the CPF's working may be mentioned. Payments into the CPF and withdrawals were tax exempt. Housing policy (and its financing) was made the task of the HDB (see p. 90). Finally, the contribution rates of both employers and employees – the latter depending on age – fluctuate. They have been used as an instrument of macroeconomic policy, notably a cut in the employers' contribution was used to fight the recession of 1985[10] (see p. 70). The trade unions have sometimes expressed their unhappiness when adversely affected by the use of this policy weapon but have nevertheless shown their understanding (see p. 123).

The CPF's functions have been greatly expanded and diversified. Beyond compulsory savings for retirement, a secondary, but related, provision was to provide at least partial support for the family in case of the death or incapacity of a CPF member. In the words of a critic, a plan with a clear central objective became transformed into a "many-headed hydra".[11] The most prominent additions were: provision for partial payment of the cost of some social services; government facilitation of investment by CPF members, and "topping up" members' accounts by the government. The first of these categories included loans for tertiary education,[12] Medisave[13] (health care), and Medishield (low-cost insurance against "catastrophic" illness). All of these changes were introduced between 1984 and 1990.[14]

The initial step toward encouraging investment by members was taken partly to support a collection of not-very-prosperous bus companies which had been consolidated by the government (1978). CPF members could use their funds to buy shares in local transportation companies. A 1986 investment scheme was more elaborate. A percentage of CPF savings could be invested in "trustee stocks", that is, shares listed on the Singapore Exchange which were approved by the CPF board. The scheme was initiated for two main reasons. The stock market was depressed at the time, and needed a boost. Also some managers and other professional people were unhappy because they wanted a wider choice in investing their savings and were willing to assume greater risks in order to exercise that choice. In 1993, a further range of investment opportunities was made available to CPF members; they were also offered Singapore Telecommunications (SingTel) shares at a subsidized rate. A similar offer was made in 1996.[15]

The topping-up scheme

Prime Minister Goh Chok Tong explained the rationale for the new "topping up" scheme through asset-enhancement in 1993.[16] There were several steps in his argument. The scheme was intended to help Singaporeans own a stake in the economy. The current system subsidized productive social programs – housing, education and health (paid for by the current surplus of the present government). In 1993, a typical Singaporean, living in a three-room flat, would receive subsidies amounting to $70,000 during his/her lifetime, for these three items. The money would come from "the more successful Singaporeans, who pay a disproportionate amount of taxes". Goh believed that this system had served Singapore well. It had created a "virtuous cycle" – economic growth, employment and wealth leading to more growth, and so on.

This summary should convey the tone of the speech. Near the end, Goh gave a brief rationale for the topping-up scheme. The government intended to make Singaporeans owners of the Singapore economy through ownership of blue chip shares. Their assets would be built up through regular declarations of dividends and capital appreciation of the shares. If a CPF member put $500 in the CPF account between 1 March and 31 August, 1993, the person would receive an immediate dividend of $200, and would also be entitled to purchase several hundred SingTel shares, at a discount. Top-ups would be made in the future, and some have since been delivered. They would not be given every year, but only when there were budgetary surpluses to warrant it. In 2000 Goh announced, at the National Day Rally, that those who had made CPF deposits between certain dates would qualify for that year, but that the amount would depend on income. Of three levels of income, the highest level would receive least, and the lowest level would receive most.[17]

The business analogy, treating Singapore, the country, as Singapore, a business, was apposite and persuasive, especially at a time when business in Singapore was being converted to the ways of the New Economy (see p. 78). Goh neatly conveyed the notion of a "trustee model" of government, and his invocation of business dispelled any whiff of "welfare".

Criticisms of the Central Provident Fund

Recent criticisms of the CPF tend to be centered on the viability of its financial assumptions, as well as questioning whether the original purpose of the CPF was not, perhaps, being imperiled by the accumulation of other functions – each by itself often quite desirable – which it had assumed.

The concern of critics varied widely. At one extreme, criticism might be personal: "How can I be sure that there will be sufficient money in the fund to meet my needs in my old age?" With a different point of view were critics who seized on apparent inconsistencies in government policies. The government, it seemed, was critical of banks which engaged in operations other than banking (see p. 76), and of GLCs which performed quite unrelated functions (see p. 74); yet the CPF was also engaged in a wide range of functions, apparently without arousing great concern.

On the first issue, financial viability, it should be noted that not all the criticisms and not all the suggestions for meeting them, have come from outside the government. As early as 1987, the government itself inaugurated a Minimum Sum Scheme as a safeguard. It was intended to require members to set aside a minimum sum in their Retirement Account a few years before retirement. The minimum is gradually raised to provide a greater supply of savings. The effective age will change in accord with general changes in the age for retirement. The idea, of course, was that the basic purpose of providing for post-retirement should not be pre-empted by other demands on a member's funds.[18]

One of the most telling indications of gloomy prospects for adequate retirement incomes came from a government minister, Mah Bow Tan: "The CPF is not sufficient. It should be supplemented. We should try as much as possible to make it sufficient, but it needs to be added to by other CPF-type schemes, preferably by the private sector".[19] At the beginning of the new millennium, one of the more disquieting statistics was the small amount available for retirement in CPF accounts. "A government-led committee on aging[20] noted in 1999 that 24 percent of CPF members who reached 55 in 1998 had less than $16,000 in their CPF accounts – an amount that runs out quickly if the retirees lack family support".[21] It was said that, to have a shot at a decent lifestyle after retirement, you would need per month at least the equivalent of what $750 can purchase today. Even assuming no debt payments were involved, the conclusion was that not many people would have that kind of money when they retired.

To avoid downgrading lifestyles, and in the absence of family help, members would obviously need more funds. Two trends are becoming clearer. One is government recognition that there is a problem after retirement and that funds must be provided to meet it. Exactly where they will come from is yet to be decided, but one suggested source is that the future retirees will be asked to undertake some of it themselves, possibly encouraged by incentives.[22] They are likely to be offered more choices, including a wider range of investment opportunities. The Supplementary Retirement Scheme, introduced in 2001, has some distinguishing features. It is separate from the CPF and applies only to employees; it offers several types of tax exemption, and will be operated by financial institutions which are approved by the Monetary Authority of Singapore. Its main distinguishing features are: it continues the trend toward liberalizing investments; it encourages Singaporeans to save for their own retirement needs.

Ironically, although the idea of investing appealed to some CPF members, those who took advantage of being allowed to invest were not very successful. Nearly three out of five who preferred investing rather than leaving their money in CPF accounts, made less than the 2.5 percent due if the money had been left in them.[23]

Something which is unknown to the vast majority of CPF members, perhaps because of a lack of transparency, is that there is no link between the returns on CPF funds and what the members receive. The former, invested by GIC, etc., are not disclosed, while the latter are known to earn only short-term interest rates, which are low.[24]

It may be appropriate to consider a puzzling aspect of the basic supplying-of-income-after-retirement, etc., scheme. It was not surprising that the scheme was compulsory. The PAP's well-known paternalism favored "save-as-you-go" and Dhanabalan's explanation (see p. 86) accounts for that. What is surprising is that most CPF members *approved of a compulsory scheme*. A sample survey, conducted by United States academics in Singapore in the early 1990s, obtained the following responses to some relevant questions. (The questions cover numerous features of the CPF and only seventy respondents out of nearly a thousand mentioned compulsory savings.) Fifty-six respondents were favorable and fourteen were unfavorable. Several answers were quoted; the prevailing reason for being favorable was that saving was contrary to human nature. The most revealing comment was, "CPF is a good idea because it forces you to save. More importantly, you cannot use the amount in your CPF account to buy whatever you like. If you save on your own, you are tempted to buy new products advertised on television".[25]

The broader question raised – on the multiplicity of tasks performed by the CPF – may be dealt with quite shortly. The comparison with banks and GLCs is not precise. Most of the CPF's functions are indeed related, insofar as they have to do with financial transactions relating to social services. A slightly different, but nevertheless fascinating, point is raised by Linda Low, when she writes that these "extra" functions "seemed an *ex post facto* event rather than a carefully planned and orchestrated policy".[26] This seems very probable (see p. 88). In 2000, the IMF suggested that the CPF should be made into "a pure retirement savings scheme"[27] – its sole purpose originally.

Short of a complete overhaul, two suggestions for reform have been made: to replace the compulsory-savings aspects of the scheme with a modified version of the Supplementary Retirement Scheme (SRS); given the high rate of home ownership, cease funding housing costs through ordinary savings.[28]

A final point concerns recent changes in employment practices. It appears that now employment for a lifetime may be rare (see p. 81), and, although CPF benefits are portable from job to job, medical benefits are not yet portable.

Housing

Housing, as an element in the PAP's achievements and electoral success, seemed a marvel in the 1970s and still stands as a memorial. In 1973, T.J.S. George, a chronicler but hardly an admirer of the PAP government, had this to say: "Spectacular as Singapore's business and industrial growth was, the greatest achievement of them all was its many-splendoured low-cost housing scheme. . . . It was what made Singapore a topic of discussion round the world".[29] Statistics as well as the visual aspects are striking, but sometimes convey a wrong impression. By the year 2000, 86 percent of Singaporeans lived in public housing and 93 percent of the occupiers were also owners. This may suggest an image of mass-production, reminiscent, according to a critic quoted later, of living in "barracks".[30] However, over time quality gradually tempered quantity, and "Design" flats and "Build and Design" flats approached the status of show-pieces.

The HDB concept, viewed as a whole, resists simple classification; its operations are neither noticeably market-based nor market-restricting. It does not fix sale or rental prices of the houses it has built (through contractors); that function is undertaken by the Ministry of National Development. It does possess extensive powers over land acquisition, and it standardizes construction methods to reduce costs. It subsidizes the sale or rent of housing, particularly for lower-income occupants. It could not operate effectively except under a strong government.[31]

The origins of the EDB were contemporaneous with those of the HDB (see p. 85). Within a year, 1960–1, they were formed to replace the Singapore Industrial Promotion Board and the Singapore Improvement Trust, respectively. Although these two were key elements in the creation of modern Singapore, functionally there was a closer working relationship between the HDB and the CPF. Provision for retirement and housing payments were the two major items handled by the CPF. The CPF was the HDB's "financing agent".[32]

The PAP's concern with housing was impelled partly by its shocking state when the party came to power. The supply was insufficient and the standards were low.[33] The PAP leaders were quick to perceive that a well-planned and executed housing policy would reap rich rewards. It would help to reduce the unemployment problem, especially in the construction industry.[34] Politically, it boosted the PAP's popularity, exhibiting visible proof that the party kept its promises. Those who hoped to be housed were potential beneficiaries and possible supporters. Lee Kuan Yew, personally, had ideas that went beyond that. He wanted not only gratitude, but *abiding* gratitude, and saw the potential appeal, not only of living in a house, but of owning it, making a home of it. Home ownership would also complement the unifying effects of national service. Thus, although the HDB Home Ownership Scheme was not launched until 1968, the idea was conceived much earlier, by Lee Kuan Yew, who discussed it with Goh Keng Swee and the trade unions.[35]

The original flats built were quite spartan, consisting of a single room, with a tiny kitchen adjoining; communal toilets and washing facilities were on each floor, which was in accordance with the standards of the time.[36] By 1999, the size and quality of new flats had greatly improved. Not only were one-room to five-room flats available, there were also superior "executive" flats, some of which were built by the private sector. The demand for larger and better-appointed flats grew stronger as ownership increased. It was met partly by the government deciding to build through the HUDC (the Housing and Urban Development Company) accommodation for mainly professional people, at current rates of not more than $4000 a month.[37] Such accommodation catered for, among other things, a desire for privacy or individuality. Other attractive features were pleasing design and greater convenience.

Beyond the HUDC possibility and similar schemes, an alternative was private residential properties. The line between public and private housing is becoming less distinct,[38] although for those who value symbols of social attainment the latter has a certain cachet.

A consequence of Singapore's small size was that, once the country began to be developed, there was a shortage of land. Accordingly, legislation was passed to make possible the acquisition of land at reasonable, non-inflated prices.[39] The main personalities in the house-building saga differed substantially in their approaches. Teh Cheang Wan, minister for national development in 1979, had previously been the CEO of the HDB. He emphasized speed in construction, but did not make sure that contractors were equally solicitous about meeting standards.[40] The shining light in the entire operation was apparently Lim Kim San, who became chairman of the HDB in 1960. A less overwhelming personality than Teh, it seems, he merited this warm tribute from Lee Kuan Yew; "We made him the chairman of the Housing and Development Board ... It was crucial, life and death. If we failed, we would not be re-elected. This was the first year of office for PAP".[41] Lee was conscious of housing's possible effect on his own future. Referring to a block of flats being put up in his constituency, he observed that, if it were not completed by the time of the next election, he might not be re-elected. This may have been only a casual pleasantry, but it was also a recognition of the political importance of the housing program at that time.[42]

Something more should be said about resistance to giving up land, which made the whole housing program contentious. Resistance occurred not only because the compensation offered was judged inadequate. The costs to some who were not willing to move were sometimes almost impossible to quantify. Three groups were particularly adversely affected. The first were squatters who, before they had to move, had almost rent-free huts to live in and hardly any amenities. After being re-housed, compensation was often insufficient to pay for the new charges. A second group was rural farmers; those who now had to live in flats, particularly if old, saw that their way of life had been taken away. A third group consisted of Malays whose numbers in flats quadrupled between 1970 and 1980. Those who had been farmers were obviously subject to the same difficulties as the second group; some felt so uprooted that they made regular nostalgic visits back to their *kampungs* (villages) to try to maintain their former social relationships. They also sometimes had to relocate their *surau* (small mosque), which could be a long process, necessitating negotiations with religious bodies.[43]

It is sometimes said that *public* housing enables the government to control those who live in it, which is legally correct, because the HDB, being a statutory board, and the housing being publicly funded, enabled the exercise of controls which do not apply to *private* housing.[44] The question is surely: how intrusive are the controls? In Singapore, some kinds of control exist which seem to be quite acceptable. An instance might be measures which are anti-crime or anti-damage, such as the Neighbourhood Police Post System, inspired by the Japanese practice – situating a small police post in the center of an area containing, say, about 30,000 residents.[45] This may be an adaptation suitable for Singapore, which, unlike Japan, has problems arising from its tall high-density flats, which enable, for example, "killer-litter" to be thrown from the windows of the higher stories. "The number of dangerous objects was not all that large, but the diversity has been impressive, and has included chairs, cupboards, iron pipes, and bicycle wheels".[46] Offenders originally could be fined, or barred from occupying flats for several years.

Another example concerns accidentally dislodged, rather than jettisoned, objects, mostly religious items, such as joss-stick holders, as well as potted plants and laundry racks. In June 2000 Buddhists and other religious leaders had to be called on to advise residents about how to secure such items from falling over parapets, which one had done recently, killing a six-year-old girl.[47]

Another opinion, on housing as a means of control, should be rejected, because the argument has been based on irrelevant considerations. Christopher Tremewan acknowledges that the PAP has supplied a comparatively high standard of housing in Singapore, but cautions that we must remember the political context – "the alliance between the PAP state and foreign capital". The latter, he argues, has enhanced the PAP state's powers of social control for the purposes of political hegemony and the development of capitalism in Singapore.[48] This deployment of abstract terms does nothing to weaken the claim that the PAP has performed well on housing and that its alliance with MNCs has, on balance, contributed to the welfare of Singapore.

A different view of control is that it does not constitute an expression of governmental, or HDB, desire to exert, or exhibit, authority. The object may also be to promote values, which are esteemed generally, not just by government. These could include "family values". In 1978 parents occupying a flat were encouraged to apply for their married children to be allocated an adjacent flat. A similar policy was announced in 1994, also intended to strengthen parent–child bonds.[49] Another policy, its purpose conveyed by its name, was the introduction of "granny flats", or later, when this failed to attract much demand, the availability of "studio flats" for elderly parents.[50] A "family" policy, although it was not "pro-family", was the "Small Families Improvement Scheme",[51] which provided educational bursaries and housing grants to parents with no more than two children. The rationale was that children who did not do well at school tended to come from large families.

When the first phase of the frenetic flat-building program was over, and attention could be turned to social aspects, a feature which deserved, and got, attention was the ethnic composition of flat occupants. The ethnic enclaves of the colonial period had been somewhat dispersed by changes in the location of jobs and by squatters. The PAP ethnic ideal concerning housing was the embodiment of a form of multiracialism (see pp. 101–3). The party leaders believed that ethnic location could not be left for chance to dictate.

When people relocated, they often preferred to have neighbors of the same ethnic group near them. Apart from pursuing similar interests, and speaking similar language, or dialect, memories of the racial riots of the 1960s were sufficiently powerful for self-protection to be a consideration. On the other hand, the PAP predilection for multi-ethnicity was re-enforced by caution against facilitating concentration of an ethnic group – with a risk of ethnic clashes. Balloting for flats introduced randomness, but, when flats were sold, this disappeared when members of an ethnic group preferred to sell to a member of the same group. The remedy adopted was to eliminate that possibility.[52] So, for example, under this "clear and open policy", the check to ethnic "congregation" comes into effect at the time of resale. If, say, the fixed "Chinese" proportion has been exceeded in a particular neighborhood, a non-Chinese there is free to sell his/her flat only to a non-Chinese. This program, introduced in 1989, has worked well. The limit on its success follows from its, necessarily limited, objectives. The aim was to create conditions which would be conducive to integration. It could not guarantee that integration would actually be achieved.

The decision to concentrate the housing program on building flats, and not houses, was not much questioned, because the urgency of the operation favored speed. (In the longer run, for instance in the early 2000s, the demands for land are so great, that "building up" seems unavoidable.) The pressures for accommodation in Singapore are expected to increase. The demand for large flats is growing, and so are competing uses for land.[53] It seems that the land shortage will make higher-rise building inevitable. By 2004, some 40-story blocks will be ready (the tallest existing blocks are 30-story).[54]

Malays and others, who had to be uprooted to live in flats, were not just having to leave their human attachments and adapt to a "flat" life. They were entering a totally alien situation, in which animals, for instance ducks, played no part. Instead they had to put up with strange noises, such as the pounding of chilies at close quarters, and the use of electric drills to install fixtures. They had to get used to elevators and do without kerosene lamps. Feelings of isolation and irritation often resulted.

Upgrading

One of the most contentious terms about housing is "upgrading". This is because the word has now acquired political overtones. Originally, upgrading referred to an individual's improving his/her housing through moving to preferable/more expensive public housing. Based on a 1998 sample survey, it was found that members of every third household were likely to move to a new home, and that many would probably move up to bigger or more expensive homes.[55] An alternative to moving from a flat, and perhaps, from a neighborhood to which the resident has become attached, might be to remain in the flat, but take advantage of the government's upgrading plan. The Main Upgrading Plan started with two pilot projects. It continued in the Plan itself, by which a certain proportion of Singapore's area is upgraded each year. The government pays for the larger share of the costs; the occupant's share may be paid from CPF savings. The alterations can include adding space to the flat. Upgrading is a consultative process, which involves the Town Councilors, the grassroots leaders, and HDB officers, who form a Working Committee.[56]

The advantage of upgrading is not only to improve one's accommodation by making it closer to what one needs for comfortable living. It also raises the value, in a typical case in mid-2000, by 60 percent over five years. Without upgrading, an estimate was that the value would have risen only 34 percent.[57] Another estimate was that the amenities after upgrading would have been on a par with those of a similar house on a new estate.[58]

The "political" element which may be present in upgrading occurs when areas thought to have voted against the government at a previous election may be "punished" by having upgrading postponed after its due date in the sequence. The tactic was described, clinically, by the Prime Minister as demonstrating the second generation leadership's ability to handle hardline politics:

> And to me it was quite clear, it's not about threatening the voters. When you go for elections, you must have a programme. Upgrading was our programme. We were saying, "If we're in charge, this is how we want to use our fund. So, if we lose, there'll be no upgrading". So, to me, it was a very clear case of getting the message through to the people.[59]

The issue was discussed in 1997. The upshot seemed to be that if the government is inflexible on showing preference in upgrading toward constituencies which have returned PAP candidates, the only recourse left to the opposition, realistically, is to wait, hoping that observers attribute neglect as a symptom of poor HDB (and PAP) performance.[60]

In the preceding section on the CPF, the government position on subsidies was referred to. While it approved of subsidized programs for education and health, it affirmed that these did not fall into the category of welfare, but actually constituted productive social investment. Housing was considered another example of this, being regarded also as a case of building up social capital. It was a means of helping people to help themselves. The government wished to avoid any claim of its being a legal entitlement. In the government's eyes, the ambiguous status of the HDB, as a statutory board, was deemed to lie outside the political arena.

The sample survey previously cited of the strong and weak points of the CPF (see p. 89), also asked questions about the HDB. In some respects it may now be dated, but some answers are worth mentioning. About three-quarters of the responses were classified as favorable. Some representative replies were; "home ownership gives a greater sense of self-worth, due to possession of something"; "allows people to have a stake, a sense of belonging"; "I have a stake, this is my country".[61] A complementary survey, expressed in a study in the 1990s, concerned occupants' characteristics, and their opinions about the amenities most and least appreciated. A typical household in 2000 consisted of two-income parents and two children, with no car, but with a personal computer. Half of the households had one or more members who had been on an overseas tour within the last twelve months.

The government's housing program transformed the Singapore scene from the 1950s squalors of Upper Nanking Street, etc. (see p. 220, n. 33). The visual transformation was accompanied by a financial one. A rising wave of property prices in Singapore had enabled a new generation to enjoy not only shelter and the necessities of living but set many of them on the road to affluence. Average HDB household income rose 40 per cent, from S$2653 in 1993 to S$3719 in 1998, and half the households had a computer. Note that originally the HDB was meant to provide "low cost public housing".[62]

Para-political organizations

Para-political organizations are mentioned below. This introduction is followed by an account of a different kind of organization – Community Development Councils.

At the apex of the para-political organizations is the People's Association,[63] established in July 1960. In order to consolidate existing community centres, the PA, as the *national* grassroots organization, was entrusted with the mission of promoting the objectives of: promoting racial harmony and social cohesion; acting as a bridge between the government and the people; and implementing schemes relevant to these two objectives. Lee Kuan Yew stated the objectives more specifically. It would be the task of the Community Centres, under the People's Association umbrella, to ensure the survival of a non-Communist state by providing the necessary "bridge" between government and the masses. The centres had to act as "... a nervous system of human beings, transmitting messages, getting people together so that they know they are a community, and not just anonymous individuals who shut their doors and live their own private lives...".[64]

When a large number of PAP branches came under Communist control in the early 1960s (see p. 40), it was discovered that a leading figure in both the PA and the Works Brigade had been planted there by the MCP. The former was also the Prime Minister's political secretary.[65]

The People's Association is firmly anchored in the structure of government. The Chairman of its Board of Management is the Prime Minister, the Deputy Chairman is a Cabinet Minister, and its Chief Executive Director is at present Press Secretary to the Prime Minister. Below this level are the grassroots "para-political" institutions. Their existence has served to blur the line between government and party, which has not been discouraged by the PAP; in fact, the PAP prefers to keep opposition MPs out of these organizations.

The four organizations concerned are: the Management Committees of Community Centres (CCs), of which there are now about 130; the Citizens' Consultative Committees (CCCs); the Residents' Committees (RCs); and the Town Councils (TCs).

Community Centres, first established in colonial times, were set up locally, and not uniformly organized until the PAP took over control after the 1959 elections. Since then there has been close liaison between each center and the local (PAP) MP. CC Management Committees were set up in 1964, which strengthened the links with the party.[66]

In 1965 the Prime Minister, Lee Kuan Yew, planned to establish a CCC in every constituency. There were two motives which prompted the expansion: to expose the lies spread by the Communists and their agents, and to facilitate links between the masses and the government. An immediate spur to the creation of the CCCs may have been the challenge of the newly-formed Barisan. Additionally, Lee wished to become acquainted with the people's grievances, which they sometimes failed to communicate through other channels.

Residents' Committees were introduced in 1978. They are found in HDB estates, on the initiative of the government.[67] Because the residents are concentrated geographically, they are likely to have more in common – as flat-dwellers do – than the more dispersed members of CCCs. RCs build on this to promote a community spirit.

The "Team-MP system", later known as "Group Representation Constituencies" (see pp. 145–6) was linked with a plan to introduce MPs as Town Councillors in charge of managing government flats in the new town areas, 1985–6. They, not the HDB, would now have to deal with complaints. In this way, voters would have to live with their choices, not only because they became MPs, but would also chair Town Councils, and in that capacity would make decisions which would closely affect the lives of their constituents. They also had to demonstrate their financial competence.[68]

All these four organizations had two things in common. Initially, they were meant to show vigilance about any signs of the revival of Communism. They also had to cooperate closely with local, non-party leaders.

Community Development Councils

Community Development Councils,[69] gradually introduced from March 1997, have been strongly promoted by Prime Minister Goh Chok Tong. Some Singaporeans, no doubt suffering from "initials fatigue", may not see anything much different in them compared with their predecessors. However, it should be clear by 2002 that there are substantial differences. The CDCs are indeed concerned with particular geographical areas. But, unlike most of the organizations described in this section, while having a similar role in strengthening links and loyalties, the emphasis is largely on their *administrative* character.

There will be two administrative tiers in Singapore – a form of devolution. For some government functions, the second tier will be a CDC. For example, the lower tier will deal, increasingly, with social services, but not with foreign policy. The bodies will be analogous to municipal, or city, government. The functions they undertake will be performed by officials who will report immediately, not to the central government, but to the appropriate CDC. In the new scheme, for some services a CDC will replace the central government. It will operate from offices closer to the people than the central government could have, both geographically, and in the sense of having greater "empathy" with them. Accordingly, some civil servants will be moved from a ministry office to a CDC office. Other civil servants who do not deal with CDC matters, will remain with their ministries. Although the scheme applies to administration, it does not have the "dry" connotation often associated with that word. The purpose is to give administration a more human face and heart, by strengthening, so to speak, the "body's" communications system. The change takes into account the fact that the needs of the CDCs will vary because the characteristics of their populations will vary. A difference might be a different distribution pattern according to age which might give two adjacent CDCs a contrasting emphasis to their needs. Particular human needs may also influence a council's pattern of interaction with voluntary bodies, an important feature of the CDC's activities.

The government has envisioned the future scope and shape of the CDC's operations.[70] Presently (2001) there are five CDCs, each will be headed by a full-time mayor. There will be considerable variations in size and population among the CDCs.

A mayor's job will not be an easy one. The role should be guided by a compassionate approach, it seems, because, for the scheme to take root, citizens' initial impressions should be favorable. Yet this will have to be accompanied by making sure that a mayor's decisions are not sharply "out of line" with those of his or her fellow mayors, for the sake of evenhandedness.

The mayor will be assisted by a corps of full-time professional staff, and will serve for a term of two or three years. Apart from leadership qualities in general, it would obviously be an advantage if the person had good fund-raising abilities, to supplement the income of the CDC derived from a government payment, initially $1 per head of the CDC population. Fund-raising ability should, ideally, be accompanied by capacity for "people-raising", that is, persuading volunteers to step forward for service.

In raising funds, the CDC's relation with voluntary welfare services is both competitive and complementary. The activities themselves can be made a basis for cooperation through mutual agreement on the allocation of tasks, etc., so as to avoid duplication. However, when it is a matter of donations, the voluntary organizations and the CDCs may feel that they are competing for aid from the same donors.

The mayor's job, being new, without an exact precedent or roots, requires all the prestige which can be summoned up for it. It must be given impressive symbolic, as well as actual, power. Research has been done by observing foreign models, for instance how ceremonial trappings proclaim the weight and dignity of the office.[71] Protocols are also worth establishing, for instance the place of seating, the sequence of entering and leaving rooms and so on. However, the typical robes and accessories for the office of mayor elsewhere are not likely to be favored. Instead, the dress will likely be simple and practical.

Looking further ahead, there has been speculation on how the position of mayor might fit in with government renewal and succession in Singapore. The Prime Minister has envisaged possible career paths for mayors, if it is deemed advisable that a mayor should not spend too long in that office.[72] The qualities demanded of mayors are, above all, the ability to deal with a great variety of people. They might be able to make use of such qualities in Cabinet positions. They might be able to "balance" the present preponderant attributes of ministers, which, reacting against "technocrats", some have criticized as over-emphasizing intellectual and academic interests. Mayors will be elevated to the level of Ministers of State or parliamentary secretaries, which could be a launching pad for yet higher office.

The process of identification might begin earlier – a person might even be seen as a possible mayor, because it might lead to the sequence just outlined.

Some other features of the scheme are worth mentioning. It is not claimed that the introduction of CDCs will save money, but it is expected that, with about the same expenditure as at present, there will be a gain in efficiency.[73] Also, beyond the services "devolved" to it, a CDC has an "overall" function, wider than any possessed by any community organization; it should organize programs that have a district-wide impact.

Some people may feel that they are adversely affected by CDCs and may be resistant to their introduction. Possible examples come to mind, some civil servants may be reluctant to move their offices to less frequented or less prestigious places, and some ministries may feel that they have diminished when they have lost personnel, now taken over by the CDCs.

Opposition parties see little to look forward to from the CDC concept. However, people living in parliamentary constituencies which have Opposition members have the Prime Minister's assurance that they will not be left out of a CDC's programs.[74]

In any case, two statements seem quite unambiguous. In May 1997, the Parliamentary Secretary to the Prime Minister's Office stated that the government decided against involving opposition MPs in the CDCs, after they expressed outright opposition to the concept.[75] The Prime Minister also stated in Parliament:

> ... CDCs are part of the governmental functions. So we are not intending to hand over this governmental function to the opposition. We will hand over to the CDC [those functions] which can be, in the case of the opposition wards, handled by non-MPs in charge.[76]

It seems that the government is dealing with the Opposition in the same distanced way as it did in most para-political organizations previous to the introduction of CDCs.

One important question remains to be answered about the CDCs – will they ever become locally-elected bodies? To some, this would set the seal of approval on the CDCs by supporting the claim that they embodied local democracy. Goh has given cautious comment on this issue. He expected growing pressure for local elections, and if this were exerted, he wouldn't mind their arrival eventually.[77]

Summary

The first two of the organizations examined in this chapter concerned the growth of the CPF and the HDB, not only in size, but also in the range of services offered. The CDCs should improve services previously supplied by other organizations by enabling the "consumers" to indicate more clearly than before what their needs and preferences are. In each of the three institutions considered in this chapter, the range of choice has been expanded. CPF clients, for example, are offered a wider selection of investments. The HDB has moved from quantity to quality, and its products have benefited by competition from the, now comparable, private sector. The CDCs, while remaining governmental, are based on a well-known principle of administration – that policy-making should be a central function, but that administration, if it is to handle local needs knowledgeably, should be local.

8 The dictates of ethnicity

Language policy, education, and self-help

Singapore is a multi-ethnic state, with 77 percent Chinese, 14 percent Malays, 7.7 percent Indians, and 1.3 percent Eurasians and Others, as noted in Chapter 2. Permanent residents and foreigners comprise 24 percent of the total population – a 10 percent increase in a decade. There is considerable heterogeneity within each community, adding to the overall diversity.

The Chinese consist of 12 or so dialect groups, Hokkien and Teochew being the largest. There has also been a deep cleavage since colonial times between the English-educated and Chinese-educated Chinese. Historically, these language and education differences have resulted in intense divisions in cultural and political orientation. The English-educated have always predominated in positions of power and status. The Chinese-educated have tended to be blue-collar and mass-based, politically left-wing and are sometimes regarded as Chinese "chauvinists". These divisions have been ameliorated considerably in the last decade, yet always remain susceptible to rekindling, such as transpired in the 1997 election when the campaign, in the Prime Minister's words, "opened up old fault lines".[1] Since the late 1990s, the two groups have been depicted as the mobile, English-educated "cosmopolitans" and the dialect-speaking "heartlanders", although some individuals fit both categories.[2]

The Malay–Muslim community is also diverse, comprising Malays, Javanese, Bugis, Indian Muslims, Minangkabau, and Arabs among others, and any person who is generally accepted as a member of the Malay community *by* the community.[3] This category is based primarily on the Islamic religion. However, there are a few Indonesian Christians in this grouping.[4] The Indian community is likewise heterogeneous, with Tamils (the largest group), Malayalam, Hindus, Sikhs and others.

Under British colonial rule, the different ethnic groups and subgroups lived in separate areas, spoke their own languages and practiced their own religions, rituals and ways of life. It represented, as noted by Raj Vasil, a very good example of J.S. Furnivall's classic depiction of ethnic groups "living side by side but separately".[5]

But inevitably with modernization these separate ethnic worlds touch one another, sometimes clashing over the most deeply held and volatile beliefs and values – language, religion, family, politics – thus making the management of ethnic conflict a difficult and high priority task for any government. This is all the more so in Singapore's case given that it has what is called a "double minority" setting: the Chinese are a majority in Singapore, but a minority in the region; the

Malays are a minority in Singapore but a strong majority in the immediate region. The seemingly intractable ethnic conflict in some other states with a double minority, such as Sri Lanka and Northern Ireland, illustrate the problem. Singapore has managed its multi-ethnic community exceedingly well, but it has not escaped totally unscathed. There have been four main sets of ethnic riots, each with significant injuries and deaths.[6]

When the PAP came to power in 1959, the PAP decided to have Malay as the national language and to have four official languages (Malay, Mandarin, Tamil, and English), and to maintain four language media of instruction in schools. Radio and television were also broadcast in all four languages. The official policy, a founding PAP principle, is called "multi-racialism". It encompasses multi-culturalism, multi-lingualism, and mutual tolerance of and protection for the major religions, mostly viewed in ethnic terms. The specter of ethnic conflict has been held up as a major threat to the survival of the state, already vulnerable. The government could not create a "Chinese Singapore" without causing serious internal tension and potentially dangerous external criticism.[7] It had to avoid the stigma of being seen as a "Third China". The Malays were given special recognition, mostly symbolic, in the Constitution. State support was given to all ethnic groups, and political minorities were included in the PAP and represented at "all levels of the state and in [most] state institutions."[8]

When considering the management of ethnicity, the emotional issues of language, education, and religion come to the forefront. These aspects of ethnicity help define the boundaries of a group and they have a direct impact on the socio-economic prospects of the group. Language interacts with education. Language groups are concerned to promote and protect the use of their languages in educational institutions and in the workplace. John Clammer says it well: "What is however of great importance is the way in which this official [multi-racial] policy is reflected in educational and linguistic policy, two areas fraught with the greatest difficulties and ambiguities".[9] In a competitive multi-ethnic setting with language policy in flux, there are likely to be winners and losers. The worst nightmare of an ethnic group is to find its language and education medium no longer of value, because then its cultural status will decline and its members' economic prospects will be diminished.[10] This is all the more so in a meritocracy such as Singapore (see pp. 55–6). One answer has been a policy of bilingualism (discussed below). The PAP government has always been acutely aware of the importance of education and language policy, and education has always been given a high priority in terms of resources. Education is viewed as an important nation-building and socialization institution, and a mechanism for the management of ethnicity.

By contrast, managing religious diversity, although it is highly volatile, is more straightforward. In Singapore, while multi-racialism is talked about, religion is carefully controlled. A host of laws, bolstered by the Maintenance of Religious Harmony Act, 1991, are designed to prevent religious flare-ups.[11] Meanwhile, the government supports the festivities and practices of all the major religions, carefully limits proselytizing, protects and subsidizes religious dwellings, and tries to be sensitive about all religious matters, especially concerning Islam. As Goh Chok Tong has reflected, "When religion is involved there is no way you quench the fire once it is started, and we are very fearful of that".[12]

The PAP government has always proclaimed a policy of multi-racialism and denied any intentions of trying to integrate the people. "Our ideal has never been a melting pot. We have not tried to amalgamate and assimilate the different communities into one".[13] For one thing, there was no overarching culture to assimilate to, and it was politically not possible to try to assimilate non-Chinese into the majority culture, even if Chinese resistance to such assimilation could be surmounted.

However, the meaning of multi-racialism has been modified over the years. Early on, there *were* some integrative policies: resettlement into integrated government housing, known as HDB flats (see pp. 86–7, 90–5); the promotion of English and the closure of Nanyang University; and two marginally integrative policies: integrated schools and national service. The primary motives for these measures were not necessarily for promoting integration, it should be noted.

Before HDB flats were built, the population resided in relatively discrete and homogeneous ethnic enclaves. Everyone knew that Geylang Serai was a Malay area, and that on Serangoon Road one would find Indians. Lee Kuan Yew explains that as part of a plan to rebuild Singapore and re-house everyone, and to demolish the shacks where Malays were concentrated, it was decided to scatter and mix the ethnic groups by setting up ethnic quotas in public housing estates.[14] This was done, starting in 1970, but by buying, selling and trading flats, the groups started re-concentrating again. So, in 1989 the government tightened the rules on ethnic quotas to include every block or unit in each estate.

By the mid-1960s, the PAP government had decided that English was the language of commerce, international trade, and science, and that a wide use of English would serve to link Singapore to the world and also give Singapore a competitive advantage. It would also provide Singaporeans with a common working language. In 1966, English was made a compulsory language in the bilingual education scheme. English had the advantage of already being the administrative language of Singapore, and it was an ethnically "neutral" language (given that Singapore did not have any serious problems with it because it had been the colonial language). Thereafter, the ascendancy of English was remarkable, speeded by its economic advantage. By 1985, the English-stream had 97 percent of all students, and soon afterwards the government announced that all schools would have to switch to English as the medium of instruction (with the three mother tongues being taught in the English schools).

The same fate befell Nanyang University (Nantah), founded in 1956 as the only Mandarin-medium university in Southeast Asia. It was the center of classical Chinese learning and a hotbed of left-wing politics. Nantah graduates found it difficult to find suitable employment, and the government was unhappy that it had to modify its strict meritocratic standards to allow some into the public service.[15] By 1975, Nantah was compelled to adopt English as a parallel language of instruction, and by 1980 it was merged into the National University of Singapore (NUS). This was a very difficult and emotional blow to the Chinese clan associations, Chinese newspapers, Chinese chambers of commerce, and Chinese teachers' union and school management committees.[16] The closure of Nantah meant that tertiary education in Singapore was entirely in English.

Two other policies had a moderate integrative effect. The first was "integrated schools", meaning the housing of two or more language streams in the same school buildings so that there would be more inter-ethnic mingling. It probably had some positive effect, but on the whole it was found that students kept largely to their own language groups. The other integrative measure was national service, introduced in July 1967. It brought together young males of diverse backgrounds and resulted in some inter-ethnic male bonding. However, given the limited enlistment of Malays, and the fact that females were not conscripted, the scheme was limited as an integrative device.

Soon the PAP realized that the ascendancy of English, coinciding with the global technological revolution, meant that Singaporeans were greatly exposed to the impact of Westernization, including many elements which the PAP leaders believed were negative influences. At the same time, it appeared that Chinese culture and language might simply fade away. Thus, beginning in the late 1970s, the PAP government made a "dramatic shift in the application of multi-racialism",[17] through language and especially education policy. It began to re-emphasize ethnicity, especially Chinese language and culture (discussed below) to strengthen the Asian roots of Singaporeans. Whereas before, ethnicity was played down and everyone was considered "Singaporean", now everyone was hyphenated: a Chinese-Singaporean, Indian-Singaporean, etc.[18] Thoughts of integration or of focusing on an overarching Singapore identity were relegated to the back burner, and Lee Kuan Yew spoke publicly of his regret that English had been allowed to become so dominant.[19]

There were a number of reasons for this shift to a more vigorously multi-racial system. One, of course, concerned the inroads of Western culture and values, especially ideas of individualism and political liberalism. Another concern was that Singapore was going to lose that vital "something" in its Asian values that possibly helped explain Singapore's economic "miracle". A third reason was that the political and economic rise of China meant that Singapore should not lose the comparative advantage of its "Chinese-ness". Still another reason concerned the electoral implications of the embittered Chinese-educated and dialect-speaking Chinese over the decline of Chinese schools and Nantah.[20] Christopher Tremewan views the switch in more conspiratorial terms. In his view, the PAP used the English-educated to demolish the Chinese-educated and destroy Chinese working class political opposition. This produced an English-educated middle class with a desire for liberal democracy. So the government is now using the Chinese language as a weapon against the English-educated to prevent them becoming a threat to the PAP.[21]

One thing is certain, the government has deliberately enhanced ethnic consciousness and ethnic identities and reinforced ethnic boundaries, and this has implications for the development of a Singaporean national identity. Nurturing a national identity involves promoting the sense of a shared history, common beliefs and values, and a sense of common destiny. However, the current emphasis on distinct ethnic identities complicates the task of formulating a Singaporean supra-identity.[22] This was shown in the government's attempts to create a National Ideology in the late 1980s (see pp. 62–4). Because of lack of consensus and suspicions that the project was intended to promote Confucian values through the back door, the proposal was downgraded and renamed "Shared Values". The government now seems to be focusing, quite successfully according to various surveys, on one element of national identity – a sense of common destiny ("We live together or we die together", in Lee Kuan Yew's words[23]) – in order to promote a key value: patriotism and loyalty to Singapore.

Education policy

Governments subsidize public education for a number of reasons: to promote literacy so that the people can understand and obey the law and act as responsible citizens; to nurture the dominant political culture; to develop human capital, a capable workforce, and a division of labor; and to socialize young people to certain ideas and values by managing (along with families and the mass media) the creation and dissemination of knowledge in a society.[24] To Tremewan, the education system of Singapore is a key social control mechanism "to provide a cheap, disciplined labor force"; to Gopinathan it is seen "almost completely as an instrument in the national development process"; and to Noronha, education is viewed "as an investment" with an emphasis on minimizing educational wastage.[25] In fact, the goals of education policy in Singapore include all of the above, and all have ethnic implications.

When the PAP came to power in 1959, it inherited an education system with four media of instruction differentiated along the lines of race and language. Not only were the schools ethnically segregated (except for the English schools), but they had different histories (Chinese education, for instance, grew out of the efforts of the Chinese community during colonial rule, as discussed earlier), their standards, syllabuses, and certificates were all different.

Many recommendations for change came out of the 1956 All Party Committee Report on education, and some of these, such as bilingualism, were implemented immediately. When it came to power, the PAP implemented the standardization of content and exams, and modified the bilingual policy to emphasize English and respective mother tongues. Because the PAP leaders were interested in merging with Malaya, learning Malay for non-Malays was also stressed. The government also began building schools at a rate of one a month, and dramatically increased the educational opportunities of young females. The education curriculum focused on bilingual (sometimes, until 1967, multi-lingual) language and math competency in primary schools and increased emphasis on science and technology in secondary schools.

By the late 1960s, the government was inclining to the view that English should be the working language and mother tongues should provide the cultural language. In 1967, the government decreed that math and science subjects be taught in English in Chinese primary schools, and in 1969 it required that civics in English schools be taught in the mother tongue language(s). However, a 1963 commission reported that second-language learning was lagging, and more extensive reports in 1978 and 1979 recommended major changes to the education system.

The *Report on the Ministry of Education, 1978*, known as the Goh Report, concluded that effective bilingualism was not being achieved and that English literacy and comprehension were low, resulting in "high wastage rates" (premature school-leaving, repetition of grades, and unemployable school-leavers).[26] The solutions, Goh Keng Swee noted, "almost suggest themselves":

streaming students with different learning capacities at different rates to suit slow, average, above average and outstanding learners.[27] Under the New Education System (NES), bilingualism was viewed as desirable and would be continued for most, with varying degrees of difficulty and pace of instruction. However, the report concluded that bilingualism was beyond the capability of some weak students, who would be better served in a monolingual stream so that as school-leavers, they would be proficient in at least one language. The streaming of pupils would be based on their school performance and intelligence tests. The report also prompted the initiation of a single national stream, beginning in 1987, wherein all students would take English as their first language and their mother tongue as a second language.[28]

A second initiative of the Goh Report was to ensure that the best Chinese schools would survive (enrollment had declined to 9 percent in 1979, down from 46 percent in 1959) by establishing Special Assistance Plan (SAP) schools and channeling the ablest Chinese students into them (discussed below).

There was another change in the education system brought about by the *Report on Moral Education 1979*. The PAP government had experimented with a number of approaches for inculcating values in the schools through civics courses, but the 1979 report concluded that the civics syllabus had shortcomings in that it included too many subjects that had little or nothing to do with morality (i.e., basic history, geography, family structure – including 40 categories of relatives!). The report recommended that moral education through Religious Knowledge (RK) courses be introduced to produce "good, useful and loyal citizens". Although the PAP government had always taken great care to play down religion and had treated it as a highly sensitive subject, the report was approved since it was not religious instruction *per se*. Originally students had a choice of taking Bible Knowledge, Buddhist Studies, Hindu Studies, Islamic Knowledge or World Religions. Confucian Ethics and Sikh Studies were soon added. However, a report on Religion and Religious Revivalism in October 1988 concluded that the RK courses appeared to be exacerbating religious differences and might be having an impact on religious revivalism in Singapore. In 1989 the government announced that it was discontinuing RK and replacing it with an expanded civics program.[29]

The experiment with moral education came about because the government was concerned that the rapid ascendancy of English was making Singaporeans more susceptible to Western cultural influences and weakening traditional Asian values. What the government preferred was that English be utilized as the language of science, technology and commerce, while cultural values and traditions would be derived through and sustained by proficiency in the various mother-tongues. The PAP did not intend to destroy the vernacular schools.[30] However, parents pragmatically enrolled their children in English schools because English proficiency provided the greatest economic opportunities. The government's move to a single English-stream in 1987 was simply acknowledging a reality.

To encourage initiative and develop niches of excellence, certain top-performing schools in the 1990s were given more freedom of action and more money by being designated independent and autonomous schools. However, an educational review concluded that students in general were learning by rote without applying any thinking skills or creativity. The review recommended that education be geared to promoting "learners, creators, and communicators", instead of simply exam-smart students.[31] In 1997 a major new initiative in education was launched: "Thinking Schools, Learning Nation", a Masterplan for information technology (IT) in education and the new National Education civics initiative. Additionally, a third (and private) university was approved – Singapore Management University (SMU) – which began operations in 2000. Modeled after Wharton School of the University of Pennsylvania, SMU stresses innovation, and aims at attracting those who are "intelligent and creative in different ways".[32]

The IT Masterplan goal is to provide students with the knowledge and tools necessary to get along in the IT future and Knowledge-Based Economy (KBE) (see pp. 78–81), and with some knowledge about Singapore's place in the world.[33] More specifically, the emphasis is on thinking and developing creative problem solvers; on accessing and processing information; and on developing the ability to use knowledge. The government has committed $2bn over five years to create an IT teaching and learning environment. In 2002, there is one personal computer for every two students, and students spend about 30 percent of their curriculum time using computers in the classroom. All 360 schools are already hooked up to the Internet, and by the end of 2000, 95 percent of the teachers were already trained in using computer technology to enhance classroom learning.[34] As with other places where there is an education performance gap that finds some minorities lagging behind, Singapore's IT emphasis could have ethnic ramifications.

The second part of the 1997 education initiative involves a new approach to civics, called the National Education (NE) program. It aims to enhance the commitment of Singaporeans to the country, and it is considered a Total Defence Initiative (see 170–1). By studying Singapore's history, geography, and demography, the program is intended to foster pride and patriotism, provide a shared sense of nationhood, and instill core values, such as racial harmony and meritocracy. Particularly, it emphasizes the unique challenges facing Singapore, its constraints and vulnerabilities. A new examination subject, social studies, was introduced in Secondary 3 classes in 2001 in order to teach students about Singapore's road to nationhood, principles of governance, and international issues which affect Singapore's survival and growth.[35] Overall, the difference with the NE initiative is that it is intended to integrate these themes into *all* subjects within the curriculum, at all levels.[36]

Accompanying these NE initiatives is an effort to improve the standard of English and arrest the spread of "Singlish" – a corrupted and ungrammatical form of English reminiscent of the local patois spoken in some former British colonies in Africa and the Caribbean. There has always been Singlish spoken in Singapore among the older non-English educated people, forced to cope with English yet possessing only rudimentary knowledge of the language. The difference recently is that Singlish has become glamorized, partly as a result of a popular television sitcom (Phua Chua Kang Pte Ltd). There is now some peer pressure exerted on children to speak Singlish, and it has become the "in-thing even amongst people who should know better".[37] This has alarmed many parents, and also the government, which believes Singaporeans need to speak standard grammatical English to be able to plug into the global economy successfully. To Lee Kuan Yew, Singlish is "a handicap we must not wish on Singaporeans".[38]

As a result, the government launched an annual Speak Good English Campaign in 2000, and the Education Ministry sent 8,000 teachers through an English course to improve their English language skills, and also revised the English language syllabus to strengthen grammar and oral skills.[39] Stifling Singlish (while leaving alone less harmful local Singaporean additions to English and current slang) is yet another language challenge facing Singapore.

Goh Chok Tong, in a speech to Parliament in October 1999, said he was shocked that 3 percent of the Primary 1 cohort were not registered in national schools. He therefore asked the Minister for Education to consider the introduction of compulsory education.[40] This seemed straightforward and quite overdue for a state as advanced as Singapore, with an education system producing students who regularly win international competitions in mathematics and science.[41] However, about one-third of those not registered in national schools are enrolled in Islamic religious schools, called Madrasahs. As will be discussed below, many Muslims viewed compulsory education as a plot to shut down the religious schools. Despite the concerns, the Compulsory Education legislation was passed and comes into effect in 2003, making six years of primary education compulsory.

Correcting the "Western" bias: "Chinese policies"

There have been several major initiatives to try to resurrect the "Chinese-ness" of Singapore Chinese: the Special Assistance Plan (SAP) schools, the "Speak Mandarin" Campaign, and the promotion of a Chinese cultural elite.

In the 1940s and 1950s, the Chinese schools were a crucial breeding ground for the Communists, and those supporting Chinese language and culture were labeled "chauvinists" and tainted as Communist supporters. After the Communists were defeated in the mid-1960s, the Chinese schools were "cleaned up". However, this did not stop the attrition from Chinese-language education, as mentioned earlier, which threatened the imminent demise of the Chinese schools. In order to keep the Chinese language alive and to recapture some of the values of the old Chinese schools, as well as to have a pool of people deeply knowledgeable about Chinese culture and traditions to engage a rising China, the government in 1987 converted four primary schools into SAP schools.[42] By 2000 the number had grown to ten primary and ten secondary SAP schools. These are the premier elite schools, with the most resources and the best students, and a strongly Chinese ambiance. The students take both Mandarin and English as first languages, although the curriculum is in English except for Chinese language. As Goh Chok Tong explained, "These schools are an attempt to preserve some very powerful assets of the Chinese community ... The SAP school students are amongst the brightest in the country. If the people at the top are proficient in Chinese and possess the strong virtues of the Chinese society, they will give Singapore its Asian ballast".[43]

The SAP schools have caused some controversy, especially in conjunction with the Speak Mandarin Campaign, the promotion of a Chinese cultural elite, and what is perceived by the minorities to be a new cultural assertiveness on the part of the Chinese-Singaporeans. Lee Kuan Yew has stated that former minister S. Dhanabalan argued strenuously in Cabinet against the SAP schools, and several ethnic minority PAP MPs have stated their respective community's concerns that the schools may be undermining multi-racialism, and nurturing a new generation of leaders who have been isolated in their school experience – their formative years – from the other ethnic groups.[44] Some Chinese PAP ministers have tried to reassure the minorities that the SAP students would know English and would be surrounded by other races in their daily lives outside of school; that there was no intention of having Mandarin replace English as the country's working language; and that SAP students would not capture *all* the best scholarships or top positions.[45]

The Chinese language was given another boost by the Speak Mandarin Campaign, which was launched in 1979 and is still on-going. The campaign was intended originally to promote the use of Mandarin instead of the various dialects, so that Chinese-Singaporeans would be united by a common Chinese language. Another reason for it was that the widespread use of dialects in the home was complicating the government's English and "mother tongue" bilingualism efforts. A 1980 census showed that 64 percent of the Chinese spoke dialect at home; 9 percent English, and only 26 percent Mandarin.[46] Since the majority of Chinese children spoke dialect at home, they were having to learn *two* new languages at school – a heavy burden. Further, proficiency in Mandarin was going to be a necessity when trade with China opened up. Fourth, the campaign was designed to placate some of the Chinese-language hardliners who remained angry over the closure of Nantah. Finally, the initiative held out the promise for the political leaders of being able to communicate with every Chinese in one language, especially during election campaigns, instead of struggling with bazaar Hokkien and half a dozen other dialects.[47]

The campaign was supported by many Chinese, especially the intellectuals and the hitherto-marginalized Chinese-educated, and it seemed to raise the stature of Chinese culture and heritage. Three groups opposed the campaign to varying degrees: the ethnic minorities, the English-educated Chinese, and the older Chinese who did not understand Mandarin.[48] The minorities felt threatened by the upsurge of Chinese language promotion, as will be discussed below. For the English-educated Chinese, there had always been a socio-political division between them and the Chinese-educated Chinese, so this "comeback" of the Chinese language was disturbing. However, originally, the group most adversely affected was the older, dialect-speaking Chinese. They were especially aggrieved when all commercials in dialect on radio and television were canceled, and shows and movies were dubbed into Mandarin. Dubbing the popular Cantonese serial, "Heaven Sword and Dragon Sabre" into Mandarin led to a torrent of objections from irate viewers.[49] Also, with the resurgence of Mandarin instruction in the schools, "gaps between generations were created because of the mismatch between languages spoken at home and at school," and dialect-speaking Chinese, especially grandparents, found it difficult to communicate with the young.[50]

While dialects have been tenacious, the opening of China has brought with it a positive change of attitude about learning Mandarin, and by 1990 more Mandarin than dialect was being spoken as the principal Chinese home language. The successful campaign then in the early 1990s shifted its target from dialect speakers to English speakers. Now Mandarin was being promoted to equal status with English, for the Chinese. Some of the English-educated have resented the implied criticism of the campaigns, which have strongly suggested that if you are Chinese, you should speak Mandarin. They remain concerned also that they might be adversely affected in terms of status and career opportunities.[51]

Another current focus of the Speak Mandarin Campaign is to get Chinese-Singaporeans to use the two hundred or so Chinese-language Internet websites. B.G. George Yeo notes that an MIT professor has predicted that in a decade Chinese will be the dominant language on the Internet.[52]

One of the problems that has arisen with the renewed emphasis on Chinese language and with making the subject compulsory for all Chinese is that a number of Chinese from English-speaking homes, strong in other subjects, have struggled with Mandarin. This has probably contributed to the emigration problem (see pp. 189–90). It has led the government to introduce a new, less rigorous Chinese language "B Syllabus". This in turn has triggered a counter-reaction from the Chinese-speakers, who fear that standards will suffer by offering a "soft option".[53]

An Education Ministry survey of Primary 1 students shows that only 2.2 percent still use dialects as the first home language, down from 64.4 percent in two decades.[54] Surveys show that almost all Chinese-Singaporeans can speak some Mandarin, at varying levels of fluency. B.G. Yeo notes that the government has "succeeded in the historical task of establishing Mandarin as the high language for Chinese-Singaporeans over the use of dialects".[55] Furthermore, among the young Chinese, the "old, bitter divide" between the English-educated and Chinese-educated seems to be subsiding.[56]

Because the campaign has been so successful, the government has started to allow the resumption of dialect for radio news broadcasts and subscription television entertainment programs (such as the very popular "Money, No Enough", largely in Hokkien). Live Chinese opera performances, usually in dialect, have always been allowed.

Despite all the successes, some problems remain. First, the use of Mandarin reached a high in 1989, with 69.1 percent using Mandarin as their first home language (primarily replacing dialect), but it has started to lose out to English since then. In 1980, only 9.3 percent used English as their first home language; by 1989 this figure had increased to 23.3 percent. By October 2000, English use had increased further to 43.2 percent and Mandarin had slipped to 53.8 percent.[57]

Another problem is that there is a declining percentage of Chinese under age 30 who are reading Chinese newspapers (*Lianhe Zaobao, Shin Min* and *Wanbao*). Also, while Chinese-language television Channel 8 remains more popular than the English-language Channel 5, more tickets are sold for English-language movies than for Chinese films.[58] Likewise, many Chinese who know Mandarin, are not using it socially. A 1997 survey showed that there was a relatively low use of Mandarin in post offices, supermarkets and HDB estate offices. The Prime Minister noted, as a "typical example", that his children, who passed Mandarin without much difficulty, do not speak the language or read Chinese newspapers.[59]

Finally, there is the political problem that despite the extensive government efforts to promote the Chinese language – often incurring the displeasure of other groups in so doing – many Chinese-educated continue to feel neglected. They want the government to do more, for example they want Chinese characters added to MRT and bus routes, and on street names.[60] And some will not be satisfied until a Chinese university is resurrected.

Lee Kuan Yew believes that the dominance of English for the next 50–100 years is "unassailable" because it is the language of the new knowledge. The government's problem is that it cannot say "Don't learn English," it can only say "Don't give up Chinese"[61] However, others are more optimistic about the future of Mandarin, especially if it captures the entertainment industry. They believe the dip since 1989 is only a temporary time-lag reflecting language policy in the 1960s, which promoted English.

Recently, and in tandem with the Speak Mandarin Campaign and the SAP school program, there have been official calls for the creation of a Chinese cultural elite for government and business, the media and the arts. Goh Chok Tong and Lee Hsien Loong have described this cultural elite as possessing a high knowledge of and proficiency in Mandarin, and as being steeped in Chinese culture, history, literature and the arts. If a critical mass of such elites could be developed, this would help Singapore maintain its Asian heritage and transmit Chinese culture and language to successive generations.[62] Clearly, many of these cultural elites (as well as political elites) would be products of the SAP schools.

Multi-racialism and the Malay–Muslims

Although they are only one of the minorities, the Malay–Muslims pose an important challenge to the government. The Malay–Muslims constitute the largest minority group in Singapore at 14 percent. Despite significant improvements, the group lags behind the others in educational attainment, its members are disproportionately employed in low-skill jobs, it perceives that the PAP leaders have no confidence in the ability of the Malay community to uplift itself, and it lacks strong political influence.[63]

The Malay community, as with the Indian, Eurasian and other communities, fully supports the concept of multi-racialism. Likewise, it supports the idea of a meritocracy. The Singapore Malay–Muslims have not pushed for preferential policies, although some believe that Article 152 of the Constitution should have accorded them more status, and more preferences than just free tertiary education (which was made subject to a means test in 1989). Despite support for multi-racialism and meritocracy, the community has a number of fears and grievances.

The most serious grievances of the Malay–Muslim community concern national service and the question of loyalty. Before independence, the Malays dominated the police and army ranks. After independence, it was decided that the military should reflect the ethnic composition of the state. Consequently, many Malays were deliberately not conscripted, which took away a chief avenue of upward mobility and restricted job opportunities because employers preferred hiring males who had already completed their national service. Since the mid-1980s, they have been called up, but they are mostly shunted off to police or civil defense units. The whole issue of loyalty came into the open in 1987 when B.G. Lee said that Malays should not be put in a position of having to choose between loyalty to their country and to their religion.[64] The issue had already been exacerbated by Muslim opposition to the visit of the Israeli president in 1986 and was once more strained by the community's criticisms of the Allies during the 1991 Gulf War. Still, the Malays feel their loyalty has been unfairly questioned, that their dissatisfaction is largely economic and has nothing to do with national loyalty,[65] and they believe continuing remarks impugning their loyalty only undermine unity.[66] Goh Chok Tong tried to reassure the Malays by saying, "I can tell you there's no mistrust of the Malay community. This is a falsehood. If we distrusted them, we would not be putting them in the armed forces. I mean, that's a very big step forward". However, he somewhat undermined this vote of confidence by using, in reference to sensitive SAF positions, the analogy of Indira Gandhi's bodyguards.[67]

There are a number of other long-standing grievances – descriptions of Singapore's history that begin with Sir Stamford Raffles and the immigrants, and ignore the earlier history of the Malay sultanate;[68] job discrimination, especially through advertisements that allow the race of the person wanted to be specified;[69] CPF wage deductions (which have led some Malays to seek only lowly casual or part-time work in order to avoid the deductions[70]); and the 25 percent quota on Malays in schools (the government believes that by keeping the numbers small they will perform better, however, critics say the quota leads to many Malays being stuck in less sought after neighborhood schools[71]). The Malays originally opposed the Group Representation Constituencies (GRCs) because they did not want Malays elected "in the armpit" of the Chinese (see pp. 145–6), but they now mostly accept the value of guaranteed representation.[72]

There are also some issues that make the Malay community fearful and insecure. They are apprehensive about the new awareness of ethnicity the government is promoting. They think the SAP schools constitute an unequal use of state resources and undermine multi-racialism, and they view the promotion of a Chinese cultural elite as a move to increase Chinese dominance. They fear the Speak Mandarin Campaign. Even though the PAP reassures them that it is a "Chinese issue" that will not have any negative impact on the other groups, they are suspicious that it will pave the way for replacing English as the *lingua franca*.[73] Another issue of deep concern is the government's campaign to attract foreign talent, including a high percentage of Chinese, to immigrate to Singapore. The Malays believe that this will increase job competition, and that it may be part of a strategy to reduce the percentage of Malays in Singapore to an insignificant proportion.[74]

Finally, a very visceral issue came to the forefront in 2000 – anxiety by the Malay–Muslim community that the government's compulsory education scheme would doom the six private Madrasah Islamic religious schools (the oldest of which was set up in 1912), whose enrollments have been on the rise. In March, PERGAS, the Association of Islamic Scholars and Religious Teachers, "stirred up an emotional storm not seen in recent memory".[75] It argued that even if it was not a plot to kill the schools, this would happen naturally by cutting off the supply of students and by making the Madrasahs follow the national education system secular curriculum in order to meet the Primary School Leaving Examination (PSLE) standards, which would change their character.[76] Additionally, implementing the national education curriculum would be very difficult without state resources. It is not difficult to believe that the government wants to reduce the number of students attending these schools, and to impose some national standards on those who do attend. Madrasah students tend to drop out early (70 percent do not complete Secondary 4), they may not be adequately prepared for the modern economy, and they tend to have poor job prospects beyond being religious teachers. Also, the government wants to socialize students to a national set of secular values, whereas the Madrasah seek to imbue students with Islamic values. However, as emotions escalated and Malay PAP MPs and the government were increasingly disparaged, Goh Chok Tong, who is viewed favorably by the Malay community, stepped into the fray and reassured the community at a dialogue session with 60 Muslim leaders.[77] By October 2000, a compromise solution had been worked out that defused the situation for the time being. The Madrasah are to be exempt from the Compulsory Education Act. They have eight years to prepare their students to sit the PSLE with their age cohorts and ensure minimal results, or they will not be allowed to have any more full-time students.[78] Still, the existence of the Madrasahs seems assured. B.G. Lee said in a television interview that the Madrasahs "will not disappear. They have a role. We acknowledge that role".[79]

There is one other issue. The PAP government, Malay MPs, Malay–Muslim community leaders and Muslim professionals all believe that there is a need to reform Malay attitudes and certain cultural values detrimental to economic progress.[80] This "cultural deficit" thesis has a long history, as Tania Li notes, going back to the turn of the century.[81] It is strongly criticized, however, by those who believe that socioeconomic disadvantages better explain Malay marginality.[82] It is reasonable to conclude that while negative stereotyping can be destructive and needs to be countered,[83] and that socioeconomic and political hurdles cannot be discounted, neither can the impact of cultural values be denied.

The self-help approach to multi-racialism

The poor educational performance of the Malays revealed by the 1980 census was a surprise, and it led to the establishment of an ethnic self-help scheme as an answer to the vexing question of how to help the lower-income group and close the Malay education gap. It was a scheme that "fits with the PAP's studious avoidance of direct state welfare provision".[84] It also seemed to provide an answer to the dilemma of Malay–Muslims resistance to participating in multi-ethnic remedial classes or support groups.

In late 1981, a group of PAP Malay MPs and the Prime Minister established Yayasan Mendaki (Council for the Education of Muslim Children).[85] Mendaki was described as a self-help body aiming to reform attitudes and raise educational performance, and not an affirmative action-based organization.[86] To finance Mendaki, 50 cents (now S$2.50) was deducted from each Malay–Muslim worker's monthly CPF contribution, and this amount was matched by the government. To maintain PAP control, Mendaki officials were appointed by the government (partly directly and partly from a list submitted by Malay organizations).

The approach was not approved by everyone. Lee Kuan Yew writes that some of his older Cabinet ministers, especially S. Rajaratnam, were opposed, and in Parliament it was also opposed by opposition MP J.B. Jeyaretnam.[87] To some it seemed an abrupt change in the meaning of multi-racialism; one that would raise ethnic consciousness and promote distinctiveness and difference.

Mendaki focused on supplementing education with Weekend Tuition Scheme classes, and between 1982 and 1992, more than 45,000 students attended its classes. Its success ratio is impressive. A 1991 study showed that the pass rate in English for those in the tuition scheme was 99.5 percent compared with 88 percent for those not in the scheme. In science, the pass rate was 99 percent as opposed to 77 percent, and in mathematics it was 69 percent as opposed to 47 percent.[88]

In 1989, Mendaki was given broader responsibilities, to help Malays enter into the business and corporate world, and to assist poor Malay families. Known as Mendaki II, it was renamed the Council for the Development of the Singaporean Muslim Community. Its subsidiaries, institutional members, clubs and committees are numerous[89] and its activities vast – from free computers and IT training for 2000 disadvantaged Malay families to new university scholarships.[90]

Despite its education and development successes, and the fact that the household income of Malays grew 150 percent between 1980 and 1990, there was a feeling that while the Malays were progressing, they were not catching up, and that Mendaki was too closely aligned to the PAP and therefore had to temper its demands. Out of this mood came the creation of several new Malay–Muslim organizations, the most interesting being the Association of Muslim Professionals (AMP), to augment, but also to challenge Mendaki.[91] The AMP was formed in 1991 by a number of young Malay professionals.[92] The government was initially suspicious of the AMP, but Goh Chok Tong said that it could establish its own version of Mendaki, which it has done, as well as also acting as a Malay–Muslim think-tank. The AMP receives government support and operates out of premises rented from the government for a nominal fee. Occasionally the AMP skirts close to the edge of political permissibility. This was the case in November 2000 when an AMP Congress put forward a plan for "collective Malay leadership" in response to the feeling that Malay MPs had failed to articulate the views of the community, especially with regard to the compulsory education issue. In reply, the Prime Minister cautioned the AMP not to split the Malay community, and said they had strayed into the political arena. Goh said, "My signals are very clear where collective leadership is concerned. You can debate it, but to implement it is no go".[93]

Not unexpectedly, the creation of Mendaki soon led to calls by other groups for similar self-help groups. In 1991, with the backing of Indian PAP MPs, the Singapore Indian Development Association (SINDA) was formed to promote Indian education and welfare. Similar to Mendaki, it has tuition classes, parent outreach, pre-schools, and a family service center.[94] In 1992, the 73-year old Eurasian Association was also given funding for self-help.[95]

Inevitably, the majority Chinese community was soon clamoring that there were poor Chinese too, and that there should be an organization to help them. Thus, in 1992, the Chinese Development Assistance Council (CDAC) was formed.[96] Its patron is the Prime Minister; its Board of Directors, headed by a senior government minister, includes an impressive list of multi-millionaires. Two founding members of the CDAC are the Singapore Chinese Chamber of Commerce and Industry, and the Singapore Federation of Chinese Clans Association. In contrast to the other ethnic self-help groups, the CDAC was almost immediately flush with money, with $5.5 million in pledges and donations before its official opening, and soon after raising over $1.7 million in six weeks (in addition to the funds from CPF contributions of Chinese workers, matched by the government).[97] This is in sharp contrast to Mendaki and SINDA, which are forced to spend considerable time simply fund-raising.

This has created a potential problem. The disadvantaged minority communities were given a self-help mechanism, with government support, in order to pull themselves up to national averages. Then the dominant majority set up a similar mechanism for its under-achievers and poorer members. But because of its stronger demographic and financial base, CDAC can offer superior assistance, a situation which could exacerbate the educational gap the government hoped to close, and give re-trained Chinese a competitive advantage for jobs over minority candidates.[98]

Conclusions

Given its ethnic composition and "double minority" setting, as mentioned earlier, Singapore has had an enviable record of maintaining ethnic peace. Years of downplaying ethnicity and sensitive issues through a mix of "multi-racial" accommodation and control accompanied by strong economic growth have defused ethnicity. It is not normally a place palpitating with ethnic tension nowadays. A telephone survey conducted in early 2000 indicates that 70 percent think ethnic relations are better today than they were ten years ago (56 percent rated ethnic relations as "good", while 42 percent said they were average), and 83 percent think that a race riot is unlikely to erupt in the next ten years. However, only 48 percent would trust someone of a different race to protect them if race riots did break out.[99]

The long-term hope of multi-racialism is that by allowing ethnic diversity, rather than suppressing it, while simultaneously discouraging ethnic group competition and treating the groups fairly (e.g., meritocracy), a supra-ethnic unity or civic nationalism/patriotism will emerge. In Singapore, there is still a question as to how effectively, "when the chips are down", ethnic identities and loyalties have been superceded by a Singapore national identity and loyalty.[100] Following the arrest of alleged clandestine Muslim terrorists in December, the Prime Minister in January 2002 announced the formation of Inter-racial Confidence Circles (ICC), operating through Citizen's Consultative Committees, to enhance ethnic interaction. Although a small measure, this contrasts sharply with the ethnic self-help initiatives.

The PAP government must be careful with its new, perhaps riskier, approach of encouraging ethnic identities and promoting a Chinese-educated, Mandarin and English-speaking elite. If it stimulates ethnic competition that disadvantages the minorities or leads to perceptions that the majority is acting to further its own interests and dominance, especially if the economy slips, it could generate all kinds of ethnic issues and tensions.

9 The successors

Leadership trends in the PAP – the search for top talent

Political succession: the founder leader steps aside

The institutional strength of a political party and a government is measured "in the first instance" by its ability to survive its founder.[1] Political succession can be a perilous and unpredictable process in developing states. Sometimes leaders are unwilling to give up power, and in order to avoid pressure from below, they will not name a successor or plan the succession. Some other times, the highly personalized nature of their rule means that, even if the succession is planned, attempts at institutionalization are overwhelmed and the leader remains more important than the office. Announcements of succession can also be dangerous in that they may heighten expectations and signal the possibility of change that can affect state–society relations and lead to instability.

Singapore is unusual in that the succession was painstakingly planned, was predictable and gradual, and that a strong leader (and the original one) voluntarily stepped aside (although he did not retire). It did not raise expectations of profound political change, nor did it destabilize the state. Of course, some elements of personalization of rule existed after 31 years of the same leader, and Lee Kuan Yew retains considerable authority even without occupying the highest office.[2]

While Lee Kuan Yew played an important role in choosing the successor team, and dismissing the old guard, he chose not to specify exactly *when* he would step down,[3] or to name an actual successor. Teamwork had been stressed, and Lee decided to let the new team members choose a successor from among themselves. He reflected that "the chances of success are much better if you select a group of people, any one of whom could be your successor. Let them contend amongst themselves and decide who will be the leader".[4] In January 1985, a group of seven young Cabinet Ministers (a majority of the 12-member Cabinet) unanimously chose Goh Chok Tong to be Deputy Prime Minister.[5] The full Cabinet concurred.

Ironically, Lee then seemed to second-guess the choice and was at times publicly critical of Goh, referring to his manner of speech and his consultative decision-making style. This nearly came to a head in 1988, when Lee made two startling speeches, saying that Goh Chok Tong had not been his first choice as successor; that he had preferred Dr. Tony Tan (who described what Lee said as "a very curious speech").[6] He also asked the Cabinet to reconsider who it wanted to succeed him. The Cabinet, following the group of seven, reconfirmed Goh Chok Tong who, clearly stung, stated firmly that the Prime Minister had said that the successor would not be decided by him "and indeed it will not be decided by him".[7]

This account of Lee Kuan Yew's behavior would be hard to believe, if one thought of him as the epitome of reason, motivated only by logic. However, Lee Kuan Yew is more complex than that. He strongly believes in the importance of meritocracy and talent (see pp. 55–6). Indeed, he regards *political* talent as the very pinnacle of talent, surpassing any other kind in importance. This belief is reaffirmed in the last words of the concluding page of his two volume 1400-page memoirs, where he sees meritocracy as consisting in appointing the best person for a particular position, especially at the level of a government's leaders.[8] He had expressed his belief in talent, years previously, not only by expressing his admiration for the presence of talent, but by venting his frustration at having to deal with the *lack* of it.

> Whenever I have had lesser men in charge, the average or slightly above-average, I have had to keep pushing and prodding them to review problems, to identify roadblocks, to suggest solutions, to come back and discover that less than the best has been achieved. To be exasperated, and often to be totally frustrated, is the price to pay for not having an able and talented man in charge.[9]

When he could not find an obvious person who conformed completely to his own exacting standards, Lee was, constructively, worried at the possibility of making the wrong choice of a successor. What was at issue was not some abstract question, but something which was in large part his own creation. A few years later, he expressed his personal commitment and concern in general terms, which sounds like a cry from the heart:

> I will be very unhappy if I felt that all I have done has been a waste of time ... Therefore I would like to spend the rest of my life making sure that what I have done has not been a waste of time.[10]

Singapore's continued existence and prosperity had been built up by him, and was now identified with him. In choosing a successor, the stakes were huge, and the choice was beyond even the "calculating" PAP's power to assess. His understandable appearance of indecision can be seen in his handing over the choice to Goh's Cabinet colleagues, then intervening in favor of Tony Tan, then returning the choice to the Cabinet, and finally accepting their (same) choice. Later, after consideration, Lee publicly revised his opinion, acknowledging that Goh had ability, determination, and drive, and had become more proficient in speaking both Mandarin and English.[11]

Irrespective of the propriety of Lee Kuan Yew's actions, their *raison d'être* could be questioned. Tony Tan was one of the top three candidates for Prime Minister, the others being Goh and Ong Teng Cheong, perhaps. There was no doubt about Goh's abilities or his popularity with the second-generation leaders or with the public. The main deficiencies which could be attributed to him were lack of toughness (incorrectly, see pp. 118–19) and lack of ability to "galvanize" crowds.[12] Curiously, there is little to show that Tony Tan was any better than Goh, when judged by these criteria. He was sometimes linked with him in contrast with the, reputedly, tougher B.G. Lee.

With Tan's experience in politics, his inclusion in Goh's Cabinet as Deputy Prime Minister greatly strengthened it. His penetrating mind, ability to convince small groups and his impeccable manners were indicative of his having been a university lecturer and of currently being seconded from his position of chief executive officer in his family bank.[13] The most cogent argument against Tan as Prime Minister could be phrased as an understatement; by most accounts, he did not actively seek the job.[14]

In November 1990, Goh Chok Tong succeeded Lee Kuan Yew as Prime Minister in a low-key ceremony. The stock market was not ruffled. Lee remained in the Cabinet with the title of Senior Minister, and both Goh and Lee continued to work one floor apart in the Istana Annex (the office wing of the former colonial government house, and where Cabinet meets). However, Lee did not quickly relinquish his party post as Secretary-General, to Goh's obvious consternation. All of this – the public criticisms, and Lee still in the Cabinet and still head of the PAP – made Goh appear almost as an ephemeral figure, or, in popular Singapore parlance, a "seat-warmer" for the rapidly rising B.G. Lee Hsien Loong (see pp. 120–1), the highly-qualified eldest son of Lee Kuan Yew. Goh, in fact, had already acknowledged B.G. Lee as his successor, but, he emphasized, only in due course.[15]

It was publicly disclosed in November 1992 that B.G. Lee had a malignant lymphoma. This had some obvious implications, and the PAP moved quickly to signal that Goh Chok Tong should not be considered a transient leader. Goh, in answer to a question, said he was "sure" he would become the PAP secretary-general one day, but, he added, "it's better not to jump to any premature conclusion, just in case you or I will be embarrassed".[16] In fact, he did not have long to wait. A PAP press statement revealed that Lee Kuan Yew had now decided to give up the post of secretary-general, and in December 1992, he proposed Goh Chok Tong for the position and the CEC unanimously accepted the recommendation. To many in Singapore and the region, this effectively completed the succession from the founder leader.

The timing of the succession from Goh Chok Tong to, presumably, B.G. Lee Hsien Loong, kept cropping up. In late 2000, Goh Chok Tong said that there was no hurry to change leaders in Singapore, and that he, the Prime Minister alone, would decide when it was time for him to step down. He also added that if someone wanted to edge him out of office, he would dig in his heels. Lee Kuan Yew, when asked about Goh's statements, replied that "What he said is what he said. I mean, that's right . . . he is the Prime Minister . . . he will decide . . . Nobody is going to edge him out. There is no hurry".[17]

This chapter considers Goh Chok Tong and B.G. Lee, as well as a few politically promising ministers who are longer-term prospects for Prime Minister. It also considers people who had prospects of becoming Prime Minister, but failed. As well, it looks at sources of recruitment for a Prime Minister, which were not obvious at the start of the PAP government in 1959, but have emerged since, namely the military and the trade unions. (Actually, the sources have been limited to quite special military and quite special trade union leaders, in both cases described as "technocrats".) It also mentions trade union leaders who have become presidents. Finally explored is the question of whether social, economic, and language-policy changes indicate that future leaders will require different qualifications than previously.

Goh Chok Tong: origins; entry into politics; how he "became his own man"

Goh Chok Tong was born without the advantages of an upper-middle class home, unlike the one in which Lee Kuan Yew was raised. He was, however, except as a very young child, spared the anxieties and disruption of living under the Japanese occupation. He did not exhibit the formidable intellectual qualities of Lee early on, but performed well at primary school and then at Raffles Institution.[18] He obtained First Class Honors in Economics at the University of Singapore, and after three years' service in the elite Singapore Administrative Service, attended the prestigious Williams College in Massachusetts on a fellowship, where he obtained a Master of Arts degree in Development Economics. Some time after his return to Singapore, he was seconded to Neptune Oriental Lines, and in 1973 became its Managing Director. He achieved impressive financial results. His career was soon interrupted by his being asked by Finance Minister Hon Sui Sen to allow his name to go forward as a PAP candidate for the 1976 election. He agreed, stood at the election, and was elected for the Marine Parade constituency. He became a Senior Minister of State for Finance[19] in 1979 and the Minister for Trade and Industry in 1981.

In addition to climbing the ministerial hierarchy, Goh began his ascent of the party hierarchy, beginning with second assistant secretary-general in 1979. He was also given another task – an important one considering the emphasis which the PAP places on the recruitment of the best talent. He was put in charge of standardizing and supervising methods of recruiting candidates, and he introduced psychological tests for prospective ministers (see p. 48).[20]

From 1985 the policies of the government were those of the second generation, led by Deputy Prime Minister Goh.[21] In January 1989, Goh explained in a letter to the Speaker of Parliament: "the members of cabinet were chosen by me and we are in charge of the day-to-day running of the government, not the prime minister. He chairs cabinet meetings and gives us the benefit of his experience. However, we settle the policies".[22] In November 1990, Goh succeeded to the prime ministership, as mentioned earlier.

A comment by a top-rank Australian journalist contrasts the two personalities concerned. Greg Sheridan found Goh as "easy, affable, friendly, solicitous as Lee [was] dry, precise and forbidding", adding that Goh's "change of style after the all dominant Lee seems to have gone down very well, although there are no real differences of substance between them".[23]

Goh has needed to defend himself from time to time against some of Lee's remarks (see p. 115): "I have told the Prime Minister many times I will not change my style. It is part of my temperament and personality. I listen, I talk, I try to persuade and try to bring as many people on board as possible, I try to accommodate. I regard this style of mine as a strength, not a weakness".[24] In a subsequent interview, when Goh was questioned on his relations with Lee, his reply was: "... we have, shall we say, a candid relationship. He gives his views. I don't take offence. He told me, quite frankly, that I am his second choice as PM, but better that than have a misunderstanding".[25]

A comment by Lee Kuan Yew suggests mutual adaptation by the two "generations". In February 1988, in reply to a question on his relations with the younger generation, he explained: "Any proposition that they reject, unless I consider it a matter of national security, I will just say 'All right, proceed your way', because then there is no need for an abrupt change after me. It has already been tailored to suit their inclinations".[26] This last remark suggests that sometimes convergence between Lee and the younger generation had been based on adjustments by the former.

A basic question about Goh Chok Tong is: how tough is he? The question might not be necessary but for two things – his own low-key manner, and the contrast, drawn by some, with Lee Kuan Yew. Goh handled the question in a way that could not be faulted in an interview with *Asiaweek*, taking care to rephrase the question first. Asked if, under his genial exterior, he was nevertheless quite tough and hard, he replied: "I would say 'firm and disciplined'. While there's always a logical mind at work, I show a more human side of government. But the PAP is not going to become soft and effete under my leadership. If the party were getting soft underneath, you can be sure I would not be here talking to you, I would be pushed out".[27] It is not too hard to provide evidence of Goh's toughness.[28] As Deputy Prime Minister, Goh and his team had to make the difficult decision to support the arrests of Christian social activist "Marxist conspirators" in 1987 (see p. 131).[29] Goh's affirmation of his toughness also demonstrates other strengths of character. He thinks before he speaks, and his comments are to the point and coolly delivered.

In several instances, Goh has practiced a gentler style and displayed a degree of liberality, but has drawn a clear line where the limits would be and has stated that he would react strongly if it were breached. He has favored allowing more NGOs to exist, but refused to let them set the agenda (see pp. 167–8). He would, he said, crack down hard on any organization that constituted a political opposition "in disguise".[30] He would also not allow other countries to dictate its policies through such organizations; it must be clear to the government that they do not have a foreign agenda.

Goh's behavior over the caning sentence handed down on Michael Fay for vandalism (see p. 131) was nicely balanced. After representations were made on Fay's behalf by President Clinton, he reduced the number of strokes to be inflicted (which, it appears, Lee Kuan Yew would not have done), showing some regard for the President's intervention, but yet reaffirming the principle involved.[31]

In one respect, Lee Kuan Yew should have been reassured by Goh's actions. Lee had feared that when Goh took over, pressure groups would test Goh and his Cabinet and that the pressures would continue until Goh and his team indicated that there were limits "beyond which there will be no give".[32] It seems that the new government reacted quite quickly against being pressured. The use of "Out of Bounds" markers, introduced by Goh, and the letters to the press by his Press Secretary rebuking offenders (see pp. 141–2), helped to clarify somewhat what was acceptable and what was not acceptable to the government by means that were stern but not Draconian. However, they were also an undeniable manifestation of toughness.

It has been surmised that an aspect of Goh's toughness is that it tends sometimes to take the form of resilience. Criticism or setbacks stiffen his resolve to do better. This trait was apparent after the PAP lost the Anson by-election in 1981 (see p. 149). Goh had been in charge of the PAP campaign, but, instead of the defeat eroding his resolve it seemed, rather, to redouble it. A similar reaction occurred when Lee Kuan Yew publicly criticized his speaking style. He did not show resentment, or loss of will; he just tried harder.

Goh Chok Tong's ups and downs, achievements, aspirations

Goh Chok Tong's feelings about being Prime Minister, and about how long he wants to stay in that post, have varied over time. In general, the longer he has been in the job, the more he likes it. Percipiently – although, with hindsight, also predictably – in 1990 Michael Leifer mused that Goh might well come to enjoy the exercise of power more than he had enjoyed being Deputy Prime Minister.[33] The correlation between time in office and enjoyment of office is not exact; it has been affected by ups and downs, external impacts and so on. Goh has had times of near-despondency, both before and after he became Prime Minister. In 1985, for example, when stories circulated that he would be only a "seat-warmer" before B.G. Lee took over, he put his position very clearly: "If Singapore will be better led by somebody else, if I'm just to warm the seat, so be it". He rested his case on the method of selection. "If the PM told me that he wants his son to succeed him he wouldn't have my support. It can't be decided by the PM against the wishes of the ministers in my generation".[34]

The other "bad time" experienced by Goh was after the 1991 election (see pp. 150–1). He called the election less than a year after he became Prime Minister, asking for a "solid endorsement" of his style and policies. The results were disappointing. The PAP lost several more seats and won with a slightly smaller percentage of the total popular vote.[35] Goh was temporarily devastated, saying that things could never be the same, but in fact he made a quick recovery.

With B.G. Lee clearly designated as his successor, Goh Chok Tong has taken some pains to state that he does not expect factions to be formed or personality conflicts to break out. He has sought to allay fears that the compassionate and consultative leadership which he has stood for would end with his handover of power. The same basic program would be carried through in spite of changes in personalities. There would be no U-turn.[36]

It is reassuring to have one's estimate of a Prime Minister's achievements confirmed by him. In 2000, the authors suggested the following list: keeping the Cabinet team together and arriving at a suitable relationship with the Senior Minister; guiding the country through the regional economic crisis in the late 1990s; fashioning the Community Development Councils scheme, which provided two-tier government in certain areas (see p. 96); being the prime initiator for the foundation of ASEM (see pp. 183–4). Prime Minister Goh agreed with the list, but pointed out that the achievements should be attributed, not to him personally, but to the government as a team.[37]

His views on how long he will stay in office have changed over the years. Terms of office which are predominantly pleasant naturally make staying in it longer a more attractive idea. In November 1992, he looked and felt relaxed, saying that he had felt that way over the last two years but not previously. It had been an effort to meet people without strain. If he could learn how to do it, anybody could.[38] In 1998 he thought it was premature to consider assuming a post such as Senior Minister after being Prime Minister.[39] By 2000, he imagined that after the upcoming election (held in November 2001), he could stay on for a little. He would consider the matter "after we have won the election". He would certainly step down by the time he was 65 (2006). After the election, he said would likely step down after leading Singapore out of the recession, probably in two to three years.[40] He would not mind assuming another role after he stepped down, not necessarily the exact equivalent of a Senior Minister role – for example, in his case, he would not attend Cabinet meetings.[41] Underlying these ideas was the thought that he constituted too great a resource not to be used in some capacity.

It seems that the concept of Senior Minister, introduced by Lee Kuan Yew, will be followed in some form by at least one of his successors. It is thoroughly in conformity with a basic tenet of the PAP – that talent should be used to the full.

In attempting to draw a contrast between the pronouncements of Lee Kuan Yew and those of Goh Chok Tong, one should look for similarities of approach rather than nuances of expression. After all, they are members of the same party, and the binding link of party is strong. The PAP has been shaped by the activities and according to the values of Lee Kuan Yew, and in joining the party Goh Chok Tong has subscribed to these values. The PAP has not moved far from Edmund Burke's eighteenth-century belief that a party is based on agreement on principles.[42] In one of Goh's major speeches, he warned Parliament not to expect from him: "any sudden shift of gears, sudden reversal of policies, or any dramatic movement heading Singapore in a different direction".[43]

B.G. Lee's entry into politics: his expanding role in the party

Politics in Singapore provides rather fewer surprises than politics in many other countries; perhaps this results from the hierarchical structure of the PAP, and the weakness of the Opposition. However, a major surprise (except to a few "insiders"), occurred in September 1984, when it was announced that Lee Kuan Yew's eldest son, B.G. Lee Hsien Loong, had been appointed Political Secretary to the Minister of Defence and chosen as a PAP candidate for the approaching general election.[44] This was more than an item of political near-trivia. It had the potential to change drastically the pattern of the top leadership, and, to those with runaway imaginations, to usher in "dynastic politics".

Lee Hsien Loong's political talents were unknown. However, his parents' intellectual abilities, and his academic successes were indicative, as was his army record. A summary of his performance may indicate his solid foundation for a political career. Lee was awarded a President's Scholarship and an SAF scholarship – which entitled him to combine military training with academic courses at Cambridge and Harvard. He graduated from Cambridge in 1974 with first-class honors in Mathematics and a diploma, with distinction, in Computer

Science. In 1979, he attended the Kennedy School of Government at Harvard University, winning a Master's degree in Public Administration. His army record was also distinguished. Beginning in the artillery, he went on to become head of joint operations and planning. He left the army with the rank of Brigadier-General.

B.G. Lee's education and training was extended in 1997, when Lee Kuan Yew became aware that the Monetary Authority of Singapore (MAS)[45] needed to be revitalized so as to conform to sweeping changes (many in the direction of liberalization) which were occurring worldwide. With the Prime Minister's approval, he decided that B.G. Lee was the person to head the MAS, and to prepare him for the job, had him meet with brokers and fund managers to learn about international trends, while also acquainting himself with the workings of Singapore's financial sectors.[46] The Prime Minister appointed B.G. Lee chair of the MAS in January 1998.

Early in his political career, in October 1989, B.G. Lee was the speaker at a Singapore luncheon talk organized by the prestigious Institute of International Affairs. There he made a favorable impression on a hard-headed reporter, who confirmed afterwards that her opinion was shared by others who had been in the audience. She wrote: "Our younger ministers may have the best brains in Singapore, but not all of them are able to express their ideas clearly ... Certainly, only a handful give the impression of being relaxed yet confident when faced with a barrage of questions".[47]

It would be too easy to conclude that B.G. Lee's beliefs were the product of his genes and upbringing leading to a predisposition to support "hard-line" policies, in contrast to the "softer" inclinations of Goh Chok Tong, and possibly Tony Tan.[48] However, when using such terms as "hard-line", it is necessary to identify the "territory". For instance, is it primarily political or economic? B.G. Lee's approach, as regards economics (in accord with his actions as Chair of the MAS) was decidedly liberal. He is in favor of competition, including competition *inside* Singapore. He also is pro-globalization to the extent that a challenge to Singapore keeps it in fighting trim without submerging its autonomy and distinctive personality.

Asked what would happen if Singapore became more liberal, B.G. Lee replied that there was no reason for it to do so – the system worked as it was. Pleasing the West was not a sufficient reason to change.[49] On some political and social issues, B.G. Lee is aware of the complexities entailed by government efforts to induce participation in the political process without weakening respect for government and authority as such.

> The question is what are the ground rules. If we respond to criticism with a sledgehammer and demolish or humiliate people every time they disagree with us, then nobody is going to speak up. On the other hand, if you just take it meekly every time somebody fires at you, not all the shots are intended to point you in the right direction. So somewhere in between you must find the right stance. It's a matter of judgment.[50]

B.G. Lee's attitude to life has changed with the years. This has not corresponded to any change in orientation towards toughness or tenderness. Neither has it seemed to be linked with any "mellowing" process. The death of his first wife (1982) and his bout with cancer, in 1992, from which he has recovered, have no doubt contributed to the change. One way of expressing what has occurred is to say that things that once seemed important to him have become less so with the passage of time. He has summarized the process thus:

> When you're young, you think you can do everything. And the sky is the limit. Then if you apply yourself, you can learn and you can be as knowledgeable as the experts. But after some time, you realise that you can't. You will understand, you will follow the logic, but you won't have the feel and the judgement and the mind is finite. You have to depend on other people. You'll get better solutions that way ...[51]

Later, when asked specifically about his wife's death and his own illness, his reply was:

> I think it makes you something different ... I suppose it's the difference between feeling young and feeling as if what you never imagined could actually take place. So when you come to deal with people or deal with things, take it with a bit less intensity and self-absorption.[52]

This having been said, B.G. Lee has retained a fount of ebullience of spirit not to be found in any other Singapore politician. It emerges when he enters the room where one is waiting to interview him or with a chance encounter when one is greeted by a wave and smile from him. It is worth commenting briefly on his relations with Goh Chok Tong and with his father, Lee Kuan Yew. His remarks on the former relationship are in tune with what is generally believed. Goh is more circumspect and careful and milder in his presentation, while Lee Hsien Loong tends to be sharper. Lee thinks he has a good relationship with Goh. He notes that Goh has established himself and that nobody calls him a seat-warmer any more. He believes that Singaporeans respect Goh and have a considerable affection for him.[53]

Sometimes assessments of B.G. Lee are colored by identifying his traits with his father's reputation. When B.G. Lee made his entrance into the political scene, he struck a hopeful chord in some young professionals, who welcomed a change from an older generation of politicians and perceived him as a vanguard of the "yuppie generation". A year or two later some of his initial glamor had worn off, and his mannerisms and image were seen as reminiscent of his father – capable, but stern. B.G. Lee's succession to Goh Chok Tong has been accepted, but the "dynasty" scenario has been revived in a different shape – that after B.G. Lee has succeeded Goh, Lee Kuan Yew will still remain as Senior Minister.

B.G. Lee believes that Lee Kuan Yew has been a big influence on him, especially when he was growing up, but also even now.

> It's the way he helps to point me in certain directions and formed even the personality to some extent and set an example of what can be done and how to do it. We're quite close. We have somewhat similar temperaments ...

> approaches to issues, but not quite the same because he grew up in tumultuous times and I grew up in orderly times. So he's very much aware of major things which can go wrong.[54]

B.G. Lee's intellectual grasp of how to devise remedies to cope with the 1997 economic crisis was referred to in the account given earlier (see p. 71). What remains to be said is that the government policies, largely crafted by Lee, were implemented with close attention to minimizing opposition, using an incremental approach.[55] The emphasis lay in cooperation between the government and the public to solve a puzzle; the "solution" was to be arrived at gradually by the government, as it were, taking people along with it, step by step.[56] For example, proposals to reduce the employers' contributions to the CPF were not produced with a flourish, out of a hat. They were gradually unveiled as a hypothetical last-resort policy, which became increasingly perceived as inevitable. The initial step was for Lim Boon Heng, Minister without Portfolio and secretary-general of the NTUC, to introduce the issues involved at a seminar in Pasir Ris. Although the presentation had been carefully prepared, the reception was quite chilly. However, the idea had really been just to broach the topic. The real presentation was done through a large number of discussions in the party, at the grassroots, and with trade unionists.[57] The policy was formally announced in November 1998. By this time, many had been convinced that the government's proposals made sense. Even then, the government's case had not been concluded. It was willing to make concessions to meet the grievances of those who were worried about their own particular problems, such as mortgage payments, increased transportation costs, and so on.

B.G. Lee summed up the outcome in numerical terms: "[Adjustments] don't cost a lot of money but I think they relieved a lot of anxiety and they actually helped to make the policy better … I wanted to do a hundred [percent] but people were not willing, so I did 70 or 80. But it's really a matter of refining and improving what we're trying to do"[58] The lesson was that, if you have to change your policy, prepare the people early and explain why the change is necessary. B.G. Lee's mastery of the economics of liberalization has been demonstrated (see pp. 75–6). His reputation as a manager of political change – as a politician – largely rests on his ability to manage *people*.

Prominent figures in the line of succession

The two people most often mentioned in the line of succession to B.G. Lee are Brigadier-General George Yeo Yong-Boon and Rear-Admiral Teo Chee Hean. The former was in the second batch of recruits into politics from the army. Like B.G. Lee, Yeo was awarded both a President's scholarship and an SAF scholarship. Yeo won a double first in Engineering at Cambridge. Later he attended the Harvard Business School, graduating with an MBA with High Distinction. After service in the army, he transferred to the air force, where he became chief-of-staff, and then director of joint operations and planning in the Ministry of Defence. He entered politics in 1988, and, once elected, followed the normal PAP pattern of gaining experience in various ministries. His appointments as Minister for Information and the Arts in 1991 (until 1999), Minister for Health in 1997, and Minister for Trade and Industry in 1999 reflected his wide interests and capabilities. In MITA, he encouraged performances and exhibitions, mostly displayed in the "Esplanade" area of Singapore (Theaters on the Bay). He is well-versed in the history of places which he enjoys comparing with Singapore, mainly the Venetian Republic, and, more recently, China. In his current ministry he has made use of his expertise in IT, and is one of the main exponents of the Knowledge-Based Economy (see p. 78). His promotion of the arts has not succeeded in winning the support of all Cabinet members. But his mastery of IT and the KBE refutes any too narrow assessment of his talents.

Rear-Admiral Teo Chee Hean (born in the same year as Yeo, 1954), also a recipient of President's and SAF scholarships, studied Electrical Engineering and Management Science at the University of Manchester Institute of Science and Technology, where he graduated as Bachelor of Science with first class honors. He continued his studies at the Imperial College in London, achieving a Master of Science degree, with distinction, in Computing Science. Later he attended the Kennedy School of Government at Harvard University, obtaining a Master's degree in Public Administration. Unlike the current trend in Singapore, he elected to join Singapore's navy, assuming command of it as chief of navy in 1991, and reaching the rank of Rear-Admiral before leaving it to enter politics in 1992. His early appointments were in the Ministries of Defence, Finance, and Communications, before becoming Minister for the Environment and then being appointed as Minister for Education in 1997. He chaired the Committee to Promote Enterprise Overseas (1993) (see p. 76), and in 1998 was appointed chair of the influential Singapore 21 Committee (see p. 165), which he has described as intended to draw up a vision of the "heartware" of Singapore in the twenty-first century.

In contrast to his reasoned presentation of issues, Teo is uncompromising when he thinks toughness is needed. Stopping corruption in China, he remarked, would require that some found guilty should be shot as an example.[59]

These two ministers are at, or near, the top of those who may move up the hierarchy when Goh Chok Tong retires as Prime Minister. Below them the sequence of succession is not so obvious. Some names are likely to be mentioned more often than others, if the topic arises. Among them – in no particular order – are: Lim Hng Kiang, the Health Minister; David Lim Tik En, whose main strengths are in technology and the use of computers; and Lim Swee Say, the former deputy head of the NTUC and also an IT expert. He is the only "rising star" who has been preeminent both in the armed services and in the hierarchy of trade union leaders. After the 2001 general election, Lim Hng Kiang remained Minister for Health while the two other Lims mentioned were promoted to the Cabinet. Lim Swee Say was made a full minister (Environment) while David Lim was made Acting Minister for Information, Communications and the Arts, and is scheduled to become a full minister in a year's time when he takes over MITA. Although they were all recruited from the military, they do not use their military ranks. It has been optional to do so, except that B.G. Lee and B.G. Yeo were instructed to use them to boost the prestige of the military. (It is likely that the government is sensitive to having too many military titles used in case a false impression might be given to other countries about the nature of the state in

Singapore.) The fact that they were all in the armed services, as were the three previous names discussed above, was not the consequence of any government policy to try to "militarize" the PAP (see p. 175). The impetus arose from a desire to counteract a traditional Chinese stereotype which stigmatized the military as a low-grade employment. If sufficient able young men – the top ten percent academically – could be induced to take SAF scholarships (see p. 170), it was hoped that its prestige would be given a boost. The military thus became a major source of political recruitment for a short time, when other sources failed to provide the desired supply.[60]

However, after the second batch of SAF scholar recruits into politics, the supply of candidates fell and has not risen again.[61] One reason for the drop was that scholarships for the brightest students were soon available from a large number of other sources. There were no SAF recruits among the 25 new PAP candidates in the 2001 election. The two most heralded newcomers, both of whom have close contact with influential ministers, come from the ranks of the civil service: Tharman Shanmugaratnam (44) and Khaw Boon Wan (42). Both became Senior Ministers of State, with good promotion possibilities; the former apparently being groomed for an economic or financial portfolio.

Assessment of recruitment from the military

When ministers who have been recruited to politics from the armed forces were asked to comment on the practice, their opinions have been favorable.[62] They thought that military service provided practice in stimulating cooperation, working as a team, and in teaching how to give orders so as to achieve the optimum results. One Minister with a military background thought that the appropriate behavior in each role was not too dissimilar, one became accustomed to dealing with the unexpected.

Another perspective takes account of the fact that the SAF scholarship holders do not spend all their tenure in military pursuits, perhaps only about 60 percent of it. Therefore, some of the benefits of "military" training should be attributed to the academic component of their programs.

Some concern has been expressed that military connections might be assuming too great importance inside the PAP.[63] At the time, ex-military personnel were less prominent than they are today in the government and will continue to be so for the next generation.

Recruitment from the trade unions: "lost leaders"

Some limited comparisons may be made between recruitment from the armed services and recruitment from the trade unions. In each case, the recruits have resembled technocrats. But the selection process was more formal for the former, because those selected had a "package" associated with SAF scholarships, whereas the latter had not.

As it happened, the first trade union technocrat, Lim Chee Onn (see p. 32), had a degree from Harvard University. Lim was unsuccessful in getting close to becoming Prime Minister, although before his "fall" some thought that he was among the top four aspirants. No trade union leader since then has come so close to being Prime Minister. Perhaps, after Lim, the nearest has been Ong Teng Cheong, who was one of three possible successors to Lee Kuan Yew, the others being Goh Chok Tong and Tony Tan. Ong's chances were reduced because his English was thought by some not to be good enough for international transactions in that language. Both he and C.V. Devan Nair attained the Presidency, although not the Prime Ministership. Each had an unhappy time, Ong because ill health deprived him of a second term and Devan Nair because of scandal.

Some trade unionists and others who have failed to meet with the success which was predicted for them have simply disappeared from public view. An example is Singapore's first Rhodes Scholar (Tan Eng Liang), who rose rapidly on his return to Singapore, to be a Senior Minister of State. Then he resigned in 1979, and never returned to political life.[64] Lim Chee Onn (see p. 125) is a conspicuous exception. He became chair of Keppel Corporation, where he had worked previously, and his name is included in one of the charts illustrating the "circles of power" in Singapore in the paper by Werner Vennewald previously cited.[65]

The shortage of political talent

The government is constantly complaining about the lack of political talent, but it is not always precise about what kind of talent and when the shortage(s) will be most serious. Some accounts of the talent shortage[66] mention several examples. In one of these, the categories include both thinkers and campaigners on the ground. Yet Lee Kuan Yew is quite adamant that the more important deficiency is not "foot-soldiers" but "generals". He would settle for ten of the latter, he said.[67]

One difficulty is that the source of recruits which is most preferred nowadays is private business, but the search has been unproductive. From about the mid-1970s to the late 1980s, only four ministers were recruited from the private sector, of whom two were originally from government.[68] Other sources have not been much productive either; from GLCs – although both Goh Chok Tong and Lim Boon Heng came from there – the civil service, the trade unions, and the army (after the brief spurt of recruits in the late 1980s–early 1990s).

Although the monetary rewards provided by government are now comparable with those paid by private business (see p. 61), the latter remains more attractive to the majority of potential aspirants. When the matter of timing and age is considered, the government's talent search seems to face even more formidable obstacles. Potential "generals" seem to be entering politics later in life (that is, winning a seat in Parliament at a later age than previously). Yet, the PAP view is that, ideally, the age distribution of ministers should match that of the population as a whole.

Lee Kuan Yew is emphatic that the government should be doing more to get candidates in their thirties rather than in their forties. At the later ages, there is a more adequate supply of talent; he cites the entry of Rear Admiral Teo into politics as an example.[69]

There is one particular problem about leadership, which could arise after B.G. Lee's retirement – or even before it – B.G. Yeo and RAdm. Teo were born in the same year and are only two years younger than B.G. Lee. At some levels, and times, Singapore's immediate problem may not be a shortage of talent, but at some high level, a surplus! The problem is even deeper than this. The "logjam" is not confined to the persons just mentioned. Close behind them are three others already mentioned (and even additional names) with claims for future advancement, Lim Hng Kiang, David Lim Tik En, and Lim Swee Say, all born in 1954 or 1955. Some years ago the age pattern of the leaders was serendipitous and conducive to an avoidance of conflict. There was a conveniently large age difference between Lee Kuan Yew and Goh Chok Tong, and between the latter and B.G. Lee. Probably two decades from now, instead of a smooth progression, there may be a bulge.[70]

It is often said that in politics it matters a great deal *who* you are and *where* you were born. Unless the timing fits, it may also make a big difference *when* you were born.

Future requirements for ministers

The government does not foresee any big changes in the type of ministers required in the future. The KBE has already resulted in a high level of competence in IT on the part of ministers. The selection process (see pp. 48–9) has been adaptable to suggestions on changes.

To a question of whether younger ministers would be especially useful, because they would be proficient on the Web, B.G Lee replied that all ministers, and all MPs were qualified in this respect.[71] Occasionally there is a special need for a minister who is exceptionally well-versed in IT. On a visit to Europe by B.G. Lee, for example, it seemed advisable to have the knowledgeable Lim Swee Say accompany him.[72]

With changing patterns of education in Singapore (see pp. 103–9) and the growing weight of China on the international scene, it has become more necessary for ministers to be proficient in Mandarin. It is said that one recently appointed Minister was told that he must reach the requisite standard within a year.

Ability in Mandarin among the top government leaders has varied. In his early campaigning days, Lee Kuan Yew resorted mainly to *ad hoc* measures, such as obtaining help from colleagues for translating.[73] Later, he adopted the more systematic practice of having a tutor.[74] B.G. Lee had difficulty with Chinese in secondary school, which led to warnings by his teachers.[75] Fortunately, he was later able to improve his Chinese by having conversations with his father, who needed practice in the language.[76] Goh Chok Tong started almost from scratch (he knew Hokkien but not Mandarin), but, with Lee Kuan Yew's advice on choosing tutors, he substantially improved his communication skills in the language.[77] It is expected that this requirement will become less onerous over time, because most Chinese ministers in the PAP will have attended the elite bilingual (Mandarin and English) SAP schools (see pp. 106–7, 109).

10 Authoritarian aspects of PAP rule

> In framing a government which is to be administered by men over men, the great difficulty lies in this: You must first enable the government to control the governed; and in the next place oblige it to control itself.
>
> James Madison, *The Federalist*, No. 51

Singapore has most of the trappings of democracy – a parliamentary system of government with, additionally, an elected president; regular, free and accurately counted elections, and universal suffrage. However, certain draconian laws, controls on political participation, and measures limiting civil and political rights and freedom of the press, mean that Singapore is, to some extent – critics vary on the degree – an authoritarian state.

Singapore has been called "non-democratic" by S.P. Huntington, "partly free/democratic" by Freedom House, and "democratic" by Francis Fukuyama.[1] The annual US Department of State Human Rights Reports for Singapore, which have been consistent, state that the Singapore government generally respects the human rights of its citizens, although some significant problems exist, and that Singaporeans have the means to change their government democratically, although formidable obstacles are placed in the way of the Opposition.[2] The Singapore government has not committed any serious violations of civil rights. There have been no extrajudicial killings or political disappearances, and there are currently no political detainees.[3]

Because of the situation described above, Singapore is sometimes described as an "illiberal democracy" or a "non-liberal communitarian democracy".[4] The illiberal democracy thesis is that the claim that the middle classes are the bearers of political liberalization in the Asia–Pacific region has little basis. Rather, the middle classes have been the "main beneficiaries of state economic paternalism, which [gives them] a strong stake in the perpetuation of authoritarian rule".[5] It is clear that economic advancement is a powerful legitimizing factor. Chua Beng-Huat relates this to Singapore, where the central idea promoted by the government is that to ensure stability and continuous economic growth it is necessary that community interests be placed above individual ones. In the government's eyes, communitarianism is a key factor explaining the Asian economic miracle. This "communitarian ideology", which has developed from earlier concepts of Confucianism and a tradition of collectivism, has the effect, Chua writes, of preventing democratization from taking the course of liberal democracy.[6]

Of course, some critics dismiss the idea of non-liberal communitarian democracy as little more than a disguise for authoritarian rule.[7] Others are puzzled about Singapore's exceptionalism. Huntington writes, "Setting aside the oil-rich states as a special case, all the wealthiest countries in the world, except Singapore, are democratic, and almost all the poorest countries in the world, with the notable exception of India and perhaps one or two others, are not democratic".[8]

Clearly, democracy has a wide array of meanings, applications, and connections. It represents a complex structure of ideas and conventions, institutions and practices that produce an arrangement for the distribution of political power in a state. Collier and Levitsky, for example, have identified 550 "subtypes" of democracy.[9]

What everyone *can* agree upon, including the PAP leaders, is that Singapore is *not* a liberal democracy. In power, the PAP government has been interested only in upholding certain democratic fundamentals, namely, in Lee Kuan Yew's words, "government by free choice of the people, by secret ballot, at periodic intervals".[10] The rational argument against mass democracy first put forward by Plato seems similar to the views held by the PAP leaders. The argument is that it seems irrational to leave difficult and important decisions to a vote of the whole people, some of whom will be ignorant or self-interested. The reasonable way to get the right decisions is to select people of intelligence and character who are educated, trained and committed. Further, like Plato, the PAP leaders also believe that there will be more willing compliance to authority if the people have some stake in selecting the leaders.[11] In this sense, Singapore probably fits Joseph Schumpeter's minimalist "delegates or elite model" best; that is, the governed have a right to elect their governors in fair, free and regular competitive elections, and to authorize these governors to act on their behalf.[12] Larry Diamond calls this conception "electoral democracy", as opposed to "liberal democracy".[13] Some critics would say that Singapore still does not qualify, because elections are not very competitive.

Communists, triads, dissent, and draconian laws

This distrust of liberal democracy on the part of the PAP leadership, combined with the memory of a difficult and bitter contest for survival against the Communists, and the street-fighter instincts of Lee Kuan Yew, have been translated into policies which restrict individual liberties and impede mass political organization, and some laws that seem draconian in their nature and punishments.

The ISA, CLA, and MDA

The Internal Security Act (ISA), Criminal Law (Temporary Provisions) Act (CLA), and the Misuse of Drugs Act (MDA) allow for arrest without warrant and detention without trial. The CLA is used almost exclusively in cases involving drugs or the Triads (secret societies) and not for political purposes. In June 2000, fewer than 400 people were being detained under the CLA. The MDA allows the government to commit suspected drug users to a rehabilitation center for up to six months.[14]

More controversial is the ISA, which was instituted during British rule and retained by the PAP government. It was used originally against suspected Communists, and it is employed also against racial and religious extremists and whenever the government determines that a serious security threat exists. From 1989–96, no one was detained under the ISA, but in 1997–8 there were six arrests for two cases alleging espionage. There have been no political detentions since 1989, when Chia Thye Poh, a former Barisan Sosialis MP who was detained with a number of others in 1966 for alleged involvement in the Malayan Communist Party, was released.[15]

The opposition and foreign critics have consistently called for the abolition of the ISA. This is no doubt because the ISA has been used in the past against left-wing pro-Communist political opposition (see p. 20), and was employed again in 1987 in what Garry Rodan describes as a "spectacular return to the use of the ISA" to detain a group of Christian social activist "Marxist conspirators", in a reaction that was perceived by many observers as an example of PAP "overkill".[16] The 22 detained were from the Young Christian Workers, the Catholic Welfare Centre and Catholic Centre for Foreign Workers. They championed workers' issues, such as higher wages, social security benefits, job security, and the conditions of foreign guest workers. However, according to the Internal Security Department (ISD), they included activists from the Workers' Party and from the Student Christian Movement that had flourished under self-exiled former student militant Tan Wah Piow, who had allied with some Roman Catholic followers of liberation theology, and together they used Christian organizations as a cover for political agitation.[17] The ISD considered them an incipient security threat, and so they were detained.[18] Many of the detainees confessed to being involved in a Marxist conspiracy, but Amnesty International in 1987 and Asia Watch in 1988 condemned the methods used (cold rooms, sleep deprivation and harsh interrogation) to elicit the confessions. At the end of 1987, five Christian missionaries were expelled and the Christian Conference of Asia was banned in Singapore.

The death penalty and caning

The death penalty raises more concern with Western human rights activists than it appears to bother Singaporeans, where it is not an issue.[19] The death penalty is mandatory for murder, drug trafficking, treason, and certain firearms offenses. Lee Kuan Yew was impressed that there was no crime in Singapore during the Japanese occupation because punishment was severe. "As a result, I have never believed those who advocate a soft approach to crime and punishment, claiming that punishment does not reduce crime".[20] Amnesty International in its 2000 report estimates there have been 190 executions since 1994, thus giving Singapore one of the highest rates per capita of executions in the world. Many of those executed are not Singaporeans. According to *The Economist*, they are often Thais and Malaysians convicted of smuggling drugs.[21]

Caning is also more objectionable to some Westerners than to most Singaporeans, although the practice was derived from the British. Caning on the buttocks for men between the ages of 16 and 50 who are deemed fit is used as punishment, in addition to imprisonment, for a number of offenses involving violence or the threat of violence, such as rape and robbery, as well as for some non-violent crimes such as vandalism, drug trafficking, and violation of immigration laws. Caning is inflicted as a deterrent, and it is meant to hurt, but not to permanently injure. The *cause célèbre* was the caning in 1994 of an American teenager after his conviction, along with some Asian students, for vandalism. The official US reaction was one of outrage, although American public opinion was divided on the issue. When the teenager was caned in spite of spirited American diplomacy on his behalf, the US retaliated with a number of sanctions, and bilateral relations were soured for a while (see pp. 180, 251, n. 89).[22]

The Societies Act

The Societies Act (1967, amended in 1988) requires most organizations of more than ten people to be registered. This practice was started by the British in the 1900s when the colony was troubled by violent triads. With the struggle against the Communists in the 1960s, the government wanted to gain some control over Communist front organizations operating out of seemingly harmless associations, such as old boys' associations and rural residents' associations. It also wanted to channel participation into organizations over which the PAP exerted some influence.

Over 200 groups are registered every year, whereas typically only two or three a year have their applications denied. Recently, a martial arts club was denied registration because many of its would-be members had criminal records; another was a cult group; and a third was the gay and lesbian group, People Like Us. Occasionally, the bureaucrats are stricter than the leaders desire. A Disabled People's Association inexplicably received no clearance for two years until Goh Chok Tong heard about it and cleared the way for quick registration.[23]

The 1988 amendments tightened the Societies Act to state that any registered society which made political statements beyond the scope of its stated constituency would be de-registered. This transpired as a result of the politicization of the Law Society. Normally traditional and conservative and focused on its own affairs, the agenda of the Law Society changed with the election of Francis Seow as its President in 1986. In 1987, the Law Society issued a press release that criticized the proposed amendments to the Newspaper and Printing Presses Act.[24] The PAP believed that the "Law Society was attempting to assume the role of a pressure group, something that still could not be accommodated …"[25] (especially given that most of the effective opposition members are/were lawyers – David Marshall, J.B. Jeyaretnam, Chiam See Tong, Francis Seow, Tang Liang Hong).

As a consequence, at least partially, of the 1987 troubles with leftist Christianity, in 1990 the Parliament passed the Maintenance of Religious Harmony Act, which prohibits members of a religious group from any actions that cause ill will among different groups, and from activities disguised as religious that promote a political cause.[26] However, to date, the Societies Act has been used for most prohibitions against religious groups, since all religious groups must be legally registered.

Under the Societies Act, the government has deregistered and barred meetings of the Jehovah's Witnesses, the Unification Church, and the Divine Light Mission. The latter two were banned as religious cults. Jehovah's Witnesses was deregistered in 1972 on the grounds that it was prejudicial to public welfare and order (because members refused to do military service, salute the flag, or swear oaths of allegiance to the state). Its publications were also banned. There have been numerous arrests of members of Jehovah's Witnesses, not for their beliefs *per se*, but for refusing to do military service (32 in 1999); for being in possession of unlawful written materials (69 in 1995; 2 in 1998); and for holding a meeting of a banned society (1996).[27] The most recent violations involving a religious group occurred on December 31, 2000, when 15 Falungong practitioners were arrested for holding an illegal assembly meant to memorialize the Falungong believers who have died in China. Although Falungong is banned in China and Japan, it is legally registered in Singapore as the Falun Buddha Society (since 1999), and the government has on the whole taken a cautiously tolerant approach to the group. The leader of the Falun Buddha stated that the demonstration was not organized by the society, and the government responded that so long as the Falun Buddha Society conducts its activities according to the law, there is no reason to disallow it. An oblique warning was issued by Prime Minister Goh in a speech, however, when he said that "religious leaders have a heavy responsibility for actions of practitioners . . . It is better for religious leaders to restrain and admonish these few [over-zealous activists], than for the government to do so. However, if necessary, the government will take firm action against such extremists and fringe groups whose actions threaten Singapore's multi-religious harmony".[28]

The judiciary, defamation law and other judicial actions

Singapore's judicial system has been lauded for its efficiency, the mediating innovations of the lower courts, and fairness of its procedures. It has been criticized in other quarters for allegedly being politically compliant and insufficiently independent of the executive. There is no doubt that the status of the judiciary in Singapore is a particularly sensitive issue. The PAP leaders have always believed that arbitrary personal rulership is the bane of the Third World, and that the rule of law is vital for progress and development. The rule of law, that is, rule according to known laws rather than arbitrary dictates or discretionary authority, means that no one is punishable except for a breach of law established in the ordinary courts, and that no one is above the law. It also assumes that public officials are aware of and accept the legal limits on their power.[29] Public confidence in the rule of law is a key factor in legitimating the state. According to Kevin Tan, the Singapore state's notion of the rule of law is formalistic: everything should be done in accordance with the law. In that sense, he writes, quoting another scholar, "it is 'an idea of rule through law rather than rule of law' ".[30]

In any political system, the judiciary is, or should be, the arbiter. It is the institution relied upon to deliver equality before the law, fairness, and justice. In Singapore, Parliament passes the laws, but the judiciary may interpret the constitutionality of the laws passed (judicial review), except since 1989 for the

ISA and, implicitly, the CLA.[31] Beyond that, judges and justices must interpret the exact meaning of the written law. In the end, however, their verdicts are based on the law as set or altered by Parliament.

Singapore's judicial system has received some high international ratings. The World Bank has recommended Singapore's subordinate courts as a model for developing and developed countries to study.[32] The head of the English judiciary, Lord High Chancellor Irvine of Lairg, praised the Singapore courts for their efficiency, adding that English judges had much to learn from Singapore.[33] The World Competitiveness Report Yearbook from the International Institute of Management Development in Switzerland regularly ranks Singapore's legal framework first in the support it gives to Singapore's economic competitiveness. Likewise, in a 1998 study, Hong Kong-based Political and Economic Risk Consultancy Ltd. (PERC) rated Singapore's police and judiciary best in Asia, and ahead of the United States and Hong Kong. As related by Minister of Law S. Jayakumar in Parliament, "PERC commented: Surprisingly, for a country where the government is often accused by foreign human rights activists of using the judiciary to pursue politically-motivated libel suits, our American respondents living in Singapore even rated the island's judicial system as being superior to that of the United States".[34]

There is virtually no criticism of Singapore's judicial handling of commercial or business law, or civil law other than for the law of defamation cases involving political opponents (and for the death penalty and caning). A US State Department country report notes that the "Constitution provides for an independent judiciary, and the Government generally respects this provision ..." and the "judicial system provides citizens with an efficient judicial process".[35] Criticism of the judiciary generally falls into two areas: one is basically concerned with judicial appointments, and the other focuses on what critics allege is a compliant judiciary concerning the law of defamation.[36]

As a result of merger into Malaysia in 1963, juries were abolished except for capital offenses, and in 1969 the jury system was abolished altogether. Cases are heard by a single judge (since 1992), although in the Court of Appeal there are three judges. The Constitution provides for the appointment of short-term (1–2 years) judicial commissioners to handle court cases in the Supreme Court. Cases are allocated by the registrar of the Supreme Court. For those with aspirations towards judgeships, the term serves as a probationary period. All High Court and Court of Appeal judges have tenure.

The President appoints judges on the recommendation of the Prime Minister in consultation with the Chief Justice. It is a perception that many judicial officials have close ties to the PAP and its leaders.[37] To take one example, it is well known in Singapore that Chief Justice Yong Pung How, who in 2001 was reappointed by the President for another three-year term (and who is well respected for the way he has streamlined and managed the courts and for his exceptionally heavy caseload), was a university classmate of Lee Kuan Yew's at Cambridge. Although no improprieties have been suggested, these ties between the judiciary and the executive have provided grist for the mill for domestic and international critics.

The Law of Defamation

> Mr. Ong reiterates the government's position that suing for defamation is the way to distinguish false statements from true, and thus develop a form of politics where public statements by politicians are taken seriously ... My guess is that despite many years of PAP politicians winning and justifying lawsuits in open court, not all Singaporeans look at the situation in the terms that Mr. Ong has described.
>
> Cherian George[38]

Since the 1980s, the PAP government seems to have shifted away from employing the ISA against opposition politicians to using legal proceedings against them, particularly for libel.[39] The constitutional right to free speech in Singapore is limited by the exception of defamation law, including the use of innuendo.[40]

The most recent defamation cases involve Tang Liang Hong and J.B. Jeyaretnam. Tang, a Chinese-educated lawyer, became the target of a "wide-ranging legal offensive by the PAP" when he stood unsuccessfully for the opposition Workers' Party in the 1997 general election.[41] However, the PAP had been aware of Tang as early as 1992. They knew of his involvement in Chinese cultural affairs and language issues, and when Tang became a candidate to become a Nominated Member of Parliament (NMP), several MPs wrote to the Speaker of Parliament saying Tang was not a suitable candidate because of his extreme views on Chinese culture.[42] In August 1994, he gave a speech saying that too many English-educated people and too many Christians occupied top government posts, and he alleged that institutions like the Defence Ministry were controlled by Christians. In December 1996, he made a similar speech as one of the speakers at a Mandarin promotion event, and he asked why the Chinese-educated majority were the ones "carrying the sedan-chair?" Lim Jim Koon, editor of *Lianhe Zaobao* and one of the speakers on the same platform, said that the tone of Tang's speech chilled the atmosphere.[43] Tang's defamation troubles began in mid-1996 when he gave an interview to a Hong Kong magazine in which he alleged corruption by Lee Kuan Yew and Lee Hsien Loong in their purchases of discounted condominium units (see p. 151). They sued him for defamation.

During the campaign for the January 1997 general election, when Prime Minister Goh Chok Tong and the PAP accused Tang of being a Chinese chauvinist who was aiming "to stoke the old fires" among the older, Chinese-educated and dialect-speaking generation, Tang countered by calling Goh and the others liars.[44] This prompted a new round of defamation suits by eleven PAP leaders. The last day of the campaign, Tang filed two police reports in which he stated that the PAP allegations against him were baseless and intended to harm his reputation, and that their actions were likely to "incite religious extremists" to hate him and cause him and his family harm. When the police reports were made public, with J.B. Jeyaretnam's assistance, seven more defamation suits were filed.[45]

After Tang and his team were narrowly defeated in the Cheng San GRC (see p. 151), he left the country, began to move his assets out of Singapore and closed his law firm, all the while making additional defamatory statements to the international press. By this time it was clear that Tang did not intend to return to

Singapore. In May 1997, the High Court awarded S$8 million in damages to the 11 PAP plaintiffs, although in November the Court of Appeal reduced the damages to S$3.6 million. That wrapped up the "Tang affair", although it legally entangled Jeyaretnam in the process, caused some divided opinion domestically, and it hurt Singapore's image internationally.[46]

J.B. Jeyaretnam, former head of the Workers' Party and a tenacious veteran politician who was first elected in 1981, has a long history of legal run-ins with the government. In November 1986 he was convicted of making false declarations in bankruptcy proceedings against his party and he lost his parliamentary seat. In 1988, he lost a defamation case to Lee Kuan Yew and paid the damages. After the 1997 general election he became a Non-Constituency Member of Parliament (NCMP). He was also sued for libel. At the end of the final election rally on January 1, 1997, Jeyaretnam told the audience that Tang had "just placed before me two reports he has made to the police against, you know, Mr. Goh Chok Tong and his team".[47] When he mentioned the police reports he was sued for defamation by Goh Chok Tong and ten other PAP leaders. In their suits, they said that the words, by way of innuendo, implied and would be understood to mean that the plaintiffs were guilty of committing an act of serious enough proportions to merit a police report.[48]

In October 1997, the High Court awarded Goh S$20,000 in damages, one-tenth of what he had sought. The judge rejected Goh's claim that it gave the impression that he was guilty of committing the offences. But he ruled that Jeyaretnam was liable on the grounds of a lesser defamatory meaning. In July 1998, the Court of Appeal upped the damages owed to Goh to S$100,000 plus expenses, after interpreting the law and meaning differently from the one determined by the High Court.[49]

Meanwhile, in December 1998, a PAP Minister and 9 other members of the Tamil Organizing Committee for the first Tamil Language Week in 1995 won large defamation damages as a result of an article in Tamil that appeared in the Workers' Party magazine, *The Hammer*, which accused the organizers of being incompetent and "nakedly prostituting themselves" to seek political gain. The suit was filed against the author of the article, Jeyaretnam as editor, and the Workers' Party.[50]

In July 1999 Goh Chok Tong withdrew his petition to make Jeyaretnam a bankrupt, which would have resulted in his losing his parliamentary seat. However, in November 2000 a bankruptcy petition was lodged against Jeyaretnam by eight plaintiffs from the Tamil organizing committee who would not withdraw their petition, and Jeyaretnam was declared a bankrupt in February 2001. After exhausting appeals, in July 2001, Jeyaretnam was expelled from Parliament for being a bankrupt.

Jeyaretnam's defamation trial as a result of mentioning the police reports was criticized by the International Commission of Jurists (ICJ) and Amnesty International, who had sent observers to the trial. The ICJ report said, in charging the Singapore High Court with being compliant, that Jeyaretnam's words would not be considered slanderous elsewhere, "least of all in the context of a bitterly fought general election campaign".[51] Amnesty International was more blunt. It said that it "believes that civil defamation suits are being misused by the

Executive to intimidate and deter those Singaporeans holding dissenting views ... Whereas imprisonment of political opponents under the ISA has declined, the Executive's use of civil defamation suits to bankrupt opponents through the courts ... constitutes an emerging pattern".[52]

Other judicial actions

Two other opposition party members, one in the 1980s and one currently active, have crossed the law in other ways: Francis Seow and Chee Soon Juan (the latter has also lost two defamation suits). Francis Seow, former Solicitor General (1967–69) and President of the Law Society, is allegedly a man with a history of questionable behavior.[53] He was arrested under the ISA in May 1988 for allegedly accepting funds from an American diplomat who was encouraging him to lead a group of lawyers in opposition to the government.[54] The diplomat was expelled for interfering in Singapore's parliamentary election process. Seow was released early so that he could contest the 1988 general election for the Workers' Party, since a perception was growing among Singaporeans that he had been detained to keep him from contesting. The Workers' Party team lost Eunos GRC, but Seow was named as one of two NCMPs since his team had the highest vote totals among losing candidates. He was a targeted man by then, and after a rigorous tax audit he was charged with tax evasion. Seow left the country for a medical check up before his trial and has not returned. He was tried *in absentia* in December 1988 and convicted. Because of the fine imposed, he was automatically disqualified from being an MP.

Dr. Chee Soon Juan, head of the Singapore Democratic Party and former academic, has had different legal problems, some of which he has courted through a civil disobedience campaign. As mentioned above, Chee has lost two defamation suits, and he had been cited three times, twice for speaking in public without a permit and once for hawking his book on the street (since not all book stores would carry it). Chee lost some credibility in 1996 when he got some facts wrong after the government gave him the opportunity to state his case on health care at select committee hearings. In the 1997 general election, Chee and his SDP were rather soundly defeated, and after that Chee spent 18 months in Australia writing a book.[55] Upon his return to Singapore, he gave two public speeches in the busy financial district without a permit. He was arrested after each speech and found guilty of breaching the Public Entertainments Act, and fined. In both cases he refused to pay his fine and subsequently was jailed for seven days and twelve days, respectively.[56] Singapore, however, seems not very enamored of martyrs. Chee's actions received a mixed reaction, or, as a Reuters reporter noted, some sympathy but little support.[57] In the November 2001 election, Chee and his team received a paltry 20 percent of the vote in Jurong (see p. 239, n. 77). Chee, who heckled the Prime Minister during the campaign, has subsequently been sued for defamation by the Prime Minister and the Senior Minister, and he is counter-suing the Senior Minister.[58]

Control of the media

The government, through government-linked companies (GLCs) and private holding companies with close ties to the government, has a near monopoly of the media. Singapore Press Holdings Ltd. (SPH) owns all but one of the local dailies and tabloids, in all the four official languages. The other is a free tabloid new in 2000, distributed to train and bus commuters, which is owned by the broadcasting group MediaCorp, a joint venture of four GLCs. Although MediaCorp has gone into publishing, and three new tabloids hit the streets in 2000 (the other two published by SPH[59]), the public perception is that MediaCorp and SPH will not be competitive and will not widen the editorial spectrum. The Radio Corporation of Singapore owns and operates twelve domestic and three international radio stations. Four of the five independent stations are owned by organizations close to the government.[60] The remaining station is the 24 hour-a-day BBC World Service. Some Malaysian and Indonesian programming can be received, as can the Voice of America, Radio Japan, Radio Moscow, and Radio Beijing. The SPH was given two radio channels and two television channels as part of its deal with MediaCorp. The Television Corporation of Singapore (TCS) owns and manages four channels, while Singapore Television Twelve Pte. Ltd, owns a Malay channel and a Tamil and arts channel. Singapore Cable Vision operates an exclusive subscription television service, offering more than 35 channels. Satellite dishes are banned. The Singapore Broadcasting Authority was set up in October 1994 as a statutory board to regulate the broadcasting industry.[61]

The government perceives the proper role of the mass media in Singapore as being one that informs and educates the public about, and encourages support for, government policies, programs, positions and ideas, and helps inculcate the values and beliefs being promoted by the state. Beyond this, its functions are to inform generally and to entertain. The government does not allow media that assume an adversarial "watchdog" position. In this sense, at least as concerns domestic news, it is a system that communicates messages and symbols to the public and serves the purposes of the dominant elite.[62] To control the undesirable aspects of the media and encourage a supportive outlook, there is an arsenal of legal measures the government can employ. As mentioned in Parliament by NMP Zulkifli bin Baharudin, these include the Sedition Act; the Undesirable Publications Act, which can ban publications contrary to the public interest, and the Newspaper and Printing Presses Act, which can restrict the circulation of any publication sold in Singapore.[63] Additionally, printing presses have to be licensed and permits are required for newspapers and magazines, etc.; these licenses and permits require regular renewals and accordingly encourage self-censorship.

The press

The 1970s–1980s were turbulent times for the press in Singapore as the government gradually extended its control over it. A number of newspapers have gone: *Nanyang Siang Pau, Sin Chew Jit Poh, Eastern Sun, Singapore Herald, Singapore Monitor,* and *New Nation.* In 1977, an amendment to the Newspaper and Printing Presses Act effectively killed off the control of newspapers by individuals and families. In 1981, after the PAP lost the Anson by-election (see p. 149) and Lee Kuan Yew blamed inaccurate news reports (about a hike in bus fares) for the narrow loss, there was a reorganization of the press and merger of two publishing houses into the Singapore Press Holdings. After this, at least as concerns the local press, calm prevailed.[64]

The Singapore press is generally viewed locally as being competent and trustworthy, except when it is perceived as compliantly adopting the government's perspective. NMP Zulkifli says that "While the press in Singapore is generally credited [with being] a reliable and accurate source of information, it suffers, quite unfairly, some credibility problems when it comes to coverage of local domestic issues".[65] An academic who studies the media and elections, writes that "Singaporeans appear to have little problem with the accuracy of the newspapers' reporting of events. But, in the case of election coverage, the provision of a 'definite perspective' apparently does create a credibility problem".[66] And a foreign journalist writes, "Singapore's English-language press is the most informative in Southeast Asia. None of the papers in neighboring countries compares with the *Straits Times* or *Business Times* for the breadth and incisiveness of their coverage". However, he continues, when it comes to coverage of local politics, it is criticized for being "slavishly" pro-government.[67] Even more apparent is the short shrift that the speeches of the Opposition in Parliament are given.

The government insists it does not control the editorial policy of newspapers, but that it will censure them if they print editorials that are inappropriate and not in the national interest; for example, a *Business Times* editorial (June 18, 1999) critical of Malaysian Prime Minister Mahathir that drew a reaction from Malaysia. The government responded with what has become known as an "Out of Bounds" marker (discussed below), whereby the Press Secretary to the Prime Minister sent a letter to the press that the *BT* editorial was "rash, unwise and inappropriate" and also "contrary" to the Singapore government's view. However, no penalties were imposed on the *BT*, nor was its license reviewed.[68] In fact, however, the English-language press, while not crusading or adversarial, does often present a diversity of views, covers the activities of opposition politicians considered newsworthy (e.g., Chee's civil disobedience speeches), and at times some of its columnists push the boundaries in defense of "fair comment".

Film – political videos

Since independence, motion pictures in Singapore have always been subject to censorship on the grounds of public morality. This has been generally supported by the public, and in fact the government had to back-track in the early 1990s when some older Chinese-educated constituents objected that liberalization was proceeding too quickly.

In 1998 the Films Act was amended to take account of new technology, and some of the changes have distinct political ramifications. As a result of the Singapore Democratic Party's efforts to make promotional videos for distribution in 1996, an amendment was passed banning political advertising using films, videos, CD-ROMs, computer files with moving images, etc.

Several of the NMPs and two opposition MPs spoke in Parliament against the amendment banning political videos and political commercials, basically complaining that the bill was too sweeping and vague, and specifically, that it seemed unnecessary to further handicap the Opposition.[69] Zulkifli noted that the bill "would deny opposition parties one way to reach out to citizens and inform them about their political platforms ... To deny them ... the small opportunity, is unnecessary".[70]

However, the government's position is that the ban protects politics from sensationalism and inaccuracy; that modern technology allows camera tricks and digital manipulation of figures and pictures, *à la* the Hollywood movie, *Forrest Gump*. Likewise, the government regards the visual media as having a greater mass impact than other media forms, and it worries about "sound bite" campaigning and political commercials – the Willie Horton ad used devastatingly against Michael Dukakis in the US presidential campaign being a prime example mentioned in Parliament of where sensationalism overshadowed the contest of ideas.[71] However sensible prohibiting political commercials on television might be, the effect of banning political party videos serves to undercut the Opposition and, in the words of the US Department of State's 1999 Human Rights Report, "to further restrict an already limited range of what was deemed acceptable political discourse".

Political cartooning

Political cartoons can provide satire and political criticism in a pictorial medium that is easily accessible to the public. Cartoons are a way of pointing out, as Lim Cheng Tju notes in an interesting article, that the Emperor has no clothes.[72] For these reasons, just as the PAP leaders do not think politics is "funny", or trivial, and certainly not a game (although they often employ sports analogies), they also do not think that ridiculing and caricaturing leaders is an acceptable practice.

Political cartoons were featured regularly under British rule, and continued to be published in the *Straits Times* after the PAP came to power. However, they disappeared by August 1961 after Lee Kuan Yew blamed the press for its part in two by-election losses earlier that year. They reappeared in 1979 as social commentary, but political content was very indirect. Political leaders were not featured or caricatured until *Hello Chok Tong, Goodbye Kuan Yew* in 1991, which received an unenthusiastic government response. Since then, and especially after the Catherine Lim affair in 1994 (see p. 141), cartoons have not aroused any controversy.[73]

Efforts to keep the foreign media at bay

Singaporeans have access to over 5,500 foreign publications that are available at book stores and newspaper stands. However, under the 1986 amendment to the Newspaper and Printing Presses Act (NPPA), the government may limit the circulation of foreign publications that it determines interfere in domestic politics. Further, since 1990, foreign newspapers with sales of over 300 copies in Singapore are required to apply for permits annually. Beyond that, the government has also taken defamation action against several publications. Likewise, under a 2001 amendment to the 1994 Singapore Broadcasting Authority Act, the same rules and standards which apply to the foreign print media stations also apply to foreign television station broadcasters in Singapore as regards disallowing them from "engaging in Singapore's domestic politics".[74]

The government has "gazetted", or limited the circulation of several foreign publications, including the *Asian Wall Street Journal* (1987), *Asiaweek* (1987/88), *Far Eastern Economic Review* (1987) and *The Economist* (1993). The *Far Eastern Economic Review* is now allowed 8,000 copies per issue, whereas before it was gazetted, it sold 10,000 copies an issue.[75]

Of the defamation suits, the one which caused the most sensation was in 1994–5 against the *International Herald Tribune* and Christopher Lingle, an American teaching at the National University of Singapore. In an article published on October 7, 1994, writing about authoritarianism in Southeast Asia, Lingle mentioned the tactic of using a "compliant judiciary" in an unnamed country to "bankrupt opposition politicians" through defamation suits.[76] In the trial, as Donald Emmerson points out, the "Attorney General was placed in the odd position of trying to prove that the American could *only* have had Singapore in mind". Emmerson concludes that the government appeared more eager to punish Lingle, presumably to deter future criticism, than to show that Singaporean judges were in fact completely independent.[77] Both the *IHT* and Lingle were found guilty and given stiff fines. The *IHT* apologized and paid the fine and was not gazetted. Lingle had by then left Singapore.

Living with the Internet

Singapore has a home computer ownership and Internet participation rate ahead of the US and most other countries. It also has a comprehensive Information Technology (IT) plan and has ambitions to become a new economy "information hub, trading in ideas rather than commodities".[78] The catch is, it still wants to exert whatever control possible over the political usage of the Internet, but is hindered by two facts. First, constraints on information have economic consequences. Second, trying to block new Internet sites is onerous, and likely will not stop those who are "cyber-savvy" anyway.[79] Rodan notes that the prevailing view seems to be that the "controllers have met their match".[80]

Singapore uses local Internet Service Providers and proxy servers through which local users must route their Internet connections, which provides some control. However, those with the know-how can just bypass the local ISPs and hook up with offshore operators.[81] Singapore blocks only about 100 of the worst pornographic Internet sites.[82] Since 1996, with regulations reminiscent of the Societies Act, political and religious web sites, among others, need to be registered and licensed as "content providers" with the Singapore Broadcasting Authority (SBA). The opposition parties have complained about this, but in fact do not make much use of websites anyway.

In August 2001, a law was passed governing election activity on the Internet during election campaigns. The law bans non-political party websites from campaigning and bars party websites from conducting election surveys or polls or appealing for funds.[83] In October 2001, the Parliamentary Election Act was extended to include email and SMS (Short Message Service) digital phone messages.[84] Although the Opposition complained, what was in fact allowed perhaps went beyond their expectations.[85]

The SBA has stated that it does not regulate private communications (chat rooms and email) and it does not monitor individual access to Web pages. However, it has been reported that government monitoring of Internet use became widely known in 1996 when Singapore assisted Interpol in tracking down a citizen who was downloading child pornography.[86] Further, in 1999, at the request of Singnet (a proxy server), the Ministry of Home Affairs (MHA) probed the computers of 200,000 Singnet customers to determine whether they had been infected with a computer virus. When the word got out, this aroused considerable public anger and dismay, and the MHA stated it would reject requests for such scans in the future.[87]

The perception in Singapore among the cyber-savvy is that the government understands that "individual governments are virtually impotent against the Internet", and therefore believe that the economic advantages of a "regulatory light-touch" should not be jeopardized in a losing cause.[88]

Out of bounds (OB) markers

To make Singapore a more attractive place to live, the government realizes that it needs to loosen the reins on political participation. Accordingly, the PAP government has decided to try to define the limits of what is acceptable politically in terms of dissent, by initiating what are called out of bounds markers (OB markers). The government maintains that those who do not openly join and support a political party should not be able to carp about political issues. But they realize that many educated Singaporeans who do not want to be involved in party politics still want to be able as citizens and taxpayers to voice their views and criticisms. Instead of the sledgehammer which is sometimes employed against members of the Opposition, as discussed above, the OB markers are simply public rebuttals in the form of letters to the press by the Press Secretary to the Prime Minister that state the government's positions and note the shortcomings of the points of view expressed by the transgressors. None of the handful of OB markers issued has led to any other actions against the offenders, but in a society where the importance of "face" makes people sensitive to public rebukes, they have had some of the desired effect. One journalist notes, "In recent years, Prime Minister Goh's government has mastered the use of the well-calibrated slap on the wrist to great effect"[89] (see pp. 166–7 for civil society's perceptions and concerns about OB markers).

OB markers began in 1994 when author Catherine Lim wrote two articles in the *Straits Times* that said there was a "great affective divide" between the PAP and the people, and that there were hard-liner and more liberal factions within the PAP, and insinuated that Prime Minister Goh was not really in charge. The Prime Minister's Press Secretary replied with a stinging rebuttal. In 1997, in a slightly different case, the Roundtable (see p. 162) published an analysis of the 1997 general election in the *Straits Times*, in which it disagreed with the PAP tactic of tying HDB upgrading priority to votes (see p. 151). The government had a minister respond and point out where the PAP thought the analysis was wrong. B.G. Lee notes, "some of them took it amiss, but they pressed on . . . They are still there. We take them seriously and that's a compliment to them".[90] OB markers were issued again in September 1999 against journalist Cherian George and historian Melanie Chew. Interestingly, George fired back a reply to the Forum in answer to the Press Secretary's rebuttal.[91] The Roundtable's published letter on the 2001 elections elicited another letter from the Press Secretary, which was more in the style of setting the record straight rather than rebuking the writers.[92]

The OB markers represent a trial-and-error approach that allows for more political commentary and gradually increasing openness, and the approach is certainly less severe than using some of the tough laws that are on the books. Still, it is criticized on the grounds that the boundaries are vague and judgmental, and that the idea itself is patronizing. The whole process of gradually loosening up some of the political boundaries is seen by the government as being fraught with dangers. It has to guard against those who see it as a signal that the PAP is softening and susceptible to pressure. Therefore, although the trend is to reduce the authoritarian aspects of PAP rule, periodic backtracking is not out of the question.

11 Elections, electoral innovations, and the Opposition

Elections contribute to the legitimacy of a government and the political system, so long as they are perceived to be conducted freely and honestly. Elections allow the citizenry to participate in the selection of their leaders, and in the process they further the political education of citizens and enhance acceptance of the institutions and principles guiding the state. They also reinforce the notion of government accountability and provide feedback for those in charge.[1]

Singapore's early elections (see Chapter 2) were quite competitive, and held against a backdrop of street agitation, riots and strikes, and social unrest. Since the late 1960s, when the PAP emerged as a dominant party (see p. 38), elections have been peaceful and orderly, but less competitive.[2]

Singapore holds parliamentary elections regularly within the five-year legal term limit for what is now 84 single- and multiple-member constituencies, and, since 1993, holds a national election for President every six years. There are no local elections at present. Singapore has a first-past-the-post, or majoritarian, electoral system (the candidate or team with the most votes in each constituency wins), as opposed to proportional representation or mixed systems.[3] This widely used system gives the strongest party a larger representation than its percentage of votes, and weaker parties conversely a smaller representation than their total votes would seem to warrant, thus discouraging the participation of small parties and a fragmentation of representation. There are provisions for by-elections to fill vacancies in Singapore, but the government is not required to fill them, and often does not.[4] Registration for voting is automatic, and voting is compulsory – an average of 95 percent of eligible voters typically cast ballots.[5] A Parliamentary Elections (Amendment) Bill passed early in 2001 to enable Singaporeans living abroad to vote was temporarily suspended by Parliament in October 2001 because of security concerns at overseas missions.[6] There is no ballot rigging, intimidation of voters, inaccurate counting of ballots, or manipulation of the electoral rolls to produce so-called "phantom" voters or multiple voters in Singapore. The US State Department regularly reports that "the voting and vote-counting systems are fair, accurate and free from tampering", while noting as well the "formidable obstacles" facing the Opposition (see below).[7] Similarly, Michael Haas, a critic of the PAP, writes that "... there is no doubt that substantive, majoritarian democracy exists at the polls", and that "the voters of Singapore baffle many observers by supporting the PAP at each election with huge majorities".[8]

Electoral innovations

Governing parties in a parliamentary system benefit not only from being able to influence electoral boundaries and select the timing of an election, but also from being able to enact electoral reforms and innovations, which may or may not be "voter neutral".[9] After a by-election shock in 1981, a confidential government study of voter opinion in 1982, and a significant electoral setback in 1984 (see below), the PAP government began making selective changes to the system to provide a cushion against sudden voting fluctuations, to help compensate for the absence of a politically stable and conservative rural electorate.[10] These innovations include: providing more non-PAP voices in Parliament with Non-Constituency Members of Parliament (NCMPs) and Nominated Members of Parliament (NMPs); creating some multiple-member Group Representation Constituencies (GRCs); linking MPs to decentralization moves; and, discussed later, creating an elected President with some blocking powers.

NCMPs

Sensing a desire on the part of many Singaporeans for more opposition in Parliament, the PAP devised two schemes for *adding* some non-PAP voices to Parliament while simultaneously weakening the sentiment for *electing* more opposition members. In 1984, Parliament passed an act allowing for the appointment of up to three NCMPs, to bring the Opposition in Parliament to a minimum of three, allocated to those unsuccessful opposition candidates with the highest percentage of votes. A NCMP was empowered to speak and take part in parliamentary debates, and vote except on no-confidence motions, constitutional amendments, and supply and money bills. In 1984, two opposition candidates were elected, and one NCMP seat was offered to a Workers' Party candidate but rejected as a "second-class seat" and "toothless alternative" to real opposition. In 1988, one of the two NCMP seats offered was accepted (by Dr. Lee Siew Choh). By 1997 the Workers' Party had changed its mind, and its leader, J.B. Jeyaretnam, accepted the seat. By raising awkward and sometimes sensitive issues in Parliament, Dr. Lee and Jeyaretnam did marginally provide more opposition voice to Parliament.

NMPs

The NMPs have turned out to be a much more successful and interesting innovation that has raised the intellectual level of debate in Parliament. The NMP scheme, beginning with two non-partisan nominated members, was passed in Parliament in 1990, although each new Parliament must decide whether or not it wants to have NMPs.[11] They have restricted voting rights but can speak on any bill or motion. The scheme has now been expanded to nine NMPs, which speaks to the success of the idea.[12] NMPs are nominated by the public and, increasingly, by functional groups such as business and industry, the professions, and the labor movement, and then selected by a Parliamentary Special Select Committee.[13] As such, they provide informed opinion on certain topics. According to Prime Minister Goh, the NMPs are intended to satisfy a desire for alternative views, to give non-partisan Singaporeans more opportunities for political participation, and to increase the number of MPs from under-represented groups, such as women.[14]

Overall, the NMPs have outperformed the Opposition and many PAP backbenchers as well, although they must "walk a delicate tightrope when they differ from the government's position".[15]

While the government and most Singaporeans appear to be positive about the NMPs, the scheme has its critics. Not surprisingly, the Opposition is adamantly opposed, finds it demeaning, thinks it ironic that there are more NMPs in Parliament than opposition MPs, and sees it as a plot to undermine the legitimate Opposition.[16] Also, some PAP backbenchers object to the NMPs, either in principle or because the NMPs have outshone them. One backbencher said in Parliament, "To me, this entry of non-elected members is very hard to swallow and, worse still, taking advice from people who have not fought for elections or worked the ground ... ".[17] Finally, according to one journalist, Parliament is "still not very interesting to Singaporeans because there is 'not much blood' ".[18]

GRCs and linking MPs to Town Councils

Following the 1984 election setback, Cabinet considered ideas for altering the political system. They rejected the idea of reserved minority constituencies, an ethnically-based PR system, and nomination of supplementary Malays if their elected numbers were insufficient. In the end, Cabinet accepted a modified version of Lee Kuan Yew's earlier idea of "twinning" constituencies.[19] In May 1988, Parliament passed a bill creating 13 multiple-member constituencies called Group Representation Constituencies (GRCs), for the express purpose of ensuring minority representation in Parliament.[20] Originally the scheme created 13 GRCs with three members each (for a total of 39 seats), while 42-single members constituencies were retained. This meant that each party contesting a GRC was required to put up a three-person team which included a designated minority (Malay, Indian, or Eurasian).[21] In each GRC, a party's team of candidates would be elected en bloc by a plurality.

In November 1996, the Parliamentary Elections Act was amended to allow larger GRCs.[22] Now Parliament has expanded to 84 seats, divided into 14 GRCs (a mixture of 6- and 5-member constituencies) and 9 single-seat wards.

The Opposition disliked the GRC concept, claiming it really aimed at "fixing" the Opposition by forcing them to win a group of constituencies at once to get any members elected, hence, in effect raising the threshold of votes needed by the Opposition.[23] It is clear that it is easier for the PAP than for the Opposition to find competent teams and suitable minority candidates. The new arrangement has also, in effect, eliminated ethnic party competition. In 1997, the Malay party, Pertubohan Kebangsaan Melayu Singapura (PKMS), decided not to participate in a general election for the first time in two decades.[24] Likewise, the GRCs discourage the formation of new parties. Further, the large size of the GRCs tends to eliminate ethnic concentrations and socioeconomic blocs which the Opposition might otherwise choose to target. Finally, the GRCs dilute the force of personality, which tends to have a more serious effect on the Opposition.

Another innovation, passed in June 1988 and linked to the GRC scheme, was the establishment of town councillors to manage the government housing (HDB) estates where most Singaporeans live (see pp. 90–5). As a move towards decentralization, the Opposition could not object. However, the sting was in the tail: the scheme would force citizens to be directly responsible for their electoral choices. MPs would become the town councillors, and since the councillors would be making decisions directly affecting the lives of the HDB constituents and managing multi-million dollar budgets, voters would have to consider carefully their choice of MPs. If they wanted to vote against the PAP come-what-may, they would have to be willing to accept the consequences if their choice performed poorly.[25]

Since 1997, two of the Town Councils have been run by opposition MPs. By 1999, opposition MP Chiam See Tong was showing his frustration about being thwarted by (among other things) the HDB, which refused to give its consent for any alterations to buildings or grounds, including "even a single nail". Chiam concluded, "Basically, as I see it, the Town Councils are nothing more than agents of the HDB. We are [the] cleaning and property managing agents".[26]

Altering one-person, one-vote?

In 1994, Lee Kuan Yew suggested that married Singaporeans between the ages of 35 and 60, and with children, should have two votes each, in order to give more weight to the votes of people with the greatest stake in the country. The public was not receptive to the idea, calling it unfair and undemocratic, and the idea slipped from public view, until it was revived briefly in February 2000 by B.G. George Yeo.[27] Singaporeans have learned that PAP trial balloons often foreshadow action at some later date. However, in mid-2000 Lee Kuan Yew said that altering the one-person, one-vote concept was not being discussed for the time being because it was not necessary demographically. He then added, "But what happens when the number of old people escalates?"[28]

The Opposition and the constraints upon it

Opposition political parties are legal in Singapore, except for the banned Malayan Communist Party, and out of just over 20 registered parties, four or five typically compete against the PAP at general elections. Surveys show that Singaporeans believe that having an Opposition in Parliament is necessary and desirable. Many of these same Singaporeans also believe that the PAP is providing strong and effective government.[29]

In dominant party systems such as Singapore, the Opposition has little hope of coming to power in the short term. The parties tend to be "parties of personality", centered around a strong leader. They also tend to be "parties of pressure", sometimes compelling the dominant party to adjust its policies and practices in order to protect its dominance. They perform a necessary task of articulating grievances. The Opposition in Singapore on the whole is poorly organized and under-financed, not very active between elections, and thin on substantive policy proposals. The parties tend to concentrate on negative features of PAP rule, supplemented by calls for more democracy and more political rights. They do not have access to para-political grassroots organizations, cannot attract many qualified candidates, and some have been wracked by internal dissension.[30] "None reflects an ability to formulate ideological alternatives to the PAP".[31] What's more, "citizens appear to offer little support for the Opposition or sympathy for its travails".[32]

There is no doubt that political opponents face formidable obstacles in challenging the governing PAP. The PAP does not view politics as a game; on the contrary it looks upon it more like war, and it can be ruthless in an election.[33] It does not mind being accused of using a "sledgehammer to kill a gnat"; it wants to remind the people of the consequences of taking on the PAP.[34]

In addition to a variety of legal barriers, lack of sympathetic media, and the threat of defamation suits (see pp. 134–6), as well as the impact of the electoral system (see above) and frequent changes of electoral laws and late announcements of constituency boundary changes, there are some additional constraints as well. Perhaps the most burdensome for the Opposition is the perception of citizens that having "more democracy" might come at the expense of having "more economic goods".[35] Likewise, as one analyst notes, "Singaporeans who want opposition voices in Parliament usually want the Opposition to represent someone else's constituency".[36]

Another major problem is fund-raising. The parties cannot put leaflets into letter boxes soliciting funds, or obtain licenses for house-to-house and street collection (restricted to charities).[37] It has become even more difficult to raise funds since the passage of the Political Donations Act in February 2001. The Act makes it illegal for political parties and associations, and parliamentary and presidential candidates, to receive foreign donations. Further, the Act put a limit of S$5,000 in any one year on anonymous political donations. It also requires that any single donation of S$10,000 or more must be declared and the donor identified. Finally, under the Act, every candidate must send in a donation report and declaration to the Registrar of Political Donations when an election is called, and be issued a political donations certificate before polling day.[38] While the Opposition supported the ban on foreign donations, they felt that the caps on anonymous donations would "hit the Opposition hard" and were aimed at crippling the financial strength of the Opposition.[39]

Active opposition parties

The opposition parties which competed in the 1997 and 2001 general elections are all to the political "left" of the PAP, while the PAP occupies the large center-right. There is no right-wing opposition. The Workers' Party (WP) is the oldest opposition party, reaching back to 1957. The WP lapsed into inactivity in the mid-1960s until it was revived in 1971 by J.B. Jeyaretnam, a lawyer and the party's secretary-general until May 2001, when he was succeeded by MP Low Thia Khiang.[40] It is a social-democratic party appealing to blue-collar workers and of all the opposition parties, it has the most "conscious ideological position".[41] It campaigns for more welfare and other benefits for low-income workers, and also for greater freedom of speech and more civil and political rights. The party has attracted some lawyers who were anathema to the PAP, including two in self-imposed exile after incurring legal problems: Francis Seow and Tang Liang Hong (see pp. 134, 136).

The Singapore Democratic Party (SDP) was founded in 1980 by Chiam See Tong, with the goal of serving as a "check on the government". Under Chiam, the SDP was moderate and centrist, appealing mainly to the middle classes. However, in mid-1993 Chiam was ousted in a messy internal party coup by current secretary-general Dr. Chee Soon Juan. When Chiam left, the SDP lost its "nice guy" image.[42] The party moved to the left and became more aggressive on national policy issues, such as health care and the cost of living, although less active at the grassroots level. The party also pushed for more transparency and accountability, greater civil and political rights, and specifically for an independent elections commission. Chee, the author of several books, was described as the "fastest rising opposition star" in 1996, and he confidently predicted that his party would win ten seats in the 1997 general election.[43] However, as *Asiaweek* noted, "Chee is not as astute a politician as Chiam",[44] and the SDP lost all the seats it contested, including those of two incumbents, while Chee himself was beaten decisively.[45]

Chee and Jeyaretnam jointly initiated an Open Singapore Centre, registered originally as a company, but declared by the government to be a political association in March 2001, for the promotion of transparency and democracy in Singapore. It has had trouble raising funds and has been inactive other than holding a few small events.[46]

The Singapore People's Party (SPP) was formed in 1994 by Sim Kek Tong as a vehicle for Chiam See Tong, its current leader, when he finally resigned from the SDP (he fought successfully against being expelled, or he would have lost his parliamentary seat). It is a moderate, centrist party much like the SDP had been, with a goal of providing a check on government without being obstructionist. In fact, the SPP is really a one-person party.

Another party is the National Solidarity Party (NSP), founded in 1987, with relatively unknown Steve Chia as its secretary-general. The NSP appeals to the middle classes, is concerned with the rising cost of living and issues such as freedom of speech. In 1997 it tried to counter voter dissatisfaction with the caliber and tone of the Opposition by fielding politically moderate and well-educated candidates. It put together a highly qualified team for the Hong Kah GRC, including two medical doctors, but still won only 31 percent of the votes.

In July 2001, the Singapore Democratic Alliance (SDA), comprising the SPP, NSP, the Pertubohan Kebangsaan Melayu Singapura (PKMS), and Singapore Justice Party, was registered as an electoral vehicle with Chiam See Tong as its chairman.[47]

The Opposition MPs

Despite all the obstacles, some opposition candidates *do* win – four in 1991 and two incumbents in 1997 and again in 2001. The two MPs, Chiam See Tong (now SDA) and Low Thia Khiang (WP) are quite different superficially. English-educated Chiam, a lawyer, first won middle class Potong Pasir in 1984. Low, educated at Nanyang University, fluent in Mandarin and Teochew (as well as English), and a small businessman, won the largely Teochew-speaking working class ward of Hougang in 1991.[48] Yet both are similar in that they are political pragmatists who do good constituency work, and both have been occasionally publicly praised by PAP ministers as being worth listening to. They have kept their seats in spite of the fact that their constituents will be last in line for upgrading their HDB flats, despite not having MRT stations or some other services and facilities in their wards, and despite some frustrating obstructions by the HDB or PAP-controlled CCCs.[49] The government cannot choke off all services to Hougang since it is a "busy town surrounded by PAP wards." However, Chiam's Potong Pasir is more self-contained and therefore more vulnerable.[50] Both MPs continue to survive politically, but neither can build his respective party or expand the Opposition by simply doing good constituency work.

Elections in Singapore

The PAP participated in competitive multi-party elections in 1955, 1959, and 1963. It came to power in 1959 with the help of the pro-Communists, and it narrowly survived a party split over the Malaysia issue by defeating the Barisan Sosialis to retain power in 1963 (see Chapter 2). However, by the 1968 general election, with the Barisan Sosialis scorning elections in favor of a "back to the streets" strategy[51] (see p. 24), the PAP emerged as a dominant party, winning every seat.[52] It repeated this feat in the next three general elections, in 1972, 1976, and 1980, gaining between 69 percent and 77 percent of the popular vote against a handful of opposition parties. Elections since then have been more interesting.

The return of the Opposition was signaled at a by-election in Anson in 1981, a largely Chinese working-class constituency that had been troublesome for the PAP in the early 1960s. In the first electoral campaign directed by Goh Chok Tong and the successor generation, an over-confident PAP was defeated by the head of the Workers' Party, J.B. Jeyaretnam. The PAP considered this loss a fluke – the Port of Singapore Authority had recently confiscated the homes of many of the port workers in the ward and had not provided alternative accommodation, so many voters were angry with the government.[53] Nonetheless, the win re-energized the Opposition by showing that the PAP was not invincible, and it ignited public interest in the idea of having an opposition.

The 1984 general election was a major watershed. It showed that Anson was not a fluke, and confirmed the return of the Opposition.[54] The election was held in the midst of extensive and difficult preparation for political transition, and on the heels of some particularly unpopular policies. The PAP won 77 of 79 seats (30 of them returned unopposed) against eight opposition parties. It lost to Jeyaretnam in Anson again and to Chiam See Tong in Potong Pasir. Seven other PAP candidates won by very slim margins. The party was stunned that a minister was nearly defeated by a candidate described by an analyst as "poorly educated ... with questionable attributes".[55] However, what really shocked the PAP was its nearly 13 percent decline in its share of the popular vote (to 62.9 percent).

There were three reasons for the decline: party renewal, unpopular policies, and a younger electorate less beholden to the PAP. Preparing for the succession to a new guard meant necessarily that the old guard needed to step down. However, many of the old guard resented the pace of renewal, and the process turned out to be divisive, with old guard, led by founder member Toh Chin Chye, pitted at times against the second generation. Further, because many of the forcibly-retired old guard were the most experienced and effective election campaigners, party renewal had a devastating effect on the party machinery.[56]

Also, because Lee Kuan Yew wanted to get some politically difficult policies in place before he stepped aside, the PAP deviated from its norm of not introducing controversial policies in an election year. The Graduate Mother Scheme (see p. 60) was one of four unpopular policies promulgated, un-pragmatically, before the election, and the one that Lee Kuan Yew later pinpointed as responsible for the PAP's decline in the popular vote.[57] Interestingly, after the election, Goh Chok Tong reportedly stated that none of the controversial policies had been promoted by the second generation leaders.[58]

The third element negatively affecting the PAP was the changing profile of the electorate – now better educated and with different expectations. The PAP did not connect with a lot of the young voters in the mid-1980s. As S. Dhanabalan, then a minister, complained at the time, "We just can't always be telling them to compare the situation to that of the '50s and ask them to be grateful".[59]

Despite instituting some electoral adjustments and constitutional innovations to provide "ballast" to the system, which some analysts at the time predicted would make future elections less competitive, the PAP was challenged in the 1988 general election in 70 of the 81 seats by seven opposition parties and four independents. The results were mixed. The PAP won 80 of 81 seats, losing only to incumbent Chiam See Tong, although, to its alarm, the PAP did not reverse the decline in its popular vote suffered in 1984, and in fact dropped another 1.1 percent (to 61.8 percent). The additional decline was attributed to a significant loss of Malay votes. Anger over lower incomes, mixed with some ethnic grievances and a feeling that the PAP was appeasing the Chinese at the expense of multiracialism, accounted for the desertion of many Malays from the PAP.[60] The Opposition was excited, "sensing a permanent shift of voter allegiance that put it on the brink of a significant breakthrough against PAP dominance".[61]

In August 1991, less than a year after Goh Chok Tong assumed the premiership, an early election was called so that Goh could seek a "solid endorsement" of his consultative leadership style and more open governance. The PAP won a majority of 41 of 81 seats uncontested, largely as a result of a successfully coordinated opposition "by-election" strategy of contesting fewer than half the seats so that the voters could support the opposition "risk-free" in the contested seats. Five opposition parties and seven independents contested.

The PAP won 77 of the 81 seats, losing middle-class Potong Pasir again and three Chinese working-class constituencies. The PAP won 61 percent of the popular vote (down 0.8 percent from the 1988 general election). Although the rate of decline was decreasing, the decline had now persisted through three general elections, and it was approaching the threshold where even in first-past-the-post electoral systems the Opposition begins to see its accumulation of votes translate into more seats won. Some analysts wondered if the PAP's long tenure as a dominant party was drawing to a close.[62]

The PAP had expected to reverse the trend in this election and the word was that the "ground was sweet" (other than the cost of living and the fact that Jeyaretnam was still barred from contesting, there did not seem to be many difficult issues). Consequently, the party was shocked by the results and Goh Chok Tong was temporarily dejected. He interpreted the results as a rejection of his style of governance, and stated that after this, nothing could be the same again.

Analysis after the election focused on the Chinese, the working class backlash against some policies designed to woo the English-speaking middle class, and anger over government assistance to poor non-Chinese (the Malays).[63] Deputy Prime Minister Ong Teng Cheong said the Chinese-educated and dialect-speakers felt neglected by the government and sent "the PAP an important signal".[64]

The PAP entered the January 1997 general election determined to reverse three successive electoral declines in the popular vote. The governing party was returned unopposed in a majority of seats (47 of 83), all of them in GRCs. The PAP contested 36 seats against four opposition parties. Although the Opposition once again used its "by-election" strategy of contesting fewer than half the seats, the PAP countered this by linking electoral support to priority in HDB estate upgrading – a major asset enhancement and redistribution scheme designed to uplift (and hence woo) the working class.[65] The promise that those precincts and constituencies which supported the PAP would be first in line for upgrading (see pp. 93–5), while those which voted for the Opposition would move "to the back of the queue", effectively destroyed the Opposition's idea of a "safe" protest vote.

The electoral issues included high ministerial salaries, the high cost of living, and the controversy over the soft-launch discounts on condominium unit purchases by Lee Kuan Yew and B.G. Lee Hsien Loong. This issue was defused when it was aired publicly in Parliament and shown that there was nothing illegal or corrupt about the transactions. However, all the issues, taken together, seemed to point to a concern shared by a number of Singaporeans about fairness and privilege in the state.[66]

The highlight of the campaign was the battle in Cheng San GRC, a blue collar primarily Chinese-speaking constituency. A Workers' Party team led by Jeyaretnam and Tang Liang Hong seemed to have hit a responsive chord with the crowds attending their campaign rallies. Alarmed, in the last few days of the campaign the PAP unleashed a ferocious attack centered on Tang (see p. 134), whom it accused of being an anti-Christian Chinese-language chauvinist who was a threat to ethnic peace.[67]

In the end, the PAP won 81 of 83 seats, squeaked by in Cheng San GRC with less than 55 percent of the votes, and reversed its decline in popular vote by winning 65 percent. As one Western diplomat observed, "The election has shown that the kinder, gentler approach loses four seats ... The tough-guy approach loses only two seats. Their tactics are vindicated. Why go soft?"[68] However, the bitter and bruising campaign and PAP hardball tactics caused disquiet, anger and distress among many Singaporeans, even among PAP supporters.[69]

The November 2001 general election

Despite a contracting economy, the PAP called a general election for November 3, 2001. Prime Minister Goh explained that he had intended to hold the election later, but the terrorist attacks in the US and the economic fallout and global security uncertainties convinced him that the government needed to get the election over with in order to focus fully on Singapore's economy.[70]

The key issues in the last quarter of 2001 in Singapore were job security and the related issue of recruiting foreign talent while retrenching local workers,[71] the cost of health care, and restoring CPF cuts (see pp. 82–3). However, the PAP went into the election having just announced a S$11.3 billion stimulus package that included more HDB (including rental units) and private estate upgrading, CPF top-ups, measures to make health care more affordable for the elderly, and "New Singapore" shares to every citizen, but with more going to the poor.[72]

Although the election had been long anticipated, it was over in a hurry, with a legal minimum nine-day campaign, which followed on the heels of the announcement of new constituency boundaries and then Nomination Day.[73] The new boundaries divided the constituencies into 9 five-member GRCs, 5 six-member GRCs, and 9 single-member constituencies. Eligible voters for the first time numbered over 2 million.

The election pitted the ruling PAP against four opposition parties, one of which was an alliance of four parties.[74] The PAP contested every seat, with the 14 GRCs all headed by political heavyweights. The PAP also put up 25 new candidates, in its latest renewal push. These included eight women, the largest group of women ever, and no SAF officers.

The Opposition agreed to divide the constituencies so as to avoid damaging three-way contests, and again agreed on a "by-election" strategy of contesting fewer than half of the seats, thus encouraging a "worry-free" protest vote (see p. 150).[75] As well as the usual disadvantages the Opposition in Singapore faces, it also labored under the handicaps of a very short notice on the new constituency boundaries, increased deposits for each candidate (to $13,000), and a new election law forbidding candidates from standing in more than one constituency.[76]

On Nomination Day, the PAP was returned to power, winning 55 of 84 seats uncontested. The opposition contested only 4 five-member GRCs and all 9 single seats. In the ensuing campaign, the PAP campaigned on its record of meeting economic challenges in the past and said that it wanted to focus on job creation. The PAP also capitalized on the Prime Minister's personal popularity, using his picture on campaign posters in every constituency. Finally, the PAP continued the strategy that proved successful in 1997 of linking priority in housing upgrading to votes. The Opposition highlighted three issues: the recession, foreign talent, and the need for political opposition. The WP and the SDP tried to shift the blame for the recession from global circumstances to the PAP. All the opposition parties complained about jobs going to foreigners while Singaporeans were being laid off, and the SDP called for a "Singapore First" hiring policy. The SDA focused on the idea that more opposition in Parliament would be good for Singapore. On the whole, it was a mild, issue-oriented campaign.[77]

Voters were clearly influenced by the economic downturn and global uncertainties, and chose in large numbers to stick with the party that had brought them prosperity and security.[78] The PAP won 82 of the 84 seats, losing only to the two opposition incumbents, Chiam See Tong (SDA) and Low Thia Khiang (WP), who won by reduced margins.[79] More spectacularly, the PAP increased its percentage of votes won to 75.3 percent, the party's best performance since

1980.[80] In winning so decisively, the PAP has added a twist to the definition of "performance legitimacy". It used to be thought that legitimacy and support built on performance was fragile, because it was dependent on *continually* delivering the goods. The PAP won in a landslide despite being in the midst of the worst economic recession since independence because the voters did not blame the PAP for the recession, and believed that the PAP was the most capable of restoring economic prosperity. As noted in the *Far Eastern Economic Review*, "At this rate, centuries may pass before Singapore sees a change of government – if ever".[81]

The elected President

With the return of the Opposition in 1984, the PAP began investigating ways of protecting its substantial national reserves from being depleted, and preserving an honest, meritocratic civil service from being dismantled should an irresponsible government be voted into power. It was decided to create an elected President as a custodian with some blocking powers over the use of the reserves and a veto over specific high civil service appointments. The elected President would replace the appointed ceremonial President. The legislation for an elected President had a long gestation period, it was misunderstood by the public from the beginning, and fine-tuning the relationship between the elected President and the government has been painstakingly slow and difficult.[82]

The 1991 White Paper explained the powers and limitations of presidential power by using the – perhaps unfortunate in retrospect – analogy of a two-key safeguard mechanism: the Prime Minister would hold one key and the President the other.[83] In November 1991, the "final" constitutional product was passed by Parliament. A direct national Presidential election for a six-year term was scheduled for August 1993.

The stringent candidacy requirements for President, including approval of the Presidential Elections Committee, constituted for that purpose, severely restricted the choice of candidates.[84] The government's choice (although sponsored as a candidate by the NTUC) was former Deputy Prime Minister Ong Teng Cheong. After some arm-twisting by PAP stalwarts Goh Keng Swee and Richard Hu, former Accountant-General Chua Kim Yeow reluctantly agreed to make it a contest. The electorate was not very interested in the election, which gave the appearance of being "stage-managed", although it did provide an opportunity to vote against the PAP without risk. Chua campaigned very little, limiting himself to two short TV broadcasts. Still, he struck a sympathetic chord by asking, "Do you want the PAP to dominate the presidency too?"[85] The results were rather embarrassing: Ong received only 58.7 percent of the vote.[86]

When he assumed office, President Ong surprised the Cabinet by stating that his duties entailed more than just "adding up numbers".[87] It quickly became apparent that many of the parameters of the office, particularly relations between an "activist" President and the government, remained vague.[88] Consequently, the President and the government engaged in a long process of devising a "common understanding" of the role of the President. At the same time, Ong was embroiled in a "festering dispute" with his former colleagues and civil servants over how much information he should be permitted to obtain to fulfill his role".[89] Beginning in 1994, the government began systematically whittling down the President's powers.

Despite the difficulties encountered, the government and the President reached agreement on many aspects of a working relationship, which was contained in a White Paper endorsed by Parliament in August 1999.[90] Ong wanted to stand for a second term and was unhappy when the Cabinet decided he should not run because of his health.[91] This left Ong angry and somewhat embittered, and he called a press conference where he itemized a "long list" of problems he had had in trying to safeguard the reserves.[92] He said that the decision to stand or not would be his alone, and that it did not require Cabinet approval. He revealed later that some government people were afraid he might turn up on Nomination Day.[93]

In order to clear up public confusion, Ong's accusations were rebutted before a packed Parliament, with the entire Cabinet present, in August 1999. Finance Minister Richard Hu explained in considerable detail some of the technical financial misunderstandings, involving such things as accrual accounting and the treatment of Net Investment Income (NII). Prime Minister Goh reiterated that the government did not have any objections to the President standing for re-election because of their working relationship, but only because of health concerns.[94]

Opposition MP Low Thai Khiang jumped in:

> In 1990, the PAP government amended the Constitution to institute the office of EP [elected President] in what was supposed to be a move to "clip the wings" of the government. Yet, in 1994, the PAP government again amended the Constitution, and this time, it was to clip the wings of the President ... Although it was said that the EP was holding the "second key", the PAP government changed the lock![95]

Goh admitted that there had indeed been difficulties with the new system, and as a result the Constitution had been amended several times to refine the provisions – in 1994, 1996, 1997 and 1998 (as well as the White Paper on principles and procedures in 1999), and the provisions were not yet entrenched. According to Goh, the President agreed to all the changes except for one – an amendment to Article 22H concerning the President's power to veto proposed legislation which circumvented or curtailed his discretionary powers. The President believed he could veto the amendment. It was taken to a constitutional tribunal which ruled in the government's favor.[96]

The government stressed that the President's discretionary powers were limited to specific areas (blocking the government from spending past accumulated reserves and from making bad appointments), and subject to the concurrence of a majority of the Council of Presidential Advisors, which must be consulted before any decisions are made.[97] Lee Kuan Yew gave several interviews emphasizing that the EP was never intended to be an executive office to challenge the government's power, nor was the President ever intended to be independent, or to provide a check on the government or interfere with the running of the government.[98]

For the August 1999 presidential election, the Cabinet unanimously endorsed the candidacy of S.R. Nathan, a distinguished civil servant and diplomat.[99] Nathan was the only one of four prospective candidates approved as meeting the strict qualifications for the position by the Presidential Elections Committee.[100] With the issue of the President extensively covered in the media, interest in the coming election increased. Although a *Straits Times* survey showed that nearly 80 percent of Singaporeans hoped for a contest, "the PAP government backed away from holding a popular election for President ... for fear that their preferred Indian candidate would lose to a credible Chinese opponent".[101] On August 18, 1999, Nathan was declared the duly elected President in a walkover. Further refinements to the EP legislation are likely, but in the meantime, the government is enjoying a much more comfortable relationship with President Nathan.

Channels of participation

The concept of "political participation" is used to describe the variety of ways in which an individual attempts to exert an influence over who his or her leaders shall be, and over public policy and the political process in general. Participation can be viewed on a spectrum ranging from armed rebellion to complete apathy. Elections are often held up as the essence of democracy, and voting the key avenue of citizen participation. A random survey of Singaporeans shows that 76 percent believe that voting gives citizens the most meaningful way to participate.[102] However, some scholars question the meaningfulness of such participation, given limited choices (and in some other countries, corruption and vote-buying), calling it the "fallacy of electoralism".[103]

Since independence, Singaporeans have gained a reputation for being politically apathetic. David S. Gibbons introduced the concept of the "Spectator Political Culture" (free-riders or fence-sitters) over thirty years ago to explain participation in Singapore. Spectators have a "cognitive orientation towards the political system" but choose not to actively participate.[104] This occurs when it is perceived that there is no real need for change because the system is more or less satisfying expectations, whereas alienation or withdrawal occur when citizens feel helpless to achieve any desired change. Fear can also be a factor, either promoting or inhibiting political action.

Singapore has to a considerable extent defied the predictions of the modernization theorists that with more education, income and status, and a growing middle class, the demand for political participation will increase.[105] Except for a minority of primarily English-educated Singaporeans pushing for a more civil society (see pp. 157–8), there has not been a strong demand for more participation. One survey reveals that half of adult Singaporeans are not interested in national issues, such as a national ideology and Town Councils, even if aware of them; however, most are aware of issues affecting their economic well-being, such as the CPF Minimum-sum Scheme. Higher interest corresponds to increased education, but not necessarily to higher status or income.[106] Much of the middle-class "Singapore Dream" concerns acquisition, consumption, and increasingly higher status lifestyles.

Despite the apparent apathy, election post-mortems since 1984 have shown that while most Singaporeans may not want to be active themselves, they favor more opposition in Parliament, more freedom to express their views on government policies and more channels for doing so, and more civil society.

The Feedback Unit

The government has responded to this desire by allowing some more space for civil society (discussed in Chapter 12), and by trying to channel participation by creating a Feedback Unit under the Ministry for Community Development in 1985. The Feedback Unit holds sessions to ascertain the views of citizens and passes on this information to the relevant ministries. It would also use the sessions to explain the government's position on policies under discussion.

The Feedback Unit was designed to cater primarily to an English-educated vocal minority that had been demanding more participation. It was not designed for the general public, and one survey showed that only 58 percent of those surveyed knew about the Unit, and only 15 percent thought it was the most effective channel of participation.[107] Most of the feedback sessions are by invitation only, involving some of the approximately 1000 individuals (1997) that the Unit considers to be "opinion-makers" whose views are solicited. Typically the sessions are conducted in English, but a few of the dialogues are in Mandarin and usually during the course of a year one each is held in Malay and Tamil. Other than occasional press releases, information about the sessions is not made public.

In 1997, the government decided to expand and enhance the Feedback Unit. It organized feedback contributors into 27 feedback groups. By the following year, the Unit announced plans to double participation and it held the first Feedback Conference, with 400 in attendance.[108] Goh Chok Tong also defined the limits on consultation and participation. First, he said, consultation did not mean consulting every Singaporean on every policy. Second, the government was interested in consulting "with people who have good knowledge of the subject". Third, if a proposal was well-argued, it would get a fair hearing, but this did not mean that every proposal would be accepted by the government. Fourth, those seeking to get a policy changed or to influence the national agenda must expect the government to challenge their views.[109]

The Feedback Unit has had a particular kind of effectiveness. Chiam See Tong believes it is not a unit designed to promote democracy, consultation, or participation. Rather, in his view, it "is a device for the government to get feedback, information or intelligence from the people".[110] On the other hand, it has served a political purpose as well by giving an educated vocal minority some sense of participation and consultation.

12 The growth of civil society

The term "civil society" has become fashionable and, perhaps as a result, contested and rather confused. The literature on civil society is extensive.[1] Garry Rodan notes that in concept it has become "romanticized", and Philip Resnick observes that it contributes very little beyond the characterization of "state–society relations".[2] Although the term has been traced back to Aristotle, its revival can be linked to the writings of Eastern European dissidents in the 1980s.

Civil society refers to the existence of networks of voluntary organizations residing in the space, or expanse of social life, between the family and the state, formed by citizens to pursue mutual interests or beliefs. The confusion arises when one attempts to become more specific: Must the associations be autonomous? Can they cooperate with and/or be financed by the state? Are business or labor organizations included or excluded? There is little consensus on these or other questions.

However, some types or models of civil society can be discerned. One model, the more traditional one, consists of a network of voluntary or secondary associations such as clubs, societies, and foundations, ranging from tennis clubs to charities, that engage in social, educational, self-help, welfare, and/or recreational activities. Proponents of this model see its virtues as residing in its capacity to generate "norms of reciprocity" and "social trust" conducive to collective action that leads to more effective governance.[3] In this model of civil society, associations are sometimes formed to fill gaps or deficiencies in the state's activities. They can operate autonomously (as purists would insist) or in cooperation with the state.

Another model for which there is currently a "clear normative preference",[4] consists of a dense network of non-governmental advocacy organizations which views its role as being adversarial – a "thorn in the side" of the state. These might include single-interest groups, such as those advancing the cause of the environment, women, socialism, human rights, animal rights, peace, democracy and so forth. In a variant on this model, the same types of group can accept money from the state but remain adversarial (e.g., the East Timor Alert Network in Canada), or, whether accepting money or not, cooperate with the state. Again, but more so, purists would reject cooperating with the state.

In Singapore, the distinction between the two major models is sometimes depicted as the distinction between "civic society" and "civil society". The former is viewed as constituting non-political interaction, such as self-help and volunteerism, whereas the latter is seen as engaging the state on political matters.[5] B.G. George Yeo, however, has stated that he uses the two terms interchangeably.[6] "Civic society" is also viewed less benignly by some as an "ideological counter-offensive" and "neo-conservative project" intended to distinguish the political from the social.[7]

Civil society organizations are usually viewed by the public as desirable. Rodan writes that "the premise is the notion that the state is inherently predisposed to oppression, whereas civil society is the natural domain of liberty".[8] Much of the work done by these groups warrants praise. However, there is a darker side that should not be overlooked. The organizations are not always progressive; they generally do not represent large cross-sections of political opinion; their motives are sometimes self-interested; and their practices are sometimes violent and disruptive, undemocratic, and uncivil, and therefore not conducive to enhancing effective governance.[9]

Civil society: the historical setting

Two quite different impulses activate civil society. The first grows out of neglect or insufficient action on the part of the authorities. The second arises from the feeling that what the authorities *are* doing needs to be changed. Civil society in colonial Singapore has been described as "vibrant"; it became so to satisfy certain social needs neglected by the state. The British felt some responsibility for the Malays, and built some Malay primary schools and provided some job preferences. Still, the Malays additionally established *khairat* self-help groups to help poor Muslims.[10] However, the Chinese immigrant community was left almost entirely to its own resources.

The Chinese community started temple committees and built their own temples and bought and managed their own burial grounds. They formed a host of clan associations and trade organizations, and they joined the triads to gain protection and also to promote the interests and welfare of their members. A Chinese Chamber of Commerce was established and was involved in welfare and education as well as business.[11] The Chinese community built hospitals and clinics for the poor, financed by the clan associations and rich Chinese philanthropists, and they also built Chinese primary and secondary schools, which were completely autonomous. Privately financed education culminated in 1956 in the establishment of the first Chinese university established outside of China (Nanyang University, see p. 101) in the twilight of colonial rule.[12]

While most of the organizations and associations were independent of the colonial state, some were closely linked to it (e.g., the Straits Chinese British Association).[13] This difference reflected the emerging divide between the English-educated and Chinese-educated Chinese.

When the PAP came to power it quickly moved into much of the space that had been occupied by civil society. Because of control of PAP branches by the pro-Communists before the party split, the PAP created a number of party-led community organizations (see pp. 95–6) to bolster its grassroots presence, and consequently pre-empted a large part of voluntary life in Singapore. It also moved to control existing organizations and associations through the Registrar of

Societies, and it monopolized many of their traditional activities and functions by taking over education and health. This was also necessary for nation-building purposes, along with its extensive public housing program. Simultaneously the PAP passed legislation to control trade union and social movement activities (see p. 17), and to undermine the triads. Its struggle against the Communists left it wary of civil society organizations being used as fronts for them, and hence suspicious of organizations which seemed to oppose the state.

Although civil society shrank under the PAP, there were always many organizations that made representations to the government – the National Council of Churches, Chinese Chambers of Commerce (and all the other chambers), Society for the Prevention of Cruelty to Animals, the Automobile Association, over 300 clan associations, and various temple and mosque organizations. Two less traditional non-governmental organizations (NGOs) from this period stand out: the Nature Society (Singapore) (NSS) and AWARE (Association of Women for Action and Research).[14]

The Nature Society (Singapore) and AWARE

The NSS started as a branch of the Malayan Nature Society in 1954, and was renamed in 1991 to avoid confusion with its Malaysian counterpart. In the 1960s, its membership was largely expatriate; now it is mostly local professional, senior administrative, and managerial/executive members. One of its patrons is Ambassador-at-Large Professor Tommy Koh. The NSS focuses on nature and wildlife conservation, and its activities include research, publications, seminars, clean-up campaigns, and reef-rescue operations, while in general it monitors the state's conservation and development policies.[15]

The NSS has lost some conservation efforts,[16] but some of its proposals have been accepted, including the establishment of an 87-hectare bird sanctuary at Sungei Buloh and the decision not to build a proposed golf course at the Lower Peirce Reservoir catchments area. Its 1990 conservation Master Plan was largely incorporated into the government's Singapore Green Plan.[17] The NSS is respected and taken seriously by the government because of its expertise, and because it cooperates with the state and is non-confrontational.

AWARE was founded in 1985, at the height of the Graduate Mother eugenics debate (see p. 60), as an avowedly feminist organization. Its membership mainly comprises professional women. It has lost more issues than it has won, but the Graduate Mother scheme was withdrawn, and more recently it has lobbied successfully for a relaxation of immigration rules for Singapore women who marry foreigners to bring their husbands to Singapore. Also, two of its members have served as Nominated Members of Parliament (see pp. 144–5).

However, AWARE lost a highly symbolic battle to get Singapore Airlines to stop using its "Singapore Girl" slogan, and it lost an important substantive issue in 1993 concerning unequal benefits for female civil servants. It has also not been able to get effective domestic violence legislation passed in Parliament,[18] and more recently a play on the theme of domestic violence called "Talaq" was banned.[19] In both these latter cases the issues were greatly complicated by Islamic sensitivities.

Its style is similar to the NSS, but it is more independent (it will not accept government funding), more attracted to taking issues to the public, and at times more aggressive. However, AWARE is also viewed as an organization that chooses its issues with care so as to avoid direct confrontation with the government. AWARE has not, for example, defended gay rights, nor has it challenged the government's actions that make getting an abortion somewhat more difficult.[20]

Perhaps the reason AWARE is listened to by the government has something to do with the PAP's early history of supporting women's issues. In 1952, the Singapore Council of Women (SCW) was formed, and it persuaded the PAP to adopt the slogan "one man, one wife" in its 1959 election manifesto. Five women candidates were elected that year. The SCW campaign against polygamy resulted in the passage of the Women's Charter in 1961.[21] After that, however, the SCW seemed to lack direction, and many of the women activists joined the Barisan Sosialis. Once the PAP became a dominant party, women's votes were not so crucial. The SCW was de-registered in 1971.

An emerging civil society

Singapore's authorities have been slowly and cautiously, and with some back-pedaling, loosening the restraints on civil society since the late 1980s. There are several reasons for this. First, Goh Chok Tong and his team wanted a "kinder and gentler" Singapore that was more open to discussion and debate. Lee Kuan Yew concurred to the extent that he saw that a change in the generations and different expectations meant that some adjustments had to be made.[22] Second, there was a growing realization that educated Singaporeans were finding the socio-political restrictions stifling, and that this was a contributing factor to the problem of emigration. Third, the government realized that it had over-extended itself in trying to manage all facets of society, and that this was less feasible in a complex, fast-moving, global setting. Finally, the PAP government was quick to realize the "new reality" presented by the Internet: Singapore might not be able to become successfully immersed in the global economy if the PAP tried to control the flow of information by attempting to regulate the Web[23] (see pp. 140–1). B.G. Yeo told Parliament that the "Internet has a large number of esoteric sites which cover subjects ranging from UFOs to Satanic cults . . . Most have no mass impact at all. But should they denigrate religious beliefs, threaten religious harmony or incite hatred, we will take action to remove them . . . If such sites are created locally and break our laws, the relevant agencies will take action against the content creators in accordance with the law".[24]

The first very mild indication of change to come occurred when Goh Chok Tong announced in 1988 the establishment of the Institute of Policy Studies (IPS) for the free and frank, but behind closed doors, discussion of issues among intellectuals, and also for conducting policy research.[25] This was followed by B.G. George Yeo's 1991 speech, which is considered by many in Singapore to represent a breakthrough, where he discussed the desirability of "civic society" in Singapore and the need to have the state "withdraw a little" and prune back the "Banyan tree" (a massive Asian tree with a dense canopy, under which nothing grows – in this case a metaphor for extensive government control).[26]

However, two months after Yeo's speech, general elections were held. The PAP was disappointed in the results (see pp. 150–1), and the conclusion it drew was that more cultural and political openness had no pay-off in votes and in fact may have alienated some of the more conservative Chinese-educated voters. Consequently, government encouragement of civil society cooled off. This was reinforced by the incident involving Catherine Lim in 1994, referred to on pp. 141–2. After the stinging rebuke from Goh Chok Tong, Lim withdrew from public view while Singaporeans waited to see if she would be sued for libel (she was not, and she has since been commended by the PAP government for her contributions to literature). This episode had a chilling effect on civil society and on the Press. At this point, some observers concluded that Goh Chok Tong had given up on his earlier idea of allowing more space for civil society.

However, the PAP's success in the 1997 general election rekindled the government's promotion of civil society. In June 1997 Goh made a major speech in Parliament in which he outlined his new vision for the future: Singapore 21. In the new vision, civil society was identified as an important element to harness the people's talents and energies, and to give Singaporeans a greater sense of participation and therefore an enhanced stake in the system. "When people participate actively and become involved in community and national issues, they build ties among themselves and bonds to the country".[27]

Goh's speech paved the way for the IPS-sponsored conference on civil society in May 1998, which attracted public interest and sparked a spirited debate in the newspapers. B.G. Yeo gave the keynote address, stating that Singapore must adapt to the changing world by opening up.[28] Goh's Singapore 21 vision (discussed later) led to the largest government–society consultative exercise in Singapore's history, resulting in a report in 1999, the recommendations from which are still unfolding.[29]

For culture and the arts, Singapore has liberalized significantly, especially in allowing plays and films covering a range of controversial topics, such as The Necessary Stage's play about AIDs, "Completely With/Out Character," and Eric Khoo's praised film about life in an HDB estate, "12 Stories".[30] It also allowed the stage play "Changi," with a critical narrative of the ideological position of the first-generation PAP leaders as seen from a pro-Marxist perspective of a political detainee in the 1960s.[31] Even more surprising, the 13th Singapore Film Festival, with the theme of "sex in the Asian cinema" was able to show more than 300 uncut films, although two, involving sadomasochism and sex with a minor were heavily censored and eventually withdrawn.[32] There are also very few sites blocked on the Internet (mostly dealing with pornography), and no topics seem off limits for the many chat rooms that exist, although they may be monitored (see pp. 140–1).

However, the floodgates have not been opened widely. While censorship has been greatly reduced, political debate is only slowly becoming more open. There have been "fits and starts" because of government anxiety about whether it is doing the right thing. According to long-time social activist Claire Chiang, a former Nominated Member of Parliament (NMP), "they fear chaos".[33] They also fear civil society organizations acting as fronts for groups with hidden agendas, such as those evident when the Communists were trying to gain power.[34]

Consequently, there are still limits to political debate and an arsenal of laws to deter offenders (see Chapter 10). There are also what Simon Tay calls "soft restraints" – out-of-bounds (OB) markers – to warn those recklessly skirting the edge of permissibility[35] (see pp. 141–2).

AMP and the Roundtable

Two organizations in particular, the Association of Muslim Professionals (AMP) and The Roundtable, have succeeded in operating within the parameters allowed and in cooperation with the government, and yet each has been able to further the cause of civil society in Singapore by carefully "pushing the envelope" on political and policy concerns. The AMP, which was formed in 1991, has already been discussed in Chapter 8 concerning its role as an organization for articulating the views and concerns of the Malay–Muslim community, and also its tutorial programs for Malay–Muslim schoolchildren. The AMP has also contributed to the development of civil society in Singapore through seminars, and articles published in its journal, *Karyawan,* by encouraging discussion, "providing feedback, differing views and alternative suggestions in areas connected to policies".[36]

The Roundtable is interesting because it was registered in 1994 as a political policy discussion group.[37] It comprises a small, multi-ethnic group of young professionals from business, law, journalism, and academia. It would like to expand its membership to around 25, but not much beyond. The members meet regularly; they post papers on the net and write letters to the *Straits Times* Forum page on selected policy issues with which they all feel comfortable. They have recently amended their constitution to allow outsiders to attend their forums, but this requires a permit. They are normally cautious, but gradually want to extend the boundaries.[38] In the 1997 general election they took a public stand against the PAP campaign tactic of linking priority in HDB upgrading to votes. Since this is when the PAP is most prickly, the fact that there were no serious repercussions shows that some civil society space has been opened up. In September 2000, at the launching of the Speaker's Corner in Hong Lim Park (discussed below), the Roundtable organized a "Speaker's Fest". In November 2000, the Roundtable sponsored a forum on the Societies Act, and took the position that it should be amended to bring it more in line with constitutional guarantees, so that any society would automatically be registered unless the Registrar could show cause why it should not be registered.[39]

Sintercom and Think Centre

Given that about 60 percent of local households owned computers and 50 percent had Internet access in mid-2001[40] – numbers that increase daily – the Internet is an increasingly important civil society mechanism for providing information and promoting diverse views and opinions. This is especially so since the government has decided to impose few controls and block few sites, as mentioned earlier. Currently, there are two political overseas-based websites, Singapore-Window and Singaporeans for Democracy, that view their respective advocacy roles as being in opposition to the state. There are also some local Internet sites of some renown.[41]

Sintercom, a current affairs website which closed down in August 2001 after eight years,[42] sought to promote openness by printing Forum letters in full if the *Straits Times* had edited them, by printing Roundtable position papers, by announcing various forums and seminars, and by reprinting news stories on Singapore from domestic and foreign sources. Sintercom was neither confrontational nor cooperative with the state, but it did expand the flow of information to Singaporeans. Others are trying to keep the Sintercom spirit alive.[43]

Think Centre, originally registered as a dotcom business in 1999, was subsequently designated as a political association by the government in March 2001,[44] which meant that it was subject to the political donations law (see p. 147). Its aims are to examine issues related to democracy, the rule of law, human rights and civil society. It started out as a one-man show, that of James Gomez, although Gomez subsequently recruited some young lieutenants to, in his words, "spread the risks".[45] He sometimes organized activities in conjunction with the head of the Socratic Circle, David Chew, and members of the Opposition, particularly Dr. Chee Soon Juan. It also helped organize and publicize some Roundtable forums. It doggedly obtained an assortment of permits enabling it to sponsor a "Save JBJ" fundraising rally in April 2001 at an outdoor stadium, which attracted some 2,000 people and raised about $19,000 for opposition politician Jeyaretnam, who was declared a bankrupt (see p. 147).[46] Think Centre has published and promoted Gomez's book and a first anniversary magazine, *Shame*.[47]

Gomez, who admits that politics gives him "a buzz", has been willing to "push the envelope" to the edge, and was given police warnings in 1999 and 2001 for holding some forums and demonstrations without a permit.[48] His goal, he says, is to promote a situation where the people are pushed into a corner and must disobey.[49] This approach has won a mixture of praise and criticism from civil society advocates. Some believe his approach will set back the cause of civil society because it may force the government to retreat from its policy of gradually opening up, while others believe that the timing is right for his approach.

The Working Committee

A problem perceived by civil society advocates in Singapore was that social organizations and associations were conducting their activities in isolation from other societies, with little awareness of what other groups were doing, and without networks. Further, in some cases groups were competing instead of cooperating. Consequently, The Working Committee (TWC) network was formed in November 1998 by some civil society activists to find links and forge bonds between groups and civil society activists, for example, to see what the Art Theatre Society had in common with the Nature Society, and how they might help each other.[50] It intended to promote "civil society without-p" (without partisan politics), so no politicians were invited to participate. It was not registered, it had no officers or premises, and it was meant to last only a year as a bridge-building initiative. The TWC network used the open house approach of meeting at different societies each time. It held some closed door forums (not advertised and with proceedings not reported) on issues like feminism and the role of foreigners in Singapore, and a civil society conference in October

1999.[51] It also organized a "Partnership for an Active Community" fair and exhibition in September 1999 at a shopping mall to show what different societies were trying to do, and it initiated an Electronic Newsletter for Civil Society, the first issue of which appeared in January 2000, containing appeals, announcements, events, and commentary. At the end of a year of activity, the TWC network had to decide whether to disband, as originally intended, or to register as a policy discussion group. The members voted to disband.

The Speaker's Corner

In a symbolically important step, if not functionally a significant one, the government decided to allow a Speaker's Corner to be established at Hong Lim Park (near Chinatown and the business district, the scene of some exciting political rallies in the 1950s–1960s), from September 2000. Home Affairs Minister Wong Kan Seng told Parliament that the government decided to go ahead despite public order concerns, because the idea (first suggested by Lee Kuan Yew a year earlier) had received support from civil society groups.[52]

The Speaker's Corner is modeled after London's Hyde Park. Speakers may talk on any subject, every day from 7 a.m. to 7 p.m., but must not provoke feelings of racial or religious hostility or grievance. Speakers may publicize their talks in advance. There is no limit on the number of speakers (even at the same time) or length of speeches, and speakers can debate with spectators. Any of the four official languages or dialects may be used. However, speakers must be Singapore citizens, they need to register to speak at the neighborhood police station (a process that takes only a few minutes), and they have no immunity from the law and can be sued for defamation.

The Opposition derided the Speaker's Corner, but many civil society advocates were enthusiastic. There was a Speaker's Fest, organized by the Roundtable with help from Think Centre at the inauguration on September 1, with more than five speakers at a time and enough spectators to make it worthwhile. It was widely reported in the media.

However, by November, the novelty had worn off. Public response was tepid, the crowds were growing smaller and increasingly elderly, the speakers (many by now familiar faces) were far from riveting, and the media now mostly ignored the Speaker's Corner.[53] In December 2000, on International Human Rights Day, a demonstration of about 50 people organized by the opposition-led Open Singapore Centre and Think Centre was held at the Speaker's Corner to protest the Internal Security Act. This led to a police investigation that determined that the Speaker's Corner was not a venue where demonstrations could take place without a permit, and the two Centres were warned.[54]

The problem with the Speaker's Corner at Hong Lim Park is similar to those of its Hyde Park model. In the last half of the nineteenth century, the latter venue flourished because without modern communications there were inadequate outlets for airing one's views. Nowadays, the Speaker's Corner at Hyde Park attracts many cranks. In Singapore, the civil society groups have not given up on Speaker's Corner, but it is not thriving. It is clear that unless some attractive speaking topic is publicized in advance, busy Singaporeans will not just drop by the park to hear whoever happens to be speaking, if anyone. In September 2001 there was a rare burst of activity at the park to celebrate Speaker's Corner's first anniversary. Many would probably rather participate more anonymously, with less travel time and fewer parking problems, through the Internet.

Still, just the existence of a Speaker's Corner is of some importance. It is something the civil society activists wanted and worked to attain. More significantly, it represents a situation where the government took a chance (albeit a small one) on expanding the boundaries of free speech, and no chaos has resulted.

"Active citizenship" – a key to the Singapore 21 vision

In his 1997 National Day Rally speech, Goh Chok Tong explained his intention to consult Singaporeans about what kind of Singapore they wanted, what vision of Singapore they had for the future. To this end, he asked RAdm. Teo Chee Hean to chair a "Singapore 21 Committee" to ascertain the views of Singaporeans. The committee and its five subject sub-committees spent the next 18 months consulting some 6,000 citizens through seminars, focus group discussions, surveys, and email. The S21 Committee released its report in April 1999, and it was approved by Parliament one month later. Perhaps the most important of the five subjects, or ideas, was that of "active citizenship" – encouraging a diversity of ideas and promoting greater civic participation to enhance citizens' stake in the system and sense of belonging.[55]

The active citizenship subject committee based its findings on a large survey conducted by the S21 Committee, and these findings were confirmed by a random sample of nearly 1100 Singaporeans carried out by the subject committee itself. The committee found that Singaporeans wanted to be consulted more on public policies, particularly before policies were publicly announced, rather than just post-implementation feedback. The committee also found that Singaporeans felt an element of fear about expressing their ideas, mainly fear of public chastisement and/or libel suits by PAP leaders. The committee recommended that ministries and departments, and the Feedback Unit itself, be more open and receptive to citizens' ideas and views, increase information-sharing, and that the OB markers be better defined. Citizens, for their part, would be expected to be well-informed and constructive, and to be actively involved, particularly at the local level.

The parliamentary debate on the report was revealing. While the Opposition either dismissed the report as a set of platitudes or complained about not being consulted, some of the comments by PAP backbenchers and NMPs were interesting. It is clear, for example, that most of the PAP backbenchers and Ministers who rose to speak about the report consider active citizenship primarily to consist of participating in existing (PAP-controlled) grassroots organizations and voluntary welfare organizations (see pp. 95–8). This was recognized by NMP Claire Chiang, who said that being engaged meant more than fund-raising for welfare organizations or following what was already decided by the government. "Engagement for many young professionals and executives means having meaningful two-way dialogues with policy-makers ... without being ostracized afterwards".[56]

The debate also revealed a problem with apathy, which can indicate either that people are satisfied with the status quo or that they feel politically ineffectual. Several MPs noted that some people had called the report a "collection of motherhood statements", or that they were unexcited by it. Dr. Ong Chit Chung, a PAP backbencher, noted that he "asked some grassroots leaders and residents about S21. It is of not much interest to them. Some have not heard about it ... What they are more interested in is what happens after this".[57]

Perhaps the most prevalent related themes expressed were about mistrust between the government and civil society, the "climate of fear" about speaking out against government policies, and the existence of OB markers[58] (see pp. 141–2). The most critical stance was taken by long-time PAP backbencher, Dr. Tan Cheng Bock. He asked first why OB markers were needed at all before people participated in debate and discussion? He recalled his own experience in Parliament when he asked that the effort to recruit foreign talent be "toned down" during the 1998–9 economic slowdown. "I, who have stood in this House with a record of nearly 19 years service, was labeled by a Minister to be doing a disservice to my country for bringing up this subject in this Chamber. Calling for toning down ... is a disservice, I asked myself? Then how can an ordinary Singaporean stand up to raise issues when such treatment was meted out to a long-standing fellow MP?" However, Senior Minister Lee Kuan Yew, speaking near the end of the debate, tried to be reassuring: "On OB markers, let me put it very simply. If your interest is to improve Singapore, you do not worry about OB markers. It is as simple as that. It is when your intention is to twist your Minister's tail, to show that you are smart, that is risking it ... But in our society, face is important. So we will try, when you twist my tail, I will only tweak your ear".[59]

The S21 exercise was popular, and the report and debate raised expectations to the point where the Prime Minister felt compelled to say that the S21 debate should be put "in perspective" and that a "strong dose of realism was necessary" to ward off unrealistic expectations of quick results.[60] Originally, S21 was intended simply as a vision – a guidepost for the future – and had no targets, no set programs, and no agency to drive implementation. However, after complaints, Acting Minister for Information, Communications and the Arts David Lim was appointed to set up a S21 Facilitation Committee to consult about what role the government could play as facilitator to guide the process along.[61] Implementation of the S21 vision is necessarily long-term and policies leading from it will unfold only slowly. However, the government is trying to reform its attitude about civil society. B.G. Lee explains that the

> "government is changing the approach of the ministries and departments. We want to explain and justify policies and decisions more. We are trying to be more open in accepting and soliciting inputs from the public ... The question is what the government should do if a political challenge comes from somewhere other than the Opposition political parties, which it sometimes will. This is a matter of judgment – if the response is too harsh and defensive, the government risks alienating people and losing support. On the other hand, to accept every criticism as constructive feedback would be naive".[62]

The future of civil society?

The emergence of civil society under the PAP is a recent phenomenon; it is too early to tell how far it will proceed, or whether it will be retrenched. Experience indicates that this is a genie that will be difficult to put back in the bottle. The perception exists in Singapore that the government's opening the way for more participation and active citizenship is correct and over-due. To backtrack now would be politically costly. At the same time, there is nothing to indicate in surveys or other analyses, or from talking to Singaporeans, that they are willing to risk disorder by dismantling all the restrictions hemming in civil society.

Some things seem clear. First, the Goh government is serious about consulting more with the people, listening to more diverse views, allowing more policy debate, and encouraging more participation. As the press secretary to Deputy Prime Minister Lee wrote, "The government is committed to developing a more open style of governance".[63]

Second, interviews conducted by the *Straits Times* confirmed the impression that mutual trust between civil society and the state is perceived to be lacking and that this constitutes "a major obstacle" to participation.[64] Constance Singam of AWARE notes that the "government is prepared to talk about wanting a civil society. That's a big change". But she goes on to say that much needs to be done about mutual trust and respect.[65] It is the OB markers that have caused the most public consternation. B.G. Lee Hsien Loong has tried to clarify the limits: "As long as the argument is over policies, the limits for debate – or the out-of-bounds markers – are very wide. There is no policy too sensitive to question, and no subject so taboo that you cannot even mention it ... But if it is an attack on the government and on its fitness to rule, then that response has to go beyond the merits of the particular issue and to address the broader question".[66] Still, in the public's mind, the boundaries remain unclearly demarcated.

Another "trust" issue concerns the propensity of the PAP's leaders to sue for defamation (see pp. 134–6). Although libel suits have been used mostly against members of the opposition and foreign print media, there is a fear that it could be more broadly applied and that an OB marker might be a kind of warning about, or possibly even precursor to, a libel suit.

Third, the kind of participation the government seeks is mostly that of voluntary welfare organizations (VWOs) and grassroots associations focused on local issues rather than action-oriented civil society groups concerned with national issues or advocating particular interests. One Minister defines civil society thus: "A civil society means people themselves doing things for the community. This means actual community and social work".[67] It is not an accident that the first concrete action announced as a result of the S21 Report was by the Minister of Community Development to set up a National Volunteer Centre to enhance the volunteer movement in Singapore. In this model of volunteerism, PAP Ministers and MPs would remain very involved and in overall control. The Prime Minister acknowledges that channeling an active citizenry into VWOs will not be enough, and has said that the government will allow an increasing number of NGOs.[68]

Fourth, the government will tolerate (and often offer to help finance) nationally-focused civil society organizations so long as their actions are seen as well-intentioned, responsible, and in the national interest, and they are apparently cooperative with the government rather than confrontational. This is the most likely route to produce changes in policy, but it requires patience and some subtlety in engaging the government. Pierre Lizee explains that the civil society "model emerging is not one of opposition to the state, in which the priorities and underlying logic of state action is constantly challenged, but rather one in which a more prudent and long-term process of engagement and improvement develops within the space permitted under the government's own focus on new civil society institutions".[69]

Fifth, the PAP government does not accept the idea that civil society must or should be opposed to the state, and it will not allow interest or pressure group tactics to be employed. The government will "crack down hard" on any NGOs that represent political opposition "in disguise".[70] The PAP regards interest group politics such as practiced in the US to be flawed systems that reward those who are the most vocal (or lobbyists who contribute the most), often at the expense of the "silent" majority. Acting Minister David Lim states the PAP position: "They may raise issues of concern, but this should not be through violent means or through pressure tactics".[71] Likewise, Goh Chok Tong says that while the government will listen to suggestions and advice, the NGOs are not elected and not responsible, and therefore cannot expect to set the agenda or have their way about how to run Singapore.[72]

Of course, cooperating with the state can be less satisfying than opposing it, and consequently some activists can be expected to keep pushing the boundaries no matter how far the government goes in lessening control and supervision. At some point, conflict between the state and some segment of civil society is possible, if not likely. Perhaps this is why B.G. Lee Hsien Loong writes that this "combination of vibrant civil society and strong government will not be easy to achieve".[73] If the goal of the PAP is not so much to establish democracy, but to build up political support, then how conflict is handled by the government, if and when it arises, will have an important bearing on the future of both the PAP and civil society.

Sixth, there are some groups that the government will not approve for registration as a society because it believes that doing so would convey tacit approval. Homosexuality is a big sticking point. The government has loosened up to the extent that it is not arresting homosexuals in sting operations, and officials are willing to consult with organizations that have openly homosexual members, such as Action for Aids. However, the Registrar of Societies has turned down the application of a homosexual group, People Like Us, and in May 2000 the government rejected a permit for gays and lesbians to hold a public forum.[74]

Finally, the opening of space for civil society in Singapore does not extend to local chapters of international groups. Noticeably, there are relatively few international non-governmental organizations (INGOs) operating in Singapore, and none of the ones well known for their social activism and political agendas.[75]

13 Deterrence and diplomacy

Deterrence

As a small state with physical and resource constraints, Singapore attaches great importance to, and expends considerable resources on, effective deterrence supported by diplomacy. Singapore has come a long way from the immediate post-independence period when Lee Kuan Yew felt compelled to declare: "We intend to fight for our stake in this part of the world, and [to] anybody who thinks they can push us around, I say: over my dead body".[1] Now, with its economic strength, political stability, technological prowess, and sophisticated armed forces, Singapore is considered by some to be a middle power, albeit one with no strategic territorial depth.[2]

Michael Leifer explains that Singapore is defined by two key features: vulnerability and exceptionalism. It is vulnerable because of its small size, its geography, wedged as it is between two much larger Malay–Muslim states, and its ethnic diversity and the fact that, alone in Southeast Asia, it has a large Chinese majority. Yet Singapore has been exceptional in its accomplishments, the international recognition it has gained, and the way it manages its vulnerability and "punches above its weight".[3] Thus, writes Leifer, Singapore does not fit neatly into the categories of small and micro-states, and it is best "represented as *sui generis*" – one of a kind.[4]

Independence for Singapore in August 1965 was a traumatic event – it had not been sought nor anticipated. Singapore had virtually no army, a two ship navy, no diplomatic corps, and it had to depend on Malaysia for its water. Singapore's army consisted of two infantry battalions, stationed outside Singapore and under Malaysian command and control, while Malaysia kept its own battalion in Singapore and refused to move out.[5] This was at a time when many Malays in Malaysia believed that Singapore should have been forcibly subdued rather than kicked out of the Malaysian Federation.[6]

Small state models

Singapore's leaders examined and evaluated a number of small state models and solicited help in building a credible deterrence force. Britain would not help, although the presence of British forces in Singapore was in itself a considerable deterrent. India and Egypt also declined to help, but Israel volunteered to send 18 advisers in late 1965 (who were called "Mexicans" to disguise their identity from Singapore's Muslim neighbors). Singapore decided on a model derived from components of the Swedish, Swiss, and Israeli systems – national conscription, a small standing army and reserves, and involvement of the entire civilian population in national defense.[7]

National service for males was instituted in 1967.[8] Conscription had been controversial in Singapore and there was rioting when the British tried to institute it earlier. However, by 1967 the PAP had succeeded in portraying Singapore as a state under siege, and there was no resistance. The army and police were traditional Malay occupations. A number of steps were taken to counter traditional Chinese prejudice against military service. The top scholastic ten percent of those who registered were conscripted in 1967. Also, cadet corps were set up in all secondary schools. In 1971, the attractive SAF (Singapore Armed Forces) Overseas Scholarship program was initiated to induce some of the ablest and brightest to become SAF officers.[9] Lee Kuan Yew's two sons became scholar-soldiers. Under the "Project Wrangler" program, promising and capable officers were tracked, given challenging assignments, promoted rapidly, and groomed for important second career appointments. Those selected have included all the President's Scholars in the SAF and SAF scholars. The PAP has not been shy in attracting the scholar-soldiers into politics, and today there are five former SAF scholars in the Cabinet. Four of these were also President's Scholars, an award open to both sexes and the most prestigious given (limited to four a year). All of these efforts raised the prestige of the SAF in the eyes of the Chinese.

Likewise, a controversial policy was enacted to reduce the proportion of Malays by not conscripting all eligible Malays for a while in order that the ethnic mix in the SAF better reflected the ethnic composition of Singapore.[10] By 1971, the year the British closed their bases in Singapore, the SAF was becoming a credible force with 17 active battalions and 14 reserve battalions, comprising approximately 27,000 men.

The deterrence psychology initially used was the feisty idiom of the "poison shrimp" – eat it and you may die. Defence Minister Goh Keng Swee noted that it should be evident "even to the meanest intellect" that "we threaten nobody, and in the course of time it will be unprofitable for anybody to threaten us".[11] After 1975, the "poison shrimp" idiom was considered too fatalistic, since Singapore now had a competent preemptive capacity. The strategy adopted was that of a "Forward Defence", based on the idea that Singapore cannot afford to fight an aggressor on its own limited territory.[12] Therefore, it cannot just be reactive. The emphasis in such a strategy is air superiority and the use of armor (Singapore began buying tanks as early as 1968).

Total Defence

The idea of involving the entire citizenry in the defense of Singapore came to be called "Total Defence", borrowed from Sweden, and it remains the cornerstone of Singapore's deterrent strategy. It helps compensate for limited manpower. The concept stresses that defense cannot be the responsibility of the SAF alone, but is the collective responsibility of all Singaporeans. It is now being taught in the schools through the national education program.[13] Total Defence has five components, each under a separate ministry: defence security, civil defence, economic defence, psychological defence, and social security. Especially critical is the psychological dimension. Singapore is such a small island state that it is very important for Total Defence that the people believe in the will and capacity of the SAF and that Singapore can and shall defend itself.[14] The importance of defense to Singapore is underscored by the fact that the SAF uses 20 percent of the land space in land-scarce Singapore for training, storage, depots, camps, and air and naval bases.[15]

In the 1980s, Singapore moved into high-tech weaponry and the use of its own defense industry; more recently, the SAF has been deeply involved with the role and use of stealth, unmanned, and information, technology. Today, the SAF is a tri-service force capable of mobilizing 350,000 active and reservist troops in just six hours in any crisis.[16] In 2000, Singapore's military budget was $4.4 billion – the highest in Southeast Asia – and 4.6 percent of the GDP.[17] The SAF is also constantly upgrading. In March 2000, it was announced that the SAF will be adding six new stealth Lafayette-class frigates (the design and first one will be built by a French firm and the rest by Singapore Technologies Engineers), to be ready between 2005 and 2009;[18] by early 2001 Singapore had taken delivery of two refurbished Swedish-built submarines and two new landing ships, while waiting for two more submarines; it was announced in July 2000 that the Air Force (RSAF) will modernize to F-16C/Ds over the next few years; and *Jane's Defence Weekly* reported that Singapore and Israel have a joint project to develop a series of photo-reconnaissance satellites.[19] *Jane's Defence Weekly* also said that in the coming decade, Singapore's "new operational capabilities" would make the SAF the region's strongest fighting force.[20]

As long ago as 1983, the SAF was described as "one of the best forces in Southeast Asia". It has remained so. *Jane's Intelligence Review* has written that "Singapore has developed one of the best-trained, best equipped and potentially most effective armies in East Asia." A US Army War College study called Singapore's ground forces "more competent technically" than those of its neighbors, and the US-based weekly, *Defense News*, ranked Singapore's navy as the best in the region.[21] The new concern in 2002 about Islamic terrorist cells in Singapore means that Singapore will spend additional funds to enlarge the SAF and police and set up a new "homeland security" framework.[22]

Singapore's defense industry

Inevitably, an effective deterrence force requires a supporting defense industry for some degree of self-sufficiency and independence from external arms' suppliers. As the industry grows, it also needs to be self-supporting and profitable. Singapore's military-industrial complex started in 1967 with a single small plant making small arms ammunition, and it has grown into a huge, diversified defense GLC-conglomerate empire under Singapore Technologies.[23] Comprising over 100 subsidiaries, Singapore Technologies is organized into four areas: ordnance, aerospace (refurbishing, modifying, and maintaining aircraft), marine (including ship-building and maintenance), and industrial (both defense and non-military).[24] An "invisible partner" of Singapore Technologies, according to Bilveer Singh, is the largest research and development organization in Singapore centralized into the Defence Science Organization (DSO), about which not much is actually known except that it comes under the direct control of the Ministry of Defence (MINDEF) and is considered a key defense component.[25]

In 2000 a new statutory body under the control of MINDEF, the Defence Science and Technology Agency (DSTA) was launched to extend knowledge-based and technology-driven expertise to the battlefield. The DSTA will acquire, develop and upgrade weapon systems for the SAF, advise the ministry on scientific and technological matters, and manage defense research and development.[26]

Apparently there was some controversy in the mid-1990s over what the primary role of Singapore Technologies should be, whether its activities should be directly related to defense strategy, or rather expand into broader political and economic activities. The latter vision of Singapore Technologies has been promoted by its hands-on president and CEO, Ho Ching, the wife of B.G. Lee Hsien Loong, and its operation now is very much as a transnational corporation.[27]

Exporting arms and military technology is a high-risk business with cut-throat competition, and the thorny matter of ethics is rarely a primary consideration. Singapore has avoided most of the criticism and adverse publicity that can accompany this enterprise, but rumors of some unsavory activities in Myanmar persist,[28] despite repeated denials by the Singapore government.[29]

Defense diplomacy: bilateral and multilateral arrangements

An important part of Singapore's deterrence is defense diplomacy. Singapore's leaders have never forgotten that theirs is a small island trading-state, and consequently Singapore has sought to establish friendly relations with all countries (although it was occasionally strident with its close neighbors just after independence). Singapore strongly endorses the international principle of territorial sovereignty and the right of small states to exist (hence Singapore sent a medical team to the Gulf in 1991 to show support for Kuwait). It has sought the best bilateral and multilateral defense arrangements possible, while side-stepping major power entanglements.

Singapore did not want British troops to leave after independence. The PAP leaders believed they were not likely to be invaded while the British had bases in Singapore (not to mention the economic benefits the bases provided). When the British announced their policy of withdrawing all troops East of Suez, Singapore faced the prospect of being on its own, vulnerable, and needing to build up an air defense system in a hurry.[30] As compensation for leaving, Britain proposed the Five Power Defence Arrangements (FPDA) comprising Britain, Australia, New Zealand, Malaysia, and Singapore, to ensure the defense of Malaysia and Singapore. This came into being in 1971, but as consultative arrangements and not any formal alliance. It was the best Singapore could get, even though it believed the benefits were marginal.[31] At least it brought Malaysia into a structure of security cooperation.[32] Singapore continues to be committed to the FPDA – now the longest standing multilateral arrangement in the region – and it participates in the annual joint air and sea exercises.

Singapore has a number of bilateral defense relations, including with the US, China, India, and South Korea, but it believes that multilateral arrangements are likely to become more important in the twenty-first century.[33] Singapore plays an important diplomatic role in the Association of Southeast Asian Nations (ASEAN), and the ASEAN Regional Forum (ARF), which was formed in 1993. The ARF is a multilateral security dialogue forum involving all of the major Asian powers (and the US), designed to defuse hostility and solve problems through dialogue and institutional cooperation. As such, it "serves a long-standing general interest of Singapore's foreign policy".[34] Singapore also participates in other multilateral regional security forums, such as the ASEAN Special Senior Officials Meeting which annually brings together foreign and defense ministry representatives from the ASEAN states.

Likewise, Singapore has considered the United Nations the key institution for maintaining international law and the right of small states to exist. Singapore first participated in UN peacekeeping operations in 1989 and it has continued to do so, but within the limits of its manpower capabilities. In September 1999, Singapore sent a 270-strong SAF team to East Timor, including a medical team, observers, liaison officers, logistics support, and two landing ship tanks.[35] In 2001, Singapore sent its first ever contingent of armed peacekeepers to East Timor as part of the United Nations Transitional Administration in East Timor. The SAF peacekeepers were asked to patrol a section of the dangerous border with West Timor, among other duties.[36]

Singapore participates in a number of joint and trilateral military training exercises, including with the US, France, Australia, New Zealand, Brunei, Malaysia, the Philippines, and Thailand. In fact, because of severe land size and air space constraints, Singapore has needed to find overseas training areas and overseas bases for many of its airplanes. The first breakthrough was achieved when Taiwan allowed the Singapore infantry to train there. Then New Zealand and Brunei and later Australia, Thailand, and, most recently, South Africa, agreed to provide training areas. Singapore's air force (RSAF) used Clark Air Base in the Philippines until the US pulled out. Now Singapore stations some of its airplanes and helicopters in the US, France, and Australia. As Lee Kuan Yew notes, these special problems required unconventional solutions.[37]

For security reasons, Singapore has always wanted a Western power presence in Southeast Asia. It has come to view the US as the most benign major power, and a positive influence for regional peace. Singapore was distressed when the Philippines turned the US out of its bases there, and was afraid that Washington might not maintain a presence in the region. Therefore Singapore signed an agreement with the US, formalized in 1998, to allow US ships and aircraft carriers to berth at Changi Naval Base (but the bases remain under Singapore control). A previous supplemental agreement led to the relocation of the US Seventh Fleet's Logistic Headquarters for surface ships in the Pacific from Subic Bay in the Philippines to Singapore. As B.G. George Yeo noted, "We built it at our own expense to facilitate the deployment of the US Seventh Fleet in Southeast Asian waters".[38] By 1998 more than 100 ships a year were stopping in Singapore, and in March 2001 the aircraft carrier USS Kitty Hawk and its battle group docked at Changi Naval Base, followed in August by the USS Constellation. At first, Singapore's neighbors were unenthusiastic about the base agreement. However,

Lee Kuan Yew noticed that perceptions changed after China published maps in 1992 that included the Spratly Islands as part of China.[39] Also, Singapore has taken pains to point out that it is not a "foreign base", and that it is open to other navies on commercial bases. One potential problem is to convince China that the US navy use of Changi is not part of a new US policy of containing China. Clearly, if Sino–US relations deteriorate, Singapore could be severely cross-pressured over the use of the base. A new problem is providing security against terrorist attacks targeting US warships at Changi Naval Base and in the waters between Changi and the island of Pulau Tekong.

Strategic problems and concerns

Singapore's relations with Malaysia have never been easy or comfortable, and Singapore remains very concerned about a strongly nationalistic or Islamic government coming to power in Kuala Lumpur. Indeed, Tim Huxley writes that Singapore's defense policy "evinces an overriding concern with the deterrence of Malaysia".[40] Of special concern to Singapore is the fact that it must rely on Malaysia for about half of its water supply. Malaysia uses this dependence as leverage against Singapore and whenever there are bilateral tensions, Malay radicals, often UMNO-connected, demand that the water pipeline from Johor be shut down.[41]

The water supply from Malaysia is governed by two agreements, which were tentatively extended and revised in an agreement reached between Lee Kuan Yew and Malaysian Prime Minister Mahathir in September 2001 (see p. 178). In 2002, proving again that "the devil is in the details", the agreement has stalled over details relating to price, amounts, and issues of filtered versus unfiltered water. Although the agreement, when it is finalized, will be reassuring to Singapore, uncertainty about Malaysia honoring its agreements in the future remains. All of this has led to the conviction by a number of Singaporeans that if the water was turned off, the SAF would immediately advance into Johor, using its armor superiority to secure Singapore's water supply.[42] In fact, Lee Kuan Yew has written that he has told Mahathir directly that if the water was stopped and the shortage was urgent, Singapore would have to go in, forcibly if need be, to restore the water flow.[43] However, this is clearly not a desirable solution, so Singapore is trying to lessen its dependency. It has opted to have the private sector construct and manage a single large desalination plant, and at the same time it has plans to reclaim treated sewage water.[44] Singapore is also trying to enlarge its storm collection ponds and reservoirs, encouraging water conservation by raising the price of water, and investigating the feasibility of a water pipeline from Indonesia, all to reduce its dependence on an occasionally difficult and sometimes unpredictable neighbor.[45]

From a security and economic standpoint, Singapore is most worried about Indonesia, its troubled giant neighbor to the south, becoming a "failed state." Specifically, Singapore is deeply concerned about the various separatist movements, religious clashes and other violence, refugees, the potential rise of militant Islam and terrorism,[46] the political infighting and instability in Jakarta, the frightening prospect of a general breakdown of law and order, and the negative economic spin-offs from a floundering Indonesia. As Huxley has noted, the "regional strategic environment" is more unstable now than it has been since the 1960s.[47]

More broadly, Singapore is worried about the conflicting claims to the Spratly Islands, particularly if oil is discovered, and the potential for regional upheaval if there is armed conflict between China and Taiwan. It is concerned that the US does not seem to be deeply engaged in Asia. Finally, it is worried about the new uncertainties in the strategic environment introduced by globalization since, as President Nathan noted in his address to Parliament, "Fundamental questions have arisen about the evolution of the international system".[48] These concerns are largely beyond the capacity of Singapore to control, hence Leifer's apt title: *Coping with Vulnerability*.[49]

Political control of the military

There is strong political control of the military by the civilian government in Singapore, despite the image portrayed by having so many retired/reservist Brigadier-Generals and other officers in high political, civil service (including key policy-making positions in MINDEF), statutory board, and GLC positions.[50] The large cluster of retired/reservist military officers is largely explainable by the fact that since 1967 *every* able-bodied male has had to do national service. To encourage respect for national service the brightest were given scholarships and became scholar-soldiers, as mentioned earlier. Because these scholars constituted a national resource, many were subsequently recruited at relatively high levels into politics or the public sector. B.G. George Yeo says there was no set plan to recruit military officers into government; rather the most able from whatever field were recruited.[51] He does not think this pattern will necessarily continue since there are now many more prestigious scholarships available that are not from the SAF.[52]

Political control of the military is exerted by the Prime Minister, the President (who can veto SAF appointments), the Minister for Defence (who thus far has always been a civilian), and Parliament, which, formally, authorizes expenditures. The Minister for Defence has considerable control over the SAF. In 1988 Goh Chok Tong, then the Minister for Defence, said, "I can tell you I am most uncomfortable [with] the authority which I have as Minister for Defence ... I can appoint [all the various service chiefs and commanders]. I can promote, I can transfer, I can demote ...".[53]

Despite the fact that the SAF is likely to remain under the control of the political leadership, it is much less likely that the top leadership will be strictly civilian (as opposed to including a number of national service officer reservists). This creates some potential liabilities. First, even with secure political control of the military, the image that is conveyed may be one of military involvement in politics and government. Second, the reservist scholars are all male, and mostly Chinese.[54] Finally, there is a possible problem with having so many former officers in important decision-making roles that a "military mindset" might favor security objectives over political goals.[55]

Diplomacy

Defense policy must necessarily be supported by a coordinated and integrated foreign policy. Further, for both deterrence and diplomacy, there should be a congruence between and continuity of interests and goals. This has been the case in Singapore. The geopolitical facts of life and the way independence was suddenly thrust upon it, have resulted in "a state whose foreign policy is rooted in a culture of siege and insecurity ..." typified by its obsession with vigilance.[56] Singapore is a small state in a rough neighborhood.

Singapore's foreign policies have been rationally calculated, and the state has exercised prudence in its international relations generally, and always when it has been vital to do so. However, Singapore has also at times irked other states by its abrasiveness. Leifer explains that Singapore has been determined to assert its right to decide its own future, and this has meant exhibiting a "don't flinch" mentality (internationally and domestically) of not showing any weaknesses, while at the same time displaying its political resolve at every opportunity.[57]

Singapore's leaders are realists who believe in a Hobbesian world where power counts and predators lurk all around looking for weaknesses and opportunity.[58] Singapore's foreign policy has been pragmatically based, and the state seeks to make itself useful to the international community and to be perceived as an asset, especially by its neighbors. In fact Lee Kuan Yew has always said that Singapore's best guarantee of survival is for it to be in the best interests of other states for it to survive. Perhaps one sees this best in the early deliberate strategy of encouraging foreign direct investment (FDI), instead of borrowing, to have a substantial foreign multinational presence in Singapore.[59]

S. Jayakumar, the Minister for Foreign Affairs, has noted Singapore's fundamental precepts of foreign policy: Singapore has sought to be friends "with all who wish to be friends with us"; it has remained non-aligned with regard to great power rivalries; it has encouraged the presence in the region of the major powers; it has maintained ASEAN as the cornerstone of its foreign policy; it has been willing to form commercial links with any state; and it has endeavored to be a good international citizen.[60]

Not surprisingly given its vulnerability, Singapore has always had a strong commitment to the development of and compliance with international law regimes, particularly respect for national sovereignty. Being a small state, Singapore has been especially opposed to armed aggression against other small states. Singapore abstained in the United Nations vote on East Timor in 1975 (the only ASEAN state to do so, thus irritating Indonesia), it opposed the US invasion of Grenada (1983), and it opposed the invasions of Cambodia, Afghanistan, and Kuwait (the last being at variance with the official positions of its two Muslim neighbors).

Bilateral relations

Singapore has diplomatic relations with 158 states, the most crucial being with its two Muslim neighbors, Malaysia and Indonesia; the rising Asian giant, China; and the world's remaining superpower, the United States.

Relations with Malaysia

Lee Kuan Yew said in a speech in October 1966 that "when you talk about foreign policy, and unless you are a big power ... you are really talking about your neighbors. Your neighbors are not your best friends, wherever you are".[61] Singapore's relations with Malaysia have always been central to its foreign policy. Theirs has been a stormy relationship, with periodic strains full of acrimonious rhetoric and media wars over unresolved issues, large and small. The citizens of both countries harbor deep prejudices about each other. Yet pragmatism and diplomacy have always prevailed.

The separation period in the mid-1960s was understandably messy, with splitting up currencies, businesses and the like. Relations were then more amenable until 1986. After that relations were marred by a series of squabbles and disputes. Malaysia still tends to regard Singapore as a state which is inferior because of its small size and absence of resources, and one that is "appropriately" dependent on Malaysia. At the same time, Malaysia exhibits considerable envy of Singapore's economic accomplishments and resentment at being adversely compared to Singapore. Some of the issues that have arisen are a result of Malaysia's relentless attempts to gain a competitive edge for its ports, airline, products, and tourist industry. Also, the UMNO-led government at times drags up old issues for domestic political purposes. Malaysia has also had a tendency, especially under Mahathir's premiership, to change its mind on agreements and memorandums of understanding.[62]

Another problem is Malaysian retaliation for real or perceived slights. In 1997, the public disclosure of Lee Kuan Yew's statement in a court affidavit, in which he stated that Johor was "notorious for shootings, muggings, and car-jackings" led to Malaysian demonstrations, official protests, and what amounted to a virtual unofficial freezing of relations. The Senior Minister apologized "unreservedly" twice, but relations remained strained for some time.[63] Then the publication of Lee Kuan Yew's first volume of memoirs in 1998 received a hostile reception in Malaysia.[64] Soon after, Malaysia gave Singapore 24-hour's notice canceling various agreements that allowed RSAF planes to fly into Malaysian airspace, and followed this by opting out of the Five Power Defence Arrangements' military exercises that year.[65] In early 2001, it was a speech by Prime Minister Goh Chok Tong which triggered an angry Malaysian reaction and the summoning of Singapore's envoy in Kuala Lumpur for an explanation. Goh, responding to Malaysian media reports claiming that Malay Singaporeans were marginalized, said that in several ways, Singaporean Malays were better off than Malays living in Malaysia.[66] A war of words ensued for several months.

Singapore, for its part, has had a tendency to arrogance and has not always been sensitive to Malaysia's feelings. This was reflected in Singapore's approval of an official visit by Israeli President Herzog in November 1986, which caused an uproar in Malaysia.[67] Likewise, there was controversy in 1987 when B.G. Lee Hsien Loong was asked why there were no Malay national servicemen in sensitive positions (air force and army) and replied that the SAF did not want to put Malay–Muslim servicemen in a position where they might find their religion and national loyalty in conflict. The PAP government has also used issues with Malaysia for domestic political purposes, such as the frightening prospect of reunification, to jolt Singaporeans out of their complacency.[68] Finally, Lee Kuan Yew's penchant for speaking his mind publicly, and not always diplomatically, has undermined relations at times.

In the midst of a deteriorating regional security environment in 2001, Singapore became more conciliatory in its determination to solve its long-standing disputes with Malaysia. Because Malaysian Prime Minister Mahathir preferred working with Lee Kuan Yew to hammer out an agreement, the Senior Minister went to Putrajaya in September 2001. Lee and Mahathir reached a breakthrough package agreement on a new water contract, restored Singapore use of Malaysian air space for the RSAF, agreed on a new bridge and rail tunnel,[69] agreed on Malaysian railway land and the location of CIQ (Customs, Immigration, and Quarantine) facilities,[70] and agreed on the early withdrawal of CPF contributions for Malaysians no longer residing in Singapore.[71]

The most controversial part of the agreement is the water contract. Singapore has been promised less than half of the water it wanted after 2061 (to 2161), and it has agreed to pay 15 times more for the water it currently receives. This led to questions as to whether the pact was a fair deal for Singapore. Lee admitted that it might not have been the best deal, but said concessions were a trade-off for long-term security.[72] Lee noted, "... we have decided to make a deal ...".[73] However, in 2002 the deal unraveled (see p. 174).

Relations with Indonesia

The relationship with Indonesia is complex, although it has not been plagued by recurring squabbles. Indonesia's stability and prosperity are very important to Singapore (and the region); but Singapore is not very important to mammoth Indonesia. Diplomatic and business relations between the two states were amicable until Indonesian President Suharto resigned in May 1998, because of the personal relationship that had developed between Suharto and Lee Kuan Yew.[74]

Singapore realized that basing foreign policy on personal ties was perilous but unavoidable, and much effort was expended in trying to identify and cultivate the possible successors. This effort was ultimately unsuccessful, and in fact the one person not thought to be presidential material, B.J. Habibie, emerged as Suharto's immediate successor.[75] Habibie smarted from the disparaging remarks made by the Senior Minister about his suitability, relations chilled, Indonesia rejected a multi-billion dollar assistance package from Singapore because of the conditions attached, and Habibie referred to Singapore menacingly as a little "red dot" on the map next to "all the green" that was Indonesia.[76]

After being caught flat-footed with Habibie, Singapore scrambled to build up good relations with other key actors, both civilian and military, and relations with Indonesia's new and eccentric President, Abdurrahman Wahid, at first seemed cordial. However, on a trip to Singapore to attend an ASEAN meeting, Wahid lashed out at Singapore, accusing the state of being selfish and only thinking about profits. More bizarre and ominous, Wahid suggested that Indonesia and Malaysia should use their strategic position as key water suppliers for Singapore to push their interests.[77] Apparently Wahid was upset by some comments made by Lee Kuan Yew in their private meeting (much of it subsequently denied by the Senior Minister),[78] and by the suggestion, mistakenly blamed on Goh Chok Tong, that English should be the official language for ASEAN (whereas it was actually

Mahathir's suggestion). Wahid also apparently threatened to "bomb" the new submarines that Singapore had acquired.[79]

Singapore initially maintained a diplomatic silence, and then replied in a firm but measured tone to set the record straight. Thereafter both Singapore and Jakarta started trying to mend diplomatic fences.[80] Relations with Indonesia improved markedly when Megawati Sukarnoputri replaced Wahid in July 2001. At the same time, Singapore remains deeply concerned about Indonesia's political stability, territorial integrity, and economic recovery, and possible spillovers from these problems.[81]

Relations with the People's Republic of China

Relations with China have been friendly and unencumbered by conflicting territorial claims in the South China Sea. Because of its majority Chinese population, and the suspicions that aroused in the region, Singapore as a matter of policy decided not to establish diplomatic relations with China until after Indonesia did, thus waiting until October 1990. However, Lee Kuan Yew had made five trips to China by then, beginning in 1976, and former Finance Minister Goh Keng Swee was already an economic adviser to Beijing. Further, by 1978, China was looking at Singapore as a socio-economic model.

The relationship has developed on the basis of the economic opportunities and Singapore's usefulness to China in dealing with the West and Taiwan, and it blossomed during Deng Xiaoping's leadership. In 1992 Deng said that there "is good social order in Singapore ... We should draw from their experience ...", resulting in visits from several hundred delegations from China to learn about Singapore's legal system and how it has resolved "contradictions" between Western technology and social stability.[82] With Singapore's "go regional" policy, initiated in 1993, China has received the most visits, and a large share of the investment, including for the controversial Suzhou Industrial Park project (see pp. 76–7). China is now Singapore's fifth largest trading partner, and trade is expected to increase. In the early 1990s, Lee Kuan Yew found himself in the role of interlocutor between China and Taiwan, and Singapore hosted their first talks in 1993.[83] He and others in Singapore have also tried to explain the US to China, and vice-versa, and have advised China about how to respond to various US charges against China of human rights violations and other abuses.[84] While Singapore has not shied away from criticizing China when it felt its interests or regional interests were involved (e.g., the provincial complications involving Suzhou (see pp. 76–7), and when China's military exercises seemed designed to intimidate Taiwan in 1996), the relationship is friendly and largely devoid of bilateral problems. In 2001, in a meeting with Senior Minister Lee, China's President Jiang Zemin said that he hoped Sino–Singapore cooperation would be further enhanced in the new century.[85]

This does not mean that Singapore is not apprehensive about China's military power. While Southeast Asia's low-cost manufacturers and assemblers are very nervous about China as an economic competitor, hi-tech Singapore remains more concerned about China's geopolitical ambitions in the region. It is for this reason that Singapore wants the US to remain a dominant player in Asia.

Relations with the United States

Singapore's relationship with the United States has been difficult at times, although the US is clearly the major power most important to Singapore. In terms of defense diplomacy, the relationship has been consistently good. However, relations with the US State Department and the US liberal media establishment have had their ups and downs.

Singapore has long supported the presence of the US in Southeast Asia and regarded it as crucial for peace and stability in the region, and it has viewed the US as a reasonably "benign hegemon".[86] Singapore supported the US intervention in Vietnam and still regards that effort as having succeeded in giving the rest of the region the time needed to develop economically and thwart local Communist insurgencies. Senior Minister Lee believes that the US is likely to remain the pre-eminent world power for the next 50 years at least.[87]

At the same time, Singapore views the US as an inconsistent and sometimes unreliable power, at the mercy of public opinion and foreign policy fads; a power with the military strength but not the political will to necessarily "stay the course".[88] Indeed, based on the little interest shown by the US in the economic crisis that hit the region and its lack of involvement in the events surrounding East Timor, Singapore has been concerned that the US is disengaging from Southeast Asian security, and that a reordering of US priorities will have it focus on Northeast Asia. The campaign against terrorism has now re-focused US attention on Southeast Asia.

The end of the Cold War reduced Singapore's usefulness to the US, and it also led to a re-emphasis in US foreign policy, strengthened by its success in the Cold War, on human rights and democratic development. This led to a clash in political values between the two countries and resultant friction in the relationship. In a series of events and incidents, Singapore showed its determination not to allow Washington to interfere with its domestic political scene,[89] and then had the audacity to critique American social and political shortcomings. Indeed, in 1997 the new US Ambassador to Singapore pointed out that while Singapore's achievements were "amazing and incredible", the state had "done a pretty poor public-relations job" in the US,[90] presumably because of its impudence. There was so much acrimony in the mid-1990s that one observer believed that the "divorce between Singapore and the US appears irreparable".[91]

The vehemence of the clash of political values is best explained by looking at the larger picture. It was not just that America's evangelical drive to democratize Asia was being rebuffed by tiny Singapore but, more to the point, it irritated the US that Singapore was providing a contrary example, even alternative model, for China – still the big prize. By the new millennium there were no new incidents and the relationship had mellowed again. Relations warmed further with the Bush Administration coming to office and Goh's visit to Washington, DC. The two countries moved still closer with the arrests in Singapore of suspected terrorists in three cells of the Jemaah Islamiah (Islamic Group), who were apparently plotting to attack US warships, navy personnel on shuttle buses, US companies, and several embassies, including that of the US.[92]

Multilateralism

Multilateral arrangements offer the advantage of strength in numbers to small states, and thus help moderate vulnerability. They also allow a small state to play an active international role and, through adept diplomacy, to make an impact that would not be possible on its own. Singapore's competent and effective engagement in multilateral organizations has enabled it to "punch above its weight".

The first multilateral organization to which Singapore was admitted, a month after becoming independent, was the United Nations in September 1965. Singapore, although sometimes despairing of the system, has remained committed to the United Nations, and believes that the UN should play *the* central role in upholding international law and world peace. Singapore has consistently defended the principle of sovereignty and non-interference, and opposed the use of force by states to affect changes in boundaries and/or governments. Singapore has also contributed to peacekeeping and humanitarian missions, although this has been necessarily limited given its resource constraints.[93] As well, Singapore has supported, and will contribute troops and equipment to, UN Standby Arrangements. Probably Singapore's most significant contribution to date was serving as chair of the Third UN Law of the Sea Conference in 1982, out of which came the first legal instruments governing the oceans. This came into force in 1994, and now binds the maritime conduct of 130 states.[94] Growing out of its efforts to get favorable maritime resolutions passed, Singapore promoted the UN Forum of Small States, which was institutionalized in 1992.[95]

Having been decisively elected by the General Assembly, after a decade-long campaign, Singapore began a two-year term in 2001 as a non-permanent member of the UN Security Council. The importance Singapore attaches to this can be seen in the fact that it named its prominent former permanent secretary of the Ministry of Foreign Affairs, Kishore Mahbubani, to be Ambassador to the United Nations.

Singapore's activism in the UN stepped up with its opposition to the Vietnamese invasion of Cambodia in late 1979. Singapore helped promote, lead and coordinate the rigorous diplomatic effort of the ASEAN states in opposing UN recognition of the new Vietnamese-imposed government in Cambodia. Singapore argued that human rights should not be the criterion for membership; that the issue at hand was respect for the principle of sovereignty. At the UN in September 1980, Foreign Minister S. Dhanabalan maintained that "when the sovereignty, territorial integrity and independence of other nations are violated by bigger nations, we feel that our security is endangered".[96] It is from the Cambodia issue, according to Leifer, that Singapore "began to register a notable lead and stridency in foreign policy . . .".[97]

Singapore has joined a number of other multilateral organizations as well, including the Association of Southeast Asian Nations (ASEAN), and its affiliates, the ASEAN Free Trade Area (AFTA), the ASEAN Regional Forum (ARF, discussed earlier), and the yearly ASEAN–EU Ministerial Conference. It also belongs to the Commonwealth, the Non-Aligned Movement, the Asia Pacific Economic Cooperation forum (APEC), the Asia–Europe Meeting (ASEM), the Forum for East Asia–Latin America Cooperation (FEALAC), the Group of 77, the

World Trade Organization (WTO), among others. Of all of these, ASEAN is the key.

Singapore joined ASEAN in 1967 as a founding member, but it did not value the organization in the early years, and in fact had strong private reservations about Indonesia's Zone of Peace, Freedom and Neutrality (ZOPFAN) concept, which it felt obliged to agree to in order to show solidarity.[98] However, by 1973 it had come to appreciate the benefits of regional cooperation and solidarity, and ASEAN emerged as the cornerstone of Singapore's foreign policy. ASEAN did not eliminate bilateral problems between the regional neighbors, but multilateral cooperation and dialogue helped ameliorate bilateral issues.

Singapore often says it had no ambition to play a leadership role in ASEAN, to avoid regional jealousies and suspicions and also to encourage Indonesia's leadership and full participation in the organization. Consequently, it has been careful to downplay its contributions to many ASEAN initiatives. For example, Lee Kuan Yew played an important role in establishing the Post-Ministerial Conference, a meeting between ASEAN and its dialogue partners (other important states) in 1979; Singapore was instrumental in persuading Brunei to join the association in 1984; and Singapore played a key role in the formation of the ARF, which held its first meeting in Singapore in 1993.[99]

Further, in order not to stymie the consensus style of decision-making in ASEAN, Singapore worked out a system of less than total unanimity, since Singapore's interests often differed from the others because it had a more urban and industrialized economy. This was the 4-minus-1, then 5-minus-1 formula where Singapore (or some other member) abstained even if it disagreed, so long as it was not detrimental to its vital interests, in order to preserve the consensus (now, with expansion, the formula is a more vague 10-minus-X). Singapore believed this concession was balanced by the benefits of membership and the perception of good neighborliness.

Until mid-1997, ASEAN was called "one of the most constructive and consequential regional groupings in the world".[100] Then a series of setbacks and disruptions undermined the association and led to diplomatic paralysis. First, in an intensely debated decision pushed hard by Indonesia and Malaysia, ASEAN expanded its membership in 1997 to include the most internationally scorned state in the region (Myanmar), thus incurring the wrath of the West over its "constructive engagement"[101] approach; the poorest state in the region (Laos), thus widening the rich-poor gap in the organization; and the (then) most unstable state in the region (Cambodia), which, because of a *coup d'état* just before its scheduled admission, was not formally admitted until April 1999.

Second, the Asian economic crisis struck in mid-1997 and spread across the region. ASEAN initially discounted the seriousness of the financial upheaval, and when it assumed crisis dimensions found itself unable to respond helpfully. Each state reverted to looking after its own interests, and ASEAN became irrelevant to the crisis or its solution. B.G. Lee, in a speech calling on ASEAN to close ranks and dispel the perception of a region in distress, noted that "ASEAN appeared divided and slow in responding to the crisis, and even now is seen as weakened and drifting".[102]

Perhaps the clearest demonstration of ASEAN impotence was seen in its inability to make any concerted response to the violence and destruction in East

Timor after the autonomy/independence referendum was held. ASEAN would not act until Indonesia asked for help. When it was clear that a peacekeeping force was going to be needed for East Timor, Malaysia and Thailand bickered over who would lead it, until finally Australia took the lead, and asked for regional participation.[103] That was perhaps ASEAN's nadir.

Singapore Foreign Minister S. Jayakumar, acknowledging that it will take some time for ASEAN to recover its international standing, said that ASEAN must reinvent itself.[104] ASEAN came to prominence as a bulwark against the spread of Communism in the region. Since that is no longer an issue, Singapore believes ASEAN should concentrate on increased economic integration and enhanced regional trade, and is its top promoter. Through the increasingly popular ASEAN+3 (China, Japan, and South Korea) meetings, the larger grouping is working out monetary agreements, such as currency swaps to deal with future financial crises, that could lead to the establishment of an Asian Monetary Fund.[105] Singapore has opposed establishing an exclusively Asian regional trading bloc, and suggested instead an "ASEAN Plus Three, Plus Two" (the latter two being Australia and New Zealand).[106] However, at the November 2001 meeting in Brunei, China and ASEAN (with Singapore concurring) agreed on constructing the world's largest free trade zone in ten years' time.[107] Further, ASEAN has set up a troika mechanism to deal with problems more quickly as they arise, and a surveillance mechanism to track the movement of short-term capital and to anticipate economic problems.

Singapore has been concerned about growing competition in the region from China, discouraged by WTO and APEC failures on trade liberalization,[108] and frustrated by the lack of progress with AFTA, particularly by Malaysia's threat in July 2000 to quit AFTA unless it was given an exemption to lower tariffs for its automobile industry – a threat which succeeded in getting ASEAN to back down.[109] As a result, Singapore has signed a number of bilateral trade deals around the world. At the ASEAN+3 Summit in Singapore in November 2000, Goh Chok Tong argued that "those who can run faster, should run faster" and should not be restrained by those who don't want to run at all. Not all of Singapore's ASEAN partners agree, notably Malaysia.[110]

ASEAN has never been a security arrangement, and multilateral defense cooperation is absent in the region. However, ASEAN's role in containing and managing tensions in Southeast Asia through diplomacy remains important, as is ASEAN's collective voice *vis-à-vis* China. As Lee Kuan Yew stated, "Where ASEAN's interests are not involved, as in issues like Taiwan, Tibet, and Hong Kong, which involve China's sovereignty, ASEAN will not back an American challenge. Over the Spratlys, ASEAN cannot remain neutral. But on other issues, ASEAN is likely to be torn between two strong pulls: the need to retain [an] American presence, and the need to develop a viable long-term relationship with a huge neighbor, China".[111]

Altogether, Singapore remains committed to ASEAN. It sees itself as inextricably linked with Southeast Asia, and believes that a strong and dynamic ASEAN strengthens the region. Prime Minister Goh has reiterated that the present difficulties should not distract from "ASEAN's relevance and potential".[112]

Another multilateral arrangement with special importance to Singapore is the Asia–Europe Meeting (ASEM), largely the brainchild of Prime Minister Goh

Chok Tong. In 1994 Singapore and France proposed a biennial Asia (ASEAN + China, Japan, and South Korea)–Europe Summit, which was endorsed by all the parties. The first summit-level bi-annual meeting was held in Bangkok in 1996. Subsequent meetings were held in London and Seoul. The next meeting will be held in Copenhagen in mid-2002. The impetus behind ASEM was to strengthen the "weak link" of the world's economic associations. The EU was alarmed that APEC would turn into a trading bloc that would exclude Europe from the major markets of Asia. Thus the EU was determined to "return to Asia", and welcomed the ASEM as a vehicle.[113] Singapore saw in ASEM the prospect of trade diversification, as well as cultural and educational exchanges, and believed this would give ASEAN leverage *vis-à-vis* the US in APEC.

ASEM has been hindered by human rights disagreements (mainly concerning Myanmar) and hampered by the EU's complex internal decision-making process. Consequently there has been little progress on a ministerial declaration or action plan, and there is also no fixed agenda at the summits. An elaborate Asia–Europe Vision Group Report in 1999 recommended, among a number of other things, moving on to a second phase that would give more importance to political and security dialogue.[114] This, however, is the European agenda, whereas Asia wants to focus on trade and is reluctant to discuss sensitive political and security issues.[115] Further, the Europeans want to discuss not only issues like arms control, but also the need for Asian economic reforms, transparency, and anti-corruption measures. More recently, as a result of the economic crisis in Southeast Asia, the EU has shifted its focus to Northeast Asia and India. In its strategic paper on Asia, only two pages concerned the ASEAN states, most of it advice on human rights.[116] Despite these problems, Singapore remains committed to making the forum work.

Foreign policy activism: the influence of Singapore abroad

Singapore's foreign policy activism can be dated back to Lee Kuan Yew's new role as Senior Minister in 1991, and the government's "go regional" economic policy, which was launched in 1993. Already by then Singapore was seen as a development model by China (see p. 179). In the 1990s, the Africa Leadership Forum was interested in any lessons that could be learned from Singapore's experience,[117] and the Labour Party in Britain, about to return to power, sent some of its shadow ministers to learn about Singapore's social security and Medisave health systems.

After he stepped down as Prime Minister in late 1990, Lee Kuan Yew became an adviser for Vietnam, Kazakhstan, and, most recently, Indonesia. He also expanded his role as a respected international figure willing to espouse his views directly and sometimes bluntly in a variety of international venues. This, as Leifer points out, has been at times "a mixed blessing for the island-state" since in some capitals "his *obiter dicta* have been deeply resented".[118] For example, in November 1992, speaking to a Philippine business conference, he angered Filipinos when he said that to develop, the Philippines had more need of discipline than democracy.[119] He has also criticized and angered the US for its unfettered individualism, and he has disparaged politics in India by saying, "Indians just love an argument . . . They never get a consensus . . . What you have is more debate".[120]

At the same time, he is very much in demand on the international stage, his contacts with world leaders are indeed extensive, as his two lengthy volumes of memoirs reveal, and his travels and international speeches have served to enhance a global recognition of tiny Singapore's "exceptionlism".

He has also served as interlocutor between China and Taiwan, as mentioned earlier (see p. 179), but his strong criticism of former Taiwan President Lee Teng-hui, and his description of President Chen Shui-bian's administration as a continuation of "the Lee administration without Lee", has meant that the Senior Minister is no longer viewed as a neutral mediator.[121]

Conclusion

Singapore is a small trading state, and much of what goes on in the world and even the region is beyond its capacity to control. Singapore's leaders are cognizant of this fact and have always been realists about Singapore's vulnerability and limitations. However, to lessen its vulnerability, Singapore has been willing to expend considerable resources on deterrence and diplomacy. Singapore has a credible defense force, generally seen as the best trained and equipped in the region, and a well developed defense industry. Diplomatically, Singapore has sought friendly relations and trade with all states in a multitude of bilateral and, increasingly, multilateral arrangements. Its foreign policy activism since the 1990s is explainable as a measure of its success, and perhaps just a touch of confidence is replacing some of its earlier insecurities.

14 Singapore in the future

Globalization and a changing regional environment

> We are living in a very dangerous period and I don't think Singaporeans understand that.
>
> Goh Chok Tong[1]

Samuel P. Huntington wrote in 1996 that the "freedom and creativity that President Lee has introduced in Taiwan will survive him. The honesty and efficiency that Senior Minister Lee has brought to Singapore are likely to follow him to the grave". Goh Chok Tong quoted this passage in his National Day Rally Speech in 1999, and asked, "What must we do to prove Huntington wrong?"[2]

Honest and efficient government may well survive Lee Kuan Yew – a great deal of effort has gone into ensuring a smooth succession, and putting in place dedicated and efficient second- and third-generation successor teams. That is probably about as far as one can realistically gaze ahead. Of course, Huntington was really referring to democratization and liberalization, which is not entirely the same thing. However, to the extent that political freedom can be linked to creativity and innovation, the challenge is relevant to Singapore's future. What can Singapore do to maintain economic progress in a rapidly changing world without sacrificing the "honesty and efficiency" of the government and societal order? Clearly, the Knowledge-Based Economy is about information and communication, and about innovation and creativity. To achieve these goals, controls are anathema, as the PAP leadership realizes. The government has largely foresworn any battle to control the Internet, and it is trying slowly to loosen the reins on civil society. Will it loosen enough, in time, is a key question? To get ahead globally in this new economy, Singapore needs to nurture an innovative, adventurous, and Internet-proficient citizenry. Economic strength will depend even less on natural resources, land size or location, and much more, as Goh Chok Tong has noted, on the "capacity to create wealth through new applications of knowledge, new ideas and new knowledge".[3] The question is, does the IT revolution undermine the Asian development model, or can the "Singapore system" now make appropriate changes to produce a culture of creativity and innovation? Further, what can Singapore do about low fertility rates and the problem of losing some of its best brains to emigration?

In preparing for the future, there is not a great deal that Singapore can do to influence many international issues and events. The environmental problems in the late 1990s caused by haze drifting from illegal fires in Indonesia demonstrated the futility of ASEAN efforts in the face of a failure of governance in a neighboring country.[4] Regional uncertainty predominates. "If you look at what's happening in the neighborhood, never before have so many countries in ASEAN suffered from political problems all at the same time ...".[5] Further, concern prevails about the US economy and the faltering electronics industry, and disquiet over the extent and duration of the global fallout as the US slips towards a recession.

But there is no backing out of globalization or the IT revolution. Governments in Asia have been the main initiators and promoters of the globalization process, and none have embraced globalization more wholeheartedly than Singapore. B.G. Lee noted, "Globalization is an imperative ... for small countries ... The alternative is not just less competitive industries or lower standards of living, but a world in which countries will be less secure and more prone to conflicts".[6] B.G. Yeo observes that globalization represents both threats and opportunities: threats because of the danger that Singapore could lose out in areas where it has been strong, and opportunities because speed and fleet-footedness may offset Singapore's size limitations.[7] Likewise, he observes that "Those who are slow to change will be outflanked and bypassed ... As a Japanese businessman remarked to me recently, 'in the past "big ate small"; in the future, it will be "fast eats slow" '."[8]

To succeed in the new global economy, Singapore's leaders believe, the government must solve the problems of adequate manpower and sufficient talent for the future.

Population problems: falling fertility rates

Singapore has had a falling Total Fertility Rate (TFR) for the last two decades. The fertility rate peaked in 1988 (an auspicious Year of the Dragon) at 1.98, and it has fallen since, including the latest cycle of the Year of the Dragon in 2000.[9] Singapore's TFR of 1.48 is amongst the lowest in the world.[10]

Prime Minister Goh has called the falling TFR one of the two major challenges facing the country (the other being emigration).[11] Each produces the same unwanted effect – loss of population. It means that, unless something changes, Singapore's population will level out well short of the population figure considered optimal (5.5–6 million). There are other ramifications as well, such as an aging workforce and graying population, and it has implications for economic growth, since growth is derived from productivity gains *and* increases in the size of the workforce. Further, although the birth rate among all ethnic groups is dropping, the Malays are reproducing themselves whereas the Chinese and Indians are not.[12]

The changing position of women is a chief reason why Singapore's TFR is falling. Modernization and rising prosperity have affected gender roles, as have equal educational opportunities for women (there are more women than men enrolled in the premier tertiary institution, the National University of Singapore), status derived from work-based achievements, and changing life-styles.[13] Women enjoy a legal status comparable to any country in the world.[14] Women have also been encouraged to join the workforce and in 1999 women comprised 53 percent of the labor force, including 35 percent in professional and managerial positions in 2000.[15] The principal remaining barrier is politics, where women remain under-represented.[16]

The dominant social values emphasize work achievement and material success, and one result is that marriage and parenthood sometimes become secondary. A Social Development Unit poll, supported by a *Straits Times* survey, showed that marriage and parenthood do not have a high priority. The 2000 Census revealed that graduates aged 50 and up have an average of 2.2 children, while those aged 30–39 have an average of only 1.3 children. From those with less than a secondary education, the corresponding figures are 4.2 and 2.1 children.[17]

Singapore has one of the highest rates of single women in the world (being single is no longer considered deviant behavior and one in seven does not marry), and the figures for unmarried women rise with their level of education.[18] "In Singapore, life as a single female fending for herself can be a good life", writes Maria Chan. She is "articulate, confident, well-educated, well-traveled, financially independent – and single. Her numbers are rising to the consternation of some."[19]

Those women who do marry, tend to wed at an increasingly later age. The average age of brides in 1998 was 26.8 years, and the trend has been upwards.[20] Marrying late usually means fewer children, and family sizes continue to shrink. Since many women work, there is also a problem of exhaustion, compounded by the persistence of traditional attitudes within the family (in some cases, social progress has not kept pace with legal progress).[21] Helen Chia sums up the problem:

> The real enemy is time, or rather, lack of it – especially given Singapore's economic and social climate. Kids suck up your time faster than you can say Pokemon ... If you take a few years off work to start a family, you have to accept being put on a slower career track while your peers surge ahead of you ... Having a third child may just mean kissing the dream condo goodbye.[22]

The Singapore government has been trying for two decades to reverse the TFR decline through a variety of incentives. Originally, the incentives were designed to encourage the best educated women and the more financially secure families to have more children, through tax relief and other incentives. Goh Chok Tong summed up the government's views in the 1980s: "The population problem ... is a sensitive subject, because it is not just about getting the birthrate up. It is about improving the quality of our population"[23] (see p. 60).

In the new century, the government has apparently shifted its views. A former Minister and now Speaker of the House, Abdullah Tarmugi, said in Parliament in March 2000 that pro-baby incentives must be targeted at a broader base of women than just university graduates.[24] Soon after, two high-powered committees were established to study the issue of marriage and procreation – one staffed by top civil servants and statutory board chiefs, headed by the Permanent Secretary to the Prime Minister's Office, and the other a ministerial committee chaired by Lim Boon Heng. The first committee recommended a package of measures in August 2000, including leave for marriage for civil servants, flexi-hours and work from home (but no five-day work week), and three days' paid paternity leave.[25]

In August 2000, the Prime Minister announced a baby bonus scheme called the Children Development Co-Saving Scheme, which requires contributions from the parents, and would offer up to $9000 for a second child and $18,000 for a third one, over six years. Also, the law was changed to allow eight weeks' paid maternity leave for the third child as well as the first two.[26] It is too early to tell whether the latest measures will have much of an impact, but the government must be sobered by a United Nations Population Fund report that states that "No national attempt to raise fertility has ever succeeded against a downward demographic trend".[27]

"Exit, voice, and loyalty"[28] – the emigration problem

> Who wins depends on who attracts the most talent.
>
> Goh Chok Tong[29]

The "brain drain" is a serious problem for many states, especially developing states which devote scarce resources to education and training only to lose some of their best talent to foreign states. With labor so mobile, the problem of highly-skilled workers who consider themselves free agents has become widespread, and it was the subject of a study session recently about the "Age of Disloyalty" at an economic summit in Davos, Switzerland.[30]

Singapore has been particularly vulnerable because it has many well-educated (particularly in sciences, mathematics, and IT), English-speaking bilingual Singaporeans who are very marketable internationally. They have choices, and if they don't like living in Singapore or have vastly greater opportunities or can earn higher incomes elsewhere, they may leave. The question of how to harness and hold the best brains against the attractions overseas offered by the IT revolution "gold rush" is a perplexing one for the Singapore government. The leaders know it is inevitable that some will go abroad; they also know that with Singapore's small population they cannot afford to lose too many.

Throughout the 1990s, about 2,000 Singaporeans emigrated every year. This number is higher than in the 1970s, comparable with the early 1980s, and considerably lower than the late 1980s.[31] More than half of those who emigrate are females, many of whom are married to foreigners and leave Singapore to join their husbands. The law was changed in 1999 to allow foreign males married to Singapore women to live in Singapore, in the hope of reducing losses. In addition to emigrants, there are also Singaporeans who work abroad and students in foreign academic institutions – for a small country this is a fairly large diaspora numbering over 100,000.

Surveys show that some are leaving because of the high cost of living, including high prices for homes and cars; work stress, including family stress derived from the highly competitive education system. Some leave because of the restrictive political atmosphere and a feeling that rules and regulations are excessive.[32] Added to this is a feeling by some that Singapore is inhospitable to cultural pursuits. Many, it appears, leave because they are "head-hunted" by top foreign companies. The government is well aware that it needs to make Singapore an attractive place to live and work, to promote and support the arts,[33] to give

Singaporeans a stake in the system and a voice in Singapore's future, and to strengthen loyalty and nationalism. The government has also become less condemnatory about those who have emigrated (unless they are bond-breakers, discussed below), and hopes that its open-door attitude might lure some emigrants back. In Perth, Australia, B.G. Lee was asked if the government was hostile to those who stayed overseas. He replied that it was not; that it accepted globalization and reality. "We hope you will keep your links, that you will come back for visits".[34] Some talent will be lost, but the main message is, like the Prime Minister has said, "study and work overseas, but come back to Singapore".[35]

The bond-breakers

The government (and most of the public) is condemnatory and unforgiving about one type of emigrant: the students who accept lucrative government scholarships for tertiary education (with overseas scholarships as high as $250,000 per scholar) and then break their moral commitment and legal obligation to serve their bonds in Singapore. There was no problem with bonds for over three decades. It has developed into a problem, for those on Singapore Inc. scholarships primarily,[36] since the mid-1980s. As B.G. Lee told Parliament, "a government scholarship recipient takes up a commitment to serve Singapore ... Scholarships represent a use of public funds to train promising young men and women ... A scholar who fails to return to serve his bond has used public funds merely to serve his personal ends ... More reprehensive, he has deprived another student of the opportunity ...".[37]

Singaporeans and the government alike were troubled in July 2000 when 11 anonymous scholarship holders out of 30 interviewed stated that they intended to break their bonds and sell their services to the highest-bidders.[38] Responding to a public outcry, one intended bond-breaker wrote to the *Straits Times* Forum page defending his decision, saying, "They are simply unaware of the plethora of opportunities open to us ... Yes, we are in demand, but for a reason – because we are worth something ... We will not reconsider ... we have been told from birth to grab opportunities ...".[39]

Singapore has nurtured a hard-working consumer society where wealth and material possessions are highly correlated to status. But it has also been a society with a strong sense of duty and obligation. Overall, the scholarship scheme has worked well, with only 1 percent of local and 0.2 percent of overseas scholars breaking their bonds before starting work.[40] However, it is a matter of concern that among some of the best young computer students, acquisitiveness, self-interest, and arrogance have been the key values gleaned.[41]

The immigration solution: bringing in foreign talent

Until the 1980s, Singapore tightly restricted immigration and work permits. It was difficult for foreigners to obtain citizenship (expensive, too), permanent residence status, work permits (even for spouses of foreigners employed in Singapore), and employment passes. Some aspects of this policy changed when the government decided that it had no choice but to augment the population with new immigrants, to increase the talent pool and the workforce. However, the admission of new immigrants was selective – focusing on foreigners who were educated and skilled, and in a productive age group.[42] Simultaneously, the government announced that ethnic percentages would be maintained.

Not only would Singapore admit talented foreigners, it would actively seek them out around the world and attempt to recruit them. Initially, a major effort was made to attract Hong Kong immigrants in the period leading up to its handover to the People's Republic of China. However, this effort fell short: while over a 1,000 professionals applied for and obtained permanent residence approval between 1985 and 1989, only 35 actually moved to Singapore (clearly many were applying to other countries as well).[43] After this, efforts were redoubled around the world, but especially in the US, Canada, UK, Australia, New Zealand, China, and India. "Every year, we send teams of Public Service Division and EDB officers to comb the universities ... They recruit people, mainly Asian, who want to work and live in Asia. But we have to compete against other talent spotters".[44] Singapore also advertises internationally. "The targets are professionals, investors, engineers, technologists, and entrepreneurs".[45]

By 1997, the immigration rules were further relaxed. In his National Day Rally speech, Goh Chok Tong said that Singapore grew on the back of immigrant labor, and that the "inflow of foreign talent will expand at all levels, from CEOs and professionals to blue collar workers from all over the world".[46] He stated that global competition for migrant talent (with the best brains in the knowledge-based IT field being wooed worldwide) required new mindsets and a review of past strategies.

In 2001, this policy continued in spite of the recession and potential political fallout. The government explained that it recognizes that the foreign talent policy impacts the middle level of the job market – the skilled workers and professionals. The government wants to attract *both* local and international talent, however, the local workforce of 1.5 million alone is "too small to support the needs of our industries".[47]

The strategy of attracting foreign talent seems to be working. Singapore now has the highest proportion of immigrants of any country in the world: more than 25 percent of people living in Singapore are foreign born. Between 1995 and mid-1999, a total of 130,000 permanent resident and 39,000 citizenship certificates were granted to immigrants.[48] B.G. Yeo observed, "For every two babies that are born in Singapore, we bring in one foreign permanent resident. Also, one in four marriages [by a] Singaporean is to a foreigner. This has doubled in the last ten years. We have become a migrant society all over again".[49]

Not surprisingly, the rapid influx of foreigners has caused some resentment among Singaporeans, and in 2001, the economic downturn made the issue more delicate. Immigrants are exempt from national service and, since 1998, from contributing to the CPF (as well as their employers). They are also provided with rental housing which is cheap by Singapore standards. Rapid immigration has also caused some apprehension among Singaporeans about jobs. There has been a lively debate in the press about immigration policy, and a 2000 poll of 500 Singaporeans conducted by Channel NewAsia found that 78 percent of respondents preferred a cut-back on immigration, mainly out of fear for their jobs.[50] In another poll in 2001, while nearly 80 percent believed foreign talent has contributed to Singapore's success, only about two-thirds believed such workers were actually necessary.[51] As Singapore's economy contracted in 2001, more graduates found it difficult to find jobs, thus complicating the issue.[52] Goh Chok Tong conceded that attracting immigrants might not be the popular thing to do, but stated that foreign talent helps create more jobs and increases Singapore's GDP growth, and reiterated that it was the best way to protect the interests of Singaporeans.[53] He urged Singaporeans to accept and help absorb the new immigrants.[54]

Singapore looking into the future

It has been pointed out that "governments are not carried forward by the tide of technology and the remorseless logic of markets but have real and difficult choices to make about how they look after their own people ...".[55] In the fast-moving, economically complex globalized world, the *quality* of governance has never been so important. Poor decision-making and bad choices, not to mention corruption, may well have serious consequences for a country.[56] For a small state like Singapore, always needing to look for market and strategic niches and to anticipate trends, with little margin for error, bad choices could change the prospects of the state in a hurry.

Good governance: providing effective and non-corrupt rule

> After years of treading carefully around the issue of why so many countries stay poor or get poorer, the UN, in a report ... put a lot of the blame on bad governance ... The report elevates good governance ... to the top priority ... What the report clearly demonstrates is that governance is a critical building block for poverty reduction. Embracing democracy is often not enough.
>
> *National Post*[57]

Good governance has a broad array of meanings. Often it is the developed West defining it for the rest of the world, although the term certainly has relevance to governance in the West as well. To many Western governments and their aid and technical assistance agencies, the term is linked to democracy and open and accountable government. The OECD ties it more narrowly to participation and human rights. However, the correlation between democracy (or democratization) and economic development remains unproven, and the fact that some agencies operate from these assumptions may have some relevance in explaining the many failures experienced by aid programs.[58]

The World Bank defines good governance as "the manner in which power is exercised in the management of a country's economic and social resources for development".[59] Clearly, the World Bank is primarily concerned about the impediments to economic development caused by government corruption, abuse of power, and incompetence. Its definition leads to a list of good traits or attributes: the rule of law and a legal framework for development, accountability, predictability, lack of corruption, and the ability to get the priorities right in the allocation of resources.[60] Likewise, Transparency International focuses on the virtues of government honesty and non-corruptibility. A related definition is "effective governance", which is concerned with the ability to govern (rather than the form of governance).[61] The key element of "effective governance" is sound leadership, which is often a neglected topic because it raises questions of values (as opposed to "universal principles").[62]

The PAP government believes that there is a strong correlation between economic performance and the quality of political leadership. Goh Chok Tong's criteria for good governance are: (1) honest, fair, and just government; (2) the capability of forging national consensus and social cohesion, and the willingness to take painful decisions; (3) the ability to anticipate the future, and to be resourceful in times of crisis; and (4) the ability to improve the standard of living of its people and maximize their potential.[63] An earlier list by Singapore officials of "Ten Easy Steps" to success include: strong government, long-term planning, welcoming FDI (foreign direct investment); clean administration; education for all; no welfarism; family values; law and order; ethnic harmony; and promotion of a national identity.[64]

Good governance in this book means a system of effective and non-corrupt rule that is responsive to people's needs and provides stability, accountability, the rule of law, increasing and shared prosperity, and socio-economic and educational opportunities. Accomplishing these is a tall order. In a few states around the world, like the US, institutions may help compensate for mediocre leadership. But for most states, while institutions matter, good leadership is still imperative for good government.

The PAP believes that the good governance it has delivered is critical to explaining Singapore's success, and some others seem to agree. Stan Sesser, who is critical about the absence of fully democratic norms in Singapore, nevertheless writes that Singapore "represents a living laboratory that shows what can be achieved by competent government, a sign to the rest of the world that cities need not plunge into the abyss of crime, pollution, and decay. On a continent where corruption, filth and poverty are the norms, Singapore is honest, clean, and prosperous".[65] PERC in 2001 rated Singapore the least corrupt country in Asia for the eighth straight year.[66] Transparency International has consistently ranked Singapore among the ten least corrupt countries in the world, and least corrupt in Asia, since its index was first published in 1995. The Swiss-based International Institute for Management Development and the World Economic Forum regularly rank Singapore as one of the world's most competitive economies, and the best in terms of government policies conducive to competitiveness. Ted Gaebler, the co-author of the book, *Reinventing Government*, when interviewed in Singapore said that there was "no question" that Singapore is an example of his 10 principles for better government, and that "Singapore is the best example of anticipatory government that I know of …". He concluded by saying that Singapore had achieved the ultimate bottom-line of good governance: maintaining and enhancing the quality of life of its citizens.[67]

How well is the Goh administration performing?: accomplishments and challenges

As *Asiaweek* aptly phrased it, "taking over from the country's founding leader, Lee Kuan Yew, is nobody's idea of an easy job".[68] What then are the major accomplishments of Prime Minister Goh Chok Tong and his team?[69] First, and most important for the PAP and domestic political stability, is the fact that Goh was able to keep the Cabinet team together and to arrive at a workable relationship with the Senior Minister. The rare glimpses the public has caught of PAP generational factions feuding, English- versus Chinese-educated differences, and perceived contention between hard-liner and consultative approaches that occurred in the 1980s and early 1990s, have now subsided (the last sign of contention was former President Ong's public tirade in 1999). Prime Minister Goh has welded a team that obviously works well together, and the PAP continues to hold off the *nemesis* of dominant parties: factional splits. Goh is, above all, a team player who is willing to share the credit for PAP successes.[70] Further, Goh was willing, from the beginning of his premiership, to state who his successor would be (Deputy Prime Minister B.G. Lee Hsien Loong), although he reserves the right to decide *when* he will step aside. He has also been willing to utilize the remarkable talent (and occasional liability) of Senior Minister Lee Kuan Yew, despite some early strains in their relationship, and at the cost to him initially of being seen as a transitory "seat warmer", and of having some of his policies perceived as bearing the imprimatur of the Senior Minister (see p. 119). Gradually his identity as the Prime Minister emerged and he is now comfortable with the relationship. Effortlessly, he exudes confidence.

Another major accomplishment for Goh and his team is that they reversed the PAP's electoral slide in 1997 after suffering declines in their percentage of votes for three successive general elections. T.J. Pempel's study of dominant parties shows that they do not necessarily decline over time *if* they are adept at creating new social bases of support.[71] The PAP has needed constantly to juggle and adjust its appeal between the English-educated and Chinese-educated Chinese; between the ethnic groups; and between the interests of the "cosmopolitans" and the "heartlanders" (see p. 81). The redistribution of wealth through the asset-enhancement scheme for HDB flats, combined with the threat of having to wait longer for housing upgrading if their constituency did not support the PAP, and the introduction of a number of subsidies and "top ups"[72] helped reverse the tide.

The first two accomplishments above were more concerned with the PAP than the country as a whole, although what happens to the PAP internally and electorally is of vital concern to Singaporeans. The third Goh accomplishment was guiding the country through the frightening 1997–8 regional financial crisis (see pp. 70–1). It is difficult sometimes to measure a government's performance until it faces a crisis. The economic crisis devastated regional economies, but left Singapore comparatively relatively unscathed (the value of the Singapore dollar declined against some currencies and a number of jobs were lost, but negative growth was avoided, and the economy bounced back quickly – see p. 71). The US Ambassador to Singapore, Steven Green, believes Singapore was affected so much less than the rest of the region by the crisis because: "In one word, it is management. Singaporeans are very fortunate to have a government that is very well managed, very far-sighted and willing to embrace change".[73]

A fourth accomplishment of the Goh government is a major administrative initiative of fashioning a second-tier government decentralization scheme featuring Community Development Councils and mayors (see pp. 96–8), so that local issues can be shaped and solved at the local level, principally by the participation of people who reside in those communities.

Another accomplishment of the Goh government is to have provided more avenues for citizens' participation and more tolerance for civil society (see Chapter 12). Despite the setback early in Goh's premiership, when his cautious liberalization efforts seemed to be rejected at the 1991 polls, mainly it seems by conservative Chinese-educated voters, Goh has made consultation and participation one of the government's top goals. Goh has said that he wants to give Singaporeans a bigger say in their future as a way of bonding them to Singapore. "We will continue to involve the private sector in major reviews of important policies ... At the same time, we have systematically opened up more channels for citizens to participate".[74] The Prime Minister clarified that the government will allow "more and more" NGOs, but will not allow them "to set the agenda". They can make suggestions and offer advice, but "they are not elected and cannot expect to have their way about how to run Singapore". Further, he added that the government will crack down on any NGOs that constitute "the political opposition in disguise".[75]

The Singapore 21 initiative was an important participatory exercise involving thousands of Singaporeans expressing their ideas on and visions for the kind of Singapore they want in the future.[76] Notably, cynicism seemed absent from the exercise, although people still feel they have little political efficacy.[77] Of course, the Goh government wants participation to be focused politically through feedback channels and socially by voluntary welfare organization service. And civil society is still in its infancy. Still, some important steps – psychological hurdles perhaps – in tolerating civil society have been taken that a decade or so ago seemed so unlikely, and now both the PAP and Singaporeans have seen that gradually allowing more voice need not be disruptive or signal the beginning of the end to the Singapore system.

A sixth accomplishment of the Goh government is its efforts to make Singapore a more cultured, refined and sophisticated place to live in future by focusing on a range of art and cultural facilities in the downtown area, enhancing the waterfront landscape, and widening the scope for downtown city living.[78] In early 2000, the government gave a $50 million top-up over five years to arts groups, activities and education, including the Singapore Symphony Orchestra and Singapore Chinese Orchestra, the National Arts Council, the Singapore Art Museum, and the Esplanade Theatres on the Bay. The aims, comprising the Renaissance City[79] report strategies, are to create a vibrant arts and cultural scene that adds a "creative buzz" to Singapore life and makes Singapore a more attractive place for talent. Another aim is to strengthen a sense of national identity by nurturing an appreciation of local arts and culture.[80] According to a 1996 survey by *Fortune Magazine*, Singapore was ranked third among the world's cities as "most conducive for living".[81]

Finally, there is one accomplishment that is Goh Chok Tong's alone: he is immensely personally popular in Singapore, spanning all classes and ethnic groups.[82] The fact that he is perceived as a "good man" who has demonstrated that he is capable and trustworthy is a great asset for the PAP government. His popularity no doubt wins votes for the PAP, and, beyond that, just liking the head of government helps take some of the rancor out of politics and keep "soft" anti-PAP opposition from becoming implacable and unreachable.

Overall, how well is the Goh government performing? Peter Schwartz, the co-founder and chair of Global Business Network, believes that Singapore may be the best-run country in the world, while at the same time becoming more democratic. He proposes, as others have done, that it be adopted as a development model.[83]

The "good life" and the "good society": living the Singapore dream

> If expectations are up and people are prepared to work to achieve them, that's good. But if everyone wants a house and a garden and a car or two, that's not achievable. Unless we can reconcile what people want with what we can actually create, we're going to have a problem on our hands.
>
> B.G. Lee Hsien Loong[84]

A society's values significantly influence what constitutes the "good life" and the "good society". Russel L. Barsh suggests that the concept of the "good society" be used to measure democracy qualitatively, based on "citizens' satisfaction". This would measure, in a broad way, governmental effectiveness and it would take political culture into account. Some societies would seek more freedom and a much higher level of participation than others, and some would expect a greater degree of expertise from their leaders and better governmental performance than others.[85] Likewise, Peter Smith asks what criteria for judging a society should be, and wonders if "a society corporately chooses to forgo individual freedom" for other values, whether it should be criticized for this?[86]

In Singapore, many surveys indicate that the "good society" gives a high priority to achieving prosperity and security, economic advancement, freedom from ordinary crime and political disorder, and general health and happiness. This has been translated into the "Singapore Dream" – the pursuit of a comfortable and rewarding life through the acquisition of material wealth, epitomized by obtaining the "5Cs": condominiums, cars, cash, credit cards, and country club memberships.[87]

However, Singaporeans and others have also criticized the "dream" for being too crassly materialistic, with too much accompanying pressure to succeed in gathering riches. Some have also criticized the "dream" for ignoring the relatively poor in affluent Singapore (see p. 81). One letter writer complained that "no one has time for those who lag behind", and another said that there should be more emphasis on the intangibles of life, and that happiness for some might mean more time to "smell the roses" and less on making money. Another writes, however, "Many think Singaporeans are in danger of becoming overwhelmed by materialism, so we should de-emphasize material achievements … But who are saying this? Surely not those still struggling up the ladder … it is coming from those who have already arrived".[88]

Since the 1980s, the PAP government has been trying to combat some of the less desirable symptoms of affluence and Westernization. These include being rude, acquisitive, and what Singaporeans have labeled "kiasuism" – a Hokkien word which literally means fear of losing, but which has come to mean two things in Singapore: risk aversion or conformity, and selfishness: "Better grab first, later no more".[89] The government does not want to dampen the materialistic spirit entirely, but it would like to curb its vulgar side through moral exhortations, by campaigns stressing courtesy, by urging volunteerism, by emphasizing creativity, and by promoting values stressing communitarianism, national pride,[90] and the concept of a shared destiny.

Among a significant minority, there is a yearning for more political openness and democratization. But for many other Singaporeans, especially since the Asian economic crisis and the turmoil in Indonesia, what may matter more is a government that maintains stability and delivers economic prosperity – "the good society". Many accept the PAP's contention that too much liberty leads to instability, and surveys show that Singaporeans consistently rank social stability and order as being more important than personal liberty.[91] What this means is that Singaporeans have learned to consider trade-offs in their political choices, such as suggested by Isaiah Berlin: "... if these ultimate human values by which we live are to be pursued, then compromises, trade-offs, arrangements, have to be made if the worst is not to happen. So much liberty for so much equality, so much individual self-expression for so much security, so much justice for so much compassion ... So we must weigh and measure, bargain, compromise ...".[92]

A recent survey of 1,407 junior college and university students is instructive. It shows that in general they respect authority (only 3 percent strongly disagree), and strongly support the maintenance of law and order and capital punishment, including 79 percent who strongly agree that criminals should be caned for serious offenses. There is high agreement that it pays to work hard and that education is valuable. They also strongly believe in the family and respect for elders; that compromise is preferable to conflict; and they are comfortable with Singapore's legal system. Finally, they have high expectations and aspirations for attaining the "good things" in life, and they are materialistic and take a short-term view in being only marginally supportive of the idea of thrift.[93] There is strong support for the idea of the "Singapore Dream".

What this survey and others indicate is that, despite restrictions on political freedoms and in spite of a desire to see more openness and more political opposition in Parliament, and a wish for less of a "nanny" state, so long as the PAP government delivers the goods and meets and contains the high expectations of Singaporeans, they will support the Singapore system and PAP rule.

Further reading

Thomas Bellows, *The People's Action Party of Singapore: Emergence of a Dominant Party System*, New Haven, CT: Yale University Southeast Asia Series, 1970. The basic source on the years preceding and during early PAP rule.

Dennis Bloodworth, *The Tiger and the Trojan Horse*, Singapore: Times Books International, 1986. A most readable account of how the PAP came to power and defeated the Communists. These early struggles are indispensable for understanding some of the party's later behavior.

Chan Heng Chee, *The Dynamics of One-Party Dominance: The PAP at the Grassroots*, Singapore: Singapore University Press, 1976. This excellent book examines the working and interactions of the party at different levels.

Chua Beng-Huat, *Communitarian Ideology and Democracy in Singapore*, London: Routledge, 1995. A Singapore sociologist's attempt to account for the evolution of the PAP's ideology. After examining pragmatism and, briefly, Confucianism, he searches for characteristics which democracy and communitarianism may have in common.

John Drysdale, *Singapore: Struggle for Success*, Singapore: Times Books International, 1984. This book is in some ways complementary to Bloodworth's. It is particularly useful in explaining the course of the PAP's economic policy and its reliance on multinational corporations, and on the advice given by UN technical assistance, notably by Dr. Albert Winsemius.

T.J.S. George, *Lee Kuan Yew's Singapore*, London: André Deutsch, 1974. Full of information, mostly via anecdotes. Useful for conveying atmosphere, with rather broad strokes.

Goh Keng Swee, *The Economics of Modernization*, Singapore: Asia-Pacific Press, 1972. Essays, economic and political, with some social implications. Goh used ideas such as those expressed in this book to create the economic infrastructure which was the basis for Singapore's success.

Michael Hill and Lien Kwen Fee, *The Politics of Nation Building and Citizenship in Singapore*, London: Routledge, 1995. The subject of the book is Singapore's efforts to create a new, and appropriate, identity. To sum up what is easier said than done: ethnic sentiments must be softened and citizenship made more vibrant. Much of the emphasis is, correctly, placed on education and language.

Gillian Koh and Ooi Giok Ling (eds.), *State–Society Relations in Singapore*, Singapore: Institute of Policy Studies and Oxford University Press, 2000. The book seeks to produce a study of "civil society" which would not envisage a zero-sum adversarial relationship. Such an approach seems congruent with Goh Chok Tong's.

Lam Peng Er and Kevin Y.L. Tan (eds.), *Lee's Lieutenants: Singapore's Old Guard*, St. Leonards, NSW: Allen & Unwin, 1999. The authors, not to coin a phrase, fill a gap.

Although the word, "lieutenants", pays little regard to their wide differences in status, it helps to make the point that, although Lee Kuan Yew was unquestionably the leader, as he himself has acknowledged, credit is also due to the *team* effort of the PAP leaders.

Albert Lau, *A Moment of Anguish: Singapore in Malaysia and the Politics of Disengagement*, Singapore: Times Academic Press, 1998. A new evaluation of Singapore's exit from Malaysia, based partly on newly-available sources.

Lee Kuan Yew, *The Singapore Story: Memoirs of Lee Kuan Yew*, Singapore: Prentice-Hall, 1998. There are two principal themes here: how in Singapore the non-Communist left triumphed over the Communist left; and how Malaysia, proposed by Malaya and eagerly welcomed by Singapore, rapidly fell apart. Agreement on general principles proved to be no protection against the disruptive effects of ethnicity harnessed to advance particular interests.

Lee Kuan Yew, *From Third World to First, The Singapore Story: 1965–2000*, Singapore: Times Media Private Ltd., 2000. The book follows the steps by which events conformed to the title and, literally, a third-world state was transformed into a first-world state. In the telling, there are pen-pictures of all the world's political elite worth writing about. Both of Lee's books contrive to be at the same time magisterial and entrancing.

Michael Leifer, *Singapore's Foreign Policy: Coping with Vulnerability*, London: Routledge, 2000. A comprehensive book, carefully planned, and felicitously expressed. The theme is briefly: how can Singapore protect its excellence from its equally apparent vulnerability?

Lim Chong Yah (ed.), *Policy Options for the Singapore Economy*, Singapore: McGraw-Hill, 1988. There are 26 contributors to this volume, on all major aspects of the economy.

Linda Low, *The Political Economy of a City-State*, Singapore: Oxford University Press, 1996. Given the shortage of resources in Singapore, how can they best be deployed? Here an economist lays the emphasis on planning. Others, such as Tremewan (see below) interpret the PAP's efforts in terms of control.

Linda Low and T.C. Aw, *Housing a Healthy, Educated and Wealthy Nation through the CPF*, Singapore: Institute of Policy Studies and Times Academic Press, 1997. The focus is on the operations of the Central Provident Fund and its twin (step-child?), the Housing and Development Board. It also deals with Prime Minister Goh Chok Tong's plans on "topping up", which distribute help to the needy while avoiding the stigma of "welfare".

Linda Low (ed.), *Singapore: Towards a Developed Status*, Singapore: Oxford University Press, 1999. The authors, mostly from the National University of Singapore, explore the criteria for attaining "developed country" status, and consider how far Singapore meets them. The main shortfall seems to be in technological capacity when compared with some other developing societies.

Arun Mahizhnan and Lee Tsao Yuan (eds.), *Singapore: Re-Engineering Success*, Singapore: Institute of Policy Studies and Oxford University Press, 1998. It explicitly looks at the future, and the contributions are partly from "official" sources, including one from Deputy Prime Minister Lee Hsien Loong, which is refreshingly unofficial in tone.

R.S. Milne and Diane K. Mauzy, *Singapore: The Legacy of Lee Kuan Yew*, Boulder, CO: Westview, 1990. An introduction to political, economic and social trends in Singapore until 1990. It concentrates on the policies of the first Prime Minister, Lee Kuan Yew, and on the probable course of events under his successor, Goh Chok Tong.

Pang Chen Liang, *Singapore's People's Action Party: Its History, Organization and*

Leadership, Singapore: Oxford University Press, 1971. A distilled account of a major crisis in the ruling party, resulting in its survival and triumph by the skin of its teeth. The statistical analysis is compelling and clearly presented.

John Quah, Chan Heng Chee and Seah Chee Meow (eds.), *Government and Politics of Singapore*, Singapore: Oxford University Press, 1985. A thorough account of how government works in Singapore. There is more "government" than "politics" in the book, perhaps reflecting that when it was written there was less "openness" than there is now.

John Quah (ed.), *In Search of Singapore's National Values*, Singapore: Institute of Policy Studies and Times Academic Press, 1990. This book is based on a Goh Chok Tong proposal of 1988, later embodied in a White Paper on shared values. The main part of the book consists of comments by Quah and other academics.

Lily Rahim, *The Singapore Dilemma: The Political and Educational Marginality of the Malay Community*, Oxford: Oxford University Press, 1998. The book does not offer any simple explanation of Malay unhappiness about its "marginality", but convincingly conveys its existence. It recognizes that the education system under the PAP offers good prospects for improvement.

Report of the Economic Committee, *The Singapore Economy: New Directions*, Singapore: Ministry of Trade and Industry, 1986. The Committee, headed by B.G. Lee Hsien Loong, was notable for two main reasons. Through its network of committees and subcommittees, it evoked massive participation. Also, most of its recommendations were adopted and implemented.

Report of the Committee on Singapore's Competitiveness, Singapore: Ministry of Trade and Industry, 1998. In some ways, this was almost a replay of the 1986 Committee report (above). It was helped by having that precedent to guide it. Some of its recommendations are forerunners of the Knowledge-Based Economy.

Garry Rodan (ed.), *Singapore Changes Guard: Social, Political and Economic Directions in the 1990s*, New York: St. Martin's Press, 1993. Some excellent contributions, including Rodan's "Introduction" and his chapter on the middle class in Singapore; others are by J. Cotton, C. Leggett, and L. Low.

Garry Rodan, "The Rise and Fall of Singapore's Second Industrial Revolution", in Richard Higgott and Kevin Hewison (eds.), *Southeast Asia in the 1980s: The Politics of Economic Crisis*, St. Leonards, NSW: Allen & Unwin, 1987. The theme is how Singapore efforts to "move upstream", technologically, in the 1980s encountered obstacles, which blunted the thrust of the policy.

Garry Rodan, "Preserving the One-Party State in Contemporary Singapore", in Kevin Hewison, Richard Robison and Garry Rodan (eds.), *Southeast Asia in the 1990s: Authoritarianism, Democracy and Capitalism*, St. Leonards, NSW: Allen & Unwin, 1993. An analysis of the PAP in class terms, emphasizing its degree of centralization, technological bent, and relation to civil society – all under Goh Chok Tong.

Garry Rodan, "State–Society Relations and Political Opposition in Singapore", in Garry Rodan (ed.), *Political Opposition in Industrialising Asia*, London: Routledge, 1994. The main theme is that a more expansive society has not yet emerged in Singapore. The role of political opposition has been limited despite the existence of a sizeable middle class.

Edgar H. Schein, *Strategic Pragmatism: The Culture of Singapore's Economic Development Board*, Cambridge, MA: MIT Press, 1996. Schein's title embodies the basic approach of the Board. Its policies, he argues, are closely linked to the values of the ruling party – the PAP.

Joseph P. Tamney, *The Struggle Over Singapore's Soul*, Berlin: Walter de Gruyter, 1995. Tamney goes beyond considering contemporary materialist evaluations of Singapore's "success". He takes into account differences between Singapore's values and those of "the West". Referring to the former, he distinguishes official programs from those of opposition movements. A satisfyingly provocative book.

Christopher Tremewan, *The Political Economy of Social Control in Singapore*, New York: St. Martin's Press, 1994. The concept concentrated on by the author is "social control", exercised by the government, which he derives from the inequitable division of income. The book ends by stating that, in spite of the apparent dominance of those in control, the working class may have the potential to extract concessions.

Mary Turnbull, *A History of Singapore, 1819–1975*, Kuala Lumpur: Oxford University Press. The standard short history of Singapore. Indispensable.

Raj Vasil, *Governing Singapore*, rev. ed., Singapore: Eastern Universities Press, 1988. Looks at how Singapore has tackled its problems, through interviews with Lee Kuan Yew and Goh Chok Tong.

Raj Vasil, *Asianising Singapore*, Singapore: Heinemann Asia, 1995. An examination of how Singapore, with its not easily tractable ethnic mix, has nevertheless handled the situation so as to cause minimum damage to its economic programs.

Notes

1 What is remarkable about Singapore?

1 Lee Kuan Yew, *From Third World to First, The Singapore Story: 1965–2000*, Singapore: Times Media Private Ltd., 2000, p. 68.

2 Lee Kuan Yew, *From Third World to First, The Singapore Story: 1965–2000*, Singapore: Times Media Private Ltd., 2000, pp. 75–84.

3 John Drysdale, *Singapore's Struggle for Success*, Singapore: Times Books International, 1984, pp. 250–2.

4 Goh Keng Swee, *The Economics of Modernization*, Singapore: Asia Pacific Press, 1972, pp. 125–6.

5 B.G. Lee Hsien Loong, "Shell – A Partner in Progress", *Speeches*, vol. 15, no. 5 (September-October 1991), pp. 40–43.

6 Lee Kuan Yew, *From Third World to First, The Singapore Story: 1965–2000*, Singapore: Times Media Private Ltd., 2000, p. 12.

7 *Straits Times*, October 21, 1995.

8 Lee Kuan Yew, *From Third World to First, The Singapore Story: 1965–2000*, Singapore: Times Media Private Ltd., 2000, pp. 201–10.

9 R.S. Milne and Diane K. Mauzy, *Singapore: The Legacy of Lee Kuan Yew*, Boulder: Westview Press, 1990, p. 5.

10 *New York Times*, June 10, 2001.

11 Lam Peng Er and Kevin Y.L. Tan (eds.), *Lee's Lieutenants: Singapore's Old Guard*, St. Leonards, NSW: Allen & Unwin, 1999, pp. xii–xiv. A good case has been made for the inclusion of Hon Sui Sen, who made a substantial contribution to directing Singapore's economic policy (p. 3). See Ho Khai Leong, *The Politics of Policy-Making in Singapore*, Singapore: Oxford University Press, 2000, p. 68. For an assessment of the relative importance of the members of Lee Kuan Yew's cabinet as regards the closeness of the "orbits" to Lee, see Robert O. Tilman, "The Political Leadership: Lee Kuan Yew and the PAP Team", in K.S. Sandhu and Paul Wheatley (eds.), *The Management of Success: The Moulding of Modern Singapore*, Singapore: Institute of Southeast Asian Studies, 1989, pp. 53–8.

12 Lam Peng Er and Kevin Y.L. Tan (eds.), *Lee's Lieutenants: Singapore's Old Guard*, St. Leonards, NSW: Allen & Unwin, 1999, pp. 5–6. The authors make the point that, even if Lee had lost the first round, he might have staged a comeback later (fn 22, p. 194).

13 Fong Sip Chee, *The PAP Story – The Pioneering Years*, Singapore: Times Periodicals, 1979, p. 154, quoting Lee's speech at the Socialist International Conference in Brussels in 1964.

14 *The Singapore Story: Memoirs of Lee Kuan Yew*, Singapore: Prentice Hall, 1998 and *From Third World to First, The Singapore Story: 1965–2000*, Singapore: Times Media Private Ltd., 2000.

15 The bust of Ferdinand Marcos carved out of the mountain can be seen from Marcos Highway, not far from the summer resort of Baguio. It was completed just before Marcos was thrown out of power in 1986.

16 Lee Kuan Yew, *From Third World to First, The Singapore Story: 1965–2000*, Singapore: Times Media Private Ltd., 2000, p. 763.

17 R.S. Milne and Diane K. Mauzy, *Singapore: The Legacy of Lee Kuan Yew*, Boulder: Westview Press, 1990, p. 106.

18 On Marcos, see D.J Steinberg (ed.), *In Search of Southeast Asia* (revised ed.), Honolulu:

University of Hawaii Press, 1987, pp. 436–42; on Suharto, see Adam Schwarz, *A Nation in Waiting*, St. Leonards, NSW: Allen & Unwin, 1994, passim.

19 Lee Kuan Yew, *From Third World to First, The Singapore Story: 1965–2000*, Singapore: Times Media Private Ltd., 2000, pp. 182–9.

20 See Thomas Bellows, review of the book by Frederic C. Deyo, *Dependent Development and Industrial Order: An Asian Case Study*, in the *Third World Quarterly*, vol. 7, no. 4 (1985), p. 1096.

21 Survey conducted by the British Consumers Association, March 12, 2001, on the Web: http://www/stuff.co.nz/inl/index/0,1008,693915a10,FF.html.

22 The Swiss-based International Institute for Management Development singled out Singapore for its "extreme resilience" during the Asian economic crisis. See *Straits Times*, April 19, 2000, forwarded by sgdaily@list.sintercom.org on April 20, 2000.

23 Edgar H. Schein, *Strategic Pragmatism*, Cambridge, MA: The MIT Press, 1996, p. 62.

24 *Straits Times Weekly Edition*, October 21, 2000.

25 *Singapore: Facts and Pictures, 1999*, Singapore: Ministry of Information and the Arts, 1999, pp. 164–5. Singapore's expertise was further demonstrated by its newly completed Changi Naval Base, designed so that huge aircraft carriers can dock (see *Far Eastern Economic Review*, May 17, 2001, and pp. 173–4).

26 It should be noted that, even before the third terminal, Changi has been almost perennially rated as the world's best airport by various international surveys.

27 *Straits Times Weekly Edition*, October 14, 2000.

28 Some would add "small population".

29 Michael Leifer, *Singapore's Foreign Policy: Coping with Vulnerability*, London and New York: Routledge, 2000, p. 5 and passim.

30 *Far Eastern Economic Review*, October 26, 1979, p. 17.

31 *Far Eastern Economic Review,* October 26, 1979, p. 17.

32 *Far Eastern Economic Review*, February 6, 1997, pp. 38–9.

33 *Straits Times*, May 5, 1986.

34 Chan Heng Chee, *The Dynamics of One Party Dominance: The PAP at the Grass-Roots*, Singapore: Singapore University Press, 1976, p. 225.

35 R.S. Milne and Diane K. Mauzy, *Singapore: The Legacy of Lee Kuan Yew*, Boulder: Westview Press, 1990, p. 33.

36 Christopher Tremewan, *The Political Economy of Social Control in Singapore*, London: Macmillan Press, 1994 (reprinted in 1996 with a new preface), pp. 45–73.

37 Iain Buchanan, *Singapore in Southeast Asia: An Economic and Political Appraisal*, London: Bell, 1972, photograph and caption, opposite p. 193.

38 Michael Haas, "Mass Society", in Michael Haas (ed.), *The Singapore Puzzle*, Westport, CT: Praeger, 1999, p. 166.

2 How Singapore became independent

1 Essential references on history are: C.M. Turnbull, *A History of Singapore, 1819–1975*, Kuala Lumpur: Oxford University Press, 1977; Edwin Lee, "The Historiography of Singapore", in Basant K. Kapur (ed.), *Singapore Studies: Critical Surveys of the Humanities and Social Sciences*, Singapore: Singapore University Press, 1986, pp. 1–32; N.J. Ryan, *The Making of Modern Malaysia and Singapore*, Kuala Lumpur: Oxford University Press, 1969; Barbara Watson Andaya and Leonard Y. Andaya, *A History of Malaysia*, London: Macmillan, 1982.

2 Raymond Flower, *Raffles: The Story of Singapore*, Beckenham, England: Croom Helm, 1984.

3 N.J. Ryan, *The Making of Modern Malaysia and Singapore*, Kuala Lumpur: Oxford University Press, 1969, p. 112.

4 C.M. Turnbull, *The Straits Settlements, 1826–1867: Indian Presidency to Crown Colony*, London: Athlone Press, 1972.

5 Lee Kuan Yew, *The Singapore Story: Memoirs of Lee Kuan Yew*, Singapore: Prentice Hall, 1998, pp. 44–83.

6 Richard Stubbs, *Hearts and Minds in Guerilla Warfare: The Malayan Emergency 1948–1960*, Singapore: Oxford University Press, 1989.

7 Earlier elections had been held in 1948 and 1951 for a handful of Legislative Council seats. The franchise was severely restricted, however, until the Rendel Constitution recommendations.

8 R.S. Milne and Diane K. Mauzy, *Singapore: The Legacy of Lee Kuan Yew*, Boulder: Westview, 1990, p. 47.

9 Dennis Bloodworth, *The Tiger and the Trojan Horse*, Singapore: Times Books International, 1986, p. 76.
10 R.S. Milne and Diane K. Mauzy, *Singapore: The Legacy of Lee Kuan Yew*, Boulder: Westview, 1990, p. 48.
11 Chan Heng Chee, *David Marshall: A Sensation of Independence*, Singapore: Oxford University Press, 1984, pp. 165–76.
12 Lee Kuan Yew, *The Singapore Story: Memoirs of Lee Kuan Yew*, Singapore: Prentice Hall, 1998, p. 251.
13 Lee Kuan Yew, *The Singapore Story: Memoirs of Lee Kuan Yew*, Singapore: Prentice Hall, 1998, p. 249.
14 Dennis Bloodworth, *The Tiger and the Trojan Horse*, Singapore: Times Books International, 1986, p. 181.
15 Dennis Bloodworth, *The Tiger and the Trojan Horse*, Singapore: Times Books International, 1986, p. 192.
16 Fong Sip Chee, *The PAP Story*, Singapore: PAP, 1979, pp. 92–3.
17 Lee Kuan Yew, *The Singapore Story: Memoirs of Lee Kuan Yew*, Singapore: Prentice Hall, 1998, p. 322.
18 Interview with Prime Minister Lee Kuan Yew on August 4, 1986.
19 Lee Kuan Yew, *The Singapore Story: Memoirs of Lee Kuan Yew*, Singapore: Prentice Hall, 1998, p. 324.
20 See Mohamed Noordin Sopiee, *From Malayan Union to Singapore's Separation*, Kuala Lumpur: Penerbit Universiti Malaya, 1974, p. 125. The author mentions some previous proposals for a similar union, pp. 127–9. According to one account, Goh Keng Swee attributed the scheme to create Malaysia to the British (Kwok Kian-Woon, "The Social Architect: Goh Keng Swee", in Lam Peng Er and Kevin Y.L. Tan (eds.), *Lee's Lieutenants*, St. Leonards: Allen & Unwin, 1999, pp. 55–6).
21 To be sure, another ethnic question was pertinent. Would the majority of natives in the Borneo territories – who were not Malays or Muslims – follow the lead of Malay Muslims? The experience of Sarawak and Sabah since the formation of Malaysia shows that they have. The conclusion is that the present federation of Malaysia operates on the basis of Malay/Muslim predominance in the Borneo states as well as outside them (R.S. Milne and Diane K. Mauzy, *Malaysian Politics Under Mahathir*, London: Routledge, 1999, pp. 97–102).
22 Martin Meadows, "The Philippine Claim to North Borneo", *Political Science Quarterly*, vol. LXVII, no. 3 (1962), pp. 321–35.
23 Somewhat guardedly, it did (Mohamed Noordin Sopiee, *From Malayan Union to Singapore's Separation*, Kuala Lumpur: Penerbit Universiti Malaya, 1974, p. 149, fn. 118).
24 Mohamed Noordin Sopiee, *From Malayan Union to Singapore's Separation*, Kuala Lumpur: Penerbit Universiti Malaya, 1974, pp. 149–55.
25 Mohamed Noordin Sopiee, *From Malayan Union to Singapore's Separation*, Kuala Lumpur: Penerbit Universiti Malaya, 1974, pp. 172–82.
26 Lee Kuan Yew, *The Singapore Story: Memoirs of Lee Kuan Yew*, Singapore: Prentice Hall, 1998, p. 481.
27 Fong Sip Chee, *The PAP Story*, Singapore: PAP, 1979, pp. 96–7.
28 Lee Kuan Yew, *The Singapore Story: Memoirs of Lee Kuan Yew*, Singapore: Prentice Hall, 1998, pp. 382–3.
29 Lee Kuan Yew, *The Singapore Story: Memoirs of Lee Kuan Yew*, Singapore: Prentice Hall, 1998, p. 393.
30 Mohamed Noordin Sopiee, *From Malayan Union to Singapore's Separation*, Kuala Lumpur: Penerbit Universiti Malaya, 1974, p. 191.
31 Lee Kuan Yew, *The Singapore Story: Memoirs of Lee Kuan Yew*, Singapore: Prentice Hall, 1998, p. 540. See also the case that it was Lee himself who took the decision that the PAP should contest the election (Michael D. Barr, "Lee Kuan Yew in Malaysia: A Reappraisal of Lee Kuan Yew's Role in the Separation of Singapore from Malaysia", *Asian Studies Review*, vol. 21, no. 1 (July 1997), pp. 1–17).
32 Lee Kuan Yew, *The Singapore Story: Memoirs of Lee Kuan Yew*, Singapore: Prentice Hall, 1998, p. 508.
33 Lee Kuan Yew, *The Singapore Story: Memoirs of Lee Kuan Yew*, Singapore: Prentice Hall, 1998, pp. 497–503.

34 R.S. Milne, "Singapore's Exit From Malaysia: The Consequences of Ambiguity", *Asian Survey*, vol. 6, no. 3 (March 1966), pp. 180–1.
35 Lee Kuan Yew, *The Singapore Story: Memoirs of Lee Kuan Yew*, Singapore: Prentice Hall, 1998, pp. 610–15.
36 R.S. Milne, "Singapore's Exit From Malaysia: The Consequences of Ambiguity", *Asian Survey*, vol. 6, no. 3 (March 1966), p. 179.
37 Noordin Sopiee has called Tunku's feelings the "pain-in-the-neck" factor (Mohamed Noordin Sopiee, *From Malayan Union to Singapore's Separation*, Kuala Lumpur: Penerbit Universiti Malaya, 1974, p. 224). Tunku's own words have often been quoted: "Every movement caused grinding pain, but the mind was alive and active; so as I laid there I was thinking of Mr. Lee Kuan Yew. The more pain I got the more I directed my anger on him..." (Tunku Abdul Rahman, "Looking Back", *The Star*, April 7, 1975). He could come to only one conclusion, which he summed up later: "If we had not separated there would have been blue murder" (*Straits Times* [Malaysia] July 4, 1969). A contentious point is whether or not there was an agreement between Lee and the Tunku about restrictions on contesting elections (and other political activities) in "the other's territory". For Toh Chin Chye's views, see Lam Peng Er, "The Organisational Utility Men: Toh Chin Chye and Lim Kim San", in Lam Peng Er and Kevin Y.L. Tan (eds.), *Lee's Lieutenants*, St. Leonards: Allen & Unwin, 1999, fn 39, p. 197.
38 The Tunku was compassionate toward Lim Yew Hock, who had converted to Islam. After having him perform diplomatic functions briefly, the Tunku, while filling a top post in an Islamic organization in Jeddah, found a place for Lim in his household entourage.
39 Mohamed Noordin Sopiee, *From Malayan Union to Singapore's Separation*, Kuala Lumpur: Penerbit Universiti Malaya, 1974, pp. 215–16.
40 Lam Peng Er, "The Organisational Utility Men: Toh Chin Chye and Lim Kim San", in Lam Peng Er and Kevin Y.L. Tan (eds.), *Lee's Lieutenants*, St. Leonards: Allen & Unwin, 1999, fn 43, p. 197.
41 Albert Lau, *A Moment of Anguish: Singapore in Malaysia and the Politics of Disengagement*, Singapore: Times Academic Press, 1998, p. 281.
42 Albert Lau, *A Moment of Anguish: Singapore in Malaysia and the Politics of Disengagement*, Singapore: Times Academic Press, 1998, p. 281.
43 Lee Kuan Yew, *The Battle for a Malaysian Malaysia*, Singapore: Ministry of Culture, 1965.
44 Mohamed Noordin Sopiee, *From Malayan Union to Singapore's Separation*, Kuala Lumpur: Penerbit Universiti Malaya, 1974, pp. 212–29.
45 Lam Peng Er, "The Organisational Utility Men: Toh Chin Chye and Lim Kim San", in Lam Peng Er and Kevin Y.L. Tan (eds.), *Lee's Lieutenants*, St. Leonards: Allen & Unwin, 1999, p. 19 and fn 120, p. 205.
46 Albert Lau, *A Moment of Anguish: Singapore in Malaysia and the Politics of Disengagement*, Singapore: Times Academic Press, 1998, pp. 257–65.
47 Kwok Kian-Woon, "The Social Architect: Goh Keng Swee", in Lam Peng Er and Kevin Y.L. Tan (eds.), *Lee's Lieutenants*, Singapore: Allen & Unwin, 1999, pp. 56–8. Apparently, on July 20, 1965, Goh recommended to Tun Razak and Tun Dr. Ismail that Singapore should secede quickly, without giving warning to the British.
48 Lee Kuan Yew, *The Singapore Story: Memoirs of Lee Kuan Yew*, Singapore: Prentice Hall, 1998, pp. 659–63.
49 Lee Kuan Yew, *The Singapore Story: Memoirs of Lee Kuan Yew*, Singapore: Prentice Hall, 1998, p. 624.

3 Locations of power

1 James Cotton, "Theorizing Singapore: State, Class, Society, Ethnicity", paper prepared for the 20th Anniversary Conference, Asian Studies Association of Australia, Melbourne: La Trobe University, July 8–11, 1996, on the Web: http://www.pol.adfa.edu.au/resources/theorise_sing/home.html.
2 For the most part, this definition is based on: H.H. Gerth and C.W. Mills, *From Max Weber: Essays in Sociology*, London: Routledge, 1948, p. 196; Alfred Stepan, *The State and Society: Peru in Comparative Perspective*, Princeton: Princeton University Press, 1978.
3 *Petir* (PAP Journal), December 1982.
4 Anthony H. Birch, *The British System of Government*, London: Unwin Hyman, 1990, p. 172.

5 This should not be confused with the Council of Presidential Advisors. The President's new powers to block spending of the accumulated reserves and veto certain senior civil service appointments are subject to the concurrence of a majority of this Council, which must be consulted. See Chapter 11, p. 153.

6 R.S. Milne and Diane K. Mauzy, *Singapore: The Legacy of Lee Kuan Yew*, Boulder: Westview, 1990, p. 78.

7 *Straits Times*, May 13, 1998.

8 Address by Deputy Prime Minister Lee Hsien Loong at the PS21 5th Anniversary Symposium, July 11, 2000, in Singapore, Singapore Government Media Release on the Web: http://www.gov.sg/sprinter/archives/0071.htm.

9 Chan Heng Chee, *The Dynamics of One Party Dominance*, Singapore: Singapore University Press, 1976, p. 232.

10 For another view, see Ho Khai Leong, *The Politics of Policy-Making in Singapore*, Singapore: Oxford University Press, 2000, p. 207.

11 Chan Heng Chee, *The Dynamics of One Party Dominance*, Singapore: Singapore University Press, 1976, p. 224. See also Chan Heng Chee, "The PAP and the Structuring of the Political System", in K.S. Sandhu and P. Wheatley (eds.), *The Management of Success*, Singapore: Institute of Southeast Asian Studies, 1989, pp. 70–89; Chan Heng Chee, "Politics in the Administrative State: Where has the Politics Gone?" in S.C. Meow (ed.), *Trends in Singapore*, Singapore: Institute of Southeast Asian Studies, 1975, pp. 51–58; Chua Beng Huat, "State and Society: Ambling Toward Greater Balance", in A. Mahizhnan and Lee Tsao Yuan (eds.), *Singapore: Re-Engineering Success*, Singapore: Institute of Political Studies and Oxford University Press, 1998, pp. 51–68.

12 It followed that those who were chosen as ministers must generally be of better quality than the top grade of civil servants (interview with B.G. Yeo, June 22, 1995).

13 Cho-Oon Khong, "Singapore: Political Legitimacy Through Managing Conformity", in M. Alagappa (ed.), *Political Legitimacy in Southeast Asia*, Stanford: Stanford University Press, 1995, pp. 108–35.

14 Werner Vennewald, "Technocrats in the State Enterprise System of Singapore", *Working Paper No. 32*, Asian Research Centre (Murdoch University), Canberra: National Library of Australia, November 1994.

15 Werner Vennewald, "Technocrats in the State Enterprise System of Singapore", *Working Paper No. 32*, Asian Research Centre (Murdoch University), Canberra: National Library of Australia, November 1994, pp. 35–7. An authoritative government source stated that the views of Vennewald (presumably excluding the opinions in his pp. 57–63) had not, in his estimation, been refuted (interview, July 2000).

16 There are also overlaps with politicians or their close relatives as is common in an elite as tightly-knit as Singapore's. Prominent posts in GLCs are held by Lim Chee Onn, chair of Keppel Corporation (see p. 126), and by Ho Ching, President and CEO of Singapore Technologies and wife of Deputy Prime Minister Lee Hsien Loong (see p. 73).

17 On early GLCs, see Lee Kuan Yew, *From Third World to First, The Singapore Story: 1965–2000*, Singapore: Times Media Private Ltd., 2000, pp. 86–7. On some financial aspects of GLCs, see Chapter 6 below.

18 *Parliamentary Debates Singapore*, vol. XX, no. 4 (February 27, 1998), cols. 462–3.

19 Werner Vennewald, "Technocrats in the State Enterprise System of Singapore", *Working Paper No. 32*, Asian Research Centre (Murdoch University), Canberra: National Library of Australia, November 1994, pp. 57–63.

20 Interview with a Singapore economist, June 2000.

21 David Marsh and Wyn Grant, "Tripartism: Reality or Myth?" *Government and Opposition*, vol. 12, no. 2, 1977, pp. 194–211.

22 Garry Rodan, *The Political Economy of Singapore's Industrialization*, Basingstoke: Macmillan, 1989, pp. 156–60.

23 Goh Keng Swee, "A Socialist Economy That Works", in C.V. Devan Nair (ed.), *Socialism That Works*, Singapore: Federal Publications, 1976, pp. 101–2.

24 Pang Cheng Lian, *Singapore's People's Action Party*, Singapore: Oxford University Press, p. 67, Table XXXVI.

25 On the occasion of the twenty-fifth anniversary of the founding of the PAP. See *Petir*, *25th Anniversary Issue*, Singapore: Central Executive Committee, People's Action Party, 1979, p. 74.

26 *Far Eastern Economic Review*, April 28, 1983, pp. 13–15.

27 Interview with Lim Boon Heng, Minister Without Portfolio and Secretary-General of the NTUC, June 8, 2000.

28 C.V. Devan Nair, "Trade Unionism in Singapore", in C.V. Devan Nair (ed.), *Socialism That Works*, Singapore: Federal Publications, 1976, pp. 100–3.

29 *Straits Times*, December 10, 1994.

30 Professor Lim Chong Yah, Chairman since 1972, gave up his post in 2001, and was universally lauded for his contribution to building the tripartite mechanism. He was succeeded by Professor Lim Pin, also an academic, who had been employed by the Economic Development Board, and has also been a board member of the Singapore Institute of Labour Studies, set up by the NTUC (*Straits Times Weekly Edition*, March 31, 2001).

31 Some MNCs, e.g., Shell, have operated in Singapore so long that they are considered almost domestic (B.G. Lee Hsien Loong, "Shell – a Partner in Progress", *Speeches*, vol. 15, no. 5 (September–October 1991), p. 40).

32 Communication from Minister Lim Boon Heng, June 22, 2001. He added that a similar impasse in the 1970s was broken by an invitation to tea from the then Prime Minister, Lee Kuan Yew.

33 Under flexi-wage, which is being quite widely adopted, the basic wage remains stable, and adjustments are made for good or bad years by increasing or reducing the annual bonus (*Far Eastern Economic Review*, September 8, 1988 p. 141). See also, *Straits Times*, November 21, 1992. As a result of the Asian financial crisis of 1997–8, the government cut employers' contributions to the CPF. It also decided to build up a monthly variable component, consisting of about 10 percent of the annual wage. By June 2001, the target had become: 70 percent stable monthly wage; 10 percent variable monthly wage; and 20 percent annual bonus. Good progress was made in implementing this target (communication from Minister Lim Boon Heng, June 22, 2001).

34 Michael Haas, "Mass Society", in Michael Haas (ed.), *The Singapore Puzzle*, Westport, CT: Praeger, 1999, p. 173.

35 M. Manoilesco, *Le Siècle du Corporatisme*, Paris: Alcan, 1934.

36 See Philippe Schmitter, whose writings include: "Still the Century of Corporatism?" *Review of Politics*, vol. 36, no. 1 (1974), pp. 92–127. See also Schmitter's "Modes of Interest Mediation and Models of Societal Change in Western Europe", in Philippe C. Schmitter and Gerhard Lehmbruch, *Trends Toward Corporatist Intermediation*, Beverly Hills: Sage, 1979, pp. 65–8.

37 *Christian Science Monitor*, April 12, 1994.

38 Lee Kuan Yew, quoted in "Singapore: Lee's Creation and Legacy", *The Economist*, November 22, 1986, p. 3.

39 Pang Eng Fong and Chan Heng Chee, "The Political Economy of Development in Singapore, 1959–1985", Singapore, 1986 (mimeo). A copy of this paper is located in the Library of the Institute of Southeast Asian Studies, Singapore. Singapore could also be classified as a "developmental state". See Linda Low, "The Developmental State in the New Economy and Polity", *The Pacific Review*, vol. 14, no. 3 (2001), pp. 413–16.

40 Garry Rodan, "Preserving the One-Party State in Contemporary Singapore", in Kevin Hewison, Richard Robison and Garry Rodan (eds.), *Southeast Asia in the 1990s*, St. Leonards: Allen & Unwin, 1993, p. 82.

41 Nico Poulantzas, *Political Power and Social Classes*, London: Verso, 1978, p. 256.

42 Garry Rodan, *The Political Economy of Singapore's Industrialization*, London: Macmillan, 1989, p. 30.

43 Garry Rodan, *The Political Economy of Singapore's Industrialization*, London: Macmillan, 1989, pp. 157–60.

44 Michael Leifer, "Priorities and Political Order in Malaysia and Singapore", *Journal of Commonwealth Studies*, vol. 11, no. 2 (July 1973), pp. 177–8; Pang Cheng Lian, *Singapore's People's Action Party: Its History, Organization and Leadership*, Singapore: Oxford University Press, 1971, p. 67, Table XXXVI.

45 F.L. Starner, "The Singapore Election of 1963", in K.J. Ratnam and R.S. Milne (eds.), *The Malayan Parliamentary Election of 1964*, Singapore: University of Malaya Press, 1967, pp. 312–58.

46 Linda Low, "The Public Sector in Contemporary Singapore: In Retreat?", in Garry Rodan (ed.), *Singapore Changes Guard*, New York: St. Martin's Press, 1993, p. 179.

47 Garry Rodan, "Preserving the One-Party State in Contemporary Singapore", in Kevin Hewison, Richard Robison and Garry Rodan (eds.), *Southeast Asia in the 1990s*, St. Leonards: Allen & Unwin, 1993, pp. 78–9, 104. Other thoughts on the middle class in Singapore are to be found in

Beng-Huat Chua, *Communitarian Ideology and Democracy in Singapore*, London: Routledge, 1995, pp. 96, 184, 206, 210.

48 Garry Rodan, "Preserving the One-Party State in Contemporary Singapore", in Kevin Hewison, Richard Robison and Garry Rodan (eds.), *Southeast Asia in the 1990s*, St. Leonards: Allen & Unwin, 1993, pp. 82–3.

49 Garry Rodan, "Preserving the One-Party State in Contemporary Singapore", in Kevin Hewison, Richard Robison and Garry Rodan (eds.), *Southeast Asia in the 1990s*, St. Leonards: Allen & Unwin, 1993, p. 83.

50 That is, not difficult for the government to work with.

4 The People's Action Party

1 Samuel P. Huntington, *Political Order in Changing Societies*, New Haven, CT: Yale University Press, 1968, p. 419.

2 See Thomas Bellows, *The People's Action Party of Singapore: The Emergence of a Dominant Party System*, New Haven, CT: Yale University Southeast Asia Series, 1970, p. 4; Chan Heng Chee, *The Dynamics of One Party Dominance: The PAP at the Grass-Roots*, Singapore: Singapore University Press, 1976.

3 Lee Kuan Yew, *The Singapore Story: Memoirs of Lee Kuan Yew*, Singapore: Prentice Hall, 1998, p. 179.

4 Lee Kuan Yew, *The Singapore Story: Memoirs of Lee Kuan Yew*, Singapore: Prentice Hall, 1998, p. 181.

5 November 28, 1954, quoted in Fong Sip Chee, *The PAP Story – The Pioneering Years*, Singapore: Times Periodicals, 1979, pp. 13–14.

6 *For People Through Action By Party* (45th Anniversary Publication), Singapore: PAP, 1999. The PAP has a symbiotic relationship with the NTUC (National Trades Union Congress), and it claims to have grown out of the trade union movement, as incongruous as that may seem today.

7 Dennis Bloodworth, *The Tiger and the Trojan Horse*, Singapore: Times Books International, 1986, p. 84.

8 Lee writes that the pro-Communists were trying to take over the Singapore Trade Union Congress, which was Lim Yew Hock's mass support base, and this prompted the sweep of subversives. See Lee Kuan Yew, *The Singapore Story: Memoirs of Lee Kuan Yew*, Singapore: Prentice Hall, 1998, pp. 270–1.

9 Lee Kuan Yew, *The Singapore Story: Memoirs of Lee Kuan Yew*, Singapore: Prentice Hall, 1998, pp. 385–6. Also see Linda Low (ed.), *Wealth of East Asian Nations: Speeches and Writings of Goh Keng Swee*, Singapore: Federal Publications, 1995, p. 146, and Pang Cheng Lian, *Singapore's People's Action Party: Its History, Organization and Leadership*, Singapore: Oxford University Press, 1971, pp. 11–15.

10 R.S. Milne and Diane K. Mauzy, *Singapore: The Legacy of Lee Kuan Yew*, Boulder: Westview Press, 1990, p. 87.

11 Cited in Lee Kuan Yew, *The Singapore Story: Memoirs of Lee Kuan Yew*, Singapore: Prentice Hall, 1998, p. 506.

12 *For People Through Action By Party* (45th Anniversary Publication), Singapore: PAP, 1999, pp. 56–8.

13 Interestingly, in 1991 the party used interactive Indoor Dialogue Sessions instead of outdoor rallies. The experiment was not successful and will not be repeated. The party found the dialogues were too serious and intellectual, and that they lacked the energy of rallies when a candidate successfully "works the crowd". See *For People Through Action By Party* (45th Anniversary Publication), Singapore: PAP, 1999, p. 101.

14 Lee Kuan Yew, *The Singapore Story: Memoirs of Lee Kuan Yew*, Singapore: Prentice Hall, 1998, p. 287. Lee was referring to the election of a new Pope in October 1958. He also noted the similarities between the mass mobilization methods of the Roman Catholic Church and the Communists. He observes that the Church must have got many things right to have survived for nearly two thousand years (p. 286).

15 Thomas Bellows, *The People's Action Party of Singapore: The Emergence of a Dominant Party System*, New Haven, CT: Yale University Southeast Asia Series, 1970, p. 26.

16 Cited in Koh Buck Song, "The 1000 PAP 'cardinals' who appoint the 'Pope' ", *Straits Times Weekly Edition*, April 11, 1998. Earlier estimates ranged between 300–500.

17 *Straits Times Weekly Edition*, December 30, 2000.

18 *PAP Youth in Action 1986–1991*, Singapore: PAP, 1991.
19 *For People Through Action By Party* (45th Anniversary Publication), Singapore: PAP, 1999, p. 75. He went on to say that the YP plays a large role in about a third of the constituencies, a middling role in another third, and a small role in the final third.
20 Koh Buck Song, "The 1000 PAP 'cardinals' who appoint the 'Pope' ", *Straits Times Weekly Edition*, April 11, 1998.
21 Thomas Bellows, *The People's Action Party of Singapore: The Emergence of a Dominant Party System*, New Haven, CT: Yale University Southeast Asia Series, 1970, p. 16.
22 *For People Through Action By Party* (45th Anniversary Publication), Singapore: PAP, 1999, p. 44.
23 *For People Through Action By Party* (45th Anniversary Publication), Singapore: PAP, 1999, p. 6.
24 See Chan Heng Chee, "Political Parties", in Jon S.T. Quah *et al.* (eds.), *Government and Politics of Singapore*, Singapore: Oxford University Press, 1985, p. 161.
25 Lee Kuan Yew, *From Third World to First: The Singapore Story: 1965–2000*, Singapore: Times Media Private Ltd., 2000, p. 145.
26 See Chan Heng Chee, "Political Parties", in Jon S.T. Quah *et al.* (eds.), *Government and Politics of Singapore*, Singapore: Oxford University Press, 1985, p. 161.
27 Likewise, as discussed in Chapter 8, the PAP has not been willing to relinquish its control over the various government-sponsored ethnic organizations, like Mendaki. See Lily Zubaidah Rahim, *The Singapore Dilemma: The Political and Educational Marginality of the Malay Community*, Kuala Lumpur: Oxford University Press, 1998, p. 214.
28 *For People Through Action By Party* (45th Anniversary Publication), Singapore: PAP, 1999, p. 82.
29 *For People Through Action By Party* (45th Anniversary Publication), Singapore: PAP, 1999, p. 61.
30 Lee Kuan Yew remains skeptical about enlarging the lower ranks. His position, seen from the perspective of someone involved in the struggle against the Communists, is that a bigger membership simply gives populists an opportunity to exercise more influence. See *For People Through Action By Party* (45th Anniversary Publication), Singapore: PAP, 1999, p. 61.
31 Lee Kuan Yew, "Picking Up the Gauntlet: Will Singapore Survive Lee Kuan Yew", *Speeches*, vol. 20, no. 3 (1996), p. 26.
32 Quoted in Lam Peng Er and Kevin Y.L. Tan (eds.), *Lee's Lieutenants: Singapore's Old Guard*, St. Leonards, NSW: Allen & Unwin, 1999, p. 161, from Lee Kuan Yew, "History is Not Made the Way it is Written", *Speeches*, vol. 3, no. 8 (January 1980), p. 7.
33 Lee Kuan Yew, *From Third World to First: The Singapore Story: 1965–2000*, Singapore: Times Media Private Ltd., 2000, p. 736.
34 Quoted in Goh Chok Tong, "Political Self-Renewal in Singapore is Well Handled", *Speeches*, vol. 13, no. 3 (1989), p. 4.
35 Chan Heng Chee, "The PAP and the Nineties: The Politics of Anticipation", in Karl D. Jackson *et al.* (eds.), *ASEAN in Regional and Global Context*, Berkeley: Institute of East Asian Studies, 1986, pp. 163–82.
36 Quoted in Lam Peng Er and Kevin Y.L. Tan (eds.), *Lee's Lieutenants: Singapore's Old Guard*, St. Leonards, NSW: Allen & Unwin, 1999, p. 166.
37 Lee Kuan Yew, "Picking Up the Gauntlet: Will Singapore Survive Lee Kuan Yew", *Speeches*, vol. 20, no. 3 (1996), p. 26.
38 Cherian George, "Old Guard Heroes Victims of Their Own Success?", *Straits Times Weekly Edition*, July 24, 1999.
39 Lee Kuan Yew, *From Third World to First: The Singapore Story: 1965–2000*, Singapore: Times Media Private Ltd., 2000, p. 742.
40 See Lam Peng Er and Kevin Y.L. Tan (eds.), *Lee's Lieutenants: Singapore's Old Guard*, St. Leonards, NSW: Allen & Unwin, 1999, pp. 1–16. Also see T.S. Selvan, *Singapore: The Ultimate Island*, Clifton Hills, Victoria: Freeway Books, 1990.
41 Chan Heng Chee, "The PAP and the Nineties: The Politics of Anticipation", in Karl D. Jackson *et al.* (eds.), *ASEAN in Regional and Global Context*, Berkeley: Institute of East Asian Studies, 1986, p. 170.
42 R.L. Clutterbuck, *Riot and Revolution in Singapore and Malaya, 1945–1960*, London: Faber and Faber, 1973, p. 150.
43 *Straits Times*, December 19, 1983 (Goh Chok Tong).

44 *For People Through Action By Party* (45th Anniversary Publication), Singapore: PAP, 1999, pp. 132–3.
45 Interview with Senior Minister Lee Kuan Yew, June 29, 2000.
46 Interview with Senior Minister Lee Kuan Yew, June 29, 2000.
47 Chan Heng Chee, "The Role of Parliamentary Politicians in Singapore", *Legislative Studies Quarterly*, vol. 1, no. 3 (August 1976), pp. 423–41.
48 Ahmad Mattar, a former Cabinet minister and the head of the party's Malay/Muslim Affairs section has said that his problems in recruiting qualified Malays were more severe than the corresponding problem faced by Goh Chok Tong. The Malay base is small, and many Malay professionals are not willing to serve because of the kinds of dilemmas faced by Malay MPs. See Lily Zubaidah Rahim, *The Singapore Dilemma: The Political and Educational Marginality of the Malay Community*, Kuala Lumpur: Oxford University Press, 1998, p. 257.
49 T.S. Selvan, *Singapore: The Ultimate Island*, Clifton Hills, Victoria: Freeway Books, 1990, p. 52.
50 Interview with the Minister for Trade and Industry, B.G. George Yeo, July 3, 2000.
51 See Tim Huxley, "The Political Role of the Singapore Armed Forces' Officer Corps: Towards A Military-Administrative State?", *Strategic and Defence Studies Centre Working Paper No. 279*, Canberra, The Australian National University (December 1993), p. 12. Also see Tim Huxley, *Defending the Lion City: The Armed Forces of Singapore*, St. Leonards: Allen & Unwin, 2000.
52 Interview with Prime Minister Goh Chok Tong, July 1, 2000.
53 Interview with Prime Minister Goh Chok Tong, July 1, 2000.
54 This is derived from a number of sources, but primarily from *For People Through Action By Party* (45th Anniversary Publication), Singapore: PAP, 1999, pp. 114–15.
55 Lee Kuan Yew, *From Third World to First: The Singapore Story: 1965–2000*, Singapore: Times Media Private Ltd., 2000, pp. 738–40.
56 Chua Lee Hoong, "No Candidates? Its More to Do with PAP", *Straits Times Weekly Edition*, December 9, 2000.
57 Chua Mui Hoong, "New PAP Faces: Most From Private Sector", *Straits Times Weekly Edition*, December 30, 2000.
58 *For People Through Action By Party* (45th Anniversary Publication), Singapore: PAP, 1999, p. 44.
59 Chan Heng Chee, "Political Parties", in Jon S.T. Quah *et al.* (eds.), *Government and Politics of Singapore*, Singapore: Oxford University Press, 1985, p. 160.
60 R.S. Milne and Diane K. Mauzy, *Singapore: The Legacy of Lee Kuan Yew*, Boulder: Westview Press, 1990, p. 55.

5 Ideology of the leaders and for the populace

1 Khoo Boo Teik, *Paradoxes of Mahathirism: An Intellectual Biography of Mahathir Mohamad*, Kuala Lumpur, Oxford University Press, 1995, pp. 1–16.
2 Goh Keng Swee, Singapore's original economic guru, came to the conclusion that socialism would not work for Singapore. Likewise, Lee Kuan Yew believed only in certain aspects of socialism, and saw "equality of opportunity" as its "fundamental premise". See Chan Heng Chee, "Political Parties", in Jon S.T. Quah *et al.* (eds.), *Government and Politics of Singapore*, Singapore: Oxford University Press, 1985, pp. 156 and 159.
3 See Chan Heng Chee, *Singapore: The Politics of Survival, 1965–1967*, Singapore: Oxford University Press, 1971, pp. 48–53.
4 Terry McCarthy, "Lee Kuan Yew", *Time*, August 23–30, 1999, pp. 88–9.
5 Chan Heng Chee, *Singapore: The Politics of Survival, 1965–1967*, Singapore: Oxford University Press, 1971, p. 53.
6 Beng-Huat Chua, *Communitarian Ideology and Democracy in Singapore*, London and New York: Routledge, 1995, p. 5. Also see John Clammer, *Singapore: Ideology, Society, Culture*, Singapore: Chopmen Pubs, 1985, p. 168.
7 H.K. Wells, *Pragmatism*, New York: 1954, p. 207, quoted in John Clammer, *Singapore: Ideology, Society, Culture*, Singapore: Chopmen Pubs, 1985, p. 168.
8 Peirce introduced the term to the Metaphysical Club in Cambridge, MA. in 1872. See Jean Strouse, "Where They Got Their Ideas", *New York Times,* book review of Louis Menand, *Metaphysical Club* (June 10, 2001). Similar ideas were propagated in Britain by F.C.S. Schiller and in Germany by Hans Vachlinger. See Edward McNall Burns, *Ideas in Conflict*, London:

Methuen and Co. Ltd., 1960, pp. 89–93. Pragmatism in the US thrived between the 1890s and 1930s, fell out of favor in the 1950s, but has re-emerged recently in scholarly debate.

9 Hsiao Kung-chuan, *A History of Chinese Political Thought*, vol. I, translated by F.W. Mote, Princeton: Princeton University Press, 1979, p. 8.

10 *Sunday Times*, August 30, 1992, cited in Joseph B. Tamney, *The Struggle Over Singapore's Soul*, Berlin and New York: Walter de Gruyter, 1996, p. 10.

11 Michael Hill and Lian Kwen Fee, *The Politics of Nation Building and Citizenship in Singapore*, London and New York: Routledge, 1995, pp. 190–1.

12 Quoted in Raj Vasil, *Governing Singapore*, rev. ed., Singapore: Times Books International, 1988, p. 163.

13 Hill and Lian point out a connection between rationality and elitism, writing that a principal component of instrumental rationality is a well articulated notion of "spheres of competence" and rule by experts. See Michael Hill and Lian Kwen Fee, *The Politics of Nation Building and Citizenship in Singapore*, London and New York: Routledge, 1995, p. 192.

14 See Gaetano Mosca, *The Ruling Class*, translated by Hanna D. Kahn, New York and London: McGraw-Hill Company, Inc., 1939; Robert Michels, *Political Parties*, translated by Eden and Cedar Paul, New York: The Free Press, 1962; and Vilfredo Pareto, *The Mind and Society*, London: Jonathan Cape, 1935. For analysis of the elitists, see T.B. Bottomore, *Elites and Society*, Harmondsworth: Penguin Books, 1964.

15 Nicholas Lemann, "Behind the SAT", *Newsweek*, September 6, 1999, on the Web: http://newsweek.com/nw-srv/issue/10_99b/printed/us/so/so0110_1.htm. Lemann notes that the idea of creating a governing intellectual elite, chosen by tests and specially educated, long predated Jefferson's letter. "Plato proposed essentially the same thing back in the third century B.C." There was another American exponent of elitism. The pragmatist William James believed that the more rapid advancement of some nations was explainable by the "exceptional concourse of brilliant leaders within a limited time". See Edward McNall Burns, *Ideas in Conflict*, London: Methuen and Co. Ltd., 1960.

16 Mosca apparently bitterly attacked Nazi racist elitism in Germany and he deplored fascism in Italy and Spain as well. See Gaetano Mosca: Philosophy, on the Web: http://library.thinkquest.org/3375/Mosca.htm.

17 For example, see Aldous Huxley's *Brave New World*, where the second-rate intellects have been conditioned to repeat, "I'm really awfully glad I'm a Beta . . ." (New York: Harper & Row, Inc., Perennial Library Edition, 1989, p. 27).

18 See Hsiao Kung-chuan, *A History of Chinese Political Thought*, vol. I, translated by F.W. Mote, Princeton: Princeton University Press, 1979, p. 87. Also see Elbert D. Thomas and Edward T. Williams, *Chinese Political Thought*, London: Williams and Norgate, 1928; James Legge, *The Four Books*, New York: Paragon Book Reprint Corp., 1966. Hsiao writes that the "ruler-preceptor" somewhat resembled Plato's "philosopher-king", however, the latter valued knowledge above all, while the former most valued ethics (p. 113), something akin to the Greek Sophists search for personal excellence.

19 Quoted in T.J.S. George, *Lee Kuan Yew's Singapore*, London: Andre Deutsch, 1973, p. 186.

20 Transcript of Senior Minister Lee Kuan Yew's Q&A Session at the Millennium Law Conference on 11 April 2000 (http://www.gov.sg/sgip/intervws/0400–01.htm).

21 *Straits Times*, February 9, 1977.

22 *Straits Times*, December 21, 1988. Singapore is perennially named the least corrupt state in Asia by the Hong Kong-based Political and Economic Risk Consultancy (PERC), and it tied for the sixth least corrupt country out of 90 indexed by the Berlin-based Transparency International in 2000 (Finland was the least corrupt; the US ranked 14th and Japan 23rd). See "Corruption Perception Index 2000", on the Web: http://www.transparancy.de, forwarded on sgdaily@list.sintercom.org, December 26, 2000.

23 See Asad Latif, "City-State: A Strong Case for Its Survival", *Sunday Times*, June 22, 1997; *Straits Times*, June 9, 1997; Chua Lee Hoong, "Papa's Package Works – In Singapore", *Straits Times Weekly Edition*, February 10, 2001.

24 On eugenics, see Charles Murray and Richard Bernstein, *The Bell Curve: Intelligence and Class Structure in American Life*, New York: The Free Press, 1994, and Roger Pearson, *Heredity and Humanity: Race, Eugenics and Modern Science*, Scott Townsend Pub., 1996. For a book critical of eugenics, see David J. Kevles, *In the Name of Eugenics: Genetics and the Uses of Human Heredity*, Cambridge: Harvard University Press, 1995.

25 Lee Kuan Yew, *From Third World To First, The Singapore Story: 1965–2000*, Singapore:

Times Media Private Ltd., 2000, p. 740. Lee writes that Eysenck reinforced his view that testing for IQ, as well as for character and personality, was useful.

26 Han Fook Kwang, Warren Fernandez, and Sumiko Tan, *Lee Kuan Yew: The Man and his Ideas*, Singapore: Times Edition, Straits Times Press, 1998, pp. 153–9.

27 Han Fook Kwang, Warren Fernandez, and Sumiko Tan, *Lee Kuan Yew: The Man and his Ideas*, Singapore: Times Edition, Straits Times Press, 1998, p. 153. The controversial book is: Charles Murray and Richard Bernstein, *The Bell Curve: Intelligence and Class Structure in American Life*, New York: The Free Press, 1994.

28 Han Fook Kwang, Warren Fernandez, and Sumiko Tan, *Lee Kuan Yew: The Man and his Ideas*, Singapore: Times Edition, 1998, pp. 157, 159.

29 *Straits Times*, August 15, 1983, cited in Lily Zubaidah Rahim, *The Singapore Dilemma: The Political and Educational Marginality of the Malay Community*, Kuala Lumpur: Oxford University Press, 1998, p. 55. Rahim contends that Goh Keng Swee also believes in eugenics. She also notes that the public eugenics debate was "particularly offensive" to Malays.

30 Interview with Senior Minister Lee Kuan Yew, June 29, 2000.

31 Interview with Senior Minister Lee Kuan Yew, June 29, 2000.

32 Joel H. Spring, *The American School 1642–1996* (4th ed.), New York: The McGraw Hill Companies, Inc., 1997, p. 254. Also see Dr. Tony Tan, speech of September 4, 1996, on the Web: http://www.mindef.gov.sg/midpa/whatsnew/yer96/04sep02.htm.

33 It has been suggested, in terms of admissions to key faculties (law, medicine) at the National University of Singapore, that interviews were added because there were too many women and Indians with top exam scores who chose those faculties (interview with a Singaporean academic in June 2000).

34 Nicholas Lemann, "Behind the SAT", *Newsweek*, September 6, 1999, on the Web: http://newsweek.com/nw-srv/issue/10_99b/printed/us/so/so0110_1.htm.

35 Ezra Vogel, "A Little Dragon Tamed", in Kernial Singh Sandhu and Paul Wheatley (eds.), *Management of Success*, Singapore: Institute of Southeast Asian Studies, 1989, p. 1053.

36 Lee Kuan Yew was attracted to the Fabian Society for a long time. However, in the 1970s he stopped subscribing to their magazines and pamphlets because he felt that they were misguided in opposing the merit principle in education and in favor of using the best teachers for the weakest students. See *The Singapore Story, Memoirs of Lee Kuan Yew*, Singapore and New York: Prentice Hall, 1998, p. 107.

37 Lee Hsien Loong, "Singapore of the Future", in Arun Mahizhnan and Lee Tsao Yuan (eds.), *Singapore: Re-Engineering Success*, Singapore: Institute of Policy Studies and Oxford University Press, 1998, p. 5.

38 Housing was a special case. It was decided to break up heavy concentrations of individual ethnic groups to try to disrupt the cycle of ethnic strife prevalent in the 1950s and 1960s. See Joseph B. Tamney, *The Struggle Over Singapore's Soul*, Berlin and New York: Walter de Gruyter, 1996, p. 92.

39 Michael D. Barr, "Lee Kuan Yew: Race, Culture and Genes", *Journal of Contemporary Asia*, vol. 29, no. 2 (1999), p. 145.

40 Interview with Dr. Arun Mahizhnan, Deputy Director of the Institute of Policy Studies, June 16, 2000.

41 It is a thorny question as to whether Asian values can be said to cover the non-Confucian states of East and Southeast Asia since it is a region of considerable diversity. Clearly, not all Asians share all "Asian values", and South Asia is completely excluded. However, there are some important commonalities in East and Southeast Asia that transcend borders and religions. One shared value is the ideal of equilibrium or moderation. Another, which encompasses not just Confucian East Asia and Singapore, but also Islamic Indonesia and Malaysia, and Buddhist Thailand, emphasizes responsibilities to the community over the rights of the individual. Another value is the preference for consultation and consensus over contention. On these themes, see Chandra Muzaffar, *Human Rights and the New World Order*, Penang: Just World Trust, 1993; Donald K. Emmerson, "Singapore and the 'Asian Values' Debate", *Journal of Democracy*, vol. 6, no. 4 (October 1995), pp. 96–100, and "Region and Recalcitrance: Rethinking Democracy Through Southeast Asia", *The Pacific Review*, vol. 8, no. 2 (1995), pp. 223–48; and Francis Fukuyama, "Confucianism and Democracy", *Journal of Democracy*, vol. 6, no. 2 (April 1995), pp. 20–33.

42 See Diane K. Mauzy, "The Human Rights and 'Asian Values' Debate in Southeast Asia: Trying to Clarify the Key Issues", *The Pacific Review*, vol. 10, no. 2 (1997), p. 212.

43 From an article by A.M. Rosenthal in the *New York Times*, reprinted in the *Straits Times*, April 2, 1994.

44 Professor Tommy Koh, Singapore's Ambassador-at-Large, recalls dining in Korea with one of his best friends from Washington, and being asked why Singapore was championing the cause of anti-Americanism in Asia (*Straits Times*, October 15, 1994). Likewise, a former US diplomat noted that "Just as America got on people's nerves, maybe Singapore is getting on American nerves" (*Straits Times*, October 15, 1994).

45 Joseph B. Tamney, *The Struggle Over Singapore's Soul*, Berlin and New York: Walter de Gruyter, 1996, pp. 153, 174–5, 180–3. He believes that Singapore's dominant ideology is a variant of Western conservatism and not Confucianism. He writes that life in Singapore "is being shaped by the demands of international capitalism, not by Asian tradition". Similarly, Garry Rodan sees Asian values as a cover for a global ideological contest between liberalism and conservatism ("The Internationalization of Ideological Conflict: Asia's New Significance", *The Pacific Review*, vol. 9, no. 3 (1996), pp. 329–36). Also see Christopher Lingle, *Singapore's Authoritarian Capitalism*, Barcelona: Edicions Sirocco SL, and the Locke Institute, 1996, p. 48.

46 Michael Backman, "Asians and Victorian Values", *Far Eastern Economic Review*, March 30, 2000, p. 32. The Baba Chinese were the early Chinese migrants to the Malay peninsula. They adopted the dress, language, and some of the customs of the Malays, but did not convert to Islam and hence did not "become" Malays. Instead they remained a separate community with a distinctive cuisine and lifestyle. Under British colonial rule, many learned English, became prominent community leaders, and many became Anglophiles.

47 Quoted in John Clammer, *Singapore: Ideology, Society, Culture*, Singapore: Chopmen Pubs, 1988, pp. 23–4.

48 Goh Keng Swee, *The Economics of Modernization and Other Essays*, Singapore: Asia Pacific Press, 1972, p. 176, quoted in Michael Hill and Lian Kwen Fee, *The Politics of Nation Building and Citizenship in Singapore*, London and New York: Routledge, 1995, p. 195.

49 *Straits Times Weekly Edition*, October 3, 1998. Likewise, Lee Kuan Yew discusses Asian values in *From Third World to First. The Singapore Story: 1965–2000*, Singapore: Times Media Private Limited, 2000, pp. 389, 545. He writes that there are many different value systems in Asia, and that there is no Asian model as such. However, there are fundamental differences between East Asian Confucian and Western liberal societies.

50 Chua Beng-Huat, sounding like an Orientalist, writes that "The East is absorbed once again and is merely reproducing, two centuries later, the Western bourgeois culture..." (*Communitarian Ideology and Democracy in Singapore*, London and New York: Routledge, 1995, p. 151). Yet, how can one dismiss such values as industry and frugality, for example, which have been exalted as virtues throughout the course of Chinese civilization? See Brigitte Sie Kok Hwa, *Singapore: A Modern Asian City-State*, PhD thesis from Katholieke Universteit, Nijmegen, published by the author, 1997. For a Western view of communitarianism, see Amitai Etzioni, *The Spirit of Community: Rights, Responsibilities, and the Communitarian Agenda*, New York: Crown Publishers, 1993.

51 Brigitte Sie Kok Hwa, *Singapore: A Modern Asian City-State*, PhD thesis from Katholieke Universteit, Nijmegen, published by the author, 1997, p. 220.

52 Alan Chong, *Goh Chok Tong: Singapore's New Premier*, Petaling Jaya: Pelanduk Pubs, Inc., 1991, p. 118.

53 Joseph B. Tamney, *The Struggle Over Singapore's Soul*, Berlin and New York: Walter de Gruyter, 1996, p. 98.

54 *Straits Times*, November 27, 1990.

55 Michael Hill and Lian Kwen Fee, *The Politics of Nation Building and Citizenship in Singapore*, London and New York: Routledge, 1995, p. 200. When Goh Keng Swee announced the five religious subjects in January 1982, Confucianism was not included because it was a secular ethical system. At Lee's suggestion, Confucian ethics was included in February 1982.

56 *Straits Times*, June 21, 1997. Also see Lee Kuan Yew, "Is Confucianism Dead?", *Newsweek Special Issue*, July–September 2000, p. 48; and David Martin Jones, "Democracy and Identity: The Paradoxical Character of Political Development", in Daniel A. Bell, *et al.* (eds.), *Towards Illiberal Democracy in Pacific Asia*, Oxford: St. Martin's Press, 1995, pp. 44–51.

57 Barry Wilkinson, "Social Engineering in Singapore", *Journal of Contemporary Asia*, vol. 18, no. 2 (1988), p. 173.

58 S. Hall, "Culture, Identity and Diaspora", in J. Rutherford (ed.), *Identity, Community, Culture, Difference,* London: Lawrence and Wishart, 1990. He writes, "Cultural identities come from

somewhere, have histories. But like everything which is historical, they undergo constant transformation" (p. 225).

59 *Straits Times Weekly Edition*, February 6, 1999.

60 Alan Chong, *Goh Chok Tong: Singapore's New Premier*, Petaling Jaya: Pelanduk Pubs., Inc., 1991, p. 110.

61 Chan Heng Chee, *The Dynamics of One-Party Dominance*, Singapore: Singapore University Press, 1976, p. 230.

62 In 1988, by age 30, only about 22 percent of tertiary-level graduate women were married. Those who married were having only 1.7 children. Women with primary education were producing 2.7 children and those with no education 3.5. See R.S. Milne and Diane K. Mauzy, *Singapore: The Legacy of Lee Kuan Yew*, Boulder: Westview Press, 1990, p. 11. The 1990 census showed that the number of single women continued to increase, with 25 percent of women with university degrees remaining single. *Straits Times*, August 27, 1990, cited in Joseph B. Tamney, *The Struggle Over Singapore's Soul*, Berlin and New York: Walter de Gruyter, 1996, pp. 120–2 (see Chapter 14 for current figures).

63 For some of the issues involved, see Chee Heng Leng and Chan Chee Khoon (eds.), *Designer Genes*, Kuala Lumpur: INSAN, 1984.

64 *Straits Times Weekly Edition*, September 1, 1990, cited in Christopher Tremewan, *The Political Economy of Social Control in Singapore*, London: Macmillan Press, 1994 (reprinted in 1996 with a new preface), p. 129.

65 *Straits Times*, July 1, 2000.

66 Ben Dolven, "Lion's Share", *Far Eastern Economic Review*, August 3, 2000, p. 24. One prominent person interviewed by the *Straits Times* said he was not persuaded that everything is money driven. He asked, "where is the commitment?" and commented, "I will not vote for someone I think is motivated by money" (*Straits Times Weekly Edition*, July 15, 2000).

67 Lee Kuan Yew, *From Third World to First, The Singapore Story: 1965–2000*, Singapore: Times Media Private Edition, 2000, p. 193.

68 The formula, as amended slightly in 2000, establishes the benchmark as 2/3rds the median income of the top eight people in six professions, with stock options discounted by 50% (*Straits Times*, June 30, 2000).

69 Goh Chok Tong, "The Philosophy Behind Salary Revision for Political Office-Holders", *Speeches*, vol. 17, no. 6 (1993), p. 1.

70 Ben Dolven, "Lion's Share", *Far Eastern Economic Review*, August 3, 2000, p. 24.

71 Ben Dolven, "Lion's Share", *Far Eastern Economic Review*, August 3, 2000, p. 24.

72 See *Straits Times*, July 1, 2000.

73 *Straits Times*, July 1, 2000.

74 The authors were in Singapore during this period (June–July 2000) and heard a constant stream of complaints about the timing of the salary revisions, from taxi drivers, casual acquaintances, friends, and various non-governmental people interviewed. Some thought the salaries were totally out of line and would further skew income disparities. However, the displeasure of most focused on the perceived unfairness that the pay raises *preceded* restoration of CPF cuts.

75 This is from the preface of the *Confucian Ethics* booklet put out by the Curriculum Development Institute of Singapore (CDIS) of the Ministry of Education, cited in Khun-Eng Kuah, "Confucian Ideology and Social Engineering in Singapore", *Journal of Contemporary Asia*, vol. 20, no. 3 (1990), p. 376.

76 See Eddie C.Y. Kuo, "Confucianism as Political Discourse in Singapore: The Case of An Incomplete Revitalization Movement", *Department of Sociology Working Papers, No. 113*, National University of Singapore, 1992, pp. 10–13. Khun-Eng Kuah writes that during the early years in Singapore, the Chinese migrants attempted to recreate a Chinese identity, and Confucian social and moral values became highly articulated and supported institutionally through clan associations ("Confucian Ideology and Social Engineering in Singapore", *Journal of Contemporary Asia*, vol. 20, no. 3 (1990), pp. 373–4).

77 See Asad Latif, "My View", *Straits Times Weekly Edition*, June 28, 1997; Eddie C.Y. Kuo, "Confucianism as Political Discourse in Singapore: The Case of An Incomplete Revitalization Movement", *Department of Sociology Working Papers, No. 113*, National University of Singapore, 1992, pp. 14–19.

78 Goh Chok Tong, "Our National Ethic", *Speeches*, vol. 12, no. 5 (September–October 1988), p. 13, quoted in Jon S.T. Quah, "National Values and Nation-Building: Defining the Problem", in

Jon S.T. Quah (ed.), *In Search of Singapore's National Values*, Singapore: The Institute of Policy Studies (reprinted edition), 1999, p. 1.

79 From the *White Paper on Shared Values* (Singapore: Singapore National Printers, 1991), quoted in "Appendix A: White Paper on Shared Values", in Jon S.T. Quah (ed.), *In Search of Singapore's National Values*, Singapore: The Institute of Policy Studies (reprinted edition), 1999, p. 107.

80 "Appendix B: Our Shared Values", prepared by the Ministry of Information and the Arts, in Jon S.T. Quah (ed.), *In Search of Singapore's National Values*, Singapore: The Institute of Policy Studies (reprinted edition), 1999, p. 118.

81 David Brown, "The Corporatist Management of Ethnicity in Contemporary Singapore", in Garry Rodan (ed.), *Singapore Changes Guard*, Melbourne: Longman Cheshire, 1993, p. 25.

82 From the *White Paper on Shared Values* (Singapore: Singapore National Printers, 1991), quoted in "Appendix A: White Paper on Shared Values", in Jon S.T. Quah (ed.), *In Search of Singapore's National Values*, Singapore: The Institute of Policy Studies (reprinted edition), 1999, p. 116.

83 Beng-Huat Chua, *Communitarian Ideology and Democracy in Singapore*, London and New York: Routledge, 1995, p. 30. This is basically the thesis of George Lodge and Ezra Vogel in their book, *Ideology and National Competitiveness: An Analysis of Nine Countries*, Boston: Harvard Business School Press, 1987. Raj Vasil suggests that the book "obviously had been carefully studied by senior PAP leaders" (*Asianising Singapore: The PAP's Management of Ethnicity*, Singapore: Heinemann Asia, 1995, p. 77).

84 Stephen A. Douglas, " 'Centrality' and 'Balance' in Southeast Asia: Official Ideologies and Regional Crises", in *Southeast Asian Journal of Social Science*, vol. 27, no. 1 (1999), p. 31.

85 John Clammer, *Race and State in Independent Singapore, 1965–1990*, Aldershot: Ashgate, 1998, chapter 11, and his "Deconstructing Values: The Establishment of a National Ideology and its Implications for Singapore's Political Future", in Garry Rodan (ed.), *Singapore Changes Guard*, Melbourne: Longman Cheshire, 1993, pp. 34–51.

86 Michael Hill and Lian Kwen Fee, *The Politics of Nation Building and Citizenship in Singapore*, London and New York: Routledge, 1995, p. 219.

6 Economic policy for an independent Singapore

1 The withdrawal (made for financial reasons) was carried out in a "considerate manner" by Harold Wilson's government (*Singapore Mirror* (Singapore: Ministry of Communications and Information), vol. 14, no. 4 (January 23, 1978), quoting a speech by Lee Kuan Yew).

2 John Drysdale, *Singapore's Struggle for Success*, Singapore: Times Books International, 1984, pp. 251–3.

3 Edgar H. Schein, *Strategic Pragmatism*, Cambridge, MA: The MIT Press, 1996, pp. 37–44.

4 Goh Keng Swee, *The Economics of Modernization*, Singapore: Asia Pacific Press, 1972, pp. 10, 79.

5 Edgar H. Schein, *Strategic Pragmatism*, Cambridge, MA: The MIT Press, 1996, p. 175. On Lee's belief, that the "acid test" was that things should work, see Lee Kuan Yew, *From Third World to First, The Singapore Story: 1965–2000*, Singapore: Times Media Private Ltd., 2000, p. 758.

6 Augustine H.H. Tan, "Foreign Investment and Multinational Corporations in Developing Countries", in C.V. Devan Nair (ed.), *Socialism That Works*, Singapore: Federal Publications, 1976, pp. 86–96.

7 See Frederic C. Deyo, *Dependent Development and Industrial Order: An Asian Case Study*, New York: Praeger, 1981, p. 74.

8 Hafiz Mirza, *Multinationals and the Growth of the Singapore Economy*, London: Croom Helm, 1986, p. 257.

9 Rachel van Elkan, "Singapore's Development Strategy", in Kenneth Bercuson (ed.), *Singapore: A Case Study in Rapid Development*, Washington, DC: International Monetary Fund, 1995, p. 17. Note that in the late 1980s about three-quarters of manufacturing output was produced by wholly-owned or partly-owned foreign firms (*ibid.*, p. 16).

10 *Straits Times Weekly Edition*, February 10, 2001.

11 *Report of the Committee on Singapore's Competitiveness*, Singapore: Ministry of Trade and Industry, 1998, pp. 75–6.

12 Goh Chok Tong, "Local Enterprises and Multinational Corporations – Complementary Roles to Singapore's Success", *Speeches*, vol. 23, no. 2 (1999), p. 3.

13 Lee Hsien Loong, "The Role of SMEs: The Singapore Experience", *Speeches*, vol. 18, no. 5 (1993), p. 64.
14 Ian Chalmers, "Weakening State Controls and Ideological Change in Singapore: The Emergence of Local Capital as a Political Force", *Working Paper No. 13*, Asia Research Centre, Murdoch University, Western Australia, 1992, pp. 11, 15.
15 *Singapore Mirror* (Singapore: Ministry of Communications and Information), vol. 22, no. 21 (1986), pp. 1–10; *Straits Times Weekly Edition*, September 16, 1998.
16 *Straits Times Weekly Edition*, January 1, 2000.
17 Garry Rodan, "The Rise and Fall of Singapore's 'Second Industrial Revolution'", in Richard Robison *et al.* (eds.), *Southeast Asia in the 1980s: The Politics of Economic Crises*, Sydney: Allen & Unwin, 1987 pp. 156–68. Wage increases had been deliberate, as part of a government "wage correction policy", based on the view that there had been too much emphasis on creating labor-intensive jobs. The new policy can be seen as a forerunner of the KBE policy (see p. 78). But in the early 1980s, high-tech products did not sell well enough to warrant high wages, and the economy faltered.
18 See Report of the Economic Committee, *The Singapore Economy: New Directions*, Singapore: Ministry of Trade and Industry, 1986; R.S. Milne and Diane K. Mauzy, *Singapore: The Legacy of Lee Kuan Yew*, Boulder: Westview, 1990, p. 135.
19 Report of the Economic Committee, *The Singapore Economy: New Directions*, Singapore: Ministry of Trade and Industry, 1986, p. 93.
20 Linda Low, "The Elusive Developed Country Status", in Linda Low (ed.), *Singapore: Towards A Developed Status*, Singapore: Oxford University Press, 1999, p. 382.
21 *Straits Times Weekly Edition*, October 25, 1997.
22 It is evident that the second group contained mostly close competitors of Singapore, while the first group was not so competitive.
23 *Report of the Committee on Singapore's Competitiveness*, Singapore: Ministry of Trade and Industry, 1998, p. 16.
24 *Report of the Committee on Singapore's Competitiveness*, Singapore: Ministry of Trade and Industry, 1998, p. 6.
25 *Report of the Committee on Singapore's Competitiveness*, Singapore: Ministry of Trade and Industry, 1998, pp. 3–4. See also p. 123.
26 *Parliamentary Debates Singapore*, vol. 69, no. 9 (November 24, 1998), col. 1439 (B.G. Lee Hsien Loong).
27 *Report of the Public Sector Divestment Committee*, Singapore: National Printers, 1987.
28 Linda Low, "State Entrepreneurship", in Lee Tsao Yuan and Linda Low, *Local Entrepreneurship in Singapore: Private and State*, Singapore: Institute of Policy Studies and Times Academic Press, 1990, p. 165.
29 Linda Low, "The Public Sector in Contemporary Singapore: In Retreat?", in Garry Rodan (ed.), *Singapore Changes Guard*, Melbourne: Longman Cheshire, 1993, p. 176.
30 *Straits Times Weekly Edition*, February 13, 1999.
31 *Straits Times Weekly Edition*, August 11, 2001.
32 R.S. Milne, "The Politics of Privatization in the ASEAN States", *ASEAN Economic Bulletin*, vol. 7, no. 3, 1991, p. 324.
33 *Straits Times Weekly Edition*, January 22, 2000.
34 *Far Eastern Economic Review*, February 3, 2000, p. 49.
35 *Straits Times*, June 10, 2000.
36 *Straits Times Weekly Edition*, May 5, 2001.
37 *Straits Times Weekly Edition*, September 15, 2001.
38 See Eric Ellis, "How Optus Deal Curries Favour with Singapore", *The Australian*, August 24, 2001, on the Web: http://australianit.news.com.au/common/storyPage/0,3811,2671991%255E501,00.html.
39 Trish Saywell, "Telecoms: Slow and Steady at SingTel", *Far Eastern Economic Review*, October 4, 2001, on the Web: http://www.feer.com/.
40 "SingTel Ringing Regional Changes", *Agence France Presse*, November 4, 2001, on the Web: http://sg.news.yahoo.com/011104/1/1o4i8.
41 Cordial family relations may co-exist with business rivalry.
42 Tan Boon Seng, "Why It Might Be Difficult for the Government to Withdraw from Business", February 10, 2002, on the Web: http://www.singapore-window.org/sw020210gl.htm.

43 Deputy Prime Minister Lee Hsien Loong's Interview with *Fortune Magazine* (April 3, 2000), on the Web: http://www.gov.sg/sgip/intervws/0300–06.htm.
44 Lee Kuan Yew, "Making Singapore Companies World-Class", *Speeches*, vol. 23, no. 6 (1999), pp. 23–6; Prime Minister Goh Chok Tong's National Day Rally 2001 Speech, August 19, 2001, on the Web: http://gov.sg/sgip/Announce/NDR.htm. See also p. 72.
45 *Parliamentary Debates Singapore*, vol. 68, no. 1 (January 14, 1998), col. 32 (Dr. Richard Hu).
46 Professor Lim Chong Yah (ed.), *Policy Options for the Singapore Economy,* Singapore: McGraw-Hill, 1988, pp. 270–1.
47 *Straits Times Weekly Edition*, December 7, 1996.
48 Further criticisms were made in 2001 about unpaid debts to the GIC incurred by the Guandong Trust and Investment Corporation (*Straits Times Weekly Edition*, April 28, 2001). On further activities of the GIC, including its part in trying to help rescue the Indonesian economy, see *Straits Times Weekly Edition*, April 28, 2001.
49 See Lynette Ong, "Singapore's GLC Debate", *Asiawise*, April 19, 2001, on the Web: http://www.asiawise.com. Substantially, the differences result from whether second- and third-tier GLCs are included or not.
50 *Straits Times Weekly Edition*, March 10, 2001. In 1999, the government sold about one-fifth of its holdings in the DBS (*Straits Times Weekly Edition*, February 13, 1999).
51 *Straits Times Weekly Edition*, February 24, 2001.
52 *Straits Times Weekly Edition*, June 26, 1999.
53 Apparently, recent recruitment policies have been more adventurous (*Straits Times Weekly Edition*, May 6, 2000). About 40 percent of the employees of the Government Investment Corporation are foreigners (*Singapore*, July–August 2001, p. 5).
54 For a balanced view by a Singaporean, see *Straits Times Weekly Edition*, July 17, 1999.
55 These points are made in a number of recent communications, mostly on the Web. For example see: Daniel Lian, "Singapore Dream – Version 2001", December 18, 2000, prepared by Morgan Stanley Dean Witter & Co., and/or its affiliates, in Special Year-End Issue: Looking to 2001: http://www.msdw.com/GERdata/digests/latest-digest.html#anchor28#anchor28, forwarded on the Web: sgdaily@list.sintercom.org. An editorial in the *Straits Times Weekly Edition*, May 19, 2001, criticizes Morgan Stanley International on some technical issues, but also questions the economic power assumed by a private United States company over foreign governments.
56 *Straits Times Weekly Edition*, February 7, 1999. In 2001, DBS made a disastrously unsuccessful bid for OUB (*Far Eastern Economic Review*, August 30, 2001, p. 47). After complex maneuvering, the OUB and the fifth-largest bank were taken over, leaving only the UOB, the DBS and the OCBC (*Straits Times Weekly Edition*, September 1 and 8, 2001). The UOB had pushed the DBS group into second place as regards domestic operations.
57 *Straits Times Weekly Edition*, May 22, 1999.
58 *Asiaweek*, July 10, 2000.
59 Interview with RAdm. Teo Chee Hean, June 28, 1995.
60 *Final Report of the Committee to Promote Enterprise Overseas*, Singapore: SNP Publishers, 1993, pp. 29–30 and 31–40.
61 *Straits Times Weekly Edition*, May 3, 1997. The first major Singapore investment in China was announced in 1992, an industrial estate in Fujian (*Business Times*, November 28–9, 1992).
62 *Parliamentary Debates Singapore*, vol. 68, no. 1 (January 14, 1998), col. 9 (B.G. Lee Hsien Loong).
63 *Far Eastern Economic Review*, August 3, 1999, p. 8.
64 *Parliamentary Debates Singapore*, vol. 70, no. 16 (August 3, 1999), col. 1832 (B.G. Lee Hsien Loong).
65 Lee Kuan Yew, *From Third World to First, The Singapore Story: 1965–2000*, Singapore: Times Media Private Ltd., 2000, pp. 719–24. In 2001, at a meeting between Senior Minister Lee and President Jiang Zemin, the latter described their cooperation as fruitful and hoped that the experience in Suzhou would be useful in later phases of the project (*Straits Times Weekly Edition*, June 9, 2001).
66 Goh Keng Swee, *Wealth of East Asian Nations: Speeches and Writings*, edited by Linda Low, Singapore: Federal Publications, 1995, p. 142.
67 Interview with Prime Minister Goh Chok Tong, June 26, 1995. For the origins and development of the triangle, see: Sree Kumar, "Johor-Singapore/Riau Growth Triangle: A Model of Subregional Cooperation", in Myo Thant, Min Tang and Kirosho Kakazu (eds.), *Growth*

Triangles in Asia, Hong Kong: Oxford University Press, 1994, pp. 175–217; R.S. Milne, "Singapore's Growth Triangle", *The Round Table*, Issue 327 (July 1993), pp. 291–304.
68 For a diagram of the "anatomy" of the KBE, see Koh Ai Tee, "Evolution and Challenges", in Yap Mui Teng (ed.), *Perspectives 2001*, Singapore: Institute of Policy Studies and Times Academic Press, 2001, p. 32.
69 Interviews with Deputy Prime Minister B.G. Lee Hsien Loong and Minister for Trade and Industry B.G. George Yeo, both in July 2000.
70 Curiously, this corresponds to economists' definition of a "recession" (see p. 71).
71 Interview with Deputy Prime Minister B.G. Lee Hsien Loong, July 4, 2000. See also his interview with *Fortune Magazine* (April 3, 2000), on the Web: http://www.gov.sg/sgip/intervws/0300–06.htm.
72 Interview with Minister for Trade and Industry B.G. George Yeo, July 3, 2000.
73 *Southeast Asia Post* (Vancouver), April 15–21, 2000.
74 *Straits Times Weekly Edition*, February 5, 2000.
75 Interview with Minister for Trade and Industry B.G. George Yeo, July 3, 2000.
76 For an exception, see an article on Kim Tan (*Far Eastern Economic Review*, August 23, 2001, pp. 30–3).
77 Lynette Ong, "The Biotech Race is On", *AsiaWise*, May 11, 2001, on the Web: http://www/asiawise.com.
78 "Singapore Set to be Hub for Stem Cell Research", August 16, 2001, on the Web: http://www.news24.co.za/News24/Technology/Science_Nature/0,1113,2-13-46_1066698,00.html (South Africa).
79 "Creativity", *The Economist*, September 21, 2000, on the Web: http://www.economist.com.
80 Goh Chok Tong is realistic, "... I am clear in my mind that the Government can only stimulate and encourage you to be innovative. It is not possible to direct and drive the population to become more innovative" (Prime Minister Goh Chok Tong's National Day Rally 2001 Speech, August 19, 2001, on the Web: http://gov.sg/sgip/Announce/NDR.htm.) Goh said he intended to set up a National Innovation Council under Lim Hng Kiang.
81 B.G. Lee Hsien Loong, "The Spirit of Innovation and Entrepreneurship", *Speeches*, vol. 23, no. 3 (1999), p. 53.
82 B.G. George Yong-Boon Yeo, "The IT Revolution and Singapore", *Speeches*, vol. 23, no. 3 (1999), pp. 70–1.
83 B.G. George Yong-Boon Yeo, "The IT Revolution and Singapore", *Speeches*, vol. 23, no. 3 (1999), p. 72.
84 B.G. George Yeo, "Information Technology and Singapore's Future", *Speeches*, vol. 22, no. 3 (1998), pp. 61–9.
85 Louise Williams, "Web of Intrigue", *Sydney Morning Herald*, April 29, 2000.
86 *Straits Times Weekly Edition*, March 24, 2001.
87 Pam Hu, "Across the Digital Divide", in Yap Mui Teng (ed.), *Perspectives 2001*, Singapore: The Institute of Policy Studies and Times Academic Press, 2001, pp. 96–9.
88 George Gilder, "The New Era", *Forbes Global*, April 3, 2000, at http://www.discovery.org, forwarded on the Web: sangkancil@lists.malaysia.net.
89 *Straits Times Weekly Edition*, January 25, 2001.
90 Goh Chok Tong, "Narrowing the Income Gap", *Speeches*, vol. 20, no. 3 (1996), p. 2.
91 Interview with Prime Minister Goh Chok Tong, July 1, 2000.
92 *Straits Times Weekly Edition*, April 1, 2000.
93 Singapore Government Press Release, Prime Minister Goh Chok Tong's National Day Rally 2001 Speech, 19 August 2001 (hereafter referred to as Goh Rally Speech), p. 17. The target is a $5bn endowment (communication from Minister Lim Boon Heng, June 22, 2001).
94 *Straits Times Weekly Edition*, May 20, 2000.
95 *Straits Times Weekly Edition*, November 18, 2000.
96 *Straits Times Weekly Edition*, August 11, 2001.
97 *Straits Times Weekly Edition*, July 18, 2001.
98 "Performance of the Singapore Economy in Third Quarter 2001", Singapore: Ministry of Trade and Industry (November 2001), p. 1.
99 *Straits Times Weekly Edition*, October 13, 2001.
100 Goh Rally Speech, p. 2.
101 Goh Rally Speech, p. 6.
102 Goh Rally Speech, p. 6.

103 Goh Rally Speech, p. 6.
104 Goh Rally Speech, pp. 9–10.
105 *Straits Times Weekly Edition*, November 10, 2001.
106 *Straits Times Weekly Edition*, October 20, 2001.
107 Goh Rally Speech, pp. 21–2.
108 *Straits Times Weekly Edition*, October 13, 2001.
109 For example, symptomatic of weak banking systems or debt problems.
110 The Economist Intelligence Unit, November 20, 2001, predicted that the Singapore economy would contract by 3.5 percent in 2001, showing only a slight growth of 0.4 percent in 2002; growth was expected to accelerate to 6.3 percent in 2003. According to the Singapore government, the "external outlook has deteriorated dramatically as a result of the terrorist attacks" and US recession. "Global prospects are expected to remain poor until the external environment improves" ("Performance of the Singapore Economy in Third Quarter 2001", Singapore: Ministry of Trade and Industry (November 2001), p. 9). By 2002 it improved.
111 Goh Rally Speech, p. 14. Lee Kuan Yew had praised the American entrepreneurial model, which is not afraid to take risks (*Straits Times Weekly Edition*, September 22, 2001).
112 A review of recent developments in biotechnology, particularly in Singapore, is given by Trish Saywell, "Medicine for the Economy", in *Far Eastern Economic Review*, November 15, 2001, pp. 40–8. Contrary to declines in other manufacturing sectors in October 2001, there was a significant expansion in the biomedical sciences cluster ("Monthly Manufacturing Performance – October 2001", Singapore: Department of Statistics, November 26, 2001, on the Web: http://singstat.gov.sg/CURRENT/current.html).
113 Goh Rally Speech, pp. 16–17.
114 Possibly to a lesser extent than previously.
115 *Straits Times Weekly Edition*, December 8, 2001. It was chaired by B.G. Lee.
116 *Straits Times Weekly Edition*, January 19, 2002.
117 *Far Eastern Economic Review*, January 10, 2002, p. 54.
118 *Straits Times Weekly Edition*, December 15, 2001.

7 Supplying social services to the people

1 The most prominent exception was that housing was financed by CPF savings (Linda Low and T.C. Aw, *Housing a Healthy, Educated and Wealthy Nation Through the CPF*, Singapore: The Institute of Policy Studies, 1997, pp. 39–40).
2 Jon S.T. Quah, "Statutory Boards", in Jon S.T. Quah *et al.* (eds.), *Government and Politics of Singapore*, Singapore: Oxford University Press, 1985, pp. 123–42.
3 For instance, the HDB built small retail shops near blocks of housing, while the EDB was concerned more with building larger business enterprises.
4 Lam Peng Er, "The Organisational Utility Men: Toh Chin Chye and Lim Kim San", in Lam Peng Er and Kevin Y.L. Tan (eds.), *Lee's Lieutenants: Singapore's Old Guard*, St. Leonards: Allen & Unwin, 1999, pp. 16–23.
5 Melanie Chew, *Leaders of Singapore*, Singapore: Resource Press, 1996, p. 166.
6 S. Dhanabalan, "The Economics of Government," *Speeches*, vol. 17, no. 4 (1993), p. 27.
7 Linda Low and T.C. Aw, *Housing a Healthy, Educated and Wealthy Nation Through the CPF*, Singapore: The Institute of Policy Studies, 1997, pp. 13–21.
8 Linda Low and T.C. Aw, *Housing a Healthy, Educated and Wealthy Nation Through the CPF*, Singapore: The Institute of Policy Studies, 1997, pp. 21–6.
9 Linda Low and T.C. Aw, *Housing a Healthy, Educated and Wealthy Nation Through the CPF*, Singapore: The Institute of Policy Studies, 1997, p. 80.
10 For changes in the most recent economic crisis, see "The Provision of Public Housing in Singapore", Report prepared by the Third World Network on public housing in Singapore, posted October 15, 2001, on the Web: http://www.undp.org/tcdc/bestprac/social/cases/02–public%20housing.htm.
11 *Straits Times Weekly Edition*, December 4, 1999. Susan Long quotes Professor Linda Low: "The CPF is slave to so many schemes, it cannot serve all its masters simultaneously".
12 Use of CPF savings for this was made easier in 2001 (*Straits Times Weekly Edition*, May 18, 2001).
13 For details of how the costs of medical services were kept down, including requiring some payments by users, see Lee Kuan Yew, *From Third World to First: The Singapore Story: 1965–*

2000, Singapore: Times Media Private Ltd., 2000, pp. 122–4. Goh Chok Tong collaborated in devising the scheme.

14 For a more complete list, see Michael Sharraden, "Social Policy Based on Assets: Singapore's Central Provident Fund", paper presented at the Annual Meeting of the Association for Asian Studies, Washington, DC, April 6–9, 1995, pp. 7–22.

15 Linda Low and T.C. Aw, *Housing a Healthy, Educated and Wealthy Nation Through the CPF*, Singapore: The Institute of Policy Studies, 1997, pp. 27–8, 70–4.

16 Goh Chok Tong, "The Philosophy Behind the CPF Top-Up Scheme", *Speeches*, vol. 17, no. 2 (1993), pp. 2–9.

17 *Straits Times Weekly Edition*, August 26, 2000.

18 Linda Low and T.C. Aw, *Housing a Healthy, Educated and Wealthy Nation Through the CPF*, Singapore: The Institute of Policy Studies, 1997, pp. 24–5.

19 Ben Dolven, "Where's My Nest Egg?", *Far Eastern Economic Review*, May 25, 2000, p. 69.

20 Before 1970, the resident population was relatively young, but since then a number of measures were adopted with the needs of an aging population in mind (Linda Low and T.C. Aw, *Housing a Healthy, Educated and Wealthy Nation Through the CPF*, Singapore: The Institute of Policy Studies, 1997, pp. 56–8).

21 Ben Dolven, "Where's My Nest Egg?", *Far Eastern Economic Review*, May 25, 2000, p. 69. See also, *Straits Times Weekly Edition*, September 2, 2000.

22 Ben Dolven, "Where's My Nest Egg?", *Far Eastern Economic Review*, May 25, 2000, p. 70.

23 *Straits Times Weekly Edition*, January 6, 2001.

24 Ben Dolven, "Where's My Nest Egg?", *Far Eastern Economic Review*, May 25, 2000, p. 69.

25 Michael Sharraden, "Social Policy Based on Assets: Singapore's Central Provident Fund", paper presented at the Annual Meeting of the Association for Asian Studies, Washington, DC, April 6–9, 1995, pp. 28–31.

26 Linda Low and T.C. Aw, *Housing a Healthy, Educated and Wealthy Nation Through the CPF*, Singapore: The Institute of Policy Studies, 1997, p. viii.

27 Ignatius Low, "IMF Gives Singapore Policies the Thumbs-Up", *Straits Times Interactive*, July 10, 2000, on the Web: http://straitstimes.asia1.com.sg/.

28 "The Central Provident Fund and Singapore's Retirement Savings Challenges", September 2001, Summary of report issued by the US Embassy in Singapore, on the Web: http://www.usembassysingapore.org/embassy/politics/CPF2001.html.

29 T.J.S. George, *Lee Kuan Yew's Singapore*, London: André Deutsch, 1974, p. 100.

30 Christopher Tremewan, *The Political Economy of Social Control in Singapore*, London: Macmillan Press Ltd., reprinted in 1996 with a new preface, pp. 44–73.

31 "The Provision of Public Housing in Singapore", Report prepared by the Third World Network on public housing in Singapore, posted October 15, 2001, on the Web: http://www.undp.org/tcdc/bestprac/social/cases/02-public%20housing.htm.

32 Linda Low and T.C. Aw, *Housing a Healthy, Educated and Wealthy Nation Through the CPF*, Singapore: The Institute of Policy Studies, 1997, p. 40.

33 Barrington Kaye, *Upper Nanking Street*, Kuala Lumpur: University of Malaya Press, 1960.

34 Goh Keng Swee, *The Economics of Modernization and Other Essays*, Singapore: Asia Pacific Press, 1973, p. 257.

35 Lee Kuan Yew, *From Third World to First: The Singapore Story: 1965–2000*, Singapore: Times Media Private Ltd., 2000, pp. 116–18.

36 James Minchin, *No Man Is An Island*, North Sydney: Allen & Unwin, 1990, p. 249.

37 Linda Low and T.C. Aw, *Housing a Healthy, Educated and Wealthy Nation Through the CPF*, Singapore: The Institute of Policy Studies, 1997, pp. 46–8.

38 Tan Sook Yee, *Private Ownership of Public Housing in Singapore*, Singapore: Times Academic Press, 1998, p. 144.

39 Michael Hill and Lian Kwen Fee, *The Politics of Nation-Building and Citizenship in Singapore*, London and New York: Routledge, 1995, pp. 119–20.

40 Lee Kuan Yew, *From Third World to First: The Singapore Story: 1965–2000*, Singapore: Times Media Private Ltd., 2000, p. 121.

41 Quoted in Lam Peng Er, "The Organisational Utility Men: Toh Chin Chye and Lim Kim San", in Lam Peng Er and Kevin Y.L. Tan (eds.), *Lee's Lieutenants: Singapore's Old Guard*, St. Leonards: Allen & Unwin, 1999, p. 18.

42 Lee Kuan Yew, *From Third World to First: The Singapore Story: 1965–2000*, Singapore: Times Media Private Ltd., 2000, pp. 116–17.

43 Lee Kuan Yew, *From Third World to First: The Singapore Story: 1965–2000*, Singapore: Times Media Private Ltd., 2000, pp. 234–7.
44 Tan Sook Yee, *Private Ownership of Public Housing in Singapore*, Singapore: Times Academic Press, 1998, p. 145.
45 Michael Hill and Lian Kwen Fee, *The Politics of Nation-Building and Citizenship in Singapore*, London and New York: Routledge, 1995, p. 128.
46 R.S. Milne and Diane K. Mauzy, *The Legacy of Lee Kuan Yew*, Boulder: Westview, 1990, p. 39.
47 *Sunday Times*, June 25, 2000.
48 Christopher Tremewan, *The Political Economy of Social Control in Singapore*, London: Macmillan Press Ltd., reprinted in 1996 with a new preface, pp. 71–2.
49 Michael Hill and Lian Kwen Fee, *The Politics of Nation-Building and Citizenship in Singapore*, London and New York: Routledge, 1995, p. 151.
50 *Straits Times Weekly Edition*, February 22, 1997.
51 Linda Low and T.C. Aw, *Housing a Healthy, Educated and Wealthy Nation Through the CPF*, Singapore: The Institute of Policy Studies, 1997, p. 50.
52 Lee Kuan Yew, *From Third World to First: The Singapore Story: 1965–2000*, Singapore: Times Media Private Ltd., 2000, p. 237; Notes for Minister's Interview with Profs Milne and Mauzy on 24 September 1990 at 10:30 am [prepared by S. Dhanabalan's staff].
53 *Straits Times Weekly Edition*, September 2, 2000.
54 *Straits Times Weekly Edition*, September 23, 2000. By 2001, 50-story blocks were planned for 2007 (*Straits Times Weekly Edition*, August 11, 2001).
55 *Straits Times Weekly Edition*, January 22, 2000.
56 Lim Hng Kiang, "HDB Upgrading Programme – Grassroots Democracy at its Best", *Speeches*, vol. 20, no. 4 (2000), pp. 75–9.
57 *Straits Times Weekly Edition*, June 3, 2000.
58 This rather happy picture needs to be put in context, both from the individual's point of view and from the advantages to the government. As regards the former, individuals must choose the right time to "sell down" their property after children leave home; otherwise they will be "asset rich but cash poor" after retirement. From the government's angle, it is interested in maintaining values through upgrading and avoiding a crash in the property market.
59 Goh Chok Tong, *For People Through Action By Party*, Singapore: People's Action Party, 1999, p. 107.
60 *Straits Times Weekly Edition*, January 10 and January 18, 1997.
61 Michael Sharraden, "Social Policy Based on Assets: Singapore's Central Provident Fund", paper presented at the Annual Meeting of the Association for Asian Studies, Washington, DC, April 6–9, 1995, pp. 45–51.
62 Jon S.T. Quah, "Statutory Boards", in Jon S.T. Quah *et al.* (eds.), *Government and Politics of Singapore*, Singapore: Oxford University Press, 1985, p. 130.
63 *People's Association Annual Report 1998–1999*, Singapore: the People's Association, 1999. The PA was reorganized in 1999. The aim was to attract young, well-educated Singaporeans and to emphasize its projects rather than its political affiliations (*Straits Times Weekly Edition*, October 9, 1999).
64 Han Fook Kwang *et al.*, *Lee Kuan Yew: The Man and His Ideas*, Singapore: Times Editions and Singapore Press Holdings, 1998, p. 342.
65 John Drysdale, *Singapore: Struggle for Success*, Singapore: Times Books International, 1984, p. 236.
66 Seah Chee Meow, "Parapolitical Institutions", in Jon S.T. Quah *et al.* (eds.), *Government and Politics in Singapore*, Singapore: Oxford University Press, 1985, pp. 178–9.
67 Seah Chee Meow, "Parapolitical Institutions", in Jon S.T. Quah *et al.* (eds.), *Government and Politics in Singapore*, Singapore: Oxford University Press, 1985, p. 190.
68 R.S. Milne and Diane K. Mauzy, *Singapore: The Legacy of Lee Kuan Yew*, Boulder: Westview, 1990, pp. 69–70.
69 *People's Association Annual Report 1998–1999*, Singapore: the People's Association, 1999, pp. 11–13.
70 Goh Chok Tong, "Community Development Councils: Building a Cohesive and Compassionate Community", *Speeches*, vol. 21, no. 2 (1997), p. 9; *Straits Times Weekly Edition*, November 17, 2001.
71 Interview with Ong Keng Yong, Chief Executive Director of the People's Association and Press Secretary to the Prime Minister, June 21, 2000.

72 Interview with Prime Minister Goh Chok Tong, July 1, 2000; *Straits Times Weekly Edition*, November 17, 2001.
73 Interview with Ong Keng Yong, Chief Executive Director of the People's Association and Press Secretary to the Prime Minister, June 21, 2000.
74 *Straits Times Weekly Edition*, November 17, 2001. CDC functions include community and welfare programs, also some health programs for the elderly.
75 *Straits Times Weekly Edition*, May 3, 1997.
76 *Parliamentary Debates Singapore*, vol. 66, no. 9 (October 28, 1996), cols. 818–19.
77 Interview with Prime Minister Goh Chok Tong, July 1, 2000.

8 The dictates of ethnicity

1 Goh Chok Tong in the *Straits Times Weekly Edition*, March 1, 1997. Warren Fernandez writes that "the chasm between the Chinese- and English-educated ... is arguably still the deepest schism in Singapore's body politic" ("Singapore Still Walks Language Tightrope", *Straits Times Weekly Edition*, January 30, 1999). Also see Koh Buck Song, "When English-Speaking Chinese Should Show More Sensitivity", *Straits Times Weekly Edition*, January 18, 1997.
2 Goh Chok Tong made reference to the two groups in his 1999 National Day Rally Speech (*Straits Times*, August 24, 1999).
3 *Straits Times*, May 11, 1988.
4 According to *Singapore in Numbers 2000* (http://www.singstat.gov.sg/FACT/SIF/sif3.html), 99.6 percent of Malays are Muslims.
5 Raj Vasil, *Asianising Singapore: The PAP's Management of Ethnicity*, Singapore: Heinemann Asia, 1995, pp. 2–3. Also see J.S. Furnivall, *Colonial Policy and Practice*, Cambridge: Cambridge University Press, 1948, p. 3.
6 The first riots, with 18 killed and 173 injured, were in December 1950 when a Dutch girl who was brought up by a Muslim family during the war was returned to her natural parents. There were riots in July and September 1964, during Singapore's short-lived and turbulent inclusion in Malaysia (see pp. 20–4), which, combined, left 36 dead and 560 injured. The most recent episode of rioting was a spill-over from the May 1969 ethnic riots in neighboring Malaysia, and resulted in 4 deaths, 60 injuries, and over a thousand arrests. See Lee Kuan Yew, *From Third World to First, The Singapore Story: 1965–2000*, Singapore: Times Media Private Ltd., 2000, pp. 38–9.
7 Raj Vasil, *Asianising Singapore: The PAP's Management of Ethnicity*, Singapore: Heinemann Asia, 1995, p. 21.
8 Joseph B. Tamney, *The Struggle Over Singapore's Soul*, Berlin and New York: Walter de Gruyter, 1996, p. 111.
9 John Clammer, *Singapore: Ideology, Society, Culture*, Singapore: Chopmen Pubs., 1985, p. 100.
10 Sri Lanka represents the classic case of a change in language policy with devastating consequences. When English was replaced by Sinhalese in the universities and civil service, the Tamil community suffered a decline of status and socio-economic standing. Violence followed.
11 The Religious Harmony Act has not yet been invoked, but a number of religious leaders have been summoned and warned of the consequences under the law of mixing politics with religion and of criticizing other faiths. See Home Affairs Minister Wong Kan Seng's discussion of the state of religious harmony in Singapore in *Straits Times Weekly Edition*, May 12, 2001.
12 *The Independent*, November 28, 1990.
13 B.G. Lee Hsien Loong, "Maintaining Social Cohesion and Racial Harmony", *Speeches*, vol. 22, no. 5 (1998), p. 43.
14 Lee Kuan Yew, *From Third World to First, The Singapore Story: 1965–2000*, Singapore: Times Media Private Ltd., 2000, pp. 234–6. The HDB estates were also mixed in terms of types of dwellings – from single room rentals to four-room luxury flats – in each estate.
15 Lee Kuan Yew, *The Singapore Story: Memoirs of Lee Kuan Yew*, Singapore: Prentice Hall, 1998, pp. 333 and 346.
16 Interview with Lim Jim Koon, the editor of *Lianhe Zaobao*, June 29, 2000.
17 Raj Vasil, *Asianising Singapore: The PAP's Management of Ethnicity*, Singapore: Heinemann Asia, 1995, p. 62.
18 Interview with Dr. Arun Mahizhnan, Deputy Director of the Institute of Policy Studies, June 16, 2000.
19 Lee has expressed this view to the authors at various times. In an interview with Taiwanese journalists in March 1989, Lee stated that if he could do it over again, he would promote

Chinese primary schools, with English as a second language in these schools. See Anne Pakir, "English-Knowing Bilingualism in Singapore", in Ban Kah Choon *et al.* (eds.), *Imagining Singapore*, Singapore: Times Academic Press, 1992, p. 248.

20 Lai Ah Eng, *Meanings of Multiethnicity*, Kuala Lumpur: Oxford University Press, 1995, p. 146. Also see the views of PAP MP Dr. Ow Chin Hock on the deeply alienated Chinese-speakers, in Raj Vasil, *Asianising Singapore: The PAP's Management of Ethnicity*, Singapore: Heinemann Asia, 1995, pp. 128–9. Dr. Ow believes some 16 percent of these feel disadvantaged and frustrated about being educated in the wrong language medium for obtaining good jobs.

21 Christopher Tremewan, *The Political Economy of Social Control in Singapore*, London: Macmillan Press, 1994 (reprinted with a new preface in 1996), p. 149.

22 On this dilemma, see Jumari Naiyan, "Does the Singaporean Identity Exist?", *Karawan*, Jan–April 1998, pp. 14–15, and Hussin Mutalib, "Singapore's Quest for National Identity: The Triumphs and Trials of Government Policies", in Bah Kah Choon *et al.* (eds.), *Imagining Singapore*, Singapore: Times Academic Press, 1992, p. 69. Jumari Naiyan contends that a Singaporean identity, such as exists, has largely been built on the economic success of Singapore (p. 15).

23 Quoted in Irene Ng, "How to Move the Race Dialogue Forward", *Straits Times Weekly Edition*, October 17, 1999.

24 See Joel H. Spring, *The American School 1642-1996* (4th ed.), New York: the McGraw Hill Companies, Inc. 1997, pp. 1–3. Also see Tham Seong Chee, "Education, Culture and Moral Values in Industrializing Plural Societies – With Special Reference to Singapore", in R.E. Vente *et al.* (eds.), *Cultural Heritage vs. Technological Development – Challenges to Education*, Singapore: Maruzen Asia, 1981, pp. 211 and 218, and Johannes Chang Han-Yin, "The Functions and Limitations of Education in Singapore", *Commentary*, vol. 15 (1998), p. 22.

25 Christopher Tremewan, *The Political Economy of Social Control in Singapore*, London: Macmillan Press, 1994 (reprinted with a new preface in 1996), p. 74; S. Gopinathan, "Education", in Jon S.T. Quah *et al.* (eds.), *Government and Politics of Singapore*, Singapore: Oxford University Press, 1985, p. 197; and a paper by Llewellyn Noronha located in the Institute of Southeast Asian Studies Library which has no reference but which is based on a conference paper "Educational Reality in Singapore – Manipulation or Management? – A Prima Facie Case", for the Conference of the Sociological Association of Australia and New Zealand, Christchurch, New Zealand, 1981, p. 15.

26 *Report on the Ministry of Education, 1978*, Singapore: Ministry of Education, 1979 (Goh Report).

27 Speech to Parliament by Goh Keng Swee on March 27, 1979, in Linda Low (ed.), *Wealth of East Asian Nations – Speeches and Writings of Goh Keng Swee*, Singapore: Federal Publications, 1995, p. 188. Streaming follows the Swiss-German model which differentiates education into a small academic sector and a much larger vocational sector. See Dr. Tony Tan Keng Yam, "Education in Modern, Industrialized Society", *Speeches*, vol. 13, no. 4 (1989), pp. 44–9.

28 See Soon Teck Wong, *Singapore's New Education System*, Singapore: Institute of Southeast Asian Studies, 1988, and Anne Pakir, "English-Knowing Bilingualism in Singapore", in Ban Kah Choon *et al.* (eds.), *Imagining Singapore*, Singapore: Times Academic Press, 1992, p. 242.

29 Jon S.T. Quah, "Government Policies and Nation-Building", in Jon S.T. Quah (ed.), *In Search of Singapore's National Values*, Singapore: Times Academic Press, 1990 (reprinted in 1999), pp. 53–4; Joseph B. Tamney, *The Struggle Over Singapore's Soul*, Berlin and New York: Walter de Gruyter, 1996, pp. 26–37.

30 See Beng-Huat Chua, *Communitarian Ideology and Democracy in Singapore*, London and New York: Routledge, 1995, p. 120.

31 *Straits Times Weekly Edition*, March 28, 1998 and March 29, 1997; Trish Saywell, "Thinking Out of the Box", *Far Eastern Economic Review*, December 14, 2000, pp. 62–4. According to Saywell, a survey showed that children aged 10 to 12 were more afraid of exams than of their parents dying (p. 62).

32 See Chiang Chie Foo, "Education: New Directions", in *Singapore – The Year in Review 1998*, Singapore: Institute of Policy Studies, 1999, pp. 65–76; Han Fook Kwang, "Thinking Aloud", *Straits Times Weekly Edition*, February 10, 2001. See also *Straits Times Weekly Edition*, January 24, 1998 (for SMU, and http://www.smu.edu.sg/) and January 15, 2000 (for autonomous schools).

33 Interview with RAdm Teo Chee Hean, Minister for Education, June 9, 2000. Also see *Straits Times Weekly Edition*, January 3, 1998; *Learning to Think, Thinking to Learn*, Singapore: Ministry of Education, 1998. There is also a pilot project called the Learning Village, a joint

venture between Singapore's Education Ministry and IBM, which will allow web-based communication and collaboration between teachers, students, parents, and interested members of the community ("A Tool for Learning", *The Economist*, June 24, 2000: http://www.economist.com/archive/view.cgi).

34 Mark Warschauer notes a potential implementation problem. After commenting that the progress has been impressive, he writes, "A recent visit to a Singaporean school revealed an outstanding technology infrastructure – with Internet connections and computer projection systems in every classroom, and with several full computer laboratories for instruction – but with students engaging in computer-based drills and exercises they would have performed on paper" ("Singapore's Dilemma: Control vs Autonomy in IT-Led Development", on the Web: http//:www.gse.uci.edu/markw/singapore.html, downloaded on September 9, 2001).

35 Theresa Tan, "New Subject Takes S'pore Story to Schools", *Straits Times Weekly Edition*, February 10, 2001. Social studies form half of the humanities subject. The other half consists of an elective course such as history, geography or literature.

36 See *Learning to Think, Thinking to Learn*, Singapore: Ministry of Education, 1998, p. 17; *Straits Times Weekly Edition*, February 1 and May 24, 1997; Goh Chok Tong, "The Key Role of Schools", *Speeches*, vol. 23, no. 2 (March–April 1999), pp. 13–21; and C.J.W.-L Wee, "The Need for National Education in Singapore", (*Trends* No. #93, Institute of Southeast Asian Studies), *Business Times*, May 30–31, 1998.

37 Liew Kai Khuin, "Setting the Standard of English for Asia From Toa Payoh", *Singapore Magazine*, January–February 2001, p. 5; Seth Mydans, "Nations In Asia Give English Their Own Flavorful Quirks", *New York Times*, July 1, 2001. For an anti-globalization and strident defense of Singlish, see *New Internationalist*, 333 (April 2001), on the Web: http://www.oneworld.org/ni/issue333/cultural.html.

38 M. Nirmala, "Moves to Prevent Erosion of English", *Straits Times Weekly Edition*, October 30, 1999.

39 Tan Dawn Wei, "No Singlish Please, We are Singaporean", *Singapore Magazine*, November–December 1999, pp. 18–22; Irene Ng, "Speak Good English Campaign Next Year", *Straits Times Weekly Edition*, September 4, 1999; *Straits Times Weekly Edition*, April 7, 2001.

40 Goh Chok Tong, "Strengthening the Singapore Heartbeat", *Speeches*, vol. 23, no. 5 (September–October 1999), p. 12: *Straits Times Weekly Edition*, November 27, 1999.

41 See the *Straits Times Weekly Edition*, September 27, 1997, for a report on international competitions in 1994 and 1996 where Singapore ranked first overall.

42 Lee Kuan Yew in the *Straits Times Weekly Edition*, April 3, 1999.

43 Raj Vasil, *Asianising Singapore: The PAP's Management of Ethnicity*, Singapore: Heinemann Asia, 1995, p. 76 (from an interview by Vasil in 1994).

44 See *Straits Times Weekly Edition*, January 23, March 27, and April 3, 1999.

45 See *Straits Times Weekly Edition*, March 27 and April 3, 1999; *Straits Times*, June 10, 2000.

46 Anne Pakir, "English-Knowing Bilingualism in Singapore", in Ban Kah Choon *et al.* (eds.), *Imagining Singapore*, Singapore: Times Academic Press, 1992, p. 252.

47 Goh Chok Tong, "Mandarin is More Than a Language", *Speeches*, vol. 15, no. 5 (1991), pp. 5–7.

48 *Mandarin: The Chinese Connection*, Singapore: Ministry of Information and the Arts, 2000, p. 45.

49 *Mandarin: The Chinese Connection*, Singapore: Ministry of Information and the Arts, 2000, pp. 47, 65.

50 Anne Pakir, "English-Knowing Bilingualism in Singapore", in Ban Kah Choon *et al.* (eds.), *Imagining Singapore*, Singapore: Times Academic Press, 1992, p. 249.

51 Goh Nguen Wah, *Mother Tongue: What it Means to Singapore*, Singapore: SNP Editions Pte, Ltd., 1999, p. 78.

52 B.G. George Yeo, "Cyberspace – New Battleground for the Speak Mandarin Campaign", *Speeches*, vol. 22, no. 5 (1998), p. 74; *Straits Times Weekly Edition*, August 23, 1997.

53 See *Parliamentary Debates Singapore*, vol. 69, no. 12 (January 20, 1999), cols. 1809–14 (Lee Hsien Loong) and cols. 1828–38 (Dr. Ow Chin Hock; Peh Chin Hua); *Straits Times Weekly Edition*, January 23, 1999; B. G. Lee Hsien Loong, "Strengthening the Use of Mandarin in Singapore", *Speeches*, vol. 21, no. 5 (1997), pp. 45–7. The Chinese-speaking community is very concerned about declining standards and the fact that a Chinese-language government brochure used to project Singapore's image internationally to attract foreign talent was "riddled with errors and inconsistencies" (see Kao Chen, "Could Chinese Become a Dumpling-House Tongue?" *Straits Times Weekly Edition*, April 7, 2001). In 2001, the Education Minister

reported, however, that more students were opting to study higher Chinese at all levels, while few were enrolling in the simpler Chinese language B syllabus (*Straits Times Weekly Edition*, July 14, 2001).

54 *Straits Times Weekly Edition*, October 21, 2000.

55 B.G. George Yeo, "Cyberspace – New Battleground for the Speak Mandarin Campaign", *Speeches*, vol. 22, no. 5 (1998), p. 69.

56 B.G. Lee Hsien Loong, "Strengthening the Use of Mandarin in Singapore", *Speeches*, vol. 21, no. 5 (1997), p. 46; Lim Jim Koon (editor, *Lianhe Zaobao*) "Forget the Sedan Chair, Let's Get on a Jetliner – Together", speech at the 3rd National Education Seminar, Singapore, January 23, 1997 (Xeroxed offprint).

57 Leong Weng Kam, "English's Great Leap Forward", *Straits Times Weekly Edition*, October 21, 2000.

58 Interview with Lim Jim Koon, editor of *Lianhe Zaobao*, June 29, 2000; B.G. George Yeo, "Cyberspace – New Battleground for the Speak Mandarin Campaign", *Speeches*, vol. 22, no. 5 (1998), p. 72.

59 *Mandarin: The Chinese Connection*, Singapore: Ministry of Information and the Arts, 2000, p. 10.

60 Interview with Lim Jim Koon, editor of *Lianhe Zaobao*, June 29, 2000.

61 *Mandarin: The Chinese Connection*, Singapore: Ministry of Information and the Arts, 2000, pp. 26, 30–2; *Straits Times*, June 10, 2000.

62 *Straits Times Weekly Edition*, January 23, 1999; *Straits Times*, June 10, 2000. Also see Warren Fernandez, "My View", *Straits Times Weekly Edition*, March 13, 1999 on the heated debate at a conference between 200 Chinese community leaders over fostering a cultural elite; Lee Kuan Yew's support for the idea, in Chua Lee Hoong, "New Chinese Elite Will Be Different", *Straits Times*, March 28, 1999.

63 Between 1990 and 1999, the median Malay household income rose almost 31 percent and the median CPF balance held by Malays more than doubled; the number of Malay workers holding administrative, managerial, professional or technical jobs nearly doubled, from 12 percent to 23 percent; and the number entering polytechnic and university education more than doubled, from 13 percent to 28 percent (whereas Chinese numbers increased from 42 percent to 68 percent and Indians from 18 percent to 37 percent). The last figures illustrate the problem of "catching up", since the other communities are also progressing. See *Straits Times Weekly Edition*, January 27, 2001. In October 2001, it was reported that 70 percent of Malay and Indian students, and 90 percent of Chinese students, from a Primary 1 cohort graduating from secondary school were going on to post-secondary education (*Straits Times Weekly Edition*, October 6, 2001).

64 Raj Vasil, *Asianising Singapore: The PAP's Management of Ethnicity*, Singapore: Heinemann Asia, 1995, p. 108.

65 John Clammer, *Singapore: Ideology, Society, Culture*, Singapore: Chopmen Pubs., 1985, pp. 124–6.

66 Most recently, when Lee Kuan Yew, responding to a forum question about ethnic bonds, said, "We must not make an error. If, for instance, you put in a Malay officer who's very religious and who has family ties in Malaysia in charge of a machine gun unit, that's a very tricky business" (*Straits Times Weekly Edition*, September 25, 1999). This led two Malay–Muslim groups, Taman Bacaan and Majlis Pusat, to ask for a dialogue with Lee to put the question of Malay–Muslim loyalty to rest "once and for all". He agreed to meet with them, but said there was no once and for all solution to ethnic issues (Mary Kwang, "'No Quick Solution' to Ethnic, Religious Issues", *Straits Times Weekly Edition*, October 2, 1999; Ahmad Osman, "AMP: Issue of Malays in SAF Must Be Answered", *Straits Times Weekly Edition*, November 4, 2000). In March 2001, a closed-door dialogue organized by Majlis Pusat and the Association of Muslim Professionals between the Senior Minister (and eight other Ministers) and about 150 Malay–Muslim Singaporeans was held. Lee explained that the role of the Malays in the SAF was an evolving one that showed considerable improvements (see *Straits Times Weekly Edition*, March 10, 2001). For an indication of just how direct and blunt the discussion was, on both sides, see Irene Ng, "Malay Leaders 'Want More Integration'", *Straits Times Weekly Edition*, March 17, 2001, and Irene Ng, "Nation's Report Card on Racial Integration: '5 or 6 Out of 10'", *Straits Times Weekly Edition*, May 5, 2001.

67 "Don't Undermine Gains Made by Malay MPs, PM Warns", *Straits Times*, November 7, 2000, posted on sgdaily@list.sintercom.org on November 23, 2000. These were excerpts of a dialogue between Goh Chok Tong and members of the Association of Muslim Professionals (AMP).

68 Lai Ah Eng, *Meanings of Multiethnicity*, Kuala Lumpur: Oxford University Press, 1995, p. 150.
69 Sheila McNulty, "Singapore: Racial Resentment Grows . . .", *Financial Times*, March 27, 1999.
70 Lily Zubaidah Rahim, *The Singapore Dilemma: The Political and Educational Marginality of the Malay Community*, Kuala Lumpur: Oxford University Press, 1998, p. 42.
71 Lily Zubaidah Rahim, *The Singapore Dilemma: The Political and Educational Marginality of the Malay Community*, Kuala Lumpur: Oxford University Press, 1998, pp. 166–7.
72 Interview with Abdullah Tarmugi, Minister for Community Development and Sports and Minister-in-Charge of Muslim Affairs, July 1, 2000.
73 Lai Ah Eng, *Meanings of Multiethnicity*, Kuala Lumpur: Oxford University Press, 1995, p. 148; also see letter to the Forum by Ismail Kassim, *Straits Times Weekly Edition*, March 17, 2001.
74 Halimah Yacob, "Wake-Up Call for Malay Workforce", *Karyawan* (January–April 1998), p. 4.
75 Ahmad Osman, "Keeping the Madrasah Relevant in the New Age", *Straits Times*, June 3, 2000. In addition to the Madrasah schools, the issue of the ban on Muslim girls wearing head-coverings (*tudong*) in national schools remains sensitive. See Trish Saywell, "Common Ground", *Far Eastern Economic Review* (January 24, 2002), pp. 20–1.
76 *Straits Times Weekly Edition*, May 6, 13, 2000; *Sunday Times*, June 4, 2000; Jamie Tarabay, "Muslims in Singapore Worry They'll Lose Schools", *Globe & Mail*, May 16, 2000; *Prime Minister's National Day Rally Speech 1999*, Singapore: MITA, 1999, pp. 4–5.
77 *Straits Times Weekly Edition*, May 27, 2000.
78 "Minimal results" have been defined as matching the average aggregate score for Malay pupils in the six lowest performing national schools who sat for the PSLE in the same year. See *Straits Times Weekly Edition*, October 14, 2000.
79 Transcript of the Channel NewAsia interview with Deputy Prime Minister Lee Hsien Loong, telecast on January 6, 2000, forwarded on sgdaily@list.sintercom.org on January 10, 2000.
80 Interview with Abdullah Tarmugi, Minister for Community Development and Sports, and Minister-in-Charge of Muslim Affairs, July 1, 2000; conversation with Sumardi Ali, CEO of Yayasan Mendaki, July 1, 2000; Haffidz A. Hamid *et al.* (eds.), *Factors Affecting Malay/Muslim Pupils' Performance in Education*, Singapore: AMP Occasional Paper Series No. 1-95, 1995; Halimah Yacob, "Wake-Up Call for Malay Workforce", *Karyawan* (January–April 1998), pp. 4–6; and Wan Hussein Zoohri, *The Singapore Malays: The Dilemma of Development*, Singapore: Singapore Malay Teachers Union, 1990.
81 See Tania Li, *Malays in Singapore: Culture, Economy, and Ideology*, Singapore: Oxford University Press, 1989, passim. She notes that as early as 1894 there was an article in a Singapore paper that identified Malay weaknesses as deriving from custom, lack of industry and ambition, and hostility to those with talent. Also, she notes that Muslim reformists in the early 1900s constantly stressed Malay cultural deficiencies (p. 168). Many academic books and analyses have perpetuated these notions, she writes (p. 169).
82 See Lily Zubaidah Rahim, *The Singapore Dilemma: The Political and Educational Marginality of the Malay Community*, Kuala Lumpur: Oxford University Press, 1998, passim; Tania Li, *Malays in Singapore: Culture, Economy, and Ideology*, Singapore: Oxford University Press, 1989, passim.
83 For example it was heartening to read that a group of 400 Malay pupils in Primary 3 and 4 were among the *best* in mathematics in an international study of 500,000 students from 45 countries conducted in October 1994. The pupils, comprising 16 percent of Singapore Malays who took part, ranked in the top 10 percent. See *Straits Times Weekly Edition*, August 30, 1997.
84 Michael Hill and Lian Kwen Fee, *The Politics of Nation Building and Citizenship in Singapore*, London and New York: Routledge, 1995, p. 234. On the advantages but also dangers of ethnic self-help groups, see Zulkifli Baharudin, "The Challenges Within", *Karyawan*, January–April 1999, pp. 8–9.
85 Yayasan Mendaki on the Web: http://www.mendaki.org.sg/about/history.htm.
86 Lily Zubaidah Rahim, *The Singapore Dilemma: The Political and Educational Marginality of the Malay Community*, Kuala Lumpur: Oxford University Press, 1998, p. 212.
87 See Lee Kuan Yew, *From Third World to First, The Singapore Story: 1965–2000*, Singapore: Times Media Private Ltd., 2000, p. 239, and "Don't Undermine Gains Made by Malay MPs, PM Warns", *Straits Times*, November 7, 2000, forwarded by sgdaily@list.sintercom.org on November 23, 2000.
88 Goh Chok Tong, "Ethnic Based Self-Help Groups: To Help, Not to Divide", *Speeches*, vol. 18, no. 4 (1994), p. 11; also see B.G. Lee Hsien Loong, "Maintaining Social Cohesion and Racial Harmony", *Speeches*, vol. 22, no. 5 (1998), pp. 42–7.

89 Malay–Muslim organizations have two pillars. The first is MUIS, the Islamic Religious Council of Singapore, which is in charge of Islamic Affairs. The second is Mendaki, which is in charge of social projects. Many major Malay–Muslim bodies, such as PERGAS (the Association of Islamic Religious Scholar and Teachers), are institutional members of Mendaki. These pillars are led by the Minister-in-Charge of Muslim Affairs, who is assisted by Malay MPs.

90 See *Straits Times Weekly Edition*, February 5, April 22, 2000; *Straits Times Interactive*, April 29, 2000, *Straits Times*, June 29, 1999, B.G. Lee Hsien Loong, "Malay/Muslims Must Prepare for Knowledge-Based Economy", *Speeches*, vol. 23, no. 4 (July–August 1999), pp. 17–22.

91 Others include Taman Bacaan and Jamiyah, grassroots organizations that provide social services to the community.

92 The AMP's goal is "to play an active and leading role in the transformation and long-term development of the Malay/Muslim Singaporean into a dynamic community to take its pride of place in the larger Singaporean society". Membership is open to all, and the AMP endeavors to work through a multi-ethnic approach. In the decade since its formation, the AMP spent $21.3 million on 37 self-help programs involving 120,000 Malay/Muslims. See the Forum letter by the chairman of the executive board of the AMP, Mohd. Amin Ibrahim, *Straits Times Weekly Edition*, May 19, 2001.

93 See *Straits Times Weekly Edition*, November 4, 11, 2000. The government also issued a veiled warning to the AMP in 2001 about possibly raising ethnic and religious tensions (see *Straits Times*, April 30, 2001; *Straits Times Weekly Edition*, May 19, 2001). In March 2001, AMP's government funding was cut by one-third, although overall funding for the Malay–Muslim community was increased (see *Straits Times Weekly Edition*, March 31, 2001).

94 On SINDA, see Raj Vasil, *Asianising Singapore: the PAP's Management of Ethnicity*, Singapore: Heinemann Asia, 1995, p. 148; Eunice Lau, "Sinda Praised for Involving Other Races", *Straits Times Weekly Edition*, March 3, 2001; and its Web page: http://www.sinda.org.sg/about.htm.

95 On the Eurasian Association, see Goh Chok Tong, "Ethnic Based Self-Help Groups: To Help, Not to Divide", *Speeches*, vol. 18, no. 4 (1994), pp. 10–14. The Eurasian community is on the whole better educated and its members are in more high skilled jobs than the other communities. In 1994, the Eurasian Association had only 31 students in its tuition program and 85 in its welfare assistance program.

96 On the CDAC, see Ho Khai Leong, *The Politics of Policy-Making in Singapore*, Singapore: Oxford University Press, 2000, pp. 124–6.

97 See Goh Chok Tong, "Self-Help in the Chinese Community", *Speeches*, vol. 16, no. 5 (1992), pp. 7–16. On the CDAC's impressive wide-ranging programs and goals, see *Straits Times Interactive*, April 29, 2000. The CDAC's Skills Upgrading Program even awards cash to those who have successfully completed each module of a course (*Straits Times*, September 5, 1992). The CDAC's web page description, however, seems singularly lacking in any spirit of multiracialism: The CDAC ... "is a self-help, non-profit organization set up BY the Chinese community and FOR the Chinese community" (see the CDAC on the Web: http://cdac.org.sg/intro.html, downloaded May 13, 2000).

98 See "Self-Help and National Integration", *AMP Occasional Paper Series*, paper # 3-96, Singapore: AMP, 1996; Lily Zubaidah Rahim, *The Singapore Dilemma: The Political and Educational Marginality of the Malay Community*, Kuala Lumpur: Oxford University Press, 1998, pp. 237–45, and "The Paradox of Ethnic-Based Self-Help Groups", in Derek da Cunha (ed.), *Debating Singapore*, Singapore: Institute of Southeast Asian Studies, 1994, pp. 46–50.

99 Irene Ng, "Race Relations and Reality", *Straits Times Weekly Edition*, March 4, 2000.

100 See a thoughtful article on ethnic policies by Chua Lee Hoong, "Time for Ethnic Experiment to Move On", *Straits Times Weekly Edition*, March 3, 2001.

9 The successors

1 Samuel P. Huntington, *Political Order in Changing Societies*, New Haven, CT: Yale University Press, 1968, p. 409.

2 Diane K. Mauzy, "Leadership Succession in Singapore: The Best Laid Plans ... ", *Asian Survey*, vol. XXXIII, no. 12 (December 1993), pp. 1163–74.

3 Both Goh Chok Tong and Lee Kuan Yew confirm that Lee did not step down immediately because he was concerned about the succession, was afraid that perhaps Goh and his team could not manage since "all the levers" over 30 years' time had been constructed for him to operate,

and he wanted to be in a position to help if need be. Goh agreed to this. Lee had intended to stay on only two or three years. Lee concedes now that Goh has done well; better than he had expected (interviews with Senior Minister Lee Kuan Yew, June 29, 2000, and Prime Minister Goh Chok Tong, July 1, 2000).

4 *Straits Times*, November 26, 1990.

5 *Asiaweek*, January 18, 1985, pp. 25–8.

6 *Straits Times*, August 24, 1988; R.S. Milne and Diane K. Mauzy, *Singapore: The Legacy of Lee Kuan Yew*, Boulder: Westview Press, 1990, p. 118.

7 See *Straits Times*, August 24 and September 2, 1988; *Far Eastern Economic Review*, September 1, 1988, p. 21, and T.S. Selvan, *Singapore: The Ultimate Island*, Clifton Hills, Victoria: Freeway Books, 1990, pp. 154–6.

8 Lee Kuan Yew, *From Third World to First: The Singapore Story: 1965–2000*, Singapore: Times Media Private Ltd., 2000, p. 763.

9 Lee Kuan Yew, "The Search for Talent", in S. Jayakumar, *Our Heritage and Beyond*, Singapore: SNTUC. 1982, pp. 13–14. Later, he repeated this view, in almost the same words, but with specific reference to ministers (Lee Kuan Yew, *From Third World to First: The Singapore Story: 1965–2000*, Singapore: Times Media Private Ltd., 2000, p. 736).

10 *Straits Times*, November 27, 1990.

11 Lee Kuan Yew, *From Third World to First: The Singapore Story: 1965–2000*, Singapore: Times Media Private Ltd., 2000, p. 745. In private, Lee Kuan Yew said in 1990 that he thought the choice of Goh was a good one, and that he had full confidence in him (Interview, September 17, 1990).

12 Lee Kuan Yew, quoted in Alan Chong, *Goh Chok Tong*, Petaling Jaya: Pelanduk, 1991, pp. 29–30.

13 See *Asiaweek*, February 6, 1981, pp. 25–7.

14 As Lee Kuan Yew recognized after the 1984 elections. See *Straits Times*, August 15, 1988.

15 Interview with Goh Chok Tong, November 12, 1990. Also see *Time International*, December 3, 1990, pp. 15–16; R.S. Milne and Diane K. Mauzy, *Singapore: The Legacy of Lee Kuan Yew*, Boulder: Westview Press, 1990, pp. 125–6.

16 *Asiaweek*, December 11, 1992, p. 32.

17 Irene Ng, "SM Lee: Nobody is Going to Edge Out PM", *Straits Times Weekly Edition*, December 16, 2000.

18 Goh was active as a Boy Scout leader. See *Asiaweek*, January 18, 1985, p. 27.

19 Originally, it was thought that Goh might have eventually become Minister of Finance, which could have destined him for a more restricted career path than the one he actually followed (Interview with Prime Minister Lee Kuan Yew, September 17, 1990).

20 His procedures were not quite as elaborate as given in *For People Through Action by Party* (45th Anniversary Edition) Singapore: People's Action Party, 1999, pp. 114–15. Interview with Prime Minister Goh Chok Tong (July 1, 2000). According to Lee Kuan Yew, Goh was responsible for finding about half of the parliamentary candidates between 1980 and 1988 (*Straits Times*, August 24, 1988). Generally, many candidates with "ministerial potential" were suggested by existing ministers.

21 This was acknowledged by Lee Kuan Yew. See R.S. Milne and Diane K. Mauzy, *Singapore: The Legacy of Lee Kuan Yew*, Boulder: Westview, 1990, p. 122.

22 *Straits Times*, January 17, 1989.

23 Greg Sheridan, *Tigers: Leaders of the New Asia-Pacific*, St. Leonards, NSW: Allen & Unwin, 1997, pp. 73 and 79.

24 *Straits Times*, August 15, 1988.

25 "Finally, Being His Own Man, Goh Chok Tong on Singapore, Asia – and Himself", *Asiaweek*, November 26, 1999 on the Web: http://www.cnn.com/ASIANOW/asiaweek/interview/goh.chok.tong/index.html.

26 *Far Eastern Economic Review*, February 25, 1988, p. 25.

27 "Finally, Being His Own Man, Goh Chok Tong on Singapore, Asia – and Himself", *Asiaweek*, November 26, 1999 on the Web: http://www.cnn.com/ASIANOW/asiaweek/interview/goh.chok.tong/index.html.

28 "He [Goh] may speak softly but he is no softie", according to Lee Kuan Yew. Cited in Alan Chong, *Goh Chok Tong*, Petaling Jaya: Pelanduk, 1991, p. 46.

29 R.S. Milne and Diane K. Mauzy, *Singapore: The Legacy of Lee Kuan Yew*, Boulder: Westview, 1990, p. 128.

30 Interview with Prime Minister Goh Chok Tong, July 1, 2000.

31 Richard Deck, "Foreign Policy", in Michael Haas (ed.), *The Singapore Puzzle*, Westport, CT: Praeger, 1999, pp. 135–8.
32 *Sunday Times*, August 16, 1992.
33 *Far Eastern Economic Review*, November 15, 1990, p. 30.
34 *Straits Times*, May 9, 1985.
35 "Finally, Being His Own Man, Goh Chok Tong on Singapore, Asia – and Himself", *Asiaweek*, November 26, 1999 on the Web: http://www.cnn.com/ASIANOW/asiaweek/interview/goh.chok.tong/index.html. He also stated that the "defining moment" of his time in office was his electoral victory at the 1997 election when he reversed the electoral trend against the PAP (*ibid.*).
36 *Straits Times Weekly Edition*, January 27, 2001.
37 Interview with Prime Minister Goh Chok Tong, July 1, 2000.
38 Interview with Prime Minster Goh Chok Tong, November 3, 1992.
39 *Far Eastern Economic Review*, September 24, 1998, p. 15.
40 "Singapore PM Plans to Step Down in Two to Three Years", *Agence France Presse*, November 22, 2001, on the Web: sg_daily@yahoogroups.com.
41 Interview with Prime Minister Goh Chok Tong, July 1, 2000.
42 J. Harvey and L. Bather, *The British Constitution*, London: Macmillan, 1964, p. 90.
43 *Straits Times*, June 21, 1989.
44 *Straits Times*, September 23, 1984.
45 "MAS is a unique organization – it is the only institution in the world that combines responsibility for monetary policy with supervisory oversight of the entire financial sector – banking, insurance and securities" (B.G. Lee, "Credibility, Confidence, Dynamism: MAS in the New Economic and Financial Landscape", MAS 30th Anniversary Conference, Keynote Address, on July 20, 2001, Singapore Government Press Release on the Web: http://app.internet.gov.sg/data/sprinter/pr/weekly/2001072005.htm.
46 Lee Kuan Yew, *From Third World to First: The Singapore Story: 1965–2000*, Singapore: Times Media Private Ltd., 2000, pp. 93–102.
47 Pang Chen Liang in the *Singapore Monitor*, October 21, 1984.
48 *Far Eastern Economic Review*, July 11, 1998, p. 59.
49 Interview with Deputy Prime Minister Lee Hsien Loong, June 15, 1995.
50 "Deputy Prime Minister Lee Hsien Loong's Interview with 'Fortune Magazine' " (April 3, 2000 issue), on the Web: http://www.gov.sg/sgip/intervws/0300-06.htm.
51 "In Conversation: Interview with DPM Lee Hsien Loong", Part 2 – Broadcast Over CNA (January 13, 1999) on the Web: http://www.gov.sg/sgip/intervws/0100-2.htm.
52 "In Conversation: Interview with DPM Lee Hsien Loong", Part 2 – Broadcast Over CNA (January 13, 1999) on the Web: http://www.gov.sg/sgip/intervws/0100-2.htm.
53 *Far Eastern Economic Review*, July 15, 1999, forwarded on sangkancil@malaysia.net on July 10, 1999.
54 "In Conversation: Interview with DPM Lee Hsien Loong", Part 2 – Broadcast Over CNA (January 13, 1999) on the Web: http://www.gov.sg/sgip/intervws/0100-2.htm.
55 The process of "testing" the ground is referred to by Ho Khai Leong, *The Politics of Policy-Making in Singapore*, Singapore: Oxford University Press, 2000, p. 133.
56 "In Conversation: Interview with DPM Lee Hsien Loong", Part 1 – Broadcast Over CNA (January 6, 1999) on the Web: http://www.gov.sg/sgip/intervws/0100-1.htm.
57 "The NTUC is not a glamorous sector, no great addition to your bio-data that will put you into a higher job. But from a good-government point of view, it's absolutely crucial because your policies have got to be sensitive to the large mass of the semi-skilled and the unskilled" (Lee Kuan Yew in the *Straits Times*, July 4, 2000).
58 "In Conversation: Interview with DPM Lee Hsien Loong", Part 1 – Broadcast Over CNA (January 6, 1999) on the Web: http://www.gov.sg/sgip/intervws/0100-1.htm.
59 Interview with Rear-Admiral Teo Chee Hean, June 28, 1995.
60 Lee Kuan Yew, *From Third World to First: The Singapore Story: 1965–2000*, Singapore: Times Media Private Ltd., 2000, p. 745.
61 In 2000, Lee Kuan Yew thought that recruiting from the military had turned out well and should continue (Interview with Senior Minister Lee Kuan Yew, June 29, 2000).
62 Interviews with B.G. Yeo, B.G. Lee, Rear-Admiral Teo, all in July 2000.
63 *Far Eastern Economic Review*, April 20, 1989, pp. 333–4. Also see Tim Huxley, *Defending the Lion City: The Armed Forces of Singapore*, St. Leonards: Allen & Unwin, 2000, pp. 245–6.

64 Beng-Huat Chua, *Communitarian Ideology and Democracy in Singapore*, London: Routledge, 1995, pp. 53–4. Tan received a PhD in chemistry at Oxford University, lectured at the University of Singapore for a while, and then joined an MNC as a chief chemist. He entered politics in 1972. Once he resigned from his political positions, he spent the rest of his work career in the privare sector. For his career, see "Who's Who in Singapore", on the Web: http://www.recordsingapore.com/.
65 Werner Vennewald, "Technocrats in the State Enterprise System of Singapore", *Working Paper no. 32*, Asian Research Centre (Murdoch University), Canberra: National Library of Australia, 1994, p. 45 and Chart 5b. In 1988 Lee Kuan Yew paid tribute to Lim, saying that he was the kind of person Singapore would need in times of crisis. However, Lim preferred to stay with Keppel rather than re-enter politics (*Straits Times*, August 15, 1988).
66 For example, *Straits Times Weekly Edition*, September 11, 1999 (Susan Long) and February 10, 2001 (Chua Mui Hoong). Some basic questions are raised by Han Fook Kwan, "Is There a Singapore System for Producing Leaders?" *Straits Times Weekly Edition*, August 13, 1994.
67 Interview with Senior Minister Lee Kuan Yew, June 29, 2000.
68 Han Fook Kwang *et al.*, *Lee Kuan Yew: The Man and His Ideas*, Singapore: Times Edition, 1998, p. 334.
69 Interview with Senior Minister Lee Kuan Yew, June 29, 2000.
70 The bulge may be benign. Given the PAP's values, it can hardly complain about a surplus of talent. It has also shown that it can survive succession sequences.
71 Interview with Deputy Prime Minister B.G. Lee Hsien Loong on July 4, 2000.
72 *Straits Times Weekly Edition*, June 5, 1999.
73 Melanie Chew, *Leaders of Singapore*, Singapore: Resource Press, 1996, p. 90.
74 *Straits Times*, November 27, 1990.
75 Ben Dolven, "Reinventing the Heir", *Far Eastern Economic Review*, July 15, 1999, on the Web: http:www.feer.com/Restricted99jul_15/cover.html. He was quite precocious in Malay, having started to learn it when only five years old.
76 "Deputy Prime Minister Lee Hsien Loong's Interview with 'Fortune Magazine' " (April 3, 2000 issue), on the Web: http://www.gov.sg/sgip/intervws/0300-06.htm.
77 Lee Kuan Yew, *From Third World to First: The Singapore Story: 1965–2000*, Singapore: Times Media Private Ltd., 2000, p. 745.

10 Authoritarian aspects of PAP rule

1 This has been noted by Chan Heng Chee, "Democracy: Evolution and Implementation; An Asian Perspective", in R. Bartley *et al.* (eds.), *Democracy and Capitalism*, Singapore: Institute of Southeast Asian Studies, 1993, pp. 3–5. For S.P. Huntington, see *The Third Wave: Democratization in the Twentieth Century*, Norman: University of Oklahoma Press, 1991; for Francis Fukuyama, see *The End of History and the Last Man*, New York: The Free Press, 1992, pp. 49–50; for Freedom House, see their annual Freedom in the World reports on the Web: http://www.freedomhouse.org/survey01/country/singapor.html.
2 See the most recent country reports on human rights practices for Singapore on the Web: http://www.state.gov/www/global/human_rights/1999_hrp/singapor.html; http://www.state.gov/g/drl/rls/hrrpt/2000.
3 See Diane K. Mauzy, "Human Rights in Indonesia, Malaysia and Singapore: Contrasting Views From ASEAN, Canada and Australia", *The Round Table*, Issue 335 (1995), pp. 279–96.
4 Beng-Huat Chua, *Communitarian Ideology and Democracy in Singapore*, London and New York: Routledge, 1995, and Daniel A. Bell *et al.* (eds.), *Towards Illiberal Democracy in Pacific Asia*, London: St. Martin's Press, 1995. For earlier similar ideas see Kishore Mahbubani, "The West and the Rest", *The National Interest*, vol. 28 (Summer 1992), pp. 3–12, and "New Areas of Asean Reaction: Environment, Human Rights, and Democracy", *ASEAN-ISIS Monitor V* (Oct.–Dec. 1992), pp. 13–14. Amitai Etzioni has called for a better balance between individual rights and communal responsibilities in the US. See his book, *The Spirit of Community: Rights, Responsibilities, and the Communitarian Agenda*, New York: Crown Publishers, 1993.
5 See Daniel A. Bell, "After the Tsunami", in *The New Republic*, March 9, 1998, p. 23.
6 Beng-Huat Chua, *Communitarian Ideology and Democracy in Singapore*, London and New York: Routledge, 1995, pp. 7, 31, and 190. As Chua points out, attributing Asian economic gains to communitarianism is essentially the thesis of the book by George Lodge and Ezra Vogel,

Ideology and National Competitiveness: An Analysis of Nine Countries, Boston: Harvard Business School Press, 1987, p. 31.

7 See, for example, Richard A. Deck, "Foreign Policy", in Michael Haas (ed.), *The Singapore Puzzle*, Westport, CT: Praeger, 1999, p. 134.

8 Samuel P. Huntington, "After Twenty Years: The Future of the Third Wave", *Journal of Democracy*, vol. 8, no. 4 (1997), p. 5. John Girling also views Singapore as an exception to the thesis that economic development and a growing middle class promote democratization ("Development and Democracy in Southeast Asia", *The Pacific Review*, vol. 1, no. 4 (1988), pp. 332–3). Interestingly, Russell Bova reports that despite being a democracy, India's human rights record is poor. According to the US Department of State, abuses include "extrajudicial executions and political killings, arbitrary arrest, long-term detention without trial, and the torture, rape and death of suspects in police custody". See "Democracy and Liberty: The Cultural Connection", *Journal of Democracy*, vol. 8, no. 1 (1997), p. 122.

9 David Collier and Steven Levitsky, "Democracy with Adjectives: Conceptual Innovation in Comparative Research", *World Politics*, vol. 49 (April 1997), pp. 430–51.

10 Quoted in Dennis Bloodworth, *The Tiger and the Trojan Horse*, Singapore: Times Books International, 1986, p. 198.

11 Plato's views are analyzed in G.C. Field, *Political Theory*, London: Methuen & Co., Ltd., 1960, Chapter VIII: "The Case Against Democracy".

12 Joseph Schumpeter, *Capitalism, Socialism and Democracy*, 2nd ed., New York: Harper, 1947.

13 Larry Diamond, "Is the Third Wave Over?" *Journal of Democracy*, vol. 7 (July 1996), pp. 20–37.

14 See *Straits Times Weekly Edition*, April 17, 1999, for a ministerial explanation of why the CLA was needed. For the statistics on arrests and procedures, see the *Straits Times*, June 28, 2000. On the MDA, see the US Department of State Human Rights report for Singapore for 1999, on the Web: http://www.state.gov/www/global/human_rights/1999_hrp_report/singapor.html.

15 For the statistics, see *Parliamentary Debates Singapore*, vol. 69, no. 12 (January 20, 1999, cols. 1991–2). On Chia, see *Asiaweek*, July 25, 1997, p. 12 and *Straits Times Weekly Edition*, July 12, 1997. Also see James Minchin, *No Man Is An Island* (2nd ed.), North Sydney: Allen & Unwin, 1990, pp. 216–18. Chia was detained much longer than the others from the Barisan Sosialis because he was not willing to make an admission that he was associated with the MCP. According to Lee Kuan Yew (*From Third World to First, The Singapore Story: 1965–2000*, Singapore: Times Media Private Ltd., 2000, p. 136), Chia's membership in the MCP was confirmed by two MCP members to whom he reported directly.

16 See Garry Rodan, "State–Society Relations and Political Opposition in Singapore", in Garry Rodan (ed.), *Political Oppositions in Industrialising Asia*, London and New York: Routledge, 1996, pp. 101–2.

17 The Student Christian Movement had hoped to raise awareness of social injustices by means of English-language classes for workers, and they denounced capitalism, class differences, and MNCs. Ironically, they were more radical than the workers, who on the whole were not very interested, and Christian activism died down until the mid-1980s. Tamney writes that their publication, *New Q*, quoted the Colombian revolutionary and Catholic priest, Camilo Torres, on the cover of its Christmas 1973 issue, saying that "It is necessary for a Christian to be revolutionary". See Joseph B. Tamney, *The Struggle Over Singapore's Soul*, Berlin and New York: Walter de Gruyter, 1996, pp. 29–32, 52–4.

18 See Lee Kuan Yew, *From Third World to First, The Singapore Story: 1965–2000*, Singapore: Times Media Private Ltd., 2000, p. 137.

19 An on-line poll conducted by the Think Centre, which opposes capital punishment, revealed that 83 percent of Singaporeans support the death penalty. See: http://sg.newd.yahoo.com/010607/l/syi0.html, posted on June 7, 2001.

20 Lee Kuan Yew, *The Singapore Story: Memoirs of Lee Kuan Yew*, Singapore: Prentice Hall, 1998, p. 74.

21 *The Economist*, April 3, 1999, p. 25; *Amnesty International Report 2000, Country Reports: Singapore*, on the Web: http://www.amnesty.org/.

22 See Richard A. Deck, "Foreign Policy", in Michael Haas (ed.), *The Singapore Puzzle*, Westport, CT: Praeger, 1999, pp. 135–42.

23 *Straits Times Weekly Edition*, January 29, 2000.

24 Matthew Gregory Towner, "Political Leaders and Democratic Change: A Comparative Study of the Republic of China and Singapore", PhD Thesis, University of Denver, 1997, pp. 306–20.

25 Garry Rodan, "Preserving the One-Party State in Contemporary Singapore", in Kevin Hewison, *et al.* (eds.), *Southeast Asia in the 1990s: Authoritarian Democracy and Capitalism*, St. Leonards: Allen & Unwin, 1993, p. 92.

26 An interesting example of how sensitive the government is about religious issues occurred with the banning (as proselytizing) of television and print advertisements promoting God by 150 churches, called the Love Singapore Movement, in May 2001, after only a week of a three month campaign. One of the ads, which the government might have thought was aimed at it, put words in God's mouth: "I hate rules. That's why I only made 10 of them". See Suh-kyung Yoon, "Prophet Warning", *Far Eastern Economic Review*, May 10, 2001, p. 37.

27 See the US Department of State Human Rights report for Singapore for 1999, on the Web: http://www.state.gov/www/global/human_rights/1999_hrp_report/singapor.html.; Garry Rodan, "State–Society Relations and Political Opposition in Singapore", in Garry Rodan (ed.), *Political Oppositions in Industrialising Asia*, London and New York: Routledge, 1996, p. 101; Jake Lloyd-Smith, "Jehovah's Witnesses Out of Step on Call-up", *South China Morning Post*, December 31, 2001.

28 *Straits Times Weekly Edition*, January 6 and 20, 2001. For a compilation of news stories on the Falun Buddha Society and the arrests, see "Media Watch: Falun Gong in Local News", by D.P. Yadav, January 2, 2001, forwarded on sgdaily@list.sintercom.org. In March 2001, seven Falungong demonstrators were sent to jail for four weeks, and the other eight were fined (*Straits Times Weekly Edition*, March 31, 2001 and *Far Eastern Economic Review*, April 12, 2001, p. 13). In May 2001, four of the demonstrators, all PRC citizens, were asked to leave Singapore (see *Straits Times Weekly Edition*, May 5, 2001).

29 David Clark, "The Many Meanings of the Rule of Law", in Kanishka Jayasuriya (ed.), *Law, Capitalism and Power in Asia*, London and New York: Routledge, 1999, pp. 31–7.

30 Kevin Tan, "A Short Legal and Constitutional History of Singapore", in Kevin Y.L. Tan (ed.), *The Singapore Legal System* (2nd ed.), Singapore: Singapore University Press, 1999. Also see Helena H.M. Chang, *The Legal System of Singapore*, Singapore: Butterworths Asia, 1995.

31 In 1998, the High Court declared a Singapore law unconstitutional and acquitted a man who worked for the Singapore Investment Corporation convicted of taking bribes (in Hong Kong). It was the first time a Singapore law had been declared unconstitutional by the courts since independence. See the *Straits Times Weekly Edition*, January 10, 1998.

32 *Straits Times Weekly Edition*, April 17, 1999.

33 Tan Ooi Boon, "Lesson in Being World Class from Singapore Judiciary", *Straits Times Weekly Edition*, October 20, 1999.

34 *Parliamentary Debates Singapore*, vol. 69, no. 11 (November 26, 1998), col. 1655.

35 US Department of State Human Rights report for Singapore for 1999, on the Web: http://www.state.gov/www/global/human_rights/1999_hrp_report/singapor.html.

36 See Christopher Tremewan, *The Political Economy of Social Control in Singapore*, London: Macmillan Press, 1994 (reprinted in 1996 with a new preface), pp. 165, 186–96; Francis T. Seow, "The Judiciary", in Michael Haas (ed.), *The Singapore Puzzle*, Westport, CT: Praeger, 1999, pp. 106–24; Francis T. Seow, "The Politics of Judicial Institutions in Singapore", on the off-shore website of Singaporeans for Democracy: http://www.gn.apc.org/sfd/ (no date, downloaded July 21, 2000); Kanishka Jayasuriya, "Corporatism and Judicial Independence Within Statist Legal Institutions in East Asia", in K. Jayasuriya (ed.), *Law, Capitalism and Power in Asia*, London and New York: Routledge, 1999, pp. 182–5; and Thio Li-Ann, "The Constitutional Framework of Powers", in Kevin Y.L. Tan (ed.), *The Singapore Legal System* (2nd ed.), Singapore: Singapore University Press, 1999, pp. 90–4.

37 US Department of State Human Rights report for Singapore for 1999, on the Web: http://www.state.gov/www/global/human_rights/1999_hrp_report/singapor.html. It is noted, however, that these ties generally do not appear to influence the judiciary's independence. See: http://www.state.gov/g/drl/rls/hrrpt/2000.

38 *Straits Times Weekly Edition*, September 14, 1999. This is from journalist Cherian George's reply to a letter in the *Straits Times* (September 9, 1999) by the Prime Minister's Press Secretary, Ong Keng Yong, rebutting an earlier article by George (*Sunday Times*, September 5, 1999).

39 The World Press Freedom Committee <http://www.wpfc.org> undertook a study of, and has written a report on, 91 states and territories that use "insult laws". According to the editor, "insult laws are used in more than 100 countries to stifle and punish political discussion and dissent, editorial comment and criticism, [and] satire..". (forwarded on the Internet from SEASIAL@LIST.MSU.EDU, on July 25, 2000).

40 Simon S.C. Tay, "The Singapore Legal System and International Law: Influence or Interference?" in Kevin Y.L. Tan (ed.), *The Singapore Legal System* (2nd ed.), Singapore: Singapore University Press, 1999, p. 483.

41 *Far Eastern Economic Review*, March 6, 1997, p. 31.

42 *Straits Times Weekly Edition*, May 10 and May 17, 1997.

43 *Straits Times Weekly Edition*, May 10, 1997; interview with Lim Jim Koon, editor of *Lianhe Zaobao*, June 29, 2000. Also see his speech, "Forget the Sedan Chair, Let's Get on a Jetliner – Together", at the 3rd National Education Seminar, Singapore, January 23, 1997 (mimeo).

44 J.B. Jeyaretnam said in Parliament that Tang could not keep silent when he was accused of being a Chinese chauvinist and anti-Christian and so he spoke to the press, and he said that they were telling lies. "But he could have said they were not telling the truth. There is no truth in what they say. And for that it was decided that libel suits should be issued against him" (*Parliamentary Debates Singapore*, vol. 69, no. 11 (November 26, 1998), col. 1735).

45 *Straits Times Weekly Edition*, January 25, 1997.

46 Bruce Gale of PERC said that "Singapore will continue to be dogged with an authoritarian image in the US where there are many human rights groups willing to be sympathetic. It gives Singapore's critics in the US added ammunition". *Bangkok Post*, May 31, 1997. One well-informed Singaporean journalist, a PAP supporter, told the authors that he thought it was disgraceful the way the PAP hounded Tang (interview, July 2000).

47 *Far Eastern Economic Review*, March 6, 1997, p. 31.

48 See *Straits Times Weekly Edition*, February 1 and October 11, 1997.

49 *Straits Times Weekly Edition*, August 22, 1998.

50 *Straits Times*, June 28, 2000; "Compliant Judiciary Rears its Ugly Head Again", Singaporeans for Democracy off-shore website: http://www.gn.apc.org/sfd/ (May 29, 1999); "J.B. Jeyaretnam Pushed towards Bankruptcy, Expulsion from Parliament", *Amnesty International News Release*, December 22, 2000, on the Web: http://www.amnesty.org/.

51 *Straits Times Weekly Edition*, October 11, 1997.

52 "J.B. Jeyaretnam – the Use of Defamation Suits for Political Purposes", *Amnesty International News Release*, October 15, 1999, on the Web: http://www.amnesty.org/news/1997/33600497.htm. Also see: http://web.amnesty.org/web/ar2001.nsf/webasacountries/SINGAPORE?OpenDocument (AI Report 2001); "The Serious Business of Politics in Singapore", *Agence France Presse*, July 29, 2001, forwarded by <sg_daily@yahoo.com>. Earlier, in December 1997, the PAP leaders, who have always insisted that the defamation suits are meant to protect the integrity of the government and its leaders and not to bankrupt opposition politicians, took out an advertisement in the *Sydney Morning Herald* to rebut an article in the paper by AI criticizing the lawsuits. Garry Rodan described the government's use of defamation suits as "a brilliant device" to divert opponents from the task of developing credible alterative programs and support bases", quoted in Fabian Dawson, "Ex-President Reveals Plot to Destroy Singapore Critics", *Southeast Asian Post*, forwarded by sangkancil@malaysia.net on March 26, 1999.

53 According to T.S. Selvan, Seow was suspended from law practice for a year (1973) as a result of his involvement in a chit fund scam; was disciplined three times; was fined in 1980 for making a false statement on his financial statement; was near bankruptcy five times; defaulted on mortgages and failed to pay his employees their salaries, in addition to owing his staff more than S$10,000 in CPF contributions (*Singapore: The Ultimate Island*, Clifton Hills, Victoria: Freeway Books, 1990, pp. 275, 288–9).

54 The diplomat was Political Counselor E. Mason Hendrickson. Some foreign critics believe that Seow was arrested because he sought to represent two of the 1987 ISA "Marxist conspiracy" re-detainees (released and then rearrested after recanting their confessions) in May 1988 (see Richard A. Deck, "Foreign Policy", in Michael Haas (ed.), *The Singapore Puzzle*, Westport, CT: Praeger, 1999, p. 131). Whatever the merits of the case, Seow admitted that he had been to Washington, DC to meet with Henderickson's boss in the State Department. Further, according to Selvan, Seow, who had been "in debt for a decade, mysteriously cleared $1.27 million in debts after meeting Hendrickson". (T.S. Selvan, *Singapore: The Ultimate Island*, Clifton Hills, Victoria: Freeway Books, 1990, pp. 280–1.) Seow said the money came from loans from friends.

55 *Far Eastern Economic Review*, January 21, 1999, p. 17. Chee's book is *To Be Free: Stories From Asia's Struggle Against Oppression*, Melbourne: Monash Asia Institute, 1998.

56 See the *Far Eastern Economic Review*, February 11 and March 11, 1999; *The Economist*, January 9, 1999, p. 28, and February 6, 1999, p. 28. The act was amended to the Public

Entertainment and Meetings Act in November 2000 and its restrictions relaxed marginally (*Straits Times Weekly Edition*, March 3, 2001).

57 See Joyce Liu (Reuters), "Little Public Backing for Someone 'Seeking Trouble'", *South China Morning Post*, February 2, 1999; Zubaidah Ibrahim, "Meet Chee and Shatter the 'Mystique'", *Straits Times Weekly Edition*, April 10, 1999.

58 See *Straits Times Weekly Edition*, December 29, 2001, and *Far Eastern Economic Review* (January 17, 2002), p. 8.

59 One tabloid, *Project Eyeball*, was closed in June 2001.

60 Two are owned by the Singapore Armed Forces Reservists' Association (SAFRA) and two by the National Trades Union Council (NTUC).

61 *Reporting from Singapore*, Singapore: MITA, 2000.

62 See Edward Herman and Noam Chomsky, *Manufacturing Consent: The Political Economy of the Mass Media*, New York: Pantheon Books, 1988, p. 1, quoted in David Birch, "Staging Crises: Media and Citizenship", in Garry Rodan (ed.), *Singapore Changes Guard*, Melbourne: Longman Cheshire, 1993, p. 77.

63 *Parliamentary Debates Singapore*, vol. 69, no. 13 (February 11, 1999), col. 2128.

64 See Derek Davies, "The Press", in Michael Haas (ed.), *The Singapore Puzzle*, Westport, CT: Praeger, 1999, pp. 77–106. For a history of 150 years of the *Straits Times*, see C.M. Turnbull, *Dateline Singapore*, Singapore: Singapore Press Holdings, 1995.

65 See *Parliamentary Debates Singapore*, vol. 69, no. 13 (February 11, 1999), col. 2128.

66 Eddie C.Y. Kuo *et al.*, *Mirror on the Wall: Media in a Singapore Election,* Singapore: Asian Mass Communications Research and Information Centre, 1993.

67 Roger Mitton, "What the Papers Say", *Asiaweek*, March 24, 2000, forwarded on the Web by sgdaily@list.sintercom.org. For an unremittingly critical essay on the Singapore press, see Eric Ellis, "Climate Control in the Singapore Press", *The Australian*, June 21, 2001, forwarded by sg_daily@yahoogroups.com.

68 *Straits Times Weekly Edition*, August 7, 1999.

69 See *Parliamentary Debates Singapore*, vol. 68, no. 4 (February 27, 1998), cols. 482–5 (Zulkifli bin Baharudin, NMP), 487–9 (Simon SC Tay, NMP), 496 (Claire Chiang, NMP), 503–6 (Chiam See Tong, MP), and 512 (J.B. Jeyaretnam, NCMP).

70 *Parliamentary Debates Singapore*, vol. 68, no. 4 (February 27, 1998), col. 485. Also see *Straits Times Weekly Edition*, March 7, 1998; Andrea Hamilton, "Questions of Censorship; A Ban on Political Film and Video Sparks Debate", *Asiaweek*, forwarded on SEASIA@MSU.EDU, March 22, 1998.

71 See *Parliamentary Debates Singapore*, vol. 68, no. 4 (February 27, 1998), cols. 491–3, 517–21.

72 Lim Cheng Tju, "Singapore Political Cartooning", *Southeast Asian Journal of Social Science*, vol. 25, no. 1 (1997), pp. 125–50.

73 Lim Cheng Tju, "Singapore Political Cartooning", *Southeast Asian Journal of Social Science*, vol. 25, no. 1 (1997), p. 140.

74 *Straits Times Weekly Edition*, March 20, 1999, March 17, 2001, April 21, 2001; Arnold Zeitlin, "Singapore's New Restrictions on International Broadcasts Assailed at Conference", May 23, 2001, on the Web: http://www.freedomforum.org.

75 *Far Eastern Economic Review*, August 12, 1999, p. 12.

76 Lingle gives some explanation of his experience in his book, *Singapore's Authoritarian Capitalism*, Barcelona: Edicions Sirocco SL, and The Locke Institute, Fairfax, VA, 1996.

77 Donald K. Emmerson, "Singapore and the 'Asian Values' Debate", *Journal of Democracy*, vol. 6, no. 4 (October 1995), p. 98. Also see Warren Fernandez, "Judge: Enough Evidence for Case Against Lingle, Four Others", *Straits Times*, December 26, 1994, cited in Emmerson (above).

78 Garry Rodan, "Information Technology and Political Control in Singapore", *Working Paper No. 26*, Japan Policy Research Institute (November 1996), p. 1.

79 Stephen Yeo Siew Chye and Arun Mahizhnan, "Developing an Intelligent Island: Dilemmas of Censorship", in Arun Mahizhnan and Lee Tsao Yuan (eds.), *Singapore: Re-Engineering Success*, Singapore: Institute of Policy Studies and Oxford University Press, 1998, pp. 141–4.

80 Garry Rodan, "Information Technology and Political Control in Singapore", *Working Paper No. 26*, Japan Policy Research Institute (November 1996), p. 2.

81 Stephen Yeo Siew Chye and Arun Mahizhnan, "Developing an Intelligent Island: Dilemmas of Censorship", in Arun Mahizhnan and Lee Tsao Yuan (eds.), *Singapore: Re-Engineering Success*, Singapore: Institute of Policy Studies and Oxford University Press, 1998, p. 143. Also see, "The Twenty Enemies of the Internet", which condemns the tactic of forcing net users to

subscribe to a state-run ISP, on the Web: http://www.rsf.fr/alaune/ennemisweb.html. Singapore is *not* one of the twenty "enemies" of the Internet, although Burma and Vietnam make the list.

82 See *Straits Times Weekly Edition*, October 25, 1997. When a network connection error message appears on the screen, it means the SBA has blocked the site. Also see *Myths and Facts about SBA and the Internet*, Singapore: SBA document, October 22, 1997.

83 "Singapore Net Law Dismays Opposition", August 14, 2001, *British Broadcasting Company*, on the Web: http://news.bbc.co.uk.

84 *Straits Times Interactive*, October 19, 2001, on the Web: http://straitstimes.asia1.com.sg.

85 Tan Tarn How, "Rules on E-Campaigning Spelt Out", *Straits Times Interactive*, October 18, 2001, on the Web: http://straitstimes.asia1.com.sg. Among the activities allowed were photos and representations of candidates, party histories, biographies and manifestos, email promoting or opposing a party or candidate, party publications, meeting notices, calls to members for volunteer activities, chatroom forums, and hypertext links.

86 US Department of State Human Rights report for Singapore for 1999, on the Web: http://www.state.gov/www/global/human_rights/1999_hrp_report/singapor.html.

87 See the US Department of State Human Rights report for Singapore for 1999, on the Web: http://www.state.gov/www/global/human_rights/1999_hrp_report/singapor.html.

88 Stephen Yeo Siew Chye and Arun Mahizhnan, "Developing an Intelligent Island: Dilemmas of Censorship", in Arun Mahizhnan and Lee Tsao Yuan (eds.), *Singapore: Re-Engineering Success*, Singapore: Institute of Policy Studies and Oxford University Press, 1998, pp. 142 and 147.

89 Chua Mui Hoong, "Allowing Diversity Without Undermining Government", *Straits Times Weekly Edition*, September 25, 1999.

90 Deputy Prime Minister Lee Hsien Loong's Interview with *Fortune Magazine*, April 3, 2000 issue, on the Web: http://www.gov.sg/sgip/intervws/0300-06.htm.

91 See p. 134 and note 38 above as well as the *Straits Times*, September 19, 1999.

92 *Straits Times*, November 22, 2001, on the Web: sg_daily@yahoogroups.com.

11 Elections, electoral innovations, and the Opposition

1 Diane K. Mauzy, "Electoral Innovation and One Party Dominance in Singapore", in John Hsieh and David Newman (eds.), *How Asia Votes*, New York and London: Chatham House, 2001, p. 240.

2 See Thomas Bellows, *The People's Action Party of Singapore: Emergence of a Dominant Party*, New Haven, CT: Yale University Southeast Asia Series, 1970. For a comparison, see T.J. Pempel, *Uncommon Democracies: The One Party Dominant Regimes*, Ithaca: Cornell University Press, 1990.

3 For types of electoral systems and their consequences, see Pippa Norris, "Choosing Electoral Systems: Proportional, Majoritarian, and Mixed Systems", *International Political Science Review*, vol. 18, no. 3 (July 1997), pp. 297–312; David Farrell, *Comparing Electoral Systems*, London: Prentice Hall, 1997; Douglas W. Rae, *The Political Consequences of Electoral Laws*, rev. ed., New Haven, CT: Yale University Press, 1971.

4 The Opposition objects that an amendment to the Parliamentary Elections Act in 1988 stipulates that by-elections in multiple-member constituencies (Group Representation Constituencies) are not necessary unless *all* the members of the team vacate their seats. The Opposition also objects to the fact that there is no provision for when by-elections must be held to fill vacancies, and hence they are often not called at all. See *Parliamentary Debates Singapore*, vol. 70, no. 15 (July 6, 1999), col. 1762 (Low Thai Khiang) and cols. 1763–4 (Chiam See Tong). Also see *Straits Times*, June 6 and 9, 1999.

5 *Parliamentary Debates Singapore*, vol. 69, no. 7 (October 12, 1998), col. 1019 (Wong Kan Seng). If one does not vote, there is a $5 fine before that person can vote again (*Straits Times Weekly Edition*, August 25, 2001).

6 See *Straits Times Weekly Edition*, February 17 and 24, 2001, May 12, 2001, October 6, 2001; *Straits Times Interactive*, March 26, 2001, on the Web: http://straitstimes.asia1.com.sg; *Singapore Magazine* (May–June 2001), p. 3.

7 *Singapore: Country Reports on Human Rights Practices – 2000*, Washington, DC: US Department of State, on the Web: http://www.state.gov/drl/rls/hrrpt/2000/eap/index.cfm?docid=770 (released February 2001). The Opposition complains, however, that just having numbers on the back of ballots intimidates voters (*Straits Times Weekly Edition*, January

25, 1997), as does the counting of votes at the precinct level (about 20 blocks and 5,000 voters) (*Straits Times Weekly Edition*, January 18 and 25, 1997).

8 Michael Haas, "Mass Society", in Michael Haas (ed.), *The Singapore Puzzle*, Westport, CT: Praeger, 1999, pp. 171, 174.

9 As popular opposition MP Low Thai Khiang notes, the PAP follows the rules where they exist, but the problem is that it keeps changing the rules (*Straits Times Weekly Edition*, September 18, 1999).

10 R.S. Milne and Diane K. Mauzy, *Singapore: The Legacy of Lee Kuan Yew*, Boulder: Westview, 1990, p. 96. Also see Christopher Tremewan, *The Political Economy of Social Control in Singapore*, London: Macmillan Press, 1994 (reprinted in 1996 with a new preface), p. 158; Kevin Y.L. Tan, "Is Singapore's Electoral System in Need of Reform?", *Commentary*, vol. 14 (1997), p. 109.

11 Irene Ng, "Have NMPs Earned their Parliamentary Spurs?" *Straits Times Weekly Edition*, August 14, 1999; *Parliamentary Debates Singapore*, vol. 67, no. 5 (June 5, 1997), cols. 415–38.

12 Interview with Dr. Lee Tsao Yuan, former director of the Institute of Policy Studies and former two-term NMP, on June 22, 2000. Also see G. Sivakkumaran and Sue-Ann Chia, "NMPs Willing to Serve Second Term in Parliament", *Straits Times Weekly Edition*, July 7, 2001.

13 See Garry Rodan, "State–Society Relations and Political Opposition in Singapore", in Garry Rodan (ed.), *Political Oppositions in Industrialising Asia*, London and New York: Routledge, 1996, p. 103.

14 Irene Ng, "Have NMPs Earned their Parliamentary Spurs?" *Straits Times Weekly Edition*, August 14, 1999. Also see *Straits Times Weekly Edition*, September 27, 1997; *Singapore Bulletin*, vol. 25, no. 9 (September 1997), p. 7.

15 Ben Dolven, "Balancing Act", *Far Eastern Economic Review*, July 15, 1998, p. 38.

16 *Parliamentary Debates Singapore*, vol. 67, no. 5 (June 5, 1997), col. 429–30 (J.B. Jeyaretnam); Lily Zubaidah Rahim, *The Singapore Dilemma: The Political and Educational Marginality of the Malay Community*, Kuala Lumpur: Oxford University Press, 1998, p. 36; James Gomez, "Proportionalising Political Representation in Singapore: Problems and Prospects", *Commentary*, vol. 14 (1997), p. 127.

17 *Parliamentary Debates Singapore*, vol. 67, no. 5 (June 5, 1997), col. 423 (Dr. Tan Cheng Bock).

18 Chua Lee Hoong, "Whither, Parliament", *Straits Times Weekly Edition*, September 18, 1999.

19 Matthew Gregory Towner, in a PhD thesis, has investigated the origins of the GRC concept. According to him, in 1982 there was a Cabinet paper advocating "twinning" a number of constituencies and requiring that one of the candidates for each party contesting in a twin constituency be a Malay. However, former minister S. Dhanabalan told Towner that the Cabinet rejected the paper and that the younger members felt it legitimized ethnic voting. In 1984, however, because of Lee's persuasiveness (Dhanabalan remained opposed), the modified GRC proposal was accepted. See Matthew Gregory Towner, "Political Leaders and Democratic Change: A Comparative Case Study of The Republic of China and Singapore", PhD Thesis, University of Denver, 1997, pp. 246–52.

20 Interestingly, despite all the evidence Towner presents concerning different Cabinet ideas for ensuring minority representation, he concludes that "... increasing demand for opposition, not ethnically-based voting, was the driving factor behind Lee's push for change". See Matthew Gregory Towner, "Political Leaders and Democratic Change: A Comparative Case Study of The Republic of China and Singapore", PhD Thesis, University of Denver, 1997, p. 247.

21 R.S. Milne and Diane K. Mauzy, *Singapore: The Legacy of Lee Kuan Yew*, Boulder: Westview, 1990, p. 71.

22 See Diane K. Mauzy, "Singapore's Dilemma: Coping with the Paradoxes of Success", *Southeast Asian Affairs 1997*, Singapore: Institute of Southeast Asian Studies, 1997, p. 266. The opposition-held constituencies were Potong Pasir, Hougang, Bukit Gombak, and Nee Soon Central. The boundaries for the last one were altered somewhat.

23 Christopher Tremewan, *The Political Economy of Social Control in Singapore*, London: Macmillan Press, 1994 (reprinted in 1996 with a new preface), p. 167. Tremewan rejects the idea that ensuring minority representation was the basic concern. He notes that all PAP minority candidates won regularly, and that the only two losses in 1984 were Chinese, one of whom was beaten by a minority candidate.

24 See Lily Zubaidah Rahim, *The Singapore Dilemma: The Political and Educational Marginality of the Malay Community*, Kuala Lumpur: Oxford University Press, 1998, pp. 77–80.

25 Diane K. Mauzy, "Electoral Innovation and One Party Dominance in Singapore", in John Hsieh and David Newman (eds.), *How Asia Votes*, London and New York: Chatham House, 2001; Matthew Gregory Towner, "Political Leaders and Democratic Change: A Comparative Case Study of The Republic of China and Singapore", PhD Thesis, University of Denver, 1997, pp. 266–77.

26 *Parliamentary Debates Singapore*, vol. 69, no. 12 (January 20, 1999), col. 1964.

27 There are numerous precedents for unequal votes – rural weightage in most states, formerly Great Britain's university graduates' vote, the US Senate and other un-proportional upper houses, etc. See *Straits Times Weekly Edition*, February 5 and 19, 2000.

28 Interview with Senior Minister Lee Kuan Yew, June 29, 2000.

29 For example, a 1996 survey of young Singaporeans showed that 77 percent wanted an opposition in Parliament while 89 percent thought the dominant PAP was delivering good government. (Cited in James V. Jesudason, "The Resilience of One-Party Dominance in Malaysia and Singapore", in Hermann Giliomee and Charles Simkins (eds.), *The Awkward Embrace: One Party-Domination and Democracy*, Cape Town: Tafelberg Publishers, Ltd., 1999, p. 155.)

30 Diane K. Mauzy, "Electoral Innovation and One Party Dominance in Singapore", in John Hsieh and David Newman (eds.), *How Asia Votes*, New York and London: Chatham House, 2001; R.S. Milne and Diane K. Mauzy, *Singapore: The Legacy of Lee Kuan Yew*, Boulder: Westview Press, 1990, p. 91.

31 Garry Rodan, "State–Society Relations and Political Opposition in Singapore", in Garry Rodan (ed.), *Political Oppositions in Industrialising Asia*, London and New York: Routledge, 1996, p. 119.

32 Andrea Hamilton, "Down and Possibly Out", *Asiaweek*, January 22, 1999, on the Web: http://www.pathfinder.com/asiaweek/99/0122/nat2.html.

33 Interview with Dr. Arun Mahizhnan, Deputy Director of the Institute of Policy Studies, June 16, 2000.

34 Interview with Prime Minister Goh Chok Tong, July 1, 2000. Prime Minister Goh believes that there are no real political costs to taking a hard-line approach or to coming down hard on opponents when necessary (when they detect a negative trend).

35 Hussin Mutalib, "Illiberal Democracy and the Future of Opposition in Singapore", *Third World Quarterly*, vol. 21, no. 2 (2000), p. 325.

36 Derek da Cunha, *The Price of Victory: The 1997 Singapore General Election and Beyond*, Singapore: Institute of Southeast Asian Studies, 1997, p. 65.

37 J.B. Jeyaretnam, *Make it Right for Singapore: Speeches in Parliament 1997–1999*, Singapore: Jeya Publishers, 2000, pp. 113–17.

38 *Straits Times Weekly Edition*, May 13, 2000 and February 17, 2001. This did not turn out to be a problem in the November 2001 general election.

39 *Straits Times Weekly Edition*, May 27, 2000.

40 Jeyaretnam was declared a bankrupt in January 2001 and lost his appeal and NCMP seat in July 2001. He quit the party in October and in November sued another WP official (the third one), for his role in the action that culminated in the defamation suit against Jeyaretnam that effectively ended his political career. See *Straits Times Weekly Edition*, July 28 and November 10, 2001; "A Worthy Legacy", *Asian Wall Street Journal* editorial, July 31, 2001.

41 Garry Rodan, "State–Society Relations and Political Opposition in Singapore", in Garry Rodan (ed.), *Political Oppositions in Industrialising Asia*, London and New York: Routledge, 1996, p. 116.

42 *Asiaweek*, February 7, 1997.

43 Seth Mydans, "Singapore Where Ruin is the Reward for Error", *New York Times*, December 12, 1996; *Southeast Asia Post*, 3, 11 (November 1996).

44 *Asiaweek*, February 7, 1997; Diane K. Mauzy, "Singapore's Dilemma: Coping with the Paradoxes of Success", *Southeast Asian Affairs 1997*, Singapore: Institute of Southeast Asian Studies, 1997, p. 264. The PAP gave him lots of public exposure in some special committee hearings on the cost of living and health care, where he lost credibility by error-filled performances.

45 See *Straits Times Weekly Edition*, January 11, 1997 and February 20, 1999.

46 James Gomez, *Self-Censorship: Singapore's Shame*, Singapore: Think Centre, 2000, p. 72; *Straits Times Weekly Edition*, May 29, 1999.

47 *Straits Times Weekly Edition*, May 26 and July 7, 2001.

48 See "Hougang – Eight Years Later", *Straits Times Weekly Edition*, November 6, 1999; Ben Dolven, "Treading Lightly", *Far Eastern Economic Review*, December 3, 1998, pp. 30–2.

49 For example, Chiam has complained about not being allowed to plant a tree for shade or hang a bulletin board on HDB property; Low had a two-year fight with a CCC over the installation of directional signs at car park entrances. However, in 2002 Potong Pasir was given an MRT station.

50 "Hougang – Eight Years Later", *Straits Times Weekly Edition*, November 6, 1999.

51 R.S. Milne and Diane K. Mauzy, *Singapore: The Legacy of Lee Kuan Yew*, Boulder: Westview Press, 1990, p. 65.

52 See Thomas Bellows, *The People's Action Party of Singapore: Emergence of a Dominant Party*, New Haven, CT: Yale University Southeast Asia Series, 1970; and Chan Heng Chee, *The Dynamics of One-Party Dominance: The PAP at the Grass-Roots*, Singapore: Singapore University Press, 1976.

53 Lee Kuan Yew writes that he was disturbed by Anson, not so much by the loss as by the PAP campaign and the fact that Goh had given him no signal that the PAP might lose. This made Lee concerned about Goh's political sensitivity. See Lee Kuan Yew, *From Third World to First, The Singapore Story: 1965–2000*, Singapore: Times Media Private Ltd., 2000, p. 146.

54 See James Cotton, "Political Innovation in Singapore: The Presidency, the Leadership and the Party", in Garry Rodan (ed.) *Singapore Changes Guard*, Melbourne: Longman Cheshire, 1993, p. 5; Bilveer Singh, *Whither PAP's Dominance: An Analysis of Singapore's 1991 General Election*, Petaling Jaya: Pelanduk, 1992, p. 15.

55 Lim Joo-Jock, "Singapore in 1985: Signs of Change in Leadership Style and the Emerging New Problems", *Southeast Asian Affairs 1986*, Singapore: Institute of Southeast Asian Studies, 1986, p. 268.

56 Chan Heng Chee, "The PAP and the Nineties: The Politics of Anticipation", in Karl D. Jackson *et al.* (eds.), *ASEAN in Regional and Global Context*, Berkeley: Institute of East Asian Studies, 1986, p. 170.

57 Lee Kuan Yew, *From Third World to First, The Singapore Story: 1965–2000*, Singapore: Times Media Private Ltd., 2000, p. 158. The policy also divided the Cabinet (pp. 163–4).

58 T.S. Selvan, *Singapore: The Ultimate Island*, Clifton Hills, Victoria: Freeway Books, 1990, p. 80.

59 *Straits Times*, September 19, 1984, cited in Beng-Huat Chua, *Communitarian Ideology and Democracy in Singapore*, London and New York: Routledge, 1995, p. 74.

60 Raj Vasil, *Asianising Singapore: The PAP's Management of Ethnicity*, Singapore: Heinemann Asia, 1995, p. 93; Chua Beng Huat, "State and Society: Ambling Towards Greater Balance", in Arun Mahizhnan and Lee Tsao Yuan (eds.), *Singapore: Re-Engineering Success*, Singapore: Institute of Policy Studies and Oxford University Press, 1998, p. 74.

61 R.S. Milne and Diane K. Mauzy, *Singapore: The Legacy of Lee Kuan Yew*, Boulder: Westview Press, 1990, p. 74.

62 Bilveer Singh, *Whither PAP's Dominance: An Analysis of Singapore's 1991 General Election*, Petaling Jaya: Pelanduk, 1992; Hussin Mutalib, "Domestic Politics", in Lee Tsao Yuan (ed.), *IPS Year in Review*, Singapore: Institute of Policy Studies and Times Academic Press, 1992, pp. 69–105.

63 Garry Rodan, "The Growth of Singapore's Middle Class and its Political Significance", in Garry Rodan (ed.), *Singapore Changes Guard*, Melbourne: Longman Cheshire, 1993, p. 59; Garry Rodan, "Singapore's Leadership Transition: Erosion or Refinement of Authoritarian Rule?", *Bulletin of Concerned Asian Scholars*, vol. 24, no. 1 (1992), pp. 15–16; David M. Jones and David Brown, "Singapore and the Myth of the Liberalizing Middle Class", *The Pacific Review*, vol. 7, no. 1 (August 1994), p. 81; Raj Vasil, *Asianising Singapore: The PAP's Management of Ethnicity*, Singapore: Heinemann Asia, 1995, pp. 123–9.

64 Ong Teng Cheong, "My Views on the Outcome of the General Election", *Speeches*, vol. 15, no. 5 (1991), pp. 34–8. Soon after Lee Kuan Yew supported this explanation. (See Raj Vasil, *Asianising Singapore: The PAP's Management of Ethnicity*, Singapore: Heinemann Asia, 1995, p. 123. Interestingly, a PAP minister told Vasil in 1993 that Lee "had obviously over-reacted in highlighting the so-called problems faced by the Chinese-speaking" (p. 125).) The grievances of the Chinese-educated never surfaced as an election issue, in the English press at least, during the campaign (see Eddie C.Y. Kuo *et al.*, *Mirror on the Wall: Media in a Singapore Election*, Singapore: Asian Mass Communication Research and Information Centre, 1993, p. 13). David Brown writes that the PAP received almost the same electoral support in 1991 as it did in 1988,

but chose to "interpret it as an expression of discontent by the poorer and older Chinese community about the way their culture had been neglected in favor of the English-speaking Chinese" ("The Corporate Management of Ethnicity in Contemporary Singapore", in Garry Rodan (ed.), *Singapore Changes Guard*, Melbourne: Longman Cheshire, 1993, p. 28).

65 Diane K. Mauzy, "Singapore's Dilemma: Coping with the Paradoxes of Success", *Southeast Asian Affairs 1997*, Singapore: Institute of Southeast Asian Studies, 1997, pp. 265–9. The upgrading is a long-term project which actually started in 1989. Under a plan spelled out in May 1996 called "A Share for All", redistribution also includes CPF top-ups for retirees, more education bursaries for the poor, and the direct transfer at a discount of HDB shops and stalls to the tenants. Moves were also made to ensure no middle-class backlash: discounted shares of SingTel, executive condominiums, and more roads, etc.

66 Diane K. Mauzy, "Singapore's Dilemma: Coping with the Paradoxes of Success", *Southeast Asian Affairs 1997*, Singapore: Institute of Southeast Asian Studies, 1997, p. 265.

67 During the campaign, Tang apparently said little that could be regarded as anti-Christian or Chinese chauvinist. However, in earlier speeches he had complained about the dominance of the English-educated and Christians in Singapore and wondered, provocatively, why those in the majority should be carrying the "sedan chair" instead of sitting on it. Lee Kuan Yew told the press that on December 27, Goh and his ministers discussed whether or not to move against Tang (see *Straits Times Weekly Edition*, January 11, 1997; Murray Hiebert, "Throwing the Book", *Far Eastern Economic Review*, March 6, 1997, p. 31).

68 *Far Eastern Economic Review*, January 16, 1997, p. 17.

69 See *Straits Times Weekly Edition*, January 11, 25 and February 1, 1997; Han Fook Kwang, "The Year of Tests and Tribulations", in *Singapore: The Year in Review 1997*, Singapore: Institute of Policy Studies, 1997, pp. 41–8; Koh Buck Song, "Commentary", in *Singapore: The Year in Review 1996*, Singapore: Institute of Policy Studies, 1996, pp. 49–60.

70 *Straits Times Interactive*, October 19, 2001, on the Web: http://straitstimes.asia1.com.sg. Opposition leader Chiam See Tong noted that while the PAP was usually reluctant to hold an election during an economic downturn, this time it had no choice (*Straits Times Weekly Edition*, September 29, 2001).

71 "Foreign Talents Become an Election Issue in Singapore", *Agence France Presse*, October 23, 2001, on the Web: sg_daily@yahoogroups.com.

72 See "A People United", *PAP Election Manifesto*, October 18, 2001, on the Web: http://www.pap.org.sg.

73 The PAP had intended allowing overseas voting for this election, but the election was called before the legislation was finalized.

74 The opposition parties were the Workers' Party, now under the leadership of Low Thia Khiang; the SDP, led by Chee Soon Juan; the Democratic Progressive Party (a father and son team); and the SDA, under the chairmanship of Chiam See Tong.

75 *Straits Times Interactive*, October 21, 2001, on the Web: http://straitstimes.asia1.com.sg.

76 *Straits Times Weekly Edition*, August 18, 2001.

77 The exception was Dr. Chee's haranguing of the Prime Minister, who was on a walkabout in Jurong GRC, by asking repeatedly "where is the money?", in reference to Chee's allegation that the government had lent S$17 billion to Indonesian President Suharto just before his downfall. In fact, it was widely known that the loan had conditions attached and had not, in fact, been taken up by Indonesia. Threatened with a defamation lawsuit, Chee issued a formal apology at an SDP rally and in the *Straits Times*. However, lawsuits were filed anyway. See "Singapore Government Fires Election Guns at SDP's Chee", *Agence France Presse*, October 29, 2001, on the Web: sg_daily@yahoogroups,com; Susan Long, "PM Goh Waves Aside 'Tailgating' SDP Team", *Straits Times Weekly Edition*, November 3, 2001; "SM Lee, PM Goh Sue Chee Soon Juan", *Yahoo! News*, November 21, 2001, on the Web: sg.news.yahoo.com/ nov 21/01. Chee and his GRC team in Jurong received only 20 percent of the vote in that constituency.

78 While the economic concerns dominated this election, local issues are important too, and in the past have cost the PAP some seats. In this election, confusion over procedure for the application of a permit for the Hungry Ghosts Festival alienated temple operators and dialect groups in Nee Soon East and threatened the candidacy of the PAP first-timer. However, Lee Kuan Yew came to the constituency, fixed the problem and soothed frayed emotions, and the PAP won. Other than the Hungry Ghosts Festival issue, there were no important Chinese community issues in this election. Economic concerns dominated. See Leong Weng Kam, "Why Was the Chinese Ground 'Silent' this Election?", *Straits Times Weekly Edition*, December 8, 2001.

79 Chiam, already the longest serving opposition MP (17 years), survived by 751 votes. See "Nail-Biting Finish for Chiam in Potong Pasir", and "A Gentleman and a Survivor", *Straits Times Interactive*, November 4, 2001, on the Web: http://straitstimes.asia1.com.sg. Low, who was considered virtually unassailable, won again with 55 percent of the vote (down 3 percent). See "Workers' Party Retains Hougang Seat", *Straits Times Interactive*, November 4, 2001, on the Web: http://straitstimes.asia1.com.sg.

80 See Amy Tan, "Reluctant Prime Minister Goh Wins Hearts", *Reuters*, November 3, 2001, on the Web: sg.news.yahoo.com/reuters/asia-70079.html; Chua Lee Hoong, "The Making of a Resounding Victory", November 4, 2001, *Straits Times Interactive*, on the Web: http://straitstimes.asia1.com.sg.

81 Trish Saywell, "Token Contest", *Far Eastern Economic Review*, November 15, 2001, p. 20.

82 It was discussed in Cabinet as early as 1982, and the first public mention of an elected President came in 1984. The idea disappeared from public view until it re-emerged in 1988 in the form of a government White Paper ("Constitutional Amendments to Safeguard Financial Assets and the Integrity of the Public Service", July 29, 1988). It was debated in Parliament (*Straits Times*, August 13, 1988) and soon became an election issue. Many believed initially that the position was being tailored for Lee Kuan Yew, who was about to step down as Prime Minister, despite his adamant denials. In 1999 a PAP backbencher noted in Parliament, unsurprisingly, that the "idea came from the mind of Lee Kuan Yew" (*Parliamentary Debates Singapore*, vol. 70, no. 19, August 18, 1999, col. 2210 (Shriniwas Rai)).

83 Lam Peng Er, "The Elected Presidency: Towards the Twenty-first Century", in Kevin Y.L. Tan and Lam Peng Er (eds.), *Managing Political Change in Singapore*, London and New York: Routledge, 1997, p. 206; James Cotton, "Political Innovation in Singapore: The Presidency, the Leadership, and the Party", in Garry Rodan (ed.), *Singapore Changes Guard*, Melbourne: Longman Cheshire, 1998, pp. 3–15.

84 J.B. Jeyaretnam and another applicant from the WP (Tan Soo Phuan) were rejected by the PEC.

85 Bilveer Singh, "Singapore: Change Amidst Continuity", *Southeast Asian Affairs 1994*, Singapore: Institute of Southeast Asian Studies, 1994, p. 276; Hussin Mutalib, "Singapore's First Elected Presidency: The Political Motivations", and Chia Shi Teck, "Notes from the Margin", in Kevin Y.L. Tan and Lam Peng Er (eds.), *Managing Political Change in Singapore*, London and New York: Routledge, 1997, pp. 167–93; *Straits Times Weekly Edition*, July 31, 1999.

86 Later Ong confessed that his colleagues were quite worried during the campaign by the swing away from him by the educated class. Interview by Roger Mitton, "I Had a Job to Do", *Asiaweek*, March 10, 2000.

87 Lee Kuan Yew said of Ong that he had the key and "he wanted to turn it" (interview, June 29, 2000). Ong was known to be independent-minded and sometimes difficult. For example, in 1986, he sanctioned a strike in the shipping industry without informing Cabinet (Roger Mitton, "Maverick Politician", *Asiaweek*, March 10, 2000). Around the same time he also resisted government pressure to impose a stiff wage restraint on the workers during a recession (Huang Jianli, "The Head of State in Singapore", in Kevin Y.L. Tan and Lam Peng Er (eds.), *Managing Political Change in Singapore*, London and New York: Routledge, 1997, p. 41). And in 1991, Ong and Goh Chok Tong openly disagreed in their respective analyses of the 1991 election. At a PAP convention afterwards, members were apparently puzzled by the exchanges between Ong and Goh (Hussin Mutalib, "Illiberal Democracy and the Future of Opposition in Singapore", *Third World Quarterly*, vol. 21, no. 2 (2000), pp. 330, 340).

88 See Thio Li-ann, "The Elected President and the Legal Control of Government", in Kevin Y.L. Tan and Lam Peng Er (eds.), *Managing Political Change in Singapore*, London and New York: Routledge, 1997, pp. 114, 125; *Business Times*, August 13, 1999.

89 Roger Mitton, "I Had a Job to Do", *Asiaweek*, March 10, 2000.

90 Chua Lee Hoong, "The Presidency: Striking a Tricky Balance", *Straits Times*, August 7, 1999; *White Paper (Paper Cmd. 5 of 1999),* "The Principles for Determining and Safeguarding the Accumulated Reserves of the Government and the Fifth Schedule Statutory Boards and Government Companies", presented to Parliament, July 2, 1999. On the motion to endorse the White Paper, see *Parliamentary Debates Singapore*, vol. 70, no. 19 (August 18 1999).

91 Interview with Senior Minister Lee Kuan Yew, June 29, 2000. Ong insisted he was in good health, however Cabinet was briefed by his specialist who was less optimistic. Ong died in February 2002. "Ong Went Most Unwillingly", *Asiaweek*, December 10, 1999, on the Web: http://cnn.com/ASIANOW/asiaweek/intelligence; *Straits Times Weekly Edition*, February 9, 2002.

92 Andrea Hamilton, "The President Speaks Out: Ong Teng Cheong Criticizes his Government", *Asiaweek*, July 30, 1999, on the Web: http://pathfinder.com/asiaweek/current/issie/nat7.html.

93 Ong Interview with Roger Mitton, "I Had a Job to Do", *Asiaweek*, March 10, 2000. Still angry in 2000, he noted that he left the announcement about whether he would run again until the last minute, apparently to worry the PAP.

94 *Parliamentary Debates Singapore*, vol. 70, no. 18 (August 17, 1999), cols. 2018–31 (Richard Hu); cols. 2032–41 (Goh Chok Tong).

95 *Parliamentary Debates Singapore*, vol. 70, no. 19 (August 18 1999), col. 2225. Low's comments prompted Lee Kuan Yew to say that Goh Chok Tong was not a lawyer by training and therefore he used words in a non-legal way. "If I had delivered that speech (moving the Second Reading of the Bill in 1990), I would not have used those words ... 'clipping one's wings' " (col. 2067).

96 *Parliamentary Debates Singapore*, vol. 70, no. 18 (August 17, 1999), cols. 2032–4 (Goh Chok Tong). Some of the alterations to the system include, an amendment allowing the government to override the President's veto by a 2/3rds majority; enlarging the Council of Presidential Advisors (CPA) from 5 to 6 members, with the additional member nominated by the Chief Justice; removing the supervision of the President over the Monetary Authority of Singapore; and removing the need for the President's consent for defense expenditure.

97 For the six member CPA, the President and the Prime Minister each appoint two members, the Chief Justice and Chair of the Public Service Commission appoint one each. Long-time PAP stalwart and friend of Lee Kuan Yew, Lim Kim San was appointed chair in 1992 and reappointed in 1999. The numbers on the powerful CPA clearly favor the government.

98 Zuraidah Ibrahim, "EP's Role Largely Ceremonial", *Straits Times Interactive*, August 11, 1999, on the Web: http://straitstimes.asia1.com.sg/one1.html; Zuraidah Ibrahim and Irene Ng, "No Such Thing as 'Independent' EP", *Straits Times Weekly Edition*, August 14, 1999.

99 *Prime Minister's National Day Rally Speech 1999*, Singapore: Ministry of Information and the Arts, 1999, pp. 57–8; Irene Ng, "Nathan is Cabinet's Choice", *Straits Times Weekly Edition*, August 14, 1999.

100 The other individuals who wanted to contest were not endorsed by the Cabinet and did not meet the candidacy requirements.

101 Michael Leifer, *Singapore's Foreign Policy: Coping with Vulnerability*, London: Routledge, 2000, p. 2. Presumably, the PAP government could have found additional qualified candidates, like it did in 1993, but chose not to do so.

102 Ooi Giok Ling, Tan Ern Ser, Gillian Koh, "Survey of State–Society Relations: Social Indicators Research Project, Executive Summary Report", *IPS Working Papers No. 5*, Singapore: Institute of Policy Studies, October 1998.

103 See, for example, Terry Karl, "Imposing Consent? Electoralism versus Democratization in El Salvador", in Paul Drake and Eduardo Silva (eds.), *Elections and Democratization in Latin America, 1980–1985*, San Diego: University of California Press, 1986, p. 24.

104 See his classic article, "The Spectator Political Culture: A Refinement of the Almond and Verba Model", *Journal of Commonwealth Political Studies*, vol. ix, no. 1 (March 1971), pp. 19–35.

105 See Samuel P. Huntington and Joan M. Nelson, *No Easy Choice*, Cambridge, MA: Harvard University Press, 1976, p. 167. The authors also mention the "free rider" option and participation as a last resort (p. 165).

106 Tan Ern Ser and Chiew Seen Kong, "Citizen Orientation Towards Political Participation in Singapore", in Ong Jin Hui *et al.* (eds.), *Understanding Singapore Society*, Singapore: Times Academic Press, 1997, pp. 328–45. Note: the survey was carried out in 1989.

107 Tan Ern Ser and Chiew Seen Kong, "Citizen Orientation Towards Political Participation in Singapore", in Ong Jin Hui *et al.* (eds.), *Understanding Singapore Society*, Singapore: Times Academic Press, 1997, pp. 340–1. The survey showed that of those surveyed , the MPs Meet the People sessions were the most widely recognized channels and they were perceived as being the most effective.

108 Goh Chok Tong, "Strengthening the Singapore Heartbeat", *Speeches*, vol. 23, no. 5 (1999), pp. 7–17. *Straits Times Weekly Edition*, June 27, 1998. Also see *Straits Times Weekly Edition*, February 22 and April 12, 1997.

109 Goh Chok Tong, "Strengthening the Singapore Heartbeat", *Speeches*, vol. 23, no. 5 (1999), pp. 7–17.

110 *Parliamentary Debates Singapore*, vol. 71, no. 2 (October 11, 1999), col. 90.

12 The growth of civil society

1 See the following: Ernest Gellner, *Conditions of Liberty: Civil Society and Its Rival*, London: Hamish Hamilton, 1994; John Keane, *Civil Society: Old Images, New Visions*, London: Polity Press, 1998; John Hall *et al.*, *Civil Society: Theory, History, Comparison*, London: Polity Press, 1995; Robert D. Putnam, *Making Democracy Work: Civic Traditions in Modern Italy*, Princeton: Princeton University Press, 1993; Robert D. Putnam, "Bowling Alone: America's Declining Social Capital", *Journal of Democracy*, vol. 6, no. 1 (January 1995), pp. 65–78; and Michael W. Foley and Bob Edwards, "The Paradox of Civil Society", *Journal of Democracy*, vol. 7, no. 3 (July 1996), pp. 38–52.

2 See Garry Rodan, "Theorising Political Opposition in East and Southeast Asia", in Garry Rodan (ed.), *Political Oppositions in Industrialising Asia*, London and New York: Routledge, 1996, p. 4; Philip Resnick, *Twenty-First Century Democracy*, Montréal: McGill-Queens University Press, 1997.

3 See Robert D. Putnam, *Making Democracy Work: Civic Traditions in Modern Italy*, Princeton: Princeton University Press, 1993; and Robert D. Putnam, "Bowling Alone: America's Declining Social Capital", *Journal of Democracy*, vol. 6, no. 1 (January 1995), pp. 65–78.

4 Garry Rodan, "Theorising Political Opposition in East and Southeast Asia", in Garry Rodan (ed.), *Political Oppositions in Industrialising Asia*, London and New York: Routledge, 1996, p. 21.

5 Garry Rodan, "Civil Society and Other Political Possibilities in Southeast Asia", *Journal of Contemporary Asia*, vol. 27, no. 2 (1997), p. 162.

6 "Civil Society in Singapore", interview with B.G. George Yeo, *Karyawan* (January–April 1999), pp. 12–20.

7 Sheila Nair, "Political Society", *Commentary*, vol. 11, no. 1 (1993), pp. 15–16. Nair's thesis is that the "civic society project" has arisen from the government's realization that the state "has over-extended itself in the management of society" and must retreat to protect its authority (p. 16). Also see "Making Space for Civil Society", editorial in *Karyawan* (January–April 1999), p. 3.

8 Garry Rodan, "Theorising Political Opposition in East and Southeast Asia", in Garry Rodan (ed.), *Political Oppositions in Industrialising Asia*, London and New York: Routledge, 1996, p. 22.

9 See Garry Rodan, "Theorising Political Opposition in East and Southeast Asia", in Garry Rodan (ed.), *Political Oppositions in Industrialising Asia*, London and New York: Routledge, 1996, p. 22; "The Uncivil Society", editorial in *The National Post*, December 13, 1999; Mancur Olson, *The Rise and Decline of Nations: Growth, Stagflation, and Social Rigidities*, New Haven, CT: Yale University Press, 1982; Michael W. Foley and Bob Edwards, "The Paradox of Civil Society", *Journal of Democracy*, vol. 7, no. 3 (July 1996), pp. 38–52.

10 "Making Space for Civil Society", editorial in *Karyawan* (January–April 1999), p. 3.

11 Pang Cheng Lian and Frances Low, "Chinese Civic Traditions in Singapore", paper prepared for the IPS [Institute of Policy Studies] Conference on Civil Society: Harnessing State–Society Synergies, in Singapore, May 6–7, 1998, p. 6.

12 Pang Cheng Lian and Frances Low, "Chinese Civic Traditions in Singapore", paper prepared for the IPS Conference on Civil Society: Harnessing State–Society Synergies, in Singapore, May 6–7, 1998, p. 7.

13 See Lee Huay Leng, " 'Boundaries and Spaces' – The State and Citizen – Commentary", paper prepared for the IPS Conference on Civil Society: Harnessing State–Society Synergies, in Singapore, May 6–7, 1998, and Chua Beng Huat, "The Changing Shape of Civil Society in Singapore", *Commentary*, vol. 11, no. 1 (1993), pp. 9–14.

14 John Clammer makes the point that these groups, except for the clan associations, were all elite organizations rather than mass based ones, and therefore, presumably, less threatening. See John Clammer, *Race and State in Independent Singapore, 1965–1990*, Aldershot: Ashgate, 1998, pp. 131–2.

15 Garry Rodan, "State–Society Relations and Political Opposition in Singapore", in Garry Rodan (ed.), *Political Oppositions in Industrialising Asia*, London and New York: Routledge, 1996, pp. 106–9.

16 These include the Kranji heronry, Marina Ponds, and, in 1994, Senoko. In the last case, the Friends of Senoko collected 25,000 signatures, with their ID numbers, which were presented to the Prime Minister, to appeal against the development of 70-hectares in Senoko because its bio-

diversity supported bird life. However, the appeal was not successful. See Garry Rodan, "State–Society Relations and Political Opposition in Singapore", in Garry Rodan (ed.), *Political Oppositions in Industrialising Asia*, London and New York: Routledge, 1996, pp. 106–9.

17 See Kirtida Mekani and Heike G. Stengel, "The Role of NGOs and Near NGOs", in Ooi Gioh Ling (ed.), *Environment and the City*, Singapore: IPS and Times Academic Press, 1995, pp. 289–90.

18 AWARE Press Statement (November 25, 2000) sent by email <aware@pacific.net.sg/>, forwarded by <sgdaily@list.sintercom.org>. AWARE's former president, Dr. Kanwaljit Soin, while serving as a Nominated Member of Parliament, introduced a private member's bill in 1995 on domestic violence. It was given a full and somewhat sympathetic hearing, but was not passed. See Simon S.C. Tay, "Towards a Singaporean Civil Society", *Southeast Asian Affairs 1998*, Singapore: Institute of Southeast Asian Studies, 1998, p. 248. Also see *Straits Times*, October 27 and November 2, 1995.

19 The play explored marital violence and rape in the Indian Muslim community. The Islamic Religious Council (MUIS) objected to the play and it was banned. See Tan Tarn How, "Cut Out the Carnage and Leave the Art Intact", *Straits Times Weekly Edition*, March 24, 2001.

20 Joseph B. Tamney, *The Struggle Over Singapore's Soul*, Berlin and New York: Walter de Gruyter, 1995, p. 143.

21 The Charter did not, however, apply to Muslim women. See Phyllis Ghim Lian Chew, *The Singapore Council of Women and the Women's Movement*, Singapore: AWARE, reprinted in 1999, p. 1; Constance Singam, "Civic Traditions in Singapore", paper for the IPS Conference on Civil Society: Harnessing State–Society Synergies, in Singapore on May 6–8, 1998.

22 *The Economist*, "Future Trends on the Loose in Singapore", May 29, 1999, on the Web: http://www.economist.com/archive/view.cgi.

23 Interview with B.G. George Yeo, Minister for International Trade and Industry, July 3, 2000. B.G. Yeo noted that it was not clear that it was feasible anyway, saying that "you can't just keep plugging holes" because one is dealing with a moving target and there are too many holes.

24 *Parliamentary Debates Singapore*, vol. 70, no. 14 (May 6, 1999), col. 1554.

25 *Straits Times*, January 16, 1988.

26 B.G. George Yong-Boon Yeo, "Civic Society – Between the Family and the State", *Speeches*, vol. 15, no. 3 (1991), pp. 78–86, especially p. 84. Interestingly, he says that this speech was not intended "as a green light" but offered only as a personal opinion (interview, July 3, 2000).

27 Simon S.C. Tay, "Towards a Singaporean Civil Society", *Southeast Asian Affairs 1998*, Singapore: Institute of Southeast Asian Studies, 1998, p. 251. Also see Simon Tay, "Civil Society: Is PM's Call Second Step Forward?", *Straits Times Weekly Edition*, June 14, 1997, April 1, 2000.

28 The conference proceedings are available in a book: Gillian Koh and Ooi Giok Ling (eds.), *State–Society Relations in Singapore*, Singapore: IPS and Oxford University Press, 2000. Also see Andrea Hamilton, "Let's Talk About Openness", *Asiaweek*, June 26, 1998, on the Web: http://www.pathfinder.com/asiaweek/98/0626/nat_5_sing.html.

29 See Goh Chok Tong, "Strengthening the Singapore Heartbeat", *Speeches*, vol. 23, no. 5 (1999), pp. 7–17.

30 Terry McCarthy with Eric Elles, "Singapore Lightens Up", *Time*, July 19, 1999, pp. 17–22. Also see Jacintha Stephens, "Lion City's Stage of Change", *Asiaweek*, July 14, 2000 on the Web: http://www.cnn.com/ASIANOW/asiaweek/magazine/2000/0714/as.theatre.html.

31 J.M. Nathan, "The Culture Industry and the Future of the Arts in Singapore", *Southeast Asian Affairs 1999*, Singapore: Institute of Southeast Asian Studies, 1999, p. 303.

32 "Little Bit on the Screen", *The Economist*, April 29, 2000 on the Web: http://www.economist.com/archive/view.cgi.

33 Andrea Hamilton, "Let's Talk About Openness", *Asiaweek*, June 26, 1998, on the Web: http://www.pathfinder.com/asiaweek/98/0626/nat_5_sing.html.

34 B.G. George Yeo says it is in Chinese and Malay cultures to work behind front organizations, pulling strings on a hidden agenda while out of sight (interview, July 3, 2000).

35 Simon S.C. Tay, "Towards a Singaporean Civil Society", *Southeast Asian Affairs 1998*, Singapore: Institute of Southeast Asian Studies, 1998, p. 255.

36 See *Karyawan*, January–April 1999, p. 21 for a résumé of its advocacy role.

37 The Socratic Circle was formed around the same time, by a group of young business professionals. In 1995 it held some lively Internet political discussion sessions. However, it was informed by the Registrar of Societies that this was illegal since it involved non-members, and

that its activities were restricted to recruitment and dissemination of club news on its website. Now it links up mostly with Think Centre activities. It has a home page: http://www.socraticcircle.org.sg/. See Garry Rodan, "Information Technology and Political Control in Singapore", *Working Paper No. 26*, Japan Policy Research Institute (November 1996), p. 5.

38 Interview with Raymond Lim, former Director-Group Chief Economist, ABN-AMRO Asia Securities, and former Vice-President and first President pro-tem of The Roundtable, June 27, 2000. Lim subsequently became Managing Director of Temasek Holdings, and in November 2001 became a PAP MP and Minister of State. Also see: http://www.roundtable.org.sg/html/committee.htm.

39 This is more a matter of "rights" and "principle" than an actual problem, since few are rejected. In 1999 (up to December), for example, the Registrar of Societies had approved 187 applications and rejected 3 for the year. Some 72 percent were approved within 3 months, while 4 percent took longer than 4 months. See *Parliamentary Debates Singapore*, vol. 71, no. 7 (January 17, 2000), col. 800. Two members of the Roundtable were later summoned to help a police investigation into the seminar, since the event was publicized on the Think Centre website, which legally made the seminar subject to licensing.

40 "Singaporeans are Living Up to Electronic Lifestyle: Survey", August 29, 2001, on the Web: http://news.catcha.com/sg. Also see Jacintha Stephens, "Testing Political Limits", *Asiaweek* (November 3, 2000), forwarded by thinkcentre@hotmail.com.

41 The most popular website is the occasionally political satirical, TalkingCock.com.

42 Tan Chong Kee, the Sintercom webmaster, said he was too tired to go on, and also that the new rules, which put responsibility for content on the shoulders of the webmaster, made it difficult to continue. See Amy Tan, "Singapore Web Sites Feel Heat of New Rules", on the Web: http://sg.news.yahoo.com/o1082/3/icn3q.html.

43 See <sg_daily@yahoogroups.com>.

44 See the release by ARTICLE 19, Global Campaign for Free Expression, April 19, 2001, on the Web: Freedom.of.Expresson/Interest@article19.org; "Singapore: No Laughing Matter", *Economist*, May 24, 2001, on the Web: http://www.economist.com. The earlier decision to register as an Internet company was taken because it apparently takes only hours or at most a few days, whereas it may take months of scrutiny to win registration approval as a society (Interview with Dr. Gillian Koh, Research Fellow, IPS, June 22, 2000).

45 Interview with James Gomez, founder and former Senior Director of Think Centre, on June 17, 2000. Gomez joined the Workers' Party in 2001 and was designated as one of the WP's candidates for a GRC. However, the team's nomination papers were rejected on a technicality.

46 See "All Permits Approved for Save JBJ Rally!", April 25, 2001, on the Web: TCsingapore@yahoogroups.com; *Straits Times Weekly Edition*, May 12, 2001.

47 The book is titled, *Self-Censorship: Singapore's Shame*, Singapore: Think Centre, 2000. Gomez was named in *Asiaweek*'s list of "Asia's 50 Most Powerful Communicators" in May 2001.

48 Gomez and three others were warned for holding a forum on "Youth and Politics" in October 1999 without a permit. The Attorney-General's Office decided not to prosecute the case. See Think Centre News Release, February 2, 2000, posted by sgdaily@list.sintercom.org. He was also warned in February and March 2001 for holding a demonstration at the Speaker's Corner in December 2000 (see note 49), and for his participation in a Roundtable seminar held in November 2000.

49 Interview with James Gomez, founder and former head of Think Centre, on June 17, 2000. For an article critical of the Think Centre approach, see Tan Tarn How, "Tolerating Mavericks, as Long as They're S'porean", *Staits Times Weekly Edition*, May 5, 2001. For Think Centre's reply to the article, see "No Foreign Funds for Think Centre", *Straits Times Weekly Edition*, May 12, 2001.

50 Interview with Dr. Gillian Koh, Research Fellow, IPS, June 22, 2000. Dr. Koh thought the TWC was a "terrific initiative". Also see the letter to the Forum, signed by Constance Singam (of AWARE) and 16 others, about the TWC (*Straits Times Weekly Edition,* October 2, 1999).

51 Terry McCarthy with Eric Elles, "Singapore Lightens Up", *Time*, July 19, 1999, p. 21; Zuraidah Ibrahim, "Give Civil Society a Chance to Grow", *Straits Times Weekly Edition*, May 22, 1999. For the conference, see the *Straits Times Weekly Edition*, October 28, 1999; Constance Singam, "Singapore Civil Society in Perspective", paper prepared for the keynote address for the TWC Civil Society Conference, in Singapore on October 30–31, 1999.

52 Lydia Lim, "Speaker's Corner . . .", *Straits Times*, April 25, 2000; Ben Dolven, "Soapbox", *Far Eastern Economic Review*, April 6, 2000, p. 30. Lee Kuan Yew apparently mentioned the idea to

the Prime Minister after it was suggested to him by Harvard Professor Joseph Nye. It was prompted by opposition politician Dr. Chee Soon Juan's insistence on speaking without a permit at a busy thoroughfare in downtown Raffles Place. See *Straits Times Weekly Edition*, March 25, 2000.

53 S. Jayasankaran, "Postcard", *Far Eastern Economic Review*, November 9, 2000, p. 75.

54 *Straits Times Weekly Edition*, February 17, 2001. Also see "Police Begin Human Rights Day Investigations", *Human Rights Watch*, January 30, 2001, and "James Gomez summoned by the Police", *Human Rights Watch*, February 6, 2001, both forwarded by the Think Centre at TCsingapore@yahoogroups.com.

55 See *Singapore 21: Together We Make the Difference*, on the Web at: http://www.gov.sg/Singapore21/keyideas5.html. The other key ideas in the report, all with catchy titles, are "Every Singaporean Matters", "Strong Families", "Opportunities for All", and "The Singapore Heartbeat".

56 *Parliamentary Debates Singapore*, vol. 70, no. 14 (May 6, 1999), col. 1584.

57 *Parliamentary Debates Singapore*, vol. 70, no. 13 (May 5, 1999), cols. 1598–9.

58 For example, see Dr. Lee Tsao Yuan (NMP) in *Parliamentary Debates Singapore*, vol. 70, no. 13 (May 5, 1999), cols. 1514–15; Clare Chiang (NMP), R. Ravindran (PAP), Simon Tay (NMP), Dr. Tan Cheng Bock (PAP) in *Parliamentary Debates Singapore*, vol. 70, no. 14 (May 6, 1999), cols. 1584–5, 1609, 1626–7, 1643–4, respectively.

59 *Parliamentary Debates Singapore*, vol. 70, no. 14 (May 6, 1999), col. 1655.

60 Zuraidah Ibrahim, "Singapore 'Not a Nation Yet'", *Straits Times Weekly Edition*, May 8, 1999.

61 This was announced in Parliament by RAdm. Teo Chee Hean. See *Parliamentary Debates Singapore*, vol. 70, no. 14 (May 6, 1999), col. 1660. Also see *Straits Times Weekly Edition*, March 18, 2000.

62 *Singapore Government Press Release*, Speech at a Singapore 21 forum by B.G. Lee Hsien Loong on January 16, 2000.

63 *Straits Times Weekly Edition*, April 24, 1999 (Pang Kin Keong). Also see Andy Ho, "Revisiting the Banyan Tree: Civil Society 10 Years On", *Straits Times Weekly Edition*, July 7, 2001; Tan Tarn How, "The Good, the Bad, and the Greater Good", *Straits Times Weekly Edition*, July 14, 2001.

64 *Straits Times Weekly Edition*, October 9, 1999.

65 *Straits Times Weekly Edition*, April 1, 2000.

66 *Straits Times Weekly Edition*, January 17, 2000.

67 *Straits Times Weekly Edition*, February 1, 1997. This was Minister Without Portfolio and head of the NTUC, Lim Boon Heng. There are now more than 200 VWOs in Singapore (*Straits Times Weekly Edition*, January 27, 2001).

68 Interview with Prime Minister Goh Chok Tong, July 1, 2000.

69 Pierre P. Lizee, "Civil Society and Regional Security: Tensions and Potentials in Post-Crisis Southeast Asia", *Contemporary Southeast Asia*, vol. 22, no. 3 (December 2000), p. 556.

70 Interview with Prime Minister Goh Chok Tong, July 1, 2000.

71 *Straits Times Weekly Edition*, February 27, 2000.

72 Interview with Prime Minister Goh Chok Tong, July 1, 2000.

73 Lee Hsien Loong, "Singapore of the Future", in Arun Mahizhnan and Lee Tsao Yuan (eds.), *Singapore: Re-Engineering Success*, Singapore: Institute of Policy Studies and Oxford University Press, 1998, p. 8.

74 See *Asiaweek*, March 24, 2000 on the web at: http://cnn.com/ASIANOW/asiaweek/magazine/2000/0324/cover.4people.html, and *Asiaweek*, June 9, 2000, p. 32.

75 Simon S.C. Tay writes that according to a New York lawyers' human rights group, Singapore refused to register Oxfam. See "Civil Society and the Law in Singapore: Three Dimensions for Change in the 21st Century", paper for the IPS Conference on Civil Society: Harnessing State–Society Synergies, in Singapore on May 6–8, 1998.

13 Deterrence and diplomacy

1 *Straits Times*, November 10, 1965, quoted in Christopher Tremewan, *The Political Economy of Social Control in Singapore*, London: Macmillan Press, 1996, p. 107.

2 Andrew T.H. Tan, "Singapore's Defence: Capabilities, Trends, and Implications", in *Contemporary Southeast Asia*, vol. 21, no. 3 (December 1999), p. 452. Also see Tommy Koh, "Size is Not Destiny", in Arun Mahizhnan and Lee Tsao Yuan (eds.), *Singapore: Re-*

Engineering Success, Singapore: Institute of Policy Studies and Oxford University Press, 1998, pp. 172–80.

3 Michael Leifer, *Singapore's Foreign Policy: Coping with Vulnerability*, London: Routledge, 2000, pp. 1–11.

4 Michael Leifer, *Singapore's Foreign Policy: Coping with Vulnerability*, London: Routledge, 2000, p. 11. Also see Michael Leifer, "Singapore in Regional and Global Context: Sustaining Exceptionalism", in Arun Mahizhnan and Lee Tsao Yuan (eds.), *Singapore: Re-Engineering Success*, Singapore: Institute of Policy Studies and Oxford University Press, 1998, pp. 19–30. Leifer notes that size, location and ethnic identity "do not in themselves add up to destiny, but they are facts of geopolitical life" (p. 20).

5 In June 1966, Britain put a financial squeeze on Malaysia to get Kuala Lumpur to act more reasonably in its defense and economic matters with Singapore. Eventually Malaysian troops vacated their barracks in Singapore and the two Singapore battalions were brought home. See Chan Heng Chee, *The Politics of Survival 1965–1967*, Singapore: Oxford University Press, 1971, p. 38.

6 See Lee Kuan Yew, *From Third World to First, The Singapore Story: 1965–2000*, Singapore: Times Media Private Ltd., 2000, p. 22.

7 See Lee Kuan Yew, *From Third World to First, The Singapore Story: 1965–2000*, Singapore: Times Media Private Ltd., 2000, pp. 31–5. Lee Kuan Yew revealed in his memoirs that he and Defence Minister Goh Keng Swee originally disagreed. Goh wanted to build up a large regular army whereas Lee wanted a small standing army and reserves, mostly because of the high recurrent costs of a large regular army (p. 35). They settled on Lee's formula. However, Lee also wanted conscription for women, but the idea was opposed by some others and eventually dropped.

8 Although women are not conscripted, there are women in the regular SAF, including in combat divisions. In mid-2000, there were four women holding the rank of lieutenant-colonel (*Straits Times*, July 1, 2000). The issue of women doing national service is periodically debated in public forums, but the Ministry of Defence (MINDEF) appears unlikely to change the status quo. See *Straits Times*, July 17, 20, 22, 29 and August 12, 2000.

9 Those selected for SAF overseas scholarships (roughly the ten best, based principally on academic merit, of the officer cadet national servicemen yearly) study at top universities, such as Oxford and Cambridge, on full pay as lieutenants and with full scholarships. They are bonded for eight years after they graduate, but during that period they are sent to the United States or Britain for graduate courses. Afterwards, they have the option of continuing in the SAF, joining the public service at the top grade, joining a statutory board, or they can opt for the private sector. See Lee Kuan Yew, *From Third World to First, The Singapore Story: 1965–2000*, Singapore: Times Media Private Ltd., 2000, pp. 44–5. Apparently, the scholarship scheme was initially modeled after the 19th century German General Staff system to produce general staff rather than commanders. However, this was soon amended to include both. See the speech of Deputy Prime Minister BG Lee Hsien Loong at the SAF Overseas Scholarship's 30th Anniversary Dinner, April 15, 2000, "SAF Scholars Make the Grade", printed in *Speeches*, vol. 24, no. 2 (2000), pp. 29–30. For a comprehensive account of the SAF and scholarships, see Tim Huxley, "The Political Role of the Singapore Armed Forces' Officer Corps: Towards a Military-Administrative State?", *SDSC Working Paper No. 279*, Strategic and Defence Studies Centre, The Australian National University, Canberra (December 1993), pp. 1–26.

10 The perceived selective recruitment and deployment of Malay Singaporeans in the SAF continues to be a sore point with the Malay–Muslim community. This is discussed in Chapter 8, pp. 109–10.

11 Quoted in Willard A. Hanna, "The New Singapore Armed Forces", *American Universities Field Staff Reports*, vol. xxi, no. 1 (January 1973), p. 8. Also see Michael Leifer, "Singapore in Regional and Global Context: Sustaining Exceptionalism", in Arun Mahizhnan and Lee Tsao Yuan (eds.), *Singapore: Re-Engineering Success*, Singapore: Institute of Policy Studies and Oxford University Press, 1998, p. 20.

12 Andrew T.H. Tan, "Singapore's Defence: Capabilities, Trends, and Implications", in *Contemporary Southeast Asia*, vol. 21, no. 3 (December 1999), pp. 454–7. On the security challenges faced by small states, and the options available, see a speech by B.G. Lee Hsien Loong published in the *Straits Times*, November 6, 1984. The strategy is reminiscent of Israel's preemptive defense policy.

13 See the speech given by Dr. Tony Tan Keng Yam in *Parliamentary Debates Singapore*, vol. 71, no. 1 (October 4, 1999), col. 52.

14 Interview with Dr. Tony Tan, Deputy Prime Minister and Minister for Defence, on July 6, 2000.

15 Michael Leifer, *Singapore's Foreign Policy: Coping with Vulnerability*, London: Routledge, 2000, p. 17.

16 *Defending Singapore in the 21st Century*, Singapore: Ministry of Defence, 2000, p. 27. Also see Andrew T.H. Tan, "Singapore's Defence: Capabilities, Trends, and Implications", in *Contemporary Southeast Asia*, vol. 21, no. 3 (December 1999), p. 458.

17 *Asiaweek*, June 9, 2000, p. 45. The Singapore government is willing to spend up to 6 percent of GDP yearly on defense (*Defending Singapore in the 21st Century*, Singapore: Ministry of Defence, 2000, p. 53). Some of these costs are incurred for reasons of economy of scale. As noted by Dr. Tony Tan, defense is very expensive, but the cost of supporting the SAF "is not an issue here" (interview with the Deputy Prime Minister and Minister for Defence, July 6, 2000).

18 Grace Sung, "France Enhances SAF Might: Tony Tan", *Straits Times Weekly Edition*, June 23, 2001.

19 See *Straits Times*, March 25 and July 5, 2000; *Straits Times Interactive*, July 15 and 23, 2000; *Far Eastern Economic Review*, April 12, 2001, p. 10. To emphasize the complexities of planning, Dr. Tony Tan remarked that it takes 12 years to procure a jet fighter and train a pilot to fly it (interview with the Deputy Prime Minister and Minister for Defence, July 6, 2000).

20 "SAF Set to Become Region's Best", *Straits Times Weekly Edition*, June 30, 2001. Also see Tim Huxley, "Singapore Sets the Pace", *Regional Security 2001*, September 17, 2001, on the Web: http://global-defence.com/webpages/RSpart3a.html; and "US Builds an Asian Tiger Cub in Singapore", *Stratfor Intelligence Report*, July 18, 2001, on the Web: http://www.stratfor.com/asia/commentary/0107181530.

21 See Andrew T.H. Tan, "Singapore's Defence: Capabilities, Trends, and Implications", in *Contemporary Southeast Asia*, vol. 21, no. 3 (December 1999), p. 455; *Jane's Intelligence Review* (April 1996), p. 180; *Straits Times Weekly Edition,* June 28, 1997; and speech by B.G. Lee Hsien Loong at the 33/98 Officer Cadets Commissioning Parade, "Professionalism in the Singapore Armed Forces", printed in *Speeches*, 23, 4 (July–August 1999), p. 14.

22 "National Security Secretariat Set Up at MINDEF', *Straits Times Weekly Edition*, January 12, 2002.

23 See *Aerospace and Defence Horizons*, Singapore: Singapore Technologies, 1990, pp. 4–5.

24 Bilveer Singh, *Singapore's Defence Industries*, Canberra Papers on Strategy and Defence, No. 70, Canberra: The Australian National University, 1990, pp. 11–14.

25 Bilveer Singh, *Singapore's Defence Industries*, Canberra Papers on Strategy and Defence, No. 70, Canberra: The Australian National University, 1990, pp. 35–6;. Tim Huxley, "The Political Role of the Singapore Armed Forces' Officer Corps: Towards a Military-Administrative State?", *SDSC Working Paper No. 279*, Strategic and Defence Studies Centre, The Australian National University, Canberra (December 1993), p. 11.

26 *Straits Times Weekly Edition*, April 1, 2000.

27 Stephen Haggard and Linda Low, "State Politics and Business in Singapore", in Edmund T. Gomez (ed.), *Political Business in East Asia*, London: Routledge, forthcoming in 2002, Chapter 10.

28 The rumors started with the airing of an Australian current affairs program, Dateline, on Australia's Special Broadcasting Service on October 12, 1996. For some other rumors concerning Myanmar, see "Burma–Singapore Axis: Globalizing the Heroin Trade", by Leslie Kean and Dennis Bernstein, in the CAQ e-magazine (*CovertAction Quarterly*), no. 64 (Spring 1998), at http://www.caq.com, forwarded on sangkancil@malaysia.net on August 7, 2000. This article states that Singapore Technologies has built a "state-of-the-art cyber-war centre" in Yangon, basically for intercepting incoming communications (the authors also published an article titled "Singapore's Blood Money", in *The Nation*, October 20, 1997). Also see William Ashton, "Burma Receives Advances from its Silent Suitors in Singapore", *Jane's Intelligence Review, ASIA*, vol. 10, no. 3 (March 1, 1998), and the *South China Morning Post*, May 13, 1998.

29 The Singapore government has consistently and strenuously denied all allegations made in these reports. See "Investment in Myanmar Fund Was Above Board", *Singapore Bulletin*, vol. 24, no. 11 (November 1996), p. 4; "Letter from the Singapore Embassy", *The Nation*, November 24, 1997. The Embassy letter says that Singapore's GIC was a passive investor in the Myanmar Fund, which had other investors like Swiss Banking Corporation, and that Bernstein and Kean were simply recycling the old allegations made by the Australian Special Broadcasting Service (see note 28 above). Also see Bilveer Singh, *Singapore's Defence Industries*, Canberra Papers on Strategy and Defence, No. 70, Canberra: The Australian National University, 1990, p. 63.

30 See Lee Kuan Yew, *From Third World To First, The Singapore Story: 1965–2000*, Singapore: Times Media Private Ltd., 2000, pp. 47–65.

31 Michael Leifer, *Singapore's Foreign Policy: Coping with Vulnerability*, London, Routledge, 2000, p. 64.

32 Michael Leifer, *Singapore's Foreign Policy: Coping with Vulnerability*, London, Routledge, 2000, p. 102.

33 *Defending Singapore in the 21st Century*, Singapore: Ministry of Defence, 2000, pp. 17–20.

34 Michael Leifer, *Singapore's Foreign Policy: Coping with Vulnerability*, London, Routledge, 2000, p. 25; Shaun Narine, *ASEAN and the East Asian Economic Crisis*, Toronto: Canadian Consortium on Asia Pacific Security (CANCAPS) Paper, No. 23 (March 2000).

35 See Lee Kuan Yew, *From Third World To First, The Singapore Story: 1965–2000*, Singapore: Times Media Private Ltd., 2000, p. 435.

36 *Straits Times Weekly Edition*, May 26 and June 30, 2001.

37 Lee Kuan Yew, *From Third World To First, The Singapore Story: 1965–2000*, Singapore: Times Media Private Ltd., 2000, p. 46.

38 Trish Saywell, " 'Places Not Bases' Puts Singapore on the Line", *Far Eastern Economic Review*, May 17, 2001.

39 Lee Kuan Yew, *From Third World To First, The Singapore Story: 1965–2000*, Singapore: Times Media Private Ltd., 2000, p. 538. A Memorandum of Understanding was signed in November 1990; a formal agreement was signed in November 1998. See *Straits Times Weekly Edition*, November 14, 1998.

40 Tim Huxley, "Singapore and Malaysia: A Precarious Balance?", *The Pacific Review*, vol. 4, no. 3 (1991), p. 204.

41 Michael Leifer, *Singapore's Foreign Policy: Coping with Vulnerability*, London, Routledge, 2000, p. 19. Just after Separation in August 1965, Malaysian Prime Minister Tunku Abdul Rahman told British and Australian diplomats that Malaysia had the "upper hand" because it could always threaten to turn off the water. See Lee Kuan Yew, *The Singapore Story: Memoirs of Lee Kuan Yew*, Singapore: Prentice Hall, 1998, p. 663, and *Parliamentary Debates Singapore*, vol. 67, no. 3 (June 3, 1997), cols 212–16. In late 2001, a Malay army officer wrote an article in an armed forces journal calling on Malaysia to use water as a "strategic weapon" (*Straits Times Interactive*, October 10, 2001, on the Web: http://straitstimes.asia1.com.sg).

42 Conversations with informed Singaporeans, June–July 2000. Also see Tim Huxley, "Singapore and Malaysia: A Precarious Balance?", *The Pacific Review*, vol. 4, no. 3 (1991), p. 208, and Andrew T.H. Tan, "Singapore's Defence: Capabilities, Trends, and Implications", *Contemporary Southeast Asia*, vol. 21, no. 3 (December 1999), pp. 455–6.

43 Lee Kuan Yew, *From Third World To First, The Singapore Story: 1965–2000*, Singapore: Times Media Private Ltd., 2000, p. 276. In September 2001, Mahathir stated that "Malaysian policy is we will not cut off the supply of water." ("Malaysia Will Not Cut Singapore's Water Supply: Mahathir", *Agence France Presse*, September 4, 2001, on the Web: http://sg.news.yahoo.com/010904/1/1e4kj.html).

44 Liang Hwee Ting, "Desalinated Water From Taps in 2005", *Straits Times Weekly Edition*, December 1, 2001. Singapore expects recycled water to supply 15 percent of its water needs by 2010. By the end of 2002, all seven water-fab plants will use reclaimed water, since it is very pure (*Straits Times Weekly Edition*, January 1, 2001 and September 1, 2001).

45 *Straits Times Weekly Edition*, March 24, 2001. The current strategies are to use both desalination and reclamation, focusing on "membrane technology". A very good 1997 article sets out the whole water supply issue: see Pang Gek Choo, "Can Singapore Ever Be Self-Sufficient in its Water Needs?" *Straits Times Weekly Edition*, July 5, 1997.

46 See Jacqueline Wong, "Singapore Walks Tightrope in Anti-Terror Stance", *Reuters*, October 4, 2001, on the Web: http://www.reuters.com; *Straits Times Weekly Edition*, October 6 and 13, 2001.

47 Tim Huxley, "Singapore in 2000: Continuing Stability and Renewed Prosperity amid Regional Disarray", *Asian Survey*, vol. 41, no. 1 (January/February 2001), p. 205. In fact, the Political and Economic Research Consultancy (PERC) has downgraded Singapore's stability rating because of its proximity to Indonesia and Malaysia, where Islamic militancy is on the rise (Zoher Abdoolcarim and Roger Mitton, "Face-Off", *Asiaweek*, November 16, 2001, on the Web: http://www.asiaweek.com).

48 President's Address (S.R. Nathan), *Parliamentary Debates Singapore*, vol. 71, no. 1 (October 1999), col. 8. As noted by Prof. S. Jayakumar, the Minister for Foreign Affairs, one question

concerns the rapid changes in the "Westphalian concept of a state with virtually absolute sovereignty within its borders". Keynote Address at the AGC-SILS International Law Seminar, July 8, 2000 in Singapore.

49 Michael Leifer, *Singapore's Foreign Policy: Coping with Vulnerability*, London, Routledge, 2000.

50 See Tim Huxley, "The Political Role of the Singapore Armed Forces' Officer Corps: Towards a Military-Administrative State?", *Strategic and Defence Studies Centre Working Paper No. 279*, Canberra: The Australian National University, December 1993. Huxley at one time believed that the tight civilian control that existed in the 1980s was eroding. He provides an extensive list of former military officers now holding high positions (pp. 7–11). See Tim Huxley, *Defending the Lion City: The Armed Forces of Singapore*, St. Leonards: Allen & Unwin, 2000.

51 Interview with B.G. George Yeo (July 3, 2000), pp. 242, 245–6.

52 Interview with B.G. George Yeo (July 3, 2000). Likewise, Deputy Prime Minister B.G. Lee Hsien Loong noted that all those recruited into politics were from the first few "batches" of SAF scholars, and none since (interview, July 4, 2000).

53 Quoted in Tim Huxley, "The Political Role of the Singapore Armed Forces' Officer Corps: Towards a Military-Administrative State?", *Strategic and Defence Studies Centre Working Paper No. 279*, Canberra: The Australian National University, December 1993, p. 18, from the *Straits Times Overseas Weekly Edition*, August 20, 1988.

54 Tim Huxley, "The Political Role of the Singapore Armed Forces' Officer Corps: Towards a Military-Administrative State?", *Strategic and Defence Studies Centre Working Paper No. 279*, Canberra: The Australian National University, December 1993, p. 14.

55 Andrew T.H. Tan, "Singapore's Defence: Capabilities, Trends, and Implications", *Contemporary Southeast Asia*, vol. 21, no. 3 (December 1999), p. 470.

56 Michael Leifer, *Singapore's Foreign Policy: Coping with Vulnerability*, London, Routledge, 2000, p. 4.

57 Michael Leifer, *Singapore's Foreign Policy: Coping with Vulnerability*, London, Routledge, 2000, pp. 8–9, and Michael Leifer, "The Conduct of Foreign Policy", in Kernial Singh Sandhu and Paul Wheatley (eds.), *Management of Success*, Singapore: Institute of Southeast Asian Studies, 1989, p. 968.

58 Lee Kuan Yew said in 1966 that "in the last resort it is power which decides what happens . . .", quoted in Michael Leifer, *Singapore's Foreign Policy: Coping with Vulnerability*, London, Routledge, 2000, p. 5.

59 Amitav Acharya and M. Ramesh, "Economic Foundations of Singapore's Security: From Globalism to Regionalism", in Garry Rodan (ed.), *Singapore Changes Guard*, Melbourne: Longman Cheshire, 1993, p. 139.

60 Prof. S. Jayakumar, "Keeping Sight of the Basics in our Foreign Diplomacy", *Speeches*, vol. 21, no. 4 (1997), p. 49. Also see Philippe Regnier, *Singapore: City-State in South-East Asia*, Honolulu: University of Hawaii Press, translated by Christopher Hurst, updated version, 1991, p. 142.

61 Obaid Ul Haq, "Foreign Policy", in Jon S.T. Quah *et al.* (eds.), *Government and Politics of Singapore*, Singapore: Oxford University Press, 1985, p. 282.

62 This was the case with the issue of water and also the long-drawn-out saga of the location of Customs, Immigration, and Quarantine (CIQ) facilities and Malayan railway land. For Prof. S. Jayakumar's speech to Parliament on July 31, 1998 on the CIQ issue, covering the sequence of events from the first Malaysian informal agreement in 1989, see http://www.asia1.com.sg/straitstimes/pages/sin12_0801.html, and Michael Leifer, *Singapore's Foreign Policy: Coping with Vulnerability*, London, Routledge, 2000, p. 153. As Leifer writes, concerning the CIQ issue, "within Singapore it served to reconfirm a belief that the government in Malaysia could not be fully trusted to keep its word and honour explicit agreements". Also see two articles in the *Straits Times Weekly Edition* by Irene Ng, "KL Seeks More Time; PM Agrees" (February 10, 2001) and "Singapore Studies Mahathir's Reply on Bilateral Issues" (March 17, 2001).

63 *Straits Times Weekly Edition,* March 15 and 22, June 7, 1997. For a comprehensive account of the bilateral issues plaguing Malaysia–Singapore relations, see Bilveer Singh, *The Vulnerability of Small States Revisited*, Yogyakarta: Gadjah Mada University Press, 1999.

64 Lee Kuan Yew, *The Singapore Story: Memoirs of Lee Kuan Yew*, Singapore: Prentice Hall, 1998. Concerning Kuala Lumpur's abrupt termination of various agreements concerning the RSAF's use of Malaysian airspace, see *Parliamentary Debates Singapore*, vol. 69, no. 7 (October 12, 1998), cols. 1021–3.

65 However, in July 2000, Kuala Lumpur hosted the two-week FPDA maritime and air defense exercises. See *Straits Times*, July 3, 2000.

66 *Straits Times Weekly Edition*, February 3, 2001; "Our Malays are Happier than Yours", *The Economist*, February 1, 2001, on the Web: http://www.economist.com. For a good brief analysis of Malaysia's and Singapore's grievances towards each other, see James Chin, "Singapore: Love-Hate Relations", *Asian Analysis* (May 2001), forwarded by bungaraya@listserve.net-gw.com on May 28, 2001.

67 In May 1998, however, Singapore rejected a request for an official visit by Israeli Prime Minister Benjamin Netanyahu.

68 For an article highly critical of Singapore's role in Singapore–Malaysia relations, see Lily Zubaidah Rahim, "Singapore-Malaysia Relations: Deep-Seated Tensions and Self-Fulfilling Prophecies", *Journal of Contemporary Asia*, vol. 29, no. 1 (1999), pp. 38–55.

69 Singapore agreed to construction of a new bridge, but not the destruction of the Causeway, and agreed to a rail tunnel, but will not pay for it (Irene Ng, "Tough Talk, Then Progress on KL Pact", *Straits Times Weekly Edition*, September 8, 2001). However, Mahathir wants Singapore to help pay for the tunnel, and may seek to renegotiate the whole pact in order to achieve that. See *Far Eastern Economic Review*, October 4, 2001, p. 10.

70 Malaysia will get some prize real estate on Shenton Way in exchange for vacating the Tanjong Pagar Railway Station. Malaysia will also be given 17 parcels of railroad land at Bukit Timah. Malaysian Customs and Immigration will move to Woodlands until its own station at Kranji is ready in 2006.

71 See Barani Krishnan, "Malaysia and Singapore Reach Landmark Agreement", *Reuters*, September 4, 2001, on the Web: http://sg.news.yahoo.com/010904/3/le4tx.html.

72 The PAP government is concerned about Malaysia after Mahathir and worried about radical Islam and the possibility of PAS (Islamic Party of Malaysia) coming to power. See S. Jayasankaran, "Moving On", *Far Eastern Economic Review*, September 20, 2001, p. 29, and Barani Krishnan, "Malaysia and Singapore Reach Landmark Agreement", *Reuters*, September 4, 2001, on the Web: http://sg.news.yahoo.com/010904/3/le4tx.html.

73 Irene Ng, "A Deal is a Deal, Now Let's Move On", *Straits Times Weekly Edition*, September 8, 2001; "Both Sides are Better Off with KL Deal, says Jaya", *Straits Times Weekly Edition*, September 29, 2001.

74 Early relations were soured when Singapore executed two Indonesian marines (for setting off a bomb in downtown Singapore which killed civilians during Confrontation) in 1968 despite a plea for leniency from Suharto. This rift was repaired when Lee Kuan Yew visited Indonesia in 1973, laid a wreath on the graves of the marines, and subsequently struck up a good rapport with Suharto. There was a small setback in relations in 1975 when Singapore abstained in the United Nations vote on Indonesia's occupation of East Timor. Otherwise the relationship was strong, much better than with Malaysia. See Lee Kuan Yew, *From Third World To First, The Singapore Story: 1965–2000*, Singapore: Times Media Private Ltd., 2000, pp. 304–15, and Michael Leifer, *Singapore's Foreign Policy: Coping with Vulnerability*, London, Routledge, 2000, pp. 38, 76–7.

75 Before Habibie was named as Suharto's running mate in early 1998, Lee said "if the market is uncomfortable with whoever is the eventual vice-president, the rupiah would weaken again" (Lee Kuan Yew, *From Third World To First, The Singapore Story: 1965–2000*, Singapore: Times Media Private Ltd., 2000, p. 315). Habibie was not identified by name, but he knew he was the one Lee meant.

76 Habibie's "red dot" statement was published in the *Asian Wall Street Journal*, August 4, 1998. Concerning the Singapore–Indonesia Bilateral Trade Finance Guarantee Scheme, Foreign Minister S. Jayakumar reported that the scheme was not acceptable to Indonesia because of conditions and safeguards, and it has not been taken up (*Parliamentary Debates Singapore*, vol. 71, no. 5 (November 23, 1999), col. 408). Habibie also made statements about discrimination against Malay–Muslims in Singapore, which were refuted strenuously by Singapore's Malay–Muslim political leaders (*Straits Times*, February 11, 1999). See also Chua Kee Hoong, "What's Happening to Singapore–Jakarta Ties?" *Straits Times Weekly Edition*, March 6, 1999.

77 "Indonesia's Wahid Lashes Money-Grabbing Singapore", *Reuters*, November 25, 2000, on the Web: http://abcnews.go.com/wire/World/reuters20001125_1338.html. Interestingly, the Malaysian opposition Democratic Action Party wondered (as did some others) if Dr. Mahathir primed Wahid for his outburst against Singapore, since the two met just beforehand, and Wahid's salvos had "unmistakable traces" of Mahathir's grievances and conspiracy theories (bungaraya@listserve.net-gw.com, December 1, 2000).

78 Wahid said that Lee Kuan Yew had told him that his days as President were numbered, and that the Senior Minister dismissed out of hand Wahid's idea of having East Timor and Papua New Guinea join ASEAN, among other things that irritated the President. Although, as one correspondent noted, this was not the first time Lee "has put the cat among the pigeons" (John McBeth, "Family Feud", *Far Eastern Economic Review*, December 2, 2000, p. 15), it was a rare occasion that the government has denied that Lee said the things he was accused of saying ("Comments by MFA Spokesman in Response to Media Queries on Indonesian Foreign Minister Alwi Shihab's Remarks on Singapore–Indonesian Relations", Ministry of Foreign Affairs press release, November 29, 2000, forwarded on sgdaily@list.sintercom.org on December 4, 2000).

79 Susan Sim, "That Outburst from Gus Dur", *Straits Times*, November 30, 2000, forwarded on sgdaily@list.sintercom.org on December 7, 2000..

80 Alan Wheatley, "Singapore Government Keeps Mum on Wahid Outburst", *Reuters*, November 27, 2000, forwarded to recipients of indonesia-act@igc.apc.org; "Comments by Press Secretary to Prime Minister Goh Chok Tong on President Abdurrahman Wahid's Remarks on the 4th ASEAN Informal Summit", Ministry of Information and the Arts press release, November 28, 2000, forwarded by sgdaily@list.sintercom.org on November 30, 2000. As the *Jakarta Post* pointed out in two editorials, this is not an easy task with Indonesian foreign policy confused and subject to abrupt shifts (see "Singapore Sling", November 28, 2000, and "Indonesian Foreign Policy is in Total Disarray", November 29, 2000).

81 See David Lamb, "Political Unrest Has Southeast Asia on Edge", *Los Angeles Times*, August 11, 2000; Ben Dolven, "Friend or Foe? Singapore Tries to Figure Out Indonesia's New Leaders", *Far Eastern Economic Review*, March 25, 1999; *Asiaweek*, June 9, 2000, pp. 34–6; *Sunday Times* (Singapore), June 11, 2000.

82 Lee Kuan Yew, *From Third World To First, The Singapore Story: 1965–2000*, Singapore: Times Media Private Ltd., 2000, p. 714.

83 There were rumors, denied by Lee, that he might be reassuming that role when he vacationed in Taiwan in September 2000. See *Far Eastern Economic Review*, October 5, 2000, p. 27.

84 For Lee Kuan Yew's ideas on US–China relations, see the *Straits Times Weekly Edition*, February 15, 1997 and September 25, 1999.

85 *Straits Times Weekly Edition*, June 9, 2001. Lee seems unperturbed that Chinese censors are deleting and rewriting parts of the second volume of his memoirs before publishing the book in China (*San Francisco Chronicle*, August 7, 2001).

86 See Michael Leifer, *Singapore's Foreign Policy: Coping with Vulnerability*, London, Routledge, 2000, p. 26, and Bilveer Singh, *The Vulnerability of Small States Revisited*, Yogyakarta: Gadjah Mada University Press, 1999, p. 298. These authors note that Singapore's relations with the US were not cordial in the immediate period following Singapore's independence, when Singapore was concerned with improving its Third World credentials and anxious to avoid being labeled "neo-colonialist" because of the presence of British troops. By 1967, however, relations had improved markedly.

87 *Straits Times Weekly Edition*, June 23, 2001. Lee believes the US will retain its power because of its technological edge, entrepreneurial nature, and conducive business environment.

88 Robert O. Tilman, *Southeast Asia and the Enemy Beyond*, Boulder: Westview Press, 1987, p. 138. Singapore has not been alone in this view. Canadian academic Andrew Cooper observes that "the US has not been able to translate its position as the one remaining superpower into a coherent vision" and instead "has offered an inconsistent form of intellectual leadership" (*Canadian Foreign Policy: Old Habits and New Directions*, Scarborough: Prentice Hall, Allyn & Bacon Canada, 1997, p. 281).

89 Among the issues, Singapore sued for libel a US-owned newspaper and restricted the domestic circulation of some other newspapers and journals; it expelled a US diplomat for offering support to an opposition candidate; and it jailed and caned a US teenager resident in Singapore for vandalism.

90 *Singapore Bulletin*, vol. 26, no. 5 (May 1998), p. 3. The new US Ambassador was Steven Green.

91 Michael Haas, "Mass Society", in Michael Haas (ed.), *The Singapore Puzzle*, Westport, CT: Praeger, 1999, p. 170. See *Far Eastern Economic Review*, April 28, 1994, p. 25, and *Straits Times Weekly Edition*, December 28, 1996.

92 Chua Lee Hoong, "Yishun Target in Group's Plans", *Straits Times Weekly Edition*, January 12, 2002; "Singapore Seeks More Al-Qaida", *Guardian*, January 12, 2002; Seth Mydans, "Singapore Stunned As Ordinary Men Are Tied to Terror", *New York Times*, January 14, 2002; "No US Tip-Off Before ISA Arrests", *Straits Times Weekly Edition*, January 19, 2002.

93 Singapore contributed both money and personnel to UN peacekeeping efforts in Namibia (1989), Kuwait (1991), Cambodia (1992–3), S. Africa (1994), and in 1999 and 2001 it participated in the UN peackeeping force in East Timor (see p. 173 above and *Straits Times Weekly Edition*, June 30, 2001). See also Alan Chong, "Analysing Singapore's Foreign Policy in the 1990s and Beyond: Limitations of the Small State Approach", *Asian Journal of Political Science*, vol. 6, no. 1 (June 1998), pp. 95–119.

94 *Straits Times Weekly Edition*, October 21, 2000.

95 See Irene Ng, "How to Make Friends and Advance Interests of Singapore", *Straits Times Weekly Edition*, November 4, 2000. This article contains an interesting story of Singapore's efforts during the period when maritime jurisdiction was being negotiated, as experienced by Foreign Minister S. Jayakumar when he was Singapore's Permanent Representative to the UN. Singapore put together a 30–40 country caucus of the "landlocked and geographically-disadvantaged countries".

96 As well as referring to Cambodia, he was arguing against the Soviet invasion of Afghanistan. See Bilveer Singh, *The Vulnerability of Small States Revisited*, Yogyakarta: Gadjah Mada University Press, 1999, p. 35.

97 Michael Leifer, *Singapore's Foreign Policy: Coping with Vulnerability*, London, Routledge, 2000, p. 84. Leifer writes that the "advocacy, lobbying and drafting skills" of Singapore diplomats "were employed to great effect within the United Nations against Vietnam and its client government in Phnom Penh" (p. 85).

98 ZOPFAN, which called for all the major powers to stay out of the region, was contrary to what Singapore believed was needed to control intra-regional conflict. See Michael Leifer, *Singapore's Foreign Policy: Coping with Vulnerability*, London, Routledge, 2000, p. 58.

99 See Derek da Cunha, "A Multiplicity of Approaches to Foreign and Defence Policy", in Arun Mahizhnan (ed.), *Singapore: The Year in Review, 1997*, Singapore: Institute of Policy Studies, pp. 63–73, and Michael Leifer, *Singapore's Foreign Policy: Coping with Vulnerability*, London, Routledge, 2000, pp. 84–5, 126.

100 Greg Sheridan, *Tigers*, St. Leonards, NSW: Allen & Unwin, 1997, p. 91.

101 For an explanation of Singapore's technical assistance to Myanmar and of "constructive engagement", see *Parliamentary Debates Singapore*, vol. 70, no. 18 (August 17, 1999), cols. 2010–13 (Prof. S. Jayakumar and J.B. Jeyaretnam).

102 *Straits Times Weekly Edition*, December 2, 2000. See Shaun Narine, *ASEAN and the East Asian Economic Crisis*, Toronto: Canadian Consortium on Asia Pacific Security (CANCAPS) Paper, No. 23 (March 2000), p. 8. Narine notes that the economic crisis undermined ASEAN's confidence and exposed both institutional flaws and structural limitations.

103 *The Economist*, February 12, 2000 survey on the Web: http://www.com/archive/view.cgi; *Far Eastern Economic Review*, August 10, 2000, p. 22.

104 *Parliamentary Debates Singapore*, vol. 71, no. 1 (October 1999), col. 48; *Straits Times Weekly Edition*, March 10, 2000. Goh Chok Tong has stated that there are "cogent geo-political reasons" why ASEAN deserves as much attention from the US as Northeast Asia (*Straits Times Weekly Edition*, June 16, 2001).

105 The ASEAN+3 is similar in constitution, and in some of the proposals being forwarded, to Malaysian Prime Minister Mahathir's proposed East Asia Economic Group/Caucus. The current arrangement falls short of a trade bloc at present and does not seem to have upset the US so much as a result.

106 "China Charms South-East Asia", *The Economist*, November 24, 2000, and "The Best Things in Life", *The Economist*, November 30, 2000, both on the Web: http://www.economist.com/.

107 *Vancouver Sun*, November 7, 2001. Soon after the ten years, Japan and South Korea will join.

108 The Shanghai Accord, signed at the October 2001 APEC summit, gave some renewed impetus to trade liberalization, although APEC's political will remains questionable. See the *Straits Times* editorial, "A Nudge for APEC", October 23, 2001.

109 See *Straits Times*, July 26, 2000.

110 "Singapore's Trade Initiatives Undermine ASEAN Economic Policy", *Stratfor*, forwarded on sgdaily@list.sintercom.org on November 28, 2000; "China Charms South-East Asia", *The Economist*, November 24, 2000, on the Web: http://www.economist.com/.

111 Lee Kuan Yew, Keynote Address at the Annual Conference of the IISS (International Institute for Strategic Studies), Singapore, September 1997 (Singapore government press release).

112 *Straits Times Weekly Edition*, June 16, 2001.

113 See Yeo Lay Hwee, "The Bangkok ASEM and the Future of Asia–Europe Relations", *Southeast Asian Affairs 1997*, Singapore: Institute of Southeast Asian Studies, 1997, pp. 35–6; D. Camroux and C. Lechervy, " 'Close Encounters of a Third Kind?': The Inaugural Asia–Europe Meeting of March 1996", *The Pacific Review*, vol. 9, no. 3 (1996), pp. 442–53; and Christopher M. Dent, "ASEM and the 'Cinderella' Complex of EU–East Asia Economic Relations", *Pacific Affairs*, vol. 74, no. 1 (Spring 2001), pp. 25–52.

114 *Asia-Europe Vision Group Report 1999*, on-line at http://www.mofat.go.kr/english/rel...ntents.html.

115 *Far Eastern Economic Review*, October 26, 2000, on-line at http://www.feer.com/_0010_26/p30region.html. Apparently the EU is determined to forge its own foreign policy and defense identity in Asia distinct from that of the US.

116 See *Far Eastern Economic Review*, July 12, 2001, p. 12, and July 26, 2001, pp. 24–5. Chris Patten, who is in charge of the EU's external relations, has been quite critical of ASEAN.

117 From an examination of the proceedings of the Conference on "The Relevance of Singapore's Experience for Africa", organized jointly by the Africa Leadership Forum and the Singapore International Foundation, November 8–10, 1993, it is difficult to see any real relevance. The advice given was good – clean and efficient government, social discipline, family planning, high savings, a priority to education, etc. – but there was less advice on *how* to get African states from their present state to achieving the above.

118 Michael Leifer, *Singapore's Foreign Policy: Coping with Vulnerability*, London, Routledge, 2000, p. 23.

119 *The Times*, November 19, 1992.

120 James V. Jesudason, "The Resilience of One-Party Dominance in Malaysia and Singapore", in Hermann Giliomee and Charles Simkins (eds.), *One Party-Dominance and Democracy*, Cape Town: Tafelberg Publishers Ltd., 1999, p. 154.

121 *Far Eastern Economic Review*, October 5, 2000.

14 Singapore in the future

1 "Singapore's Survival a Big Issue in Coming GE: PM Goh", *Yahoo! News Singapore*, May 9, 2001, on the Web: http://sg.news.yahoo.com/.

2 *Prime Minister's National Day Rally Speech 1999*, Singapore: Ministry of Information and the Arts, 1999, p. 53.

3 Goh Chok Tong, speech titled "Education – Meeting the Challenge of Globalization", April 6, 2000, forwarded on sgdaily@list.sintercom.org.

4 On the haze problem, see Ian Stewart, "Singapore Officials Fear New Disaster On the Way", *South China Morning Post*, March 8, 2000.

5 "Singapore's Survival a Big Issue in Coming GE: PM Goh", *Yahoo! News Singapore*, May 9, 2001, on the Web: http://sg.news.yahoo.com/.

6 Lee Hsien Loong, "Whither Globalization – A World In Crisis", speech at the Economic Strategy Conference, on May 6, 1998 in Washington, DC, quoted in Amitav Acharya, *The Quest for Identity: International Relations of Southeast Asia*, Singapore: Oxford University Press, 2000, p. 157. Also see Hadi Soesastro, "Synthesis Report: The Globalization, Development, and Security Task Force", *DSSEA Update*, ISDS, Quezon City, Philippines, no. 8 (2000), pp. 6–13.

7 See B.G. George Yeo, Interview by the *Wall Street Journal*, December 31, 1999, "Talking About Tomorrow", transcript on the Web: http://www.gov.sg/sgip/inervws/0200-2.htm; B.G. George Yeo, Interview with Irene Ng, "Sink or Swim in Ocean of Global League", *Straits Times*, March 6, 2000, forwarded by sgdaily@list.sintercom.org.

8 B.G. George Yeo, "The IT Revolution and Singapore", *Speeches*, vol. 23, no. 3 (1999), p. 69.

9 Sharon Vasoo, "No Bumper Crop of Dragon Babies", *Straits Times Weekly Edition*, February 10, 2001.

10 *Singapore Magazine* (January–February 2001), pp. 7–11.

11 See Siti Andrianie, "High-Level Fertility Panel Set Up", *Straits Times Weekly Edition*, April 29, 2000; *Parliamentary Debates Singapore*, vol. 71, no. 4 (October 13, 1999), cols. 345–56 (Goh Chok Tong). Also see "Statistical Highlights" for every year from the Department of Statistics.

12 The birthrate among Malays has dropped from 2.71 in 1990 to 2.42 in 1999; for Indians the decline has been from 1.95 to 1.58; and for the Chinese the birthrate has fallen from 1.68 to 1.3. See *Singapore Magazine* (January–February 2001), pp. 7–11.

13 See: *Population: An Issue of Current Concern*, Singapore: AWARE, 1988. Also see Joseph B. Tamney, *The Struggle Over Singapore's Soul*, Berlin and New York: Walter de Gruyter, 1996, pp. 117–39.

14 Aline K. Wong and Leong Wai Kum, "Introduction", in Aline K. Wong and Leong Wai Kum (eds.), *Singapore Women – Three Decades of Change*, Singapore: Times Academic Press, 1993; Liew Geok Heok and Leong Chooi Peng, "Legal Status", in Aline K. Wong and Leong Wai Kum (eds.), *Singapore Women – Three Decades of Change*, Singapore: Times Academic Press, 1993, pp. 252–83.

15 *Straits Times*, June 9, 2000. Also see "More Women Enter All-Male Arenas", *Straits Times Weekly Edition*, April 15, 2000.

16 In the past, women were not encouraged by the PAP to pursue political careers, although there has been an effort in recent years to increase their parliamentary presence, where their percentage was below the world average. Lee Kuan Yew's position has been that women should not be encouraged to take jobs where they cannot, at the same time, be mothers. Socially, politics is seen as unfeminine; there are few role models and no old boy's network; and the political culture is not conducive to women politicians. Goh Chok Tong's thinking has evolved. In 1980 he said that the PAP was not fielding any female candidates because of the problem of whether the husband or boyfriend would "allow her to enter politics". He added that "most women will not allow the men to do the housework" and concluded that "women play a more beneficial role at home . . ." (Quoted in Linda Lim, "A New Order with Some Old Prejudices", *Far Eastern Economic Review*, January 5, 1984, pp. 37–8). By the mid-1990s, Goh's thinking had progressed: ". . . I wring my hands in desperation. I cannot get women candidates . . . It is not for want of trying" (Quoted in Kanwaljit Soin, "About That Missing Half in Singapore Politics . . .", *Trends*, 64 (December 30–31, 1995). In November 2001, the PAP increased its number of women candidates significantly to 9 of 25 new candidates, including, for the first time, 3 single women, the first Malay woman since 1959, and the first Indian woman since 1965.

17 Jason Leow, "Marriage Not a Priority for Young S'preans – SDU Survey", *Straits Times Weekly Edition*, April 26, 1997; *Singapore Magazine* (January–February 2002), p. 11.

18 *Straits Times Weekly Edition*, October 30, 1999. The percentage of single women between the ages of 40–44 is 14.1 percent (*Singapore Magazine* (January–February 2002), p. 11.

19 Maria Chan, "Single and Female. So What?" *Singapore Magazine* (March–April 2001), pp. 13–16.

20 Lydia Lim, "Marriages Dipped by 10 Per Cent Last Year", *Straits Times Weekly Edition*, October 23, 1999. Also see *ibid*, October 16, 1999, and P. Parameswaran, "Singapore's 1987 Plan to Increase Births Fails", *National Post* (Canada), October 18, 1999. Marriage is also complicated at times by predictions of fortune-tellers and the occurrence, and use, of auspicious lunar years. Also, the 2000 Census revealed that divorce is increasing (nearly two-thirds being initiated by women), while the rate of remarriage is declining (*Singapore Magazine* (January–February 2002), p. 11.

21 Letter to Forum by Dana Lam-Teo, the President of AWARE, *Straits Times Weekly Edition*, April 29, 2000. Also see Chua Lee Hoong, "Time is Right to be Fair to 'Fairer' Sex", *Straits Times Weekly Edition*, March 10, 2001.

22 Helen Chia, "Having Babies Cannot be Calculated on Cold Terms", *Straits Times Weekly Edition*, May 13, 2000.

23 Goh Chok Tong, "The Challenge and Reward of Managing Success", *Speeches*, vol. 13, no. 4 (1989), p. 27.

24 Irene Ng, "Government Looks to Non-Grads to Boost Births", *Straits Times Weekly Edition*, March 18, 2000. Many believe, however, that the government is still ambivalent as to whether or not it wants all babies, regardless of genes and ethnicity. There is still a fine, called an "accounchement fee" levied against families with four or more children, to dissuade the poor from having large families. See Susan Long, "What is Still Holding Back the Stork?" *Straits Times Weekly Edition*, March 17, 2001.

25 Susan Long, "Flexi-Hours, Marriage Leave for Civil Servants", *Straits Times Weekly Edition*, September 2, 2000.

26 *Straits Times Weekly Edition*, August 26, 2000.

27 Cited in *Singapore Magazine* (January–February 2001), pp. 7–11. The UN report was issued in 1988; evidence since then does not appear to contradict it.

28 This is the title of Albert O. Hirschman's influential book. It was published in Cambridge, MA by Harvard University Press in 1970. The point of "exit, voice, and loyalty" is that if a

consumer/citizen has some objections about a product/state, the choices are to exit (not buy the product or leave the state); voice (use avenues available to declare objections and seek changes); and loyalty (the propensity of the consumer/citizen to stay with the product/state even if some things are not perfect).

29 *Prime Minister's National Day Rally Speech 1999*, Singapore: Ministry of Information and the Arts, 1999, p. 20.

30 B.G. George Yeo, "Sink or Swim in Ocean of Global League", Interview with Irene Ng, *Straits Times*, March 6, 2000, forwarded by sgdaily@list.sintercom.org.

31 *Parliamentary Debates Singapore*, vol. 71, no. 4 (October 13, 1999), cols. 349–50 (Goh Chok Tong); Goh Chok Tong, "The Challenge and Reward of Managing Success", *Speeches*, vol. 13, no. 4 (1989), p. 28; Lee Kuan Yew, "Prime Minister's Eve of National Day (Speech by Mr. Lee Kuan Yew)", *Speeches*, vol. 13, no. 4 (1989), p. 3. The ISA arrests in 1987 may have contributed to the temporarily higher numbers, especially in 1988 and 1989.

32 A *Straits Times* survey on emigration in 1997 found that only 4 percent of those who said they had ever considered emigrating, said that they might not leave if there was more freedom of speech in Singapore. The main complaint was the cost of living.

33 See "Arts for Business's Sake", *Far Eastern Economic Review*, September 20, 2001, p. 77.

34 *Singapore Magazine* (July–August 2000), p. 14.

35 Ahmad Osman, "Come Home, Generation M", *Straits Times Weekly Edition*, April 14, 2001.

36 The Singapore Inc. scholarships are those awarded by a number of statutory boards, such as the Economic Development Board and GLCs, such as Singapore Technologies. There have been very few bonds broken by recipients of the overseas PSC (Public Service Commission) scholarships. The difference may be attributable to the differing global marketability of the scholarship recipients.

37 *Parliamentary Debates Singapore*, vol. 68, no. 7 (March 11, 1998), col. 855.

38 See *Straits Times*, July 11, 2000 (editorial); *Straits Times Interactive*, July 12, 15, 19; *Straits Times Weekly Edition*, July 29, 2000; "In the Era of War for Talent: The Issue of Bond-Breakers", *Socratic Circle Publication*, August 7, 2000, forwarded by thinkcentre@hotmail.com.

39 *Straits Times Interactive*, July 19, 2000.

40 *Straits Times*, June 24, 2000.

41 See the *Straits Times* editorial, July 11, 2000. The youthful arrogance of one bond-breaker, a case mentioned in Parliament, is startling. The bond-breaker wrote a letter to say he would not be returning to serve his bond because "I cannot deprive the world of the potential benefits that can be derived from my research". (*Parliamentary Debates Singapore*, vol. 68, no. 7 (March 11, 1998), col. 862 (B.G. Lee Hsien Loong).)

42 *Singapore Parliamentary Debates*, vol. 71, no. 4 (October 13, 1999), cols. 349–50 (Goh Chok Tong); Goh Chok Tong, "The Challenge and Reward of Managing Success", *Speeches*, vol. 13, no. 4 (1989), pp. 24–30.

43 Lee Kuan Yew, "Prime Minister's Eve of National Day (Speech by Mr. Lee Kuan Yew)", *Speeches*, vol. 13, no. 4 (1989), p. 3.

44 Lee Kuan Yew, "Prime Minister's Eve of National Day (Speech by Mr. Lee Kuan Yew)", *Speeches*, vol. 13, no. 4 (1989), p. 3.

45 William Mellor, "The Risks of Playing It Safe", *Asiaweek*, May 4, 2001.

46 Chua Mui Hoong, "Singapore to Cast Net Worldwide for Talent", *Straits Times Weekly Edition*, August 30, 1997.

47 See the letter to the *Straits Times* Forum section from the Ministry of Manpower, *Straits Times Weekly Edition*, November 10, 2001.

48 *Parliamentary Debates Singapore*, vol. 70, no. 17 (August 4, 1999), cols. 1977–8 (Wong Kan Seng); *Straits Times Weekly Edition*, September 2, 2000.

49 Excerpt of interview B.G. George Yeo gave to *Business Week*, in the *Sunday Times*, June 11, 2000.

50 *Straits Times*, June 3, 2000.

51 Chan Kay Min, "4 in 5 Think Foreign Talent has Helped", *Straits Times Interactive*, October 20, 2001.

52 "Downturn Hits Mature Grads", *Straits Times Weekly Edition*, September 15, 2001; Amy Tan, "Singaporean Graduates Struggle to Find Jobs", *Reuters*, September 26, 2001, on the Web: http://sg.news.yahoo.com/010926/3/1iqie.html.

53 *Prime Minister's National Day Rally Speech 1999*, Singapore: Ministry of Information and the Arts, 1999, p. 52; Goh Chok Tong, "The Key Role of Schools", *Speeches*, vol. 23, no. 2 (1999), pp. 13–21.

54 See Andy Ho, "Is S'pore Inc Doing Enough to Help Foreigners Settle In?" *Straits Times Weekly Edition*, November 11, 2000.

55 Lawrence Freedman, "Moral and Material Grounds Will Mark the Front Lines of the Future", *Jane's Intelligence Review*, January 4, 2000.

56 Just consider the billions of dollars lost in California, the sixth largest economy in the world, as a result of a disastrous decision by the state government to deregulate energy in 1996. After years of growth and budget surpluses, it may take years for California to climb back out of the huge debt caused by the state having to pay exorbitant prices to buy energy from suppliers on the spot market. Meanwhile, consumers are paying the price, literally, for poor political decision-making and the entire economy is suffering.

57 *National Post* (Canada), April 5, 2000. The World Bank came to the same position in 1989 when, in its report on Sub-Saharan Africa, it identified the key problem as a "crisis of governance". (See *Sub-Saharan Africa: From Crisis to Sustainable Growth*, Washington, DC: World Bank, 1989.) This conclusion was reached following the failures of the Structural Adjustment Programs in Africa in the 1980s. See Peter Larmour, "Making Sense of Good Governance", *State Society and Governance in Melanesia Discussion Paper 5*, Research School of Pacific and Asian Studies, Canberra: Australia National University, 1998.

58 See S. Ersson and J.E. Lane, "Democracy and Development: A Statistical Exploration", in Adrian Leftwich (ed.), *Democracy and Development*, Cambridge: Polity Press, 1996, pp. 45–73. They found few strongly positive correlations and could only conclude that democracy was "not an obstacle" to development (p. 67). Some would even dispute that.

59 *Governance and Development*, Washington, DC: World Bank, 1992, p. 3.

60 R.S. Milne, "Good Governance: Its Relation to Human Rights", in Rodolphe De Koninck and Christine Veilleux (eds.), *L'Asie du Sud-Est Face à la Mondialisation: Les Nouveaux Champs D'Analyse*, Quebec City: Documents du GÉRAC, Université Laval, 1997, pp. 55–7; Peter Larmour, "Making Sense of Good Governance", *State Society and Governance in Melanesia Discussion Paper 5*, Research School of Pacific and Asian Studies, Canberra: Australia National University, 1998.

61 See A. Leftwich (ed.), *Democracy and Development*, Cambridge: Polity Press, 1996.

62 R.S. Milne, "Good Governance: Its Relation to Human Rights", in Rodolphe De Koninck and Christine Veilleux (eds.), *L'Asie du Sud-Est Face à la Mondialisation: Les Nouveaux Champs D'Analyse*, Quebec City: Documents du GÉRAC, Université Laval, 1997, p. 57.

63 "Cost of Good Government and Price of Bad Government", speech in Parliament by Prime Minister Goh Chok Tong, June 30, 2000 (mimeo). Also see *Straits Times Weekly Edition*, February 24, 2000.

64 R.S. Milne, "Good Governance: Its Relation to Human Rights", in Rodolphe De Koninck and Christine Veilleux (eds.), *L'Asie du Sud-Est Face à la Mondialisation: Les Nouveaux Champs D'Analyse*, Quebec City: Documents du GÉRAC, Université Laval, 1997, p. 60.

65 Stan Sesser, *The Lands of Charm and Cruelty*, New York: Alfred A. Knopf, 1993, p. xv.

66 *Vancouver Sun*, March 20, 2001. In its 1998 report, PERC noted that "Singapore remains tough on corruption, with both determined enforcement and heavy penalties". The report added that one of the state's features was that the rule of law rather than "rule by law" prevailed. See *Singapore Bulletin*, vol. 26, no. 5 (May 1998), pp. 13–14.

67 Ravi Veloo, "10 Principles for Better Government", *Straits Times Weekly Edition*, March 22, 1997.

68 "A Testing Time", *Asiaweek*, August 11, 1995, pp. 26–31.

69 In addition to the ones discussed, the Goh government can take credit for maintaining ethnic harmony while shifting to an explicit multicultural approach emphasizing separate community organizations; making Singapore more competitive by moving headlong into the knowledge-based economy; being the prime initiator for the founding of ASEM (see pp. 183–4); and by responding to ASEAN foot-dragging on free trade by initiating a series of creative bilateral free trade agreements (see p. 82).

70 In fact, Goh states emphatically that whatever the accomplishments of his administration, the credit must go also to the entire Cabinet team (interview, July 1, 2000). This was not just a conventional gesture by him. It was the only addition made by him to a list of eight to ten of his achievements suggested by the authors.

71 James V. Jesudason observes the relevance of Pemple's study to Singapore. See his "The Resilience of One-Party Dominance in Malaysia and Singapore", in Hermann Giliomee and Charles Simkins (eds.), *The Awkward Embrace: One Party-Domination and Democracy*, Cape

Town: Tafelberg Publishers Ltd., 1999, pp. 127–72. Also see T.J. Pempel, "Conclusion: One Party Dominance and the Creation of Regimes", in T.J. Pempel (ed.), *Uncommon Democracies: The One-Party Dominant Regimes*, Ithaca: Cornell University Press, 1990.

72 See Chapter 7.

73 *Straits Times*, June 21, 2000.

74 Goh Chok Tong, "Strengthening the Singapore Heartbeat", *Speeches*, vol. 23, no. 5 (Sept.–Oct. 1999), p. 13.

75 Interview with Goh Chok Tong, July 1, 2000.

76 See *Staying Ahead*, Singapore: Ministry of Information and the Arts, 1997 (Address by President Ong Teng Cheong at the Opening of the Ninth Parliament on May 26, 1997); *Straits Times Weekly Edition*, May 15, 1999.

77 Ho Khai Leong, *The Politics of Policy-Making in Singapore*, Singapore: Oxford University Press, 2000, p. 211. Ho believes that despite consultation mechanisms, people feel they have no influence on policy-making.

78 *Straits Times Weekly Edition*, January 24, 1998. The fourth key area of focus is building up business infrastructure.

79 Lee Kuan Yew is clearly not enamored of the idea of calling Singapore a "Renaissance City". To him, it means reviving something old and focusing on arts and culture. He noted that to attempt to become a world class cultural center is a very expensive project, and even then, "the Bolshoi won't come here with only four million people". He thinks government should concentrate on the basics: economic development. He mentioned that the Renaissance City idea arose in the pre-Cabinet meetings that are held without him (interview with the Senior Minister, June 29, 2000).

80 Lydia Lim, "A $50m Boost for the Arts", *Straits Times Weekly Edition*, March 20, 2000.

81 Quoted in Goh Chok Tong, "Building a World Class City", *Speeches*, vol. 22, no. 1 (1998), p. 11.

82 We have been impressed on our visits to Singapore in the last decade that virtually everyone we have talked to, from academics and business people to taxi drivers, shopkeepers, and restaurant waiters, some of whom profess to support the Opposition, yet have had positive things to say about Prime Minister Goh personally.

83 Peter Schwartz, "Scenarios: 1,000 Singapores: The Way to End Poverty", *Red Herring Magazine*, August 2000, forwarded by sgdaily@list.singtercom.org on September 6, 2000.

84 *Asiaweek*, August 11, 1995, on the Web: http://www.cnn.com/ASIANOW/asiaweek;95/0811/nat5.html.

85 Russel Laurence Barsh, "Democratization and Development", *Human Rights Quarterly*, vol. 14, no. 1 (February 1992), p. 123.

86 Peter Smith, "Evaluating the Quality of Life in Singapore", *CAS Working Paper Series* (Centre for Advanced Studies, National University of Singapore), June 1994, p. 4.

87 See "Panel Discussion: Reflections on 'The Singapore Dream'", in *Singapore: The Year in Review 1996*, Singapore: Institute of Policy Studies, 1996, pp. 75–94.

88 Tan Sai Siong, "Who Says Slow Down? Just the Rich", *Straits Times Weekly Edition*, September 20, 1997.

89 David Chan Kum Wah, "Kiasuism and the Withering of Singapore Creativity", in Derek de Cunha (ed.), *Debating Singapore*, Singapore: Institute of Southeast Asian Studies, 1994, p. 71.

90 In a survey on national pride developed by the National Opinion Research Center in Chicago, a survey of 23 countries, Singapore tied for second place with the United States (Austria placed first). See *Singapore Magazine* (June–July 2000), pp. 17–19. Singaporeans scored high on national pride in all categories: gender, ethnicity, age, education, and income.

91 See the survey done by Tham Seong Chee, *Values and Development in Singapore*, Singapore: Department of Malay Studies, National University of Singapore, 1994, cited in Clark C. Neher, "The Case for Singapore", in Michael Haas (ed.), *The Singapore Puzzle*, Westport, CT: Praeger, 1999, pp. 46–8. Also see Donald K. Emmerson, "Singapore and the 'Asian Values' Debate", *Journal of Democracy*, vol. 6, no. 4 (October 1995), pp. 96–100; *Far Eastern Economic Review*, September 12, 1996; and David I. Hitchcock, *Asian Values and the United States: How Much Conflict?*, Washington, DC: Center for Strategic and International Studies, 1994.

92 Quoted in the *Globe and Mail*, November 25, 1994.

93 Chew Soon Beng *et al.*, *Values and Lifestyles of Young Singaporeans*, Singapore: Prentice Hall, 1998.

Index

Action for Aids 165
"Active Citizenship": *see* Singapore 21
Adams, John 53
administrative state 25, 29
Afghanistan 176
Africa 21
Air New Zealand 8, 73
Airbus 9
Albar, Syed Ja'afar 21–2
All-Party Constitutional Mission 15
America/American: *see* United States
America, Latin 34–5, 181
Amnesty International 130, 135
Ansett Holdings 73
Anson (constituency) 20, 46, 119, 138, 149
anti-colonialism 39
Arabs 99
arbitration 34
Aristotle 157
arrests 118, 130, 132, 180
Art Theatre Society 163
ASEAN (Association of Southeast Asian Nations) 2, 77, 82, 173, 176, 178, 181–4, 187
ASEAN+3 183
ASEAN Free Trade Area (AFTA) 181, 183
ASEAN Post-Ministerial Conference 182
ASEAN Regional Forum (ARF) 173, 181–2
ASEAN Special Officials Meeting 173
ASEAN-EU Ministerial Conference 181
Asia/Asian 1, 6, 8, 41, 61–2, 67, 71, 83, 102, 106, 109, 128, 131, 133, 160–1, 173, 175–6, 179–80, 182–4, 187, 191, 193, 197
Asia–Europe Meeting (ASEM) 119, 181, 183–4
Asia–Europe Vision Group Report (1999) 184
Asia–Pacific 128
Asia Pacific Economic Cooperation forum (APEC) 181, 183–4
Asia Watch 130
Asiaweek 118, 140, 148, 193
Asian development model 186
Asian Monetary Fund 183
Asian values 52, 57, 62, 102, 104
Asian Wall Street Journal 27, 140
Assembly, Legislative 5, 14, 20
Association of Muslim Professionals (AMP) (1991) 112, 162
Association of Women for Action and Research (AWARE) (1985) 159–60, 167
Attorney-General 27
Australia/Australian 18, 73, 79, 82, 117, 136, 172–3, 183, 190–1
authoritarian/authoritarianism 2, 53, 59, 62, 128–9, 140, 142
Automobile Association (of Singapore) 159
autonomy, state 36–7

Bangsar 21
banking, liberalization of: *see* Lee Hsien Loong
bankruptcy laws 80, 135
"Banyan tree" analogy 160
Barisan Sosialis 18, 20–1, 24, 31, 35–7, 40, 42–4, 96, 130, 149, 160
Barker, Eddie 38
Barsh, Russel L. 196
BBC World Service 137
Bell Curve 55
Bellows, Thomas J. 7
Berlin, Isaiah 197
bilateral relations 313, 176
bilingualism: *see* education
bio-medical sciences 83
bond-breakers 190
Borneo states (Sabah and Sarawak) 3, 18–19
Boston 71
"brain drain" 189
Britain/British (UK) 1–3, 5, 13–16, 18, 20, 22–3, 28, 32, 38–40, 57, 86, 99, 105, 130–1, 139, 158, 169, 170, 172, 184; withdrawal from military bases 66, 170, 172
British East India Company 2, 13
broadband: *see* Information Technology
Brunei 18–19, 173, 182–3
Buddhism/Buddhists 62, 92
Buena Vista Science Hub 69

buildings, ancient, in Southeast Asia 2, 5; old, in Singapore 2, 4–5
Bukit Merah 86
bureaucracy/bureaucrats 28–9, 40, 42, 131
Burke, Edmund 120
Bush Administration 180
business 4, 9, 16, 29, 33–6, 68–71, 74–6, 78, 80–1, 88, 90, 109, 112, 123, 126, 133, 144, 148, 157–8, 162–3, 172, 177, 178, 184, 187
Business Times, 138
"busyness" 35, 37

cabinet 15, 23, 26–7, 29, 33, 36, 40, 45–9, 95, 97, 111, 114–20, 124, 145, 153–4, 170, 194
Cable and Wireless 73
Cable and Wireless Optus Communications 73
Cambodia 5, 176, 181–2
Cambridge 5, 38, 120, 123, 133
campaigns (social, by the government) 11, 17, 59, 108, 159, 197
Canada 157, 191
caning 118, 130–1, 133
Cantonese 107
capital 30, 34, 36–7, 67–8, 72, 79, 87, 92, 183
capitalists/capitalism 37, 51, 64, 92
Cardinals (Roman Catholic) 41
Caribbean 105
Catholic Centre for Foreign Workers 130
Catholic priests and liberation theology 59
Catholic Welfare Centre 130
census (1824) 13
census (1980) 60, 107, 111
census (2000) 188
Central Provident Fund (CPF) 28, 32, 61–2, 70–1, 75, 82, 85–90, 94, 98, 110–11, 113, 123, 152, 155, 178, 191; compulsory nature 89; financial viability 88; functions 88; investments by members 87, 89; Minimum Sum Scheme 155; and reduction in employers' contributions 32, 61–2, 70–1, 82, 86, 123, 152; Supplementary Retirement Scheme 89; Topping-up Scheme 87–8, 152; wage deductions 110–11, 113
Chalmers, Ian 69
Chan Heng Chee 28, 46–7, 49, 52
Changi International Airport 9
Changi Jail 14, 161
Changi Naval Base 173–4
Channel NewAsia 191
checks and balances 27, 75
Chee Soon Juan 136, 138, 148, 163
Chen Shui-bian (Taiwan) 185
Cheng San (Group Representation Constituency) 134, 151
Chew, David 163
Chew, Melanie 142
Chia, Helen 188
Chia, Steve 148
Chia Thye Poh 130
Chiam See Tong 131, 146, 148–50, 152, 156
Chiang, Claire 161, 165
Chief Minister 14–15
Children Development Co-Saving Scheme 189
China 14, 17
China (People's Republic of China) 76–8, 82, 100, 102, 106–7, 124, 127, 132, 158, 172–6, 179–80, 183–5, 191; trade competition to Singapore and Southeast Asia from 82
China–Singapore Industrial Park (SIP): *see* Suzhou
"Chinatown" 5, 164
Chinese 18, 22, 39, 54, 56, 62, 64, 93, 99, 101–2, 108–9, 150, 155; Baba Chinese 57; businesses 68–9; chambers of commerce (*also see* Singapore Chinese Chambers of Commerce and Industry) 68, 101, 112, 158–9; clans and guilds (*also see* Singapore Federation of Chinese Clan Associations) 39, 101, 112; Communists 2, 106; cultural elite 106, 109–10; cultural values 5, 56–9, 62–4, 102, 106–7, 109, 134; and dialects 49, 99, 102, 107–8, 151; -educated 38–9, 47, 57, 99, 102, 106–8, 113, 134, 138, 151, 158, 161, 194–5; and education 46, 101–3, 106, 158; English-educated 45, 62, 102, 107–8, 134, 194; fertility rates 60, 187; immigration 13–14, 57, 110, 158; income 22; and Japanese occupation 14; language "chauvinists" 99, 106–7, 134, 151; and language issues 46, 56–7, 102, 106–7, 134; and Mandarin 46, 106–8, 110, 113, 127, 134; and the military 125, 170, 175; newspapers (*also see Lianhe Zaobao, Shin Min, Wanbao*) 101, 108; opera 38; philanthropy 158; political thought 52; "Protectorate" 14; secret societies: *see* Triads; -speaking 15, 40, 108, 151; and Special Assistance Plan (SAP) schools 47, 56, 104, 106, 109, 127; working class, 36, 39, 99, 102, 113, 149–51
Chinese Development Assistance Council (CDAC) 112–13
Christian Conference of Asia 130
Christians/Christianity (*also see* Student Christian Movement) 99, 131, 134
Chua Beng-Huat 52, 63, 128
Chua Kim Yeow 153
Chua Lee Hoong 49
CIQ (Customs, Immigration and Quarantine) facilities 178
Citizens' Consultative Committees (CCCs) 95–6, 149

"civic society" (*also see* civil society) 157–8, 160
civil defense 109
civil rights 128
civil service 27–9, 32, 37, 48, 55–6, 125–6, 153, 175; and top civil servants salaries 54, 56, 60–1
civil society (*also see* "civic society") 2, 141, 155–68; emergence in Singapore 160–7; future 167–8; historical setting 158–9; models or types of 157–8
Clammer, John 64, 100
Clark Air Base (Philippines) 173
class (*also see* middle class) 25, 36–7, 39, 44, 52–6, 102, 117, 128, 148–51, 155, 195
Clinton, Bill 118
Cobbold Commission Report 18
Cold War 180
commerce 69–70, 78, 101, 104
Committee to Promote Enterprise Overseas 124
Committee on Singapore's Competitiveness 68–9, 71
Common Market (Singapore-Malaysia) 3, 19, 23, 66–7
Commonwealth 181
communism/Communists 2, 14–18, 20–1, 39–42, 49, 96, 106, 129–31, 149, 158–9, 161, 183
communitarianism 52, 57–8, 63–4, 128, 197
Community Centres 95; and Management Committees of 43, 95
Community Development Councils (CDCs) 85, 96–8
competitiveness 8, 68–9, 71, 133, 193
confrontation 66
Confucian thought/Confucianism 6, 52–3, 57–8, 62–4, 102, 104, 128
conscription: *see* National Service
consensus 34, 63–4, 102, 157, 182, 184, 193
Constitution/constitutional 13–14, 16, 20, 23, 25, 28, 36, 51, 59, 64, 77, 100, 109, 132–4, 144, 150, 153–4, 162
constitutional conferences, 1957 and 1958 16
constitutionalism 7
consumer culture 64
Core values: *see* Asian values, Shared Values
corporatism 34–5
Corrupt Practices Investigation Bureau 27
corruption 4, 7, 16–17, 27, 29, 44, 54, 61, 70, 72, 124, 134, 155, 184, 192–3
"cosmopolitans" 81, 99, 194
cost of living 148, 150–1, 189
Cotton, James 25
Council of Presidential Advisors 45, 154
creativity 10, 79, 104, 186, 197
Criminal Law (Temporary Provisions) Act (CLA) 129, 133
crown colony 13–14
Cuba 18
currencies 71, 177, 194

Davos (Switzerland) 189
death penalty 130, 133
debts 70, 74
Defence Minister, Australia 73
Defence Science and Technology Agency (DSTA) 172
Defence Science Organization (DSO) 172
defense (*also see* deterrence, Ministry of Defence (MINDEF), Singapore Armed Forces, "Total Defence Initiative") 8, 16, 19, 74, 109, 134, 170–5, 180, 185
defense industry 171–2
Defense News 177
deficits 70
democracy 2, 6, 128, 147–8, 155–7, 163, 168, 189, 192, 196; types of 6, 57, 64, 98, 102, 128–9, 143
democratic 6, 128–9, 180, 193, 196
Democratic Party 15
democratization 128, 186, 192, 197
Deng Xiaping 179
dependency school 67
depoliticization 28
detainees 16, 20, 128, 130, 161
detention without trial 129
deterrence 169–75
Deutsche Bank 82
Development Bank of Singapore (DBS) 62, 72–3, 75
Dewey, John 52
Dhanabalan, S. 46–7, 75, 84, 86, 89, 106, 150, 181
Diamond, Larry 129
diplomacy 175–85
Directorship and Consultancy Appointments Council (DCAC) 29
Disabled People's Association 131
Divine Light Mission 132
drugs/drug trafficking 129–31
Dukakis, Michael 139
Dutch 13

East India Company: *see* British East India Company
"East of Suez" 172
East Timor 173, 176, 180, 183
East Timor Alert Network 157
Eastern European dissidents 157
Eastern Sun 137
Economic Development Board (EDB) 4, 8–9, 67–9, 77–8, 85–6, 90, 191
economic recessions, crises: 1985, 1997, 2001 8, 61–2, 70–1, 81–3, 86, 119–20, 123, 152–3, 180, 182, 184, 187, 191, 194, 197
Economist, The 130, 140

education 1, 4, 17, 19, 35, 42, 44, 46–7, 55–9, 76, 80–1, 83, 87, 92, 94, 99–113, 127, 155–6, 159, 170, 184, 187–90, 193, 195, 197; All Party Committee Report (1956) 10; bilingual schemes 100–1, 103–4; Chinese language "B" syllabus 108; compulsory education 106, 110–12; drop outs 103, 110; and economic advancement 60, 83, 100, 109; English and "mother tongue" bilingualism 47, 100, 103, 107, 127, 189; examinations 55, 110; Goh Report (Report on the Ministry of Education, 1978) 103–4; and Information Technology 105; integrated schools 101; kindergartens 44; Madrasah schools (*also see* Muslim–Malays) 106, 110–11; moral education 53, 58, 63, 104; Moral Education, Report on (1979) 104; National Education Program (NE) 105; national schools 106; New Education System (NES) 104, 110; policy 53, 102–6; Primary School Leaving Examination (PSLE) 110–11; Religious Knowledge 62, 104; Special Assistance Plan schools (SAP): *see* Chinese; streaming 55, 104; tertiary 47, 53, 56, 60, 87, 101, 105, 109, 112, 158, 187–8, 190, 197; "Thinking Schools, Learning Nation" 105; vernacular schools 104 (*also see* Chinese, Indians, Malays; women)
Egypt 169
elections and campaigns for 2, 38, 41–3, 49, 64, 94, 107, 138, 140, 143, 147; 1948, 1949, 1951 elections 2; 1955 election 3, 5, 14; 1957 (city council) election 16–17; 1959 election 3, 5, 16–17, 36, 38, 67, 160; 1961 by-elections 20, 139; 1963 election 16, 21, 36, 40; 1965 by-election 24; 1968, 1972, 1976, 1980 elections 24, 48, 117, 149; 1981 by-election 46, 119, 138, 144, 149; 1988 election 136, 150; 1991 election 46, 69, 119, 150–1; 1997 election 46, 99, 134–6, 141, 145, 148, 151, 161–2; 2001 election 83, 120, 124–5, 136, 140–1, 151–3 (*also see* Presidential elections); reasons for holding elections 14, 38, 143, 155
elections (Malaysia, 1964) 11, 19, 21
electoral innovations (*also see* Group Representation Constituency, Nominated Member of Parliament, Non-Constituency Member of Parliament, Town Councils) 144–6; automatic registration 143; compulsory voting 143; electoral system 143–6; first-past-the-post (majoritarian) 143, 150; honest and accurate voting and vote-counting conduct 143; one-person, one-vote 146; rejection of proportional representation or mixed system 143; single and multiple-member constituencies 143–5, 152; universal suffrage 128
electorate 2, 21, 40, 144, 149–50, 153
electronic road pricing 10
electronics 68, 70, 78–9, 82–4, 187
elites/elitism 1, 38, 44–5, 51–5, 59–60, 64–5, 109
"Emergency, the" 1, 14
emigration 108, 160, 186–7, 189–90
Emmerson, Donald 140
"employability" 81
employers (*also see* business, capital) 8, 31–2, 34, 49, 61–3, 66, 81–3, 86, 109, 123, 191
employment 10, 31, 69, 74, 81–2, 87, 90, 101, 125, 190
Employment Act (1968) 31
England 26
England, Victorian 57
English 26, 133; language 57, 62, 100–10, 126, 138, 151, 156, 178, 189
environment 4, 124, 157, 159, 174–5, 178, 186
"Esplanade" (Theatres on the Bay) 124, 195
ethnic groups 14, 56, 99–101, 107, 187, 194–5
ethnicity 1, 25, 56, 62, 93, 99–100, 102, 110, 113
eugenics 54–5, 60, 159
Eunos (constituency) 136
Eurasian Association 112
Eurasians 56, 99
Europe 1, 30, 34–5, 67, 127, 184
EU (European Union) 181, 184
exports 3, 70–1, 82–3
Eysenck, H. J. 55

Falun Buddha Society: *see* Falungong
Falungong 132
family 35, 41–2, 57, 62–3, 69, 73, 87–8, 92, 99, 104, 112, 116, 134, 157, 188–9, 193, 197
Far Eastern Economic Review 40, 153
fascism 53
Fay, Michael 118
Feedback Conference 156
Feedback Unit 63, 156
Films Act 138–9
Finland 80
First World "oasis" 4, 79
Five Power Defence Arrangements (FPDA) 172, 177
flexi-wage 34
Fong Sip Chee 45
Fong Swee Suan 39
Foreign Affairs, creation of a department of 8
Foreign Direct Investment (FDI), 176, 193
foreign policy: *see* deterrence, diplomacy
foreign talent (*also see* talent, shortage of), 110, 152, 166, 190–2
foreign technologies 68

foreign workers 54, 69, 130
Fortune Magazine 195
Forum for East Asia-Latin America Cooperation (FEALAC) 181
"Forward Defence" 170
free trade 82, 183
Freedom House 128
Fukuyama, Francis 128
Furnivall, J.S. 99

Gaebler, Ted 193
Gandhi, Indira 110
George, Cherian 45, 134, 142
George, T.J.S. 90
German business (in China) 76
Geylang 21, 101
Gibbons, David S. 155
Global Business Network 196
globalization 2, 70, 72, 78, 81–2, 121, 175, 186–7, 190
"Go Regional" economic policy (1993) 179, 184
Goh Chok Tong (principal references only) 9, 54, 63, 96–8, 122, 126–7, 156, 160–1, 168, 175, 186, 189, 191–6; achievements 119, 193–6; and ASEAN 173, 176, 181–4; on corruption 7, 54, 192–3; on criteria for good governance 193; and defamation suits 134–6; early days 117; on the economy 69, 73, 76, 78, 82, 87–8, 186, 193; and education 99–100, 106, 109, 111–12; and ethnicity 99–100, 106, 109–12, 132; on foreign policy 175, 177–8, 183; future plans 120; ideology and values 58–9, 62–3; leadership style 118–19, 121, 131, 152, 160; and Lee Kuan Yew 58, 114, 116–20, 122, 193; National Day speeches 82, 87, 165, 186, 191; and OB Markers 141–2, 161–2, 165, 167; and PAP 41–2, 44, 48; political career before becoming PM 32, 41, 44, 47–8, 117; on population 187–9: and salaries 61; and Singapore's image 48; and his succession as PM 8, 28, 114–16; ups and downs 119–20, 149–53 (*also see* Lee Hsien Loong, Lee Kuan Yew)
Goh Keng Swee 4, 9, 31, 38, 45, 57, 66–7, 76–7, 79, 90, 103
Gomez, James 163
good governance 192–3
good government 9, 17, 59, 62, 193
Gopinathan, S. 103
government (principal references only) 25–6, 30, 32–5 (*also see* People's Action Party)
Government of Singapore Investment Corporation (GIC) 74, 89
Government-linked Companies (GLCs) 29, 32, 36–7, 72–6, 88–9, 126, 137
Graduate Mother Scheme 6, 11, 53–4, 60, 64, 150, 159
Grenada 176
Group of 77 181
Group Representation Constituency (GRC) 110, 144–6, 151–2
growth, economic 5, 31, 58, 61–2, 66, 68–71, 73, 82, 84, 87, 90, 113, 128, 187, 192, 194
Growth Triangle 77–8
"Guanxi" 41
Gulf War 110

Habibie, B. J. 178
Hammer, The 135
Harvard 79, 120–1, 123–5
Head, Lord Antony 23
"heartlanders" 81, 99, 194
Hello Chok Tong, Goodbye Kuan Yew 139
High Court: *see* judiciary
Hindus 99, 104
Ho Ching 73–4, 172
Hobbesian world 176
Hock Lee Bus riots (1955) 39
Hokkien (*also see* Chinese language, dialects) 4, 16, 99, 107–8, 127, 196
homeland security framework 171
Hon Sui Sen 3, 45, 117
Hong Kah (Group Representation Constituency) 148
Hong Kong 8, 14, 71, 133–4, 183, 191
Hong Lim (constituency) 6
Hong Lim Park 162, 164
hostility towards Singapore's PAP government 11
Hougang (constituency) 149
housing 2–4, 9, 11, 36, 41, 52, 56, 87, 89–95, 146, 191, 194
Housing and Development Board (HDB) 9, 85–6, 90–5; emphasis on flats 91, 93; ethnic considerations 56, 92–93, 101; government need to control 92; improvements in quality 91; ownership 90, 94; resistance to giving up land 91–3; upgrading 93–4, 152, 194; variations in value 95
Housing and Urban Development Company 91
Hsiao Kung-chuan 52
Hu Tsu Tao, Richard 30, 71, 74, 82, 153–4
human rights 57, 64, 128, 130, 133, 157, 163, 179–81, 184, 192
Huntington, S. P. 128–9, 186
Huxley, Tim 174
Hyde Park (London) 164

ideology (*also see* Confucianism, elitism, multiculturalism, National Ideology, pragmatism, Shared Values, values) 1, 51–65, 102, 128, 155

immigration 14, 54, 131, 159, 178, 190–1
import substitution 3, 66–7
incentives 35, 55, 60, 69, 79, 89, 188
income gap (resulting from globalization) 81
India 13, 42, 76, 82, 129, 145, 155, 169, 172, 184–5, 191
Indians 13, 47, 56, 63, 99, 101–2, 109, 112; education 112; language 56, 100, 135, 137, 156; Muslims 99
Indonesia 5, 10, 13, 18, 23–4, 66, 73, 77, 99, 137, 174, 176, 178–9, 182–4, 187, 197
industrial relations 66
Industrial Relations (Amendment) Act 1969 31
industrialization 3, 5, 8, 31, 36, 66, 68–9
inequality 55
Information Technology (IT) 49, 71, 80–2, 105, 112, 124, 127–8, 187–7, 189, 191 (*also see* Knowledge-based Economy)
innovation 28, 79–80, 83, 105, 132, 144–6, 150, 186
Institute of East Asian Philosophies 58
Institute of International Affairs (Singapore) 121
Institute of Policy Studies 63, 160
Internal Security Act (ISA) 18–20, 39, 129–30, 133–4, 136
Internal Security Department (ISD) 130
International Commission of Jurists (IJC) 135
International Herald Tribune 140
International Human Rights Day (2000) 133
International Institute of Management Development (Switzerland) 133
international non-governmental organizations (INGOs) 168
International Singapore Companies (ISCs) 74
Internet 42, 61, 80–1, 105, 108, 140–1, 160–2, 165, 186
Internet Service Providers 140
Inter-racial Confidence Circles (ICC) 113
investment abroad by Singapore ("external wing") 9, 76–7
investment, foreign 9, 67, 77, 79
Irvine of Lairg, Lord High Chancellor 133
Islam/Islamic 99–100, 104, 106, 174, 179; Madrasah Islamic schools 106, 110–11; terrorist cells 113, 151, 171, 274, 180 (*also see* Jemaah Islamiah); values 111, 159
Israel/Israeli 3, 109, 169–71, 177
Istana Annex 116

Jakarta: *see* Indonesia
James, William 52
Jane's Intelligence Review 171
Japan 14, 69, 82, 92, 132, 137, 183–4, 187
Japanese invasion and occupation 1, 13–14, 46, 117, 130
Javanese 99
Jayakumar, S. 133, 176, 183
Jefferson, Thomas 53
Jehovah's Witnesses 132
Jek Yuen Thong 45
Jemaah Islamiah (Islamic Group) 180
Jeyaretnam, J.B. 7, 111, 131, 134–5, 144, 147–51, 163
Jiang Zemin 76, 179
Johor 13, 77, 174, 177
Johor, Sultan of 13
judiciary 26–7, 132–6; appointments 133; Chief Justice 133; civil law 133; commercial law 133; Court of Appeal 133; criticism of being compliant 132–3, 140; High Court 27, 133; international praise for 132–3; judicial commissioners 133; judicial review 132–3; jury system 133; "strict construction" 27, 132; subordinate courts 133; Supreme Court 133 (*also see* Law of Defamation)
Jurong (constituency) 136
Jurong bird park 5
Jurong project 3, 8–9, 67, 78
Jurong Town Corporation 67

Kallang Basin 4
Karyawan (journal of AMP) 162
Kazakhstan 184
KBE: *see* Knowledge-Based Economy
Keppel Corporation 72–3, 126
Khairat (Malay self-help groups) 158
Khaw Boon Wan 125
Khoo, Eric 161
"kiasuism" 196
"killer-litter" 92
Knowledge-Based Economy (KBE) 1, 12, 27, 68, 75, 78, 83, 105, 124, 127, 186
Koh, Tommy 159
Kuala Lumpur: *see* Malaysia
Kuwait 176

Labor 19, 30–1, 33–4, 36–7, 66–7, 69, 77, 103, 144, 157, 188–9, 191
Labour Front 15–16
Labour Party (UK) 5, 184
land 4, 9, 14, 22, 36, 71, 77, 86, 90–1, 93, 171, 173, 178, 186
languages 81, 99, 106–7; official 56, 100, 137, 164
Laos 182
Latif, Asad 54
Latin America 34–5, 181
Lau, Albert 23
Law of Defamation (Libel) 133–6, 140, 161, 165, 167
law, rule of 2, 7, 132, 163, 192–3
Law Society 131, 136
Lee, B.G.: *see* Lee Hsien Loong

Lee Hsien Loong (B.G. Lee) (principal references only) 7, 10, 29, 42, 48, 56, 63, 69, 72–7, 79, 109, 111, 116, 126–7, 134, 142, 151, 166–8, 172, 177, 182, 194, 196; and banking, liberalization of 75–6; early life, education, and military career 120–1; and economic crises of 1985, 1997, 2001 70; and economic globalization 78; enters politics 120–1; and GLCs 73, 75; and Goh Chok Tong 116, 119, 122, 194; and KBE 78; and Lee Kuan Yew 122–3; and MAS 121; personality and outlook 116, 121–2; political adeptness in making policies acceptable 123; and values 63, 121
Lee Hsien Yang 73
Lee Khoon Choy (K.C. Lee) 45
Lee Kuan Yew (principal references only) 15–16, 25, 32, 59, 74, 76–7, 79, 103, 105–6, 111, 127, 130, 134–5, 138–9, 145–6; on absence of personality cult 6; and Asian values 57–8, 61, 102; and Confucianism 58; and corruption 7, 41, 134; dealings with Communists/pro-Communists 6, 17, 20, 31, 39–40, 129; and the economy 3–4, 55, 70; as elitist 54; on English 62, 102, 109; and eugenics 55; and foreign policy 169–70, 173–4, 176–9, 182–4; and formation of the PAP 38–40; and Goh Chok Tong 114–16, 118–19, 127, 193–4; and the "greening" of Singapore 4; and housing 90–2, 101; and ideologies 51; and joining and leaving Malaysia 18–24; and Lee Hsien Loong 116, 121–3; and "Lee's Lieutenants" 5, 38; and liberal democracy 6–7, 129; and meritocracy 6, 115; and National Day speeches 55, 62; and OB Markers 166; and the "Old Guard" (*also see* PAP, party renewal *below*) 45–6; on PAP policies on coming to power 3–5; and para-political organizations 95–6; and party renewal 44–6; and population policies 60, 150; and rationality 52; on search for talent 6, 47–9, 115, 126; as Senior Minister 8, 61, 120, 184, 194; study in Singapore and at Cambridge 5; succession policy 7–8, 28–9, 45–6, 114–16; as world statesman 184–5 (*also see* PAP, Suzhou)
Lee Siew Choh 24, 144
Lee Teng-hui (Taiwan) 185–6
Lee Tsao Yuan 30
Legislative Assembly: *see* Assembly, Legislative
Leifer, Michael 9, 36, 119, 169, 175–6, 181, 184
Lianhe Zaobao 108, 134
Li Ka-shing 73
Li, Richard 73
Li, Tania 111
libel: *see* Law of Defamation
life sciences 78, 83
Lim Boon Heng 32, 34, 81, 123, 126, 188
Lim, Catherine 139, 141, 161
Lim Chee Onn 32–3, 125–6
Lim Cheng Tju 139
Lim Chin Siong 24, 39
Lim Chong Yah 74
Lim, David Tik En 124, 127, 166, 168
Lim Hng Kiang 124, 127
Lim Jim Koon 134
Lim Kim San 23, 45, 85, 91
Lim Yew Hock 15–16, 18, 39
Lingle, Christopher 140
lingua franca 110
"Little India" 5
Lizee, Pierre 168
location, importance for Singapore 9, 176, 186
London 15–16, 19, 38, 124, 164, 184
Louis XIV 25
Low, Linda 70, 72, 89
Low Thia Khiang 30, 147–8, 152
Lower Peirce Reservoir 159

Machinda (Sarawak party) 22
Mah Bow Tan 88
Mahathir Mohamad 4, 51, 73, 138, 174, 177–9; "Mahathirism" 51
Mahbubani, Kishore 181
Maintenance of Religious Harmony Act 100, 131
Malacca 13
Malacca, Straits of 13
Malays, Malay-Muslims (*also see* education, ethnicity, self-help, Mendaki) 13, 21, 56, 99–100, 110–12, 145, 150–1, 158, 177, 187; and cultural deficit thesis 111; language 56, 103; in the military 102, 109–10, 170, 177; and religion 100, 110–11; special position of 19, 23, 100; uprooted when giving up land 91, 93, 101; views of Malaysian Malays 22, 169, 177
Malay sultanate 110
Malaya, Federation of (1957) (*also see* "Emergency") 1–3, 5, 14, 16, 18–19, 22, 40, 59, 103
Malayalam 99
Malayan/Malaysian Chinese Association (MCA) 19, 21–2, 24
Malayan/Malaysian Communist Party (MCP) 15, 40, 95
Malayan Forum 38
Malayan Nature Society (1954) 159
Malaysia, Federation of (1963) 3, 10, 42, 47, 67, 133, 173, 176–8, 182–3; concern by Singapore over Islam 174; conflict between Singapore and Malaysia in 19, 21–3; formation of 3, 18–20, 66, 149; in

FPDA 172, 177; Johor Baru incident (1997) 177; Singapore Malays "better off" 177; Singapore separation 3, 10, 20–3, 169; stormy relations since separation 23, 73, 138, 174, 177, 183; visit of Israeli President to Singapore (1986) 177
"Malaysian Malaysia" 22–4
Malaysian Solidarity Convention 22
Management Committees: *see* Community Centres
Mandarin (*also see* Chinese) 11, 45–6, 56, 58, 100–1, 106–10, 113, 115
Manoilesco, M. 34
manufacturing 3, 67, 69–71, 79, 82–4
Marcos, Ferdinand 6–7
Marine Parade (constituency) 117
Marshall, David 15–16, 18, 20, 131
Marxist plot (*also see* arrests) 118, 130, 161
MAS: *see* Monetary Authority of Singapore
mass beliefs 60–2, 64
mass media 2, 20, 38, 63, 103, 109, 137–41, 147, 155, 164, 167, 177, 180
Mass Rapid Transit (MRT) 109, 149
masses 15, 17, 51, 59, 64, 95–6
Matsushita Electric Co 69
mayors (of CDCs) 97–8, 194
MediaCorp 137
Medisave 87, 184
Medishield 87
Megawati Sukarnoputri 179
"melting pot" 56, 101
Mendaki (Yayasan Mendaki: Council for the Education of Muslim Children) 111–12
Mendaki II (Council for the Development of the Singaporean Muslim Community) 112
meritocracy 6–7, 27, 52, 55–6, 65, 79, 100, 105, 109, 113, 115
"Mexicans", Israeli advisors described as 169–70
Michels, Robert 53
Micropolis 74
middle class 36–7, 39, 102, 117, 128, 148, 150–1, 155
Middle Road 15
military, the 27–8 (*also see* SAF)
Minangkabau 99
Minister for/Ministry of Defence (MINDEF) 123–4, 170, 172, 175
Minister for/Ministry of Education 76, 103, 106, 124
Minister for/Ministry of the Environment 124
Minister for/Ministry of Finance 7, 66, 71, 82, 117, 124, 154, 179
Minister for/Ministry of Foreign Affairs 176, 181
Minister for/Ministry of Home Affairs (MHA) 41, 141, 164
Minister for/Ministry of Information and the Arts (MITA) 123–4, 166
Minister for/Ministry of National Development 23, 90–1
Minister for/Ministry of Trade and Industry 42, 71, 74, 117, 124
ministerial and top civil servants salaries 7, 54, 56, 60–2, 83, 151
Monetary Authority of Singapore (MAS) 75, 121
"Money, No Enough" 108
Moore, British Deputy High Commissioner Philip 40
moral education: *see* education
Mosca, Gaetano 53
multiculturalism: *see* multiracialism
multilateral defense arrangements 172–4
multinational corporations (MNCs) 3–4, 34, 36–7, 66–9, 92; investment by 67–8; transfer of technology by 68
multiracialism 52, 56, 59, 64, 93
Murray, Charles and Richard Bernstein 55
Myanmar 172, 182, 184

Nair, C.V. Devan 21, 32, 126
"Nanny state" 11, 35, 197
Nantah: *see* Nanyang University
Nanyang University (Nantah) 53, 101–2, 107, 148, 158
Napier Road 43
Nathan, S.R. 154–5, 175
National Aero-Space Administration (NASA) 49
National Arts Council 195
National Council of Churches 159
National Ideology (*also see* ideology, Shared Values) 62–3, 102, 155
National Innovation Council 83
National Service 83, 90, 101–2, 109, 170, 175, 191
National Solidarity Party (1987) 148
National Trades Union Congress (NTUC) 7, 31–7, 81, 123–4, 153; Education and Training Fund 81; Lifelong Learning Fund 81; Skills Development Programme 81
National University of Singapore (NUS) 101
National Volunteer Centre (*also see* Singapore 21, Voluntary Welfare Organizations) 167
National Wages Council (NWC) 4, 31, 33–4, 70, 82
nation-building 100, 159
nationalism 5, 46, 59, 113, 190
Nature Society (Singapore) (NSS) (1991) 159, 163
Neptune Orient Lines 32, 117
Net Investment Income (NII) 154
Netherlands, The 66
New Economy 78–80, 88, 140, 186
New Education System: *see* education
New Nation 137

New York 22
New Zealand 8, 18, 73, 82, 172–3, 183, 191
Newspaper and Printing Presses Act 27, 131, 137–9
Nominated Member of Parliament (NMP) (*also see* electoral innovations) 26, 134, 137–9, 144–5, 161, 165
Non-aligned Movement 181
Non-Constituency Member of Parliament (NCMP) (*also see* electoral innovations, opposition) 135–6, 144
Non-Governmental Organization (NGO) 59, 118, 159, 167–8, 195
Noronha, Llewellyn 103
North Borneo: *see* Sabah
Northeast Asia 180, 184
Northern Ireland 100

OECD (Organization for Economic Co-Operation and Development) 192
oil 19, 66, 70, 129, 175
old guard: *see* People's Action Party
Ong Chit Chung 166
Ong Eng Guan 5, 16–17, 24
Ong Keng Yong (as Press Secretary to the PM) 10, 95, 118, 138, 141–2
Ong Pang Boon 21, 45–6
Ong Teng Cheong 29, 115, 126, 151, 153–4, 194
Open Singapore Centre 148, 164
Opposition, The 2, 26, 28, 35, 38, 43, 45, 60, 64, 94–5, 98, 102, 109, 111, 118, 120, 128, 130–1, 144–5, 149–53, 155, 163–6, 196; "by-election strategy" 150–2; obstacles and constraints 128, 134–6, 138–41, 143, 146–9, 152; parties of personality 145–6; parties of pressure 146 (*also see* Law of Defamation)
Optus Communications: *see* Cable and Wireless Optus Communications
"Out of Bounds" Markers (OB Markers) (*also see* Goh Chok Tong) 141–2, 162, 165–7
Oversea Chinese Banking Corporation (OCBC) 45
Overseas Union Bank (OUB) 45

"Papa knows best" 35
para-political organizations 40, 43, 95–8
Pareto, Vilfredo 53
Paris 15
Parliament 5, 7, 26–7, 30–1, 33, 37, 45–6, 49, 61, 63–4, 71, 74, 76, 98, 106, 111, 117, 120, 126, 131–5, 137–9, 143–8, 153–5, 159–61, 164–6, 175, 188, 190, 197
Parliament (Malaysian) 19, 22
Parliamentary Elections Act (1996) 145
Parliamentary Elections (Amendment) Act (2001, suspended October 2001) 143
Parliamentary Pensions Act 46
Parliamentary Special Select Committee 144
Pasir Ris 123
patriotism 59, 65, 103, 105, 113
Peirce, Charles 52
Pempel, T.J. 194
Penang 13
People Like Us 168
People's Action Party (PAP) (1954) (principal references only) 1–12, 38–60; backbenchers 46, 145, 165–6; branches 20, 39–44, 95, 158; and Cabinet (principal references only) 26–7, 29, 36, 40, 45–9, 97, 106, 111, 114–20, 145, 153–4, 194; cadre system 39–41, 47, 54; candidate selection 48–9; Central Executive Committee (CEC) (formerly Executive Committee) 16, 21, 32, 39–43, 45, 48–8, 116; and centralization of power 38–9; committees 39, 43–4; conferences 16, 39; and contributions from Ministers and MPs 43; and co-opting talent 10, 38, 44–5, 47–9, 115, 117, 126–7; as dominant party 38, 40, 42, 49, 143, 146, 149–50, 160, 194; and the economy 67–84; founder generation (*also see individual names*) 13, 114; fund-raising 43; General Elections Committee 40–1; and grassroots organizations 43–4; HQ Executive Committee (HQ Exco) 42; and institutionalization 44; and kindergartens 44; and meet-the-people sessions 43; membership 41, 44; and merger referendum (1962) 20; Ops Centre 42; origins 38–9; and PAP Community Foundation (PFC) 44; party bureaucracy 42; party elections 39–41; party officials 40; party workers 41, 43; and "performance legitimacy" 153; and political succession 45, 114–16; recruitment 46–8; renewal 44–6; Secretary-General 40, 44. 116; and the split (1961) 20, 40, 43, 149; structure and organization 17, 40–1, 44; support for 53, 143, 149–53; as a team 48, 114–15, 194; and "united front" 39; and walkabouts 43–4; Women's League (1955) 42; Women's Wing (1989) 40, 42, 44; Young PAP (YP) (1986) 40–2, 44 (*also see* defense, deterrence, diplomacy, education, elections, ethnicity, housing, ideology, Law of Defamation, mass media, MCP, NTUC, Opposition, para-political organizations)
People's Association (PA) 95
People's Progressive Party (Malaya/Malaysia) 22
People's Republic of China: *see* China
PERC (Political and Economic Risk Consultancy, Ltd) 133, 193

PERGAS (Association of Islamic Scholars and Religious Teachers) 110
Permanent Secretary to the Prime Minister's Office 188
Perth 190
Pertubohan Kebangsaan Melayu Singapura (PKMS) [Singapore Malay National Association] 145, 148
Petir (PAP journal) (*also see* People's Action Party) 44–5
Petro-chemicals 70
Petroleum 68, 70
Phey Yew Kok 7
Philippines, the/Filipinos 6, 18, 59, 173, 184
Phua Chua Kang Pte. Ltd. (television comedy) 105
Pioneer Industries Employees Union (PIEU) 31
Plato 129
"Poison shrimp" idiom 170
Police 11, 109, 133–5, 163–4, 170–1; neighborhood police posts 92, 164
Political Donations Act (2001) 147
Political and Economic Risk Consultancy Ltd: see PERC
political participation 42, 121, 128, 131, 140–1, 145, 155–6, 161, 165, 167, 192, 195–6
political rights 2, 128, 147–8
Political Secretary 95, 120
political socialization 1, 58–60, 64–6, 100
Political Study Centre 27
political succession 7–8, 29, 38, 46, 97, 114, 116, 122–7, 149, 186
Pope, The 41
population 2, 13, 54, 59, 66, 97 99, 101, 170, 187–90
population growth 10, 66
population policy 10, 52–3, 55, 190
Port of Singapore Authority 9, 149
Porter, Michael 79
Portugal 34–5
Positivists 53
Potong Pasir (constituency) 148–50
Poulantzas, Nico 36
power, location of 25–37
pragmatism 4, 52–3, 64, 177
President (elected) 26, 37, 117, 128, 133, 143–4, 153–4, 175, 194; misunderstandings about discretionary powers 26, 28, 153–4, 194; national elections for (1993, 1999) 153–5; reasons for 153; refining presidential powers (1994, 1996, 1997, 1998, 1999) 154; requirements for candidacy (*also see* Presidential Elections Committee) 153; White papers on (1991, 1999) 153–4
Presidential Advisors, Council of: *see* Council of Presidential Advisors
Presidential Council 26, 56
Presidential Elections Committee 155
President's Scholars 120, 123–4, 170
press, the (*also see* mass media) 137–8, 161
Press Secretary to the Prime Minister 10, 95, 118, 134, 141–2
pressure groups 118 (*also see* civil society)
Prime Minister's Office (PMO) 27, 43
privatization 72
Pro-Communists: *see* communism/Communists
procreation pattern 60, 188
Progressive Party 15
"Project Wrangler": *see* Singapore Armed Forces
Protestant ethic 57
Public Entertainments Act 136
Public Sector Divestment Committee 72
Public Service Division 191
Pulau Tekong (island) 174
Puthucheary, James 20
Putrajaya: *see* Malaysia

Radio Beijing 137
Radio Corporation of Singapore 137
Radio Japan 137
Radio Moscow 137
R&D (Research and Development) 69
Raffles College 5, 47
Raffles Hotel 1
Raffles Institution 117
Raffles, Sir Stamford 13, 110
Rahman, Tunku Abdul: *see* Tunku Abdul Rahman
Rajaratnam, S. 21, 23, 38, 45, 49, 51, 53, 58, 111
Referendum on Singapore joining Malaysia (1962) 20
Registrar of Societies (*also see* Societies Act) 168
religion 53, 58, 99–100, 103, 109, 177
Religious Knowledge courses 62, 104
Renaissance City report 195
Rendel Commission 14
Renong group 73
Report of the Committee on Singapore's Competitiveness (1998) 68–9, 71
Report of the Economic Committee (1986) 10
Report on Moral Education 1979 104
reserves (economic) 26, 70–1, 153–4
Residents' Committees 43, 95–6
Resnick, Philip 157
Reuters 136
Review Committee 2001 83
Riau islands 24, 77
riots 15, 20–1, 39, 93, 100, 113
risks (business) 68, 74, 78–80, 83–4, 87, 172
Ritz Hotel, London 19
Rodan, Garry 35–7, 130, 140, 157–8
Roundtable (1994) 141–2
Rousseau, Jean-Jacques 53

"rugged society" 51
Rulers (Malaya/Malaysia) 19

Sabah 3, 18–19
salaries: *see* ministerial salaries, wages
sanctions 131
Sarawak 3, 18–19, 22
Sarawak United People's Party (SUPP) 22
savings 11, 35, 81, 86–9, 94
Schmitter, Philippe 34–5
scholastic achievement 47, 55–6, 170
Schumpeter, Joseph 129
Schwartz, Peter 196
secondary associations 157
secret societies: *see* triads
Sedition Act 137
self-help 111–13, 157–8 (*also see* Chinese Development Assistance Council, Eurasian Association, Mendaki, Singapore Indian Development Association)
Selkirk, Lord 20
Sembawang Corporation 73
Seoul 184
Seow, Francis 131, 136, 148
Separation from Malaysia 3, 23, 66, 69
Serangoon Road 101
Sesser, Stan 193
Shanmugaratnam, Tharman 125
Shared Values 63–4, 102 (*also see* National Ideology)
Shares, "New Singapore" 82, 152
Shell 4, 49
Sheridan, Greg 117
Shin Min 108
Sikhs 99, 104
Sim Kek Tong 148
Sin Chew Jit Poh 137
Singam, Constance 167
Singapore, location of 9, 169, 186; size 9–10, 42, 54, 60, 78, 91, 169, 173, 177, 186–7
Singapore Airlines 72–3
Singapore Armed Forces (SAF) (tri-service) 194; civilian control of 175; ethnicity 110, 170, 177; peacekeepers 173; and politics 48, 120, 123–5, 152, 170, 175; "Project Wrangler" 170; SAF overseas scholarship program 48, 120, 123–5, 170, 175; scholar-soldiers 48, 170; size 171; technology and weapons 171–2
Singapore Art Museum 195
Singapore Association of Trade Unions (SATU) 31
Singapore Broadcasting Authority (SBA) 137, 140
Singapore Broadcasting Authority Act 140
Singapore Business Federation 78
Singapore Cable Vision 137
Singapore Chinese Chambers of Commerce and Industry 68, 101, 159 (*also see* Chinese)
Singapore Chinese Orchestra 195
Singapore City Council 16
Singapore Council of Women (SCW) (1952) 160
Singapore Democratic Alliance (SDA) 148
Singapore Democratic Party (SDP) 136, 148
Singapore Diaspora 189
"Singapore Dream" 155, 196–7
Singapore Federation of Chinese Clans Association 68, 101, 159 (*also see* Chinese)
Singapore Film Festival 161
Singapore Green Plan 159
Singapore Herald 137
Singapore Improvement Trust 90
Singapore Indian Development Association (SINDA) 112–13
Singapore Industrial Labour Organization (SILO) 31
Singapore Industrial Promotion Board 90
Singapore Justice Party 148
Singapore Management University 105
Singapore Monitor 137
Singapore People's Party (SPP) 148
Singapore Press Holdings (SPH) 137–8
Singapore Stock Exchange 74
Singapore Symphony Orchestra 195
"Singapore system" 56, 186, 195, 197
Singapore Technologies 73–4, 171–2
Singapore Telecommunications: *see* SingTel
Singapore Television Twelve Pte, Ltd 137
Singapore 21 (vision) 83, 161, 165–7, 195
Singapore 21 Committee 124
Singapore 21 Facilitation Committee 166
Singapore-Window (overseas-based website) 162
Singapore's achievements 1–2, 4–5, 8–10
Singapore's mistakes 10–11
Singaporeans 4, 27, 38, 42–3, 49, 52, 54, 56–7, 61–5, 76, 80–1, 83, 87, 89–90, 96, 101–2, 104–6, 122, 128, 130, 134, 136, 138–9, 141, 143–7, 151–2, 155, 160–1, 163–5, 167, 170, 174, 177, 186, 189–92, 194–7
Singaporeans for Democracy (overseas-based website) 162
Singh, Bilveer 172
"Singlish" 105–6
Singnet 141
SingTel 72–3, 87
Sintercom (website) 162–3
sit-ins 15, 39
Skills Development Fund 69
small and medium enterprises (SMEs) 68–9
small state models 169–71
Smith, Peter 196
Social Development Unit 188
"social engineering" 59–60

social forces 25
social trust 157
socialism 51, 68, 157
socialization: *see* political socialization
Societies Act (1967, 1988) 131–2, 140, 162
society 2, 6, 25, 49, 53–4, 56–9, 62–4, 78, 103, 106, 114, 141, 190, 196–7
Society for the Prevention of Cruelty to Animals 159
Socratic Circle 163
Solicitor General 136
South Africa 173
South Asia 54
South Korea 172, 183–4
Southeast Asia 2, 8, 19, 29, 54, 67, 72, 82, 101, 138, 140, 169, 171, 173, 179–80, 183–4
Spain 34–5
"Speak Good English" Campaign 106
"Speak Mandarin" Campaign 106–10
Speaker's Corner in Hong Lim Park 162, 164–5
Special rights (of Malays) 19, 22–3 (*also see* Malays, special position of)
Spratly Islands 174–5, 183
Sri Lanka 100
Standard and Poor 8
Star Hub 73
state, the (principal references only) 2, 6, 8, 25–6, 33, 35–7; bureaucratic state 28–9; and the PAP government 25–30, 36, 50
statutory boards 28–9, 31, 37, 71–2, 85–6, 92, 94, 134, 175, 188
stem cell research 79
sterilization, voluntary 60
Straits Chinese British Association 158
Straits Settlements 13
Straits Times 54, 61, 81, 138–9, 141, 155, 162–3, 167, 188, 190
streaming: *see* education
strikes 15, 143
Student Christian Movement 130
Subic Bay (Philippines) 173
subsidies 87, 94, 194
Suez Canal 14
Suharto 7, 178
Sumitomo Electric 78
Sungei Buloh 159
surplus(es) 28, 71, 75, 87
survival 51–2, 95, 100, 105, 129, 176
Suzhou 76–7
Sweden/Swedish 170–1
Switzerland/Swiss 133, 170, 189, 193

Taiwan 79, 173, 175, 179, 185–6
talent, shortage of 6, 9–10, 38, 44–9, 54–6, 60–1, 78–9, 114–15, 117, 120, 126–7, 161, 187, 189–90, 195 (*also see* foreign talent)
Tamil Language Week 135
Tamil Organizing Committee 135
Tamils 56, 99–100, 135, 137, 156
Tamney, Joseph 58
Tan Cheng Bock 166
Tan Eng Liang 126
Tan Keng Yam, Tony 33, 46–7, 114–16, 121, 126
Tan Siew Sin 19
Tan Wah Piow 130
Tang Liang Hong 131, 134–5, 148, 151
Tarmugi, Abdullah 188
tax/taxes 19, 60, 70–1, 77, 82, 86–7, 89, 136, 188
Tay, Simon 162
technocrats 28–30, 32, 37, 45–7, 52, 61, 97, 117, 125
technocrats (trade union) 32–3, 125
technology 3, 10, 51, 68–9, 71, 73, 79, 103–5, 124, 138–9, 171–2 (*also see* Information Technology)
Teh Cheang Wan 7, 91
Television Corporation of Singapore (TCS) 137
Temasek 29–30, 72, 74–5, 84
Teo Chee Hean 76, 123–4, 126, 165
Teochew 48, 99, 148
terrorism/terrorists 151, 171, 174, 180; arrests in Singapore 180
Thailand/Thais 7, 130, 173, 183
Think Centre 162–4
"Thinking Schools, Learning Nation": *see* education
"Third China" 100
Thomson Electronics 78
Tibet 183
tin 13
Toh Chin Chye 21–2, 38, 46, 150
Toshiba 78
"Total Defence" 170–1
"Total Defence Initiative" 105
Total Fertility Rate (TFR): *see* population growth
Town Councils/town councillors 95–6, 145–6, 155
trade unions/trade unionists 2, 15, 17, 20–1, 30–3, 36–9, 47, 78, 83, 86, 90, 116–17, 123–6, 159
Transparency International 192
Tremewan, Christopher 92, 102–3
triads 14, 129, 131, 158–9
tripartism 25, 33–4
trustee stocks 87
TUC (Trades Union Congress in Britain) 32
Tunku Abdul Rahman 3, 17–19, 21–3

"ultras" 21
Undesirable Publications Act 137
unemployment 3, 31, 69–71, 81–2, 86, 90
Unification Church 132

United Democratic Party (Malaysia) 22
United Malays National Organization (UMNO) 21–2, 174, 177
United Nations 66, 173, 176, 181; general assembly 181; security council, Singapore member of 181
United Nations Forum of Small States (1992) 182
United Nations Law of the Sea Conference (1982) 181
United Nations peacekeeping 173, 181
United Nations Population Fund 189
United Nations Standby Arrangements 181
United Nations Transitional Administration in East Timor 173
United Overseas Bank (UOB) 75
United States (US) 3, 8, 27, 67, 70–1, 74, 82–3, 89, 133, 180, 186; economy 70, 74; Singapore's relations with 180; and values 57, 180
United States Army War College Study 177
United States Department of State Human Rights Reports 128, 139
United States Embassy, Singapore 74, 180
United States Seventh Fleet 173; USS Constellation 173; USS Kitty Hawk 173
US Ambassador to Singapore (Steve Green) 180

values 1, 4, 27, 29, 31, 37, 51–2, 57–60, 62–4, 86, 92, 99, 102–6, 111, 120, 137, 180, 188, 190, 193, 196–7 (*also see* Asian values, Shared Values)
Vasil, Raj 99
Vatican 41
Venetian Republic 124
Vennewald, Werner 29–30, 126
Victoria Memorial Hall 39
Victorian ethos 57 (*also see* Protestant ethic),
Vietnam/Vietnamese 78, 180–1, 184
Vogel, Ezra 65
Voice of America 137
voluntary organizations 17, 97, 157–8, 165, 167, 195
Voluntary Welfare Organizations (VWOs) 167, 195
volunteerism 57, 65, 158, 167, 197

Wage Correction Policy 10, 71
wages 8, 33–4, 54, 62, 70–1, 81–2, 130 (*also see* ministerial salaries, National Wages Council)
Wahid, Abdurrahman 178–9
Wanbao 108
Wang Gung Wu 58
Washington Naval Treaties (1921) 14
water, Singapore's problems with Malaysia about 9, 169, 174, 178
welfarism 57, 193
West, the 53, 57–8, 64, 127, 176, 182, 192
Westernization 56–7, 102, 196
West Timor 173
White Papers concerning the elected president (1988, 1999), 153–4
White Paper on Competitive Salaries for Competent and Honest Government 61
White Paper on Shared Values 63–4
Wilkinson, Barry 58
Williams College 117
Wilson, Harold 23
Winsemius, Albert 4, 76
women 60, 86, 157, 187, 189–90; education and children 55, 60, 188; education and marriage 60, 188; election candidates (2001) 152; and motherhood 187–9; organizations 157, 159–60; and politics 40–2, 44, 145, 188; status 58, 187; in work force 187–8
Women's Charter (1961) 42, 160
Wong Kan Seng 41, 164
Working Committee, The (TWC) (1998) 163–4
Works Brigade 17, 40
World Bank 19, 133, 192
World Competitiveness Report Yearbook (Switzerland) 8, 133
World Economic Forum 79, 193
World Trade Organization (WTO) 77, 182–3
Workers' Party 2, 7, 16, 130, 134–6, 144, 149, 151

Yayasan Mendaki: *see* Mendaki
Year of the Dragon (1988, 2000) 187
"yellow culture" 17
Yeo, George 42, 48, 74, 78–80, 82, 108, 123–4, 126, 146, 158, 160–1, 173, 175, 187, 191
Yeo Ning Hong 46
Young Christian Workers 130

Zone of Peace, Freedom and Neutrality (ZOPFAN) 182
Zulkifli bin Baharudin 137–9